A LEFTIST ONTOLOGY

A LEFTIST ONTOLOGY

Beyond Relativism and Identity Politics

Carsten Strathausen

Editor

Foreword by
William E. Connolly

UNIVERSITY OF MINNESOTA PRESS

MINNEAPOLIS • LONDON

An earlier version of chapter 3 was published as "What's Left of the Dialectic? A Polemic," *English Studies in Canada* 29, no. 1 (2003): 16–25. Reprinted with permission of *ESC: English Studies in Canada*.

Published by the University of Minnesota Press
111 Third Avenue South, Suite 290
Minneapolis, MN 55401-2520
http://www.upress.umn.edu

Library of Congress Cataloging-in-Publication Data

A leftist ontology : beyond relativism and identity politics / Carsten Strathausen, editor ; Foreword by William E. Connolly.
    p. cm.
  Includes bibliographical references and index.
  ISBN 978-0-8166-5029-3 (hc : alk. paper) —
  ISBN 978-0-8166-5030-9 (pb : alk. paper)
  1. Political science—Philosophy. 2. Philosophy, Marxist. 3. Socialism.
 I. Strathausen, Carsten.
  JA71.I4425 2009
  320.01—dc22

                       2009007475

Printed in the United States of America on acid-free paper

The University of Minnesota is an equal-opportunity educator and employer.

18 17 16 15 14 13 12 11 10 09   10 9 8 7 6 5 4 3 2 1

To Valerie and Clara

CONTENTS

The Left and Ontopolitics

WILLIAM E. CONNOLLY

In *Sustaining Affirmation* (2000), Stephen White examines four contemporary political theorists to ascertain how the ontology each adopts filters into his or her political theory and how the latter infiltrates into ontology.[1] By *ontology*, he means the most fundamental assumptions each makes about the world, including within that compass assumptions about time, nature, human subjectivity, the final source of morality, the territorial space of politics, and the often vexed relations between these elements. White does not make a sharp distinction between ontology and metaphysics, finding that the two terms have moved close to each other in recent discourse. His contention is that the postmetaphysical politics peddled by Habermas, Rorty, and Rawls in different ways loses credibility as soon as you compare theorists who acknowledge the active role of ontology (or metaphysics) in their work. This study also calls into question the valiant attempts by thinkers such as Lyotard and Derrida to escape metaphysics, even though each realizes from the start that the planned escape can never be complete. The ontological dimension of political thought and practice is robust, even while it may be marked by internal tensions, and a case can be made that the attempt to expunge this element from political thought recoils back on theory, making it less active and robust than it otherwise might be.

The theorists White selects for examination—George Kateb, Charles Taylor, Judith Butler, and me—disagree on several critical matters. But we tend to converge on three. First, each embraces a positive ontological orientation, as when Taylor focuses on the complexity of human embodiment, supports a fugitive philosophy of transcendence, seeks to become more closely attuned to a final moral source that cannot be known in a classical epistemic way, and defines ethical life in terms of a plastic set of intrinsic purposes to be pursued rather than a set of universal laws to be obeyed. Each of the others takes different stances on the same issues. Second, each theorist discerns a loose set of relations between the ontology adopted, the ethical–political priorities endorsed, and specific dangers and possibilities to be identified. None suggests that an ontology *determines* a political stance, but all contend that it filters into politics, so that it would be a mistake to say that ontology has no influence on politics. Taylor's faith in the grace of a loving God, for instance, enters into his politics, even if the element of mystery he discerns in divinity means that he does not delineate the tight set of moral commands presented by Pope Benedict XVI and a large section of the evangelical movement in America. Third, each figure acknowledges the ontology he or she embraces to be susceptible to reflective and comparative defense; but most conclude that it is unlikely to be established either by such airtight arguments or universal recognition that it rules every other possibility out of court. Each party—though perhaps to different degrees—is thus a pluralist, seeking to bring their onto-orientation into the public realm while recoiling back on tensions and uncertainties in it enough to invite open-textured negotiations with others. Each advances a bicameral orientation to citizenship, seeking to give his or her own orientation public presence while conceding a place to others. Discernible in the differences between them is the common appreciation of a paradoxical element in politics.

None is a relativist, because each advances arguments and invitations designed to draw others to his or her orientation. And each thinks that some possible ontopolitical orientations fall below a minimal threshold for inclusion in the contest. But each is a pluralist, seeking to convince others while inviting relations of agonistic respect with them when the first invitation is not accepted. A couple also address the question of what pluralists should do when some parties are intransigent, when dogmatists define a set of minorities as enemies in order to squash or defeat them. How to cope with intransigence is a tough issue for pluralists. It involves resisting antipluralism without recapitulating by one's own actions the tone and temper of their exclusionary politics. It is not an easy issue to resolve. One senses that the neoconservative and evangelical right knows how its own intransigence places the left into difficult binds. Watch how Fox News regularly baits the left if you want to test this claim.

There is no necessity that the four conceptions of ontopolitics examined by White must issue in a presumptive commitment to pluralism. Carl Schmitt, for instance, could move close to the ontology of Judith Butler but fold a different sensibility into it. He might concur that national unity is not inscribed in a higher purpose of Being but, because of the implacable will to dominance inhabiting him, exploit that absence to impose artificial unity on the state by treating selective minorities as enemies to be conquered, excluded, or both. This means that ontology by itself does not "determine" either an ethical or political orientation. But it does not preclude more loosely woven relations of interdetermination between ontology and politics.

The key difference between Schmitt and Butler is one of sensibility, an element that helps to define the tone and spirit of a lived ontology. The relation between Butler and Taylor, on the other hand, is that of an affinity of sensibility mediated by differences of ontology. If either Taylor or Butler was to convert to the ontology of the other, an even closer alliance between them would emerge. As it is now, a discernible affinity of sensibility across ontological difference makes it likely that they will be allied on specific issues. Similarly, if Schmitt and Leo Strauss diverge on ontology but converge in temper, they may adopt a bellicose disposition toward the adversaries they define.

By temper or sensibility, I mean a set of affectively imbued dispositions to judgment and action embedded in ideas set on different levels of body/ brain complexity. Affect-imbued ideas on the visceral register are not as complex as those on more refined levels, but each region nonetheless communicates with the others. Sensibility and thought are interinvolved in a way that allows neither to be exhausted by the other. Nietzsche, Heidegger, and Merleau-Ponty all appreciated the complexity of this interinvolvement. That is one reason you can find out more about your ontology through comparison with that of others. You do so first by drawing implicit elements into the foreground through critical comparison, and second by working on intensive thought fragments below articulation until they are altered and polished enough to be rendered articulate. The unarticulated dimension of an ontology is thus not only tacit; some of its elements are incipient in the sense that some embedded, ideationally imbued intensities must be altered in this way or that in order to be drawn into an intersubjective network of articulation. Maybe some things Freud said about memory traces are relevant here. At any rate, to the extent that such work is accomplished, the ontological problematic has been changed to some degree as it has been rendered more conscious. A sensibility is composed of a dense network of thought-imbued affects, with the thought element finding different levels of refinement and the affective element different degrees of intensity. Jokes, as Freud knew, often tap into tacit ideas or unconscious fragments that have not previously been articulated; and what is a joke to some believers is often blasphemy to others.

Ontology, sensibility, ethics, politics—a network of partly interfused and partly separate elements with none simply determining the others and all entering into complex patterns of circulation. To come to terms with the role of ontology in politics, then, it may be essential to reformulate classical ideas of causality that have both constrained the social sciences and encouraged a section of narrative theorists to turn away from the idea of cause altogether.

When the element of sensibility is folded into the question of ontopolitical connections, it becomes clear—if it wasn't already—how impossible it is to grow up without being possessed by preliminary dispositions to being before you reflect on them. Is a God central to you? If so, what are Her salient characteristics? That yes or no, and the closer determinations that follow, do not exhaust the issue. The specific theistic or nontheistic faith involved may be burned deeply into the visceral register of being or sit lightly on life, being open to possible revision in the future without throwing you into crisis. On another register, you may find yourself acting as if ethics is grounded in the first instance in a universal law; or alternatively acting as if it is set in an intrinsic purpose, or, alternatively yet, as if it grows out of a rich experience of gratitude for being refracted through the cultivation of sensitivity to new and unexpected circumstances. You may respond affirmatively to the idea that time is best understood as a series of punctual moments, or, alternatively, that it is governed by divine providence, or alternatively yet, that it flows through an open universe of becoming. You may be drawn to one of these alternatives even before you explore a philosophical treatise on it. You may feel in your gut that nature is explicable in the last instance by universal laws, or, against that, that it possesses a vitality that exceeds available modes of explanation. And so on and on. William James is right when he says that each of us comes to adulthood primed with preliminary existential faiths, some of which are burned deeply into us and others of which sit lightly upon us. Similar things can be said about the cultural commonalities and differences in which we are set. An intense feeling of disgust can be shared viscerally by a large section of a population, and it may carry fundamental judgments about the way of the world within it.

To change a set of preliminary ontological dispositions is to go through a conversion process rather than merely to shift a set of conclusions readily separable from your identity and the larger culture. That is why disputes at this level are often so intense: our lives are staked on some of the differences. So a conversion from one ontological stance to another involves intellectual arguments and affective movements entangled together.

I mention the above issues and entanglements because they may help to set the stage for the questions and debates in this book. While Stephen White sought to establish the ineliminability of ontology from politics and political thought, while I explore the links between ontology, sensibility, and politics, the authors of the essays in this volume ask whether there is such a thing as an ontology of the left. To pursue that question they engage thinkers such as Agamben, Jameson, Mouffe, Laclau, Lacan, Badiou, and Hardt/Negri. Some readers may assert at the outset that it is a category mistake to place the terms *left* and *ontology* together in such a way. Perhaps by coming to terms with the link between ontology and sensibility, we can see how this is not necessarily so. The question of an ontology of the left makes sense if, first, you relax the demand that the relation must be causal in the classic sense of efficient causality, and second, fold the issue of sensibility into the equation. One ontopolitical orientation on the left, then, could fold care for the future of the earth and the diversity of life into a reading of time as becoming and of political space as susceptible to multiple modes of organization. Michel Foucault eventually advanced such a combination of themes. Within that compass—and stretching well beyond it—there might be a few ontopolitical orientations on the left, with each entering into contact and competition with the others.

Perhaps the question inspiring this volume can be parsed into a series of questions. What does it mean to be on the left today? If it includes a focus on economic equality, diversity, and ecology, what else is involved? Does it mean that you acknowledge an aporia in "the political" that can be negotiated but never resolved? Does it mean that you rework the public/ private division that defines liberal secularism? That you explore how the acceleration of pace in several zones of life both unsettles traditions and opens a window to rethink classical images of time? That you engage the micropolitics of the contemporary media to counter the power the right now exerts over the unconscious presumptions of everyday judgment? What conceptions of space are appropriate to the left today? What combination of historical and ontological considerations might draw care for this world into closer attunement to the needs and dangers of the day?

Cutting closer to the heart of things, how wide is the range of ontosensibilities that can be counted as part of the left? What relations should be fostered between divergent ontosensibilities on the left? By what means can more people be drawn toward one of these stances? Is the appropriate goal today to construct an ontopolitical assemblage on the left? Or is it to pursue a more tightly ordered unity?

Several of these questions are addressed in the essays to follow, and others, too. Together, they show that the left is on the move again—and not a moment too soon. If the horrors of the Bush–Cheney regime have helped to trigger a new resurgence, it is imperative that this time we find ways to evade some of the traps into which the left has fallen in the past.

It is particularly pertinent to revisit Marxism, as several essays in this volume do through engagements with the work of Jameson, Laclau, and Hardt/Negri. Today may be a propitious moment to forge a new materialism, one that gains sustenance from Marx as it also draws insight from Deleuzian studies of vital materiality, time as becoming, and the complexity of space, from new work in physics and biology on the complexity and vitality of matter, and from work in neuroscience that reopens the body/mind issue as it pursues a revised concept of causality. Now may be the moment to craft such a new materialism, one that bears recognizable debts to the materialist traditions that precede it.

What could it look like? It might reconsider Marx's break with Democritus and Epicurus in his early work, folding more volatility and becoming into nature and time themselves; and it might carry those understandings into the very heart of state–capital processes. One exploration has been launched by Gilles Deleuze and Félix Guattari in their ontoconceptions of energy-matter, of a capitalist "axiomatic," and of complex capitalist assemblages that exceed both the quest for smooth explanation in neoliberal theory and the theme of dialectical progression in classical Marxism. Consider one element in the thought of Deleuze and Guattari:

> So how are we to define this matter-movement, this matter-energy, this matter-flow, this matter in variation that enters assemblages and leaves them? It is a destratified, deterritorialized matter. It seems to us that Husserl brought thought a decisive step forward when he discovered the region of *vague and material essences* (in other words, essences that are vagabond, anexact and yet rigorous), distinguishing them from fixed, metric and formal essences. . . . They constitute fuzzy aggregates. They relate to a *corporeality* (materiality) that is not to be confused either with an intelligible formal essentiality or a sensible, formed thinghood.[2]

Intensive matter-energy flows, moving through and exceeding already formed entities and patterns. These two theorists would not be inordinately surprised, for instance, by the recent "discovery" of rogue waves—or the scientific vindication of mariners' reports about them for several centuries previously dismissed as superstitions. Rogue waves in some instances form out of the collision between ocean currents and storms; they generate powers of self-amplification that exceed our current powers to predict their development; they sometimes reach the height of a ten-story building and the width of a street block; and they periodically wreak havoc on oil rigs and oceangoing vessels. They are thus linked to capitalism, just as hurricanes, earthquakes, volcanoes, virus mutations, tsunamis, and asteroid showers are. Thousands of them appear in the Bermuda Triangle and the North Sea. Deleuze and Guattari expect such roguish elements to find expression in nature and in the innumerable nature–culture exchanges that define capitalism. Moreover, an element of volatility also enters human life and cultural institutions on its own, even as it is transmitted by exchanges between culture and the inorganic world.

When Deleuze and Guattari speak of a capitalist axiomatic, it now becomes clear why it is reducible neither to the rational processes of neoliberal theory nor to the mode of production in classical Marxism, though it is closer to the latter. An axiomatic consists of a set of elements knotted together in tangles that resist capture by either a dialectical or formal analysis. The capitalist axiomatic ties together the priority of private profit, wealth applied to free labor, and commodities as consumption goods. Once so knotted, it creates specific constraints and possibilities as it bumps along through the contingencies of history, adding new components here, dropping others there, and facing unexpected obstacles at other moments. Capitalism consists of both knots and flows.

A capitalist axiomatic never exists in a pure form; it is always intertwined with specific regimes of the state, religious practices, science, exchanges with nature, and educational institutions. It could not be without them. The relations between the axiomatic and specific versions of these practices are partly internal and partly external, in a way that disrupts classic concepts of causality and suggests the idea of emergent causality developed recently in complexity theory. Thus a specific religious spirituality could both fold into habits of work, investment, and consumption to some degree *and* operate as a force impinging on them from the outside. The latter practices could then recoil back on the shape of the spirituality. Given the complexity and bounciness of such patterns of circulation a specific capitalist assemblage stretches and twists its own axiomatic in this way or that, endowing capitalism with a degree of historical plasticity and volatility that renders futile attempts to give a formal analysis of capitalism as such. Such a volatile and variable assemblage resists deep explanation. The thing to do, rather, is to identify specific historical dangers, possibilities, and potential sites of action, moving from the quest for deep explanation to the pursuit of strategic sites of intervention. You might find yourself focusing on the priorities of the state at one moment, the relation between global warming and the infrastructure of consumption at another, an incipient strain in dominant patterns of spirituality at another, and several of these as they circulate back and forth at yet another. Deleuze and Guattari explore creative intersections between micropolitics and macropolitics.

Deleuze and Guattari, holding that the dialectic fits being like loose clothing, nonetheless display debts to the structure and aspirations of classical Marxism. They fold revised conceptions of nature, time, and politics into that schema. A series of other such attempts is identified in this book as the authors respond to Jameson, Derrida, Foucault, Hardt/Negri, and Laclau.

Perhaps it is also important to learn from the politics of the recent past as we assess the contemporary promise and limits of nineteenth-century Marxism. The last time the left gained a real foothold in Euro-American states, it made a minor contribution to its own demise. In the early 1970s, one faction insisted that you cannot really be on the left unless you adopt an Althusserian reading of Marx. Today, however, Marxism itself must both be reworked and pluralized. It must be reworked to speak to distinctive changes in territorial diversity, the acceleration of speed, global capital, regional stratification, religious resurgence, and the recoil effects capitalism now has on nature itself. And it must be pluralized.

As ontological differences between twenty-first-century thinkers indebted to Marx become more visible, a corollary drive to draw stark lines of inclusion and exclusion within the left could reemerge. The need today is to negotiate relations of agonistic respect within the left so that a new left assemblage can be organized and invigorated. Rawlsian–Habermasian secular perspectives must be engaged, too. They may have lost their power to inspire many, as the emergence of the evangelical–capitalist machine in America makes clear, and as the intensity of religious–territorial struggles in Europe, the Middle East, and Asia also show.[3] Even if that is true, it is important to forge lines of communication and reciprocal influence across these differences. There are significant affinities of sensibility to draw on here. It is also critical to forge alliances with Christians, Jews, Muslims, and Hindus in a variety of places whose concern for the future of the earth pulls them toward the left. The need today is to construct a widely based assemblage on the left informed by militance and the desire to counter the media/think tank/party/church/courthouse machine on the right that has reduced liberalism to a series of whimpers.

The essays in this collection thus open up urgently needed conversations. They define several issues that must be engaged by reflective intellectuals today. Do they also nudge us closer to the day when an ontopolitics of the left deepens attachment to life and the earth while speaking to pressing issues of class, regional stratification, ecology, and diversity? That would be sweet.

NOTES

1. Stephen White, *Sustaining Affirmation: The Strengths of Weak Ontology in Political Theory* (Princeton: Princeton University Press, 2000).

2. Gilles Deleuze and Félix Guattari, *A Thousand Plateaus,* trans. Brian Massumi (Minneapolis: University of Minnesota Press, 1987), 407. This quotation is taken from the plateau on "Nomadism." The discussion of the capitalist "axiomatic" is drawn from the plateau on "The Apparatus of Capture."

3. I address this machine in an American context in "The Evangelical–Capitalist Resonance Machine," *Political Theory* (Winter 2005): 869–86.

INTRODUCTION
Thinking Outside In

CARSTEN STRATHAUSEN

Political philosophy forces us to enter the terrain of ontology.
—HARDT AND NEGRI, *Empire*

I contend that it is the lack of understanding of "the political" in its
ontological dimension which is at the origin of our current incapacity
to think in a political way.
—CHANTAL MOUFFE, *On the Political*

WHAT'S LEFT?

The title of this anthology calls for an explanation. It has become customary
these days to denounce any reference to the Left as mere rhetoric devoid of
substance—a position propagated not only by John Stossel and mainstream
media, but also in academic circles. A typical example is the increasingly
positive reception of Carl Schmitt by the former left-wing academic journal *Telos*. Paul Piccone, one of its senior editors, recently argued that "the
Left/Right split has actually been a political Trojan horse" ever since the
French Revolution. Hence, it retains "some validity" from a historical perspective, but "makes very little sense today."[1] Similarly, Hans Ulrich Gumbrecht continues to denounce the "soft terrorism" exerted by the various
doxa that allegedly prevail in the humanities today—the exhortation to be
on the "left," to be "critical," and to denounce everything else as inherently
conservative, naive, or even fascist.[2] Such academic conformism, Gumbrecht insists, restricts the very freedom of thought it claims to defend.
Self-proclaimed leftists, in other words, are the true conservatives in today's
pervasive neoliberal landscape, a view largely shared by "third way" proponents (Anthony Giddens and Ulrich Beck) and contemporary media theorists (such as Jean Baudrillard and Norbert Bolz). All of them have moved
"Beyond Left and Right."[3]

In response, the Left has vigorously defended this distinction as vital for the continued pursuit of a progressive, egalitarian politics. Norberto Bobbio, in his excellent study *Left and Right* from 1994, draws this line between the two camps: "on the one side, there are those who think men are more equal than unequal, while on the other are those who think them more unequal than equal."[4] Because the Left regards human equality as ontologically primary, it considers many existing inequalities to be socially constructed and hence able to be eliminated, whereas the Right regards these same inequalities as natural and unchangeable. The strength of Bobbio's distinction is not only its broad historical perspective, but its analytical diligence as well. Careful to avoid undue generalizations or moral judgments, Bobbio repeatedly insists that "the concept of equality is relative, not absolute," meaning that "the assertion that the Left is egalitarian does not mean that it is egalitarianist."[5] Inspired by Bobbio's study, *A Leftist Ontology* strives for a similar balance between its (absolute) anthropological assumptions—"men are more equal than unequal"—and the (relative) historical flexibility to provide changing answers to such questions as "equality between whom? In what? On what basis?"[6]

Unfortunately, Bobbio's theses found little resonance among political philosophers outside of Italy. Of the few who did engage him, Perry Anderson contends that Bobbio "run[s] together a number of propositions that are logically independent of each other" as he sets out to bring scientific clarity to Bobbio's conceptual frailty:[7]

> To base the distinction between Left and Right on ontological judgments of the balance between human equality and inequality, in other words, is to rest it on a frail foundation—which the further development of science could strike away, by imposing inescapable convergence on a common empirical standpoint. (133)

For Anderson, there is simply no room between the dialectical poles of scientific certainty and historical change to accommodate Bobbio's split position in between. Although he supports Bobbio's effort to maintain the Left/Right distinction in principle, he cautions that "the opposition between Left and Right has no axiomatic guarantee." It follows that Bobbio's ontological (that is, allegedly ahistorical) distinction falsely implies a stable ground for the "categories of Right, Centre and Left," when, in fact, "the locations and boundaries of each are far from fixed" and constantly changing (138, xi).

This critique, I believe, is based on a reductionist account of Bobbio's theory. Like most Marxists, Anderson overemphasizes the historical flexibility of philosophical concepts—always historicize!—at the expense of some ontological assumptions he, too, must endorse—for example, the belief that "the *Leitkultur* of the international Left," namely "historical materialism," still remains the most valid scientific-empirical explanation of human nature and behavior (xvi). Other beliefs, by contrast, he considers either fundamentalist and thus ahistorical (like Bobbio's) or subject to postmodern relativism (like Laclau's and Mouffe's).[8] For Anderson, there is only one theoretical framework able to supply a sophisticated Left/Right distinction without falling prey to rigid ontological axioms: Marxism. "That a Marxism capable of informing works of such magnitude as Therborn's or Brenner's or Habsbawm's . . . can scarcely be pronounced dead, is self-evident," Anderson concluded in 2005 (xvi).

One concern of this volume is to question the alleged self-evidence of Anderson's logic according to which Marxism might live forever—a position also endorsed by Fredric Jameson, Arif Dirlik, and other leading Marxists.[9] What is at stake is not simply the performative contradiction at work here, according to which all philosophical ideas and concepts change over time—except those that adequately express this insight. As Barbara Herrnstein Smith and Boris Groys have convincingly argued, it is virtually impossible for philosophical discourse not to succumb to this malleable charge of performative self-contradiction.[10] The real question today is rather how to engage this contradiction differently, outside and beyond the Marxist dialectic and the confines of historical materialism— by deconstructing it, or psychoanalyzing it, or affirming it without remainder or negativity. Materialist philosophy existed long before the arrival of Marxism, and the political left will surely survive the latter's demise as well.

RELATIVISM UNDONE

This leads us to the second challenge implicit in the title of this anthology, this time raised from a philosophical perspective. Whereas Marxist critics like Anderson deny the possibility of a leftist *ontology* that exceeds the pragmatic frame of historical materialism, others point to the logical impossibility of a *leftist* ontology—an oxymoron that merges the (contingent) political and the (timeless) philosophical dimension. How could an ontology (that is, an absolute philosophical statement as to the essence or nature of Being) be relativized by as nebulous an adjective as "leftist"? To be sure, we might reasonably refer to a "political ontology" or an "ontology of the political" as the attempt to examine the nature or essence of what Carl Schmitt named "the political."[11] An effective leftist politics would then have to take this political ontology into account as it seeks to implement its political demands. By contrast, to speak of a leftist ontology implicitly acknowledges the existence of a rightist one (and perhaps a centrist one) as well. There would then be as many ontologies as there are political opinions, giving rise to a postmodern potpourri of pseudophilosophical inquiries—in a word, Relativism.

Let me mention up front what I consider to be a naive cop-out to this challenge, namely to welcome the unlimited heterogeneity of differing opinions as the adequate expression of a fundamental disagreement in Western society about its basic values. Such a cliché form of postmodernism cannot be defended against the charge of Relativism. However, Relativism loses its bite against epistemological theories that explicitly recognize the contextual nature of human beliefs. The fact that "it's contexts all the way down" does not annul the validity of our beliefs in everyday life, as Richard Rorty tirelessly explained in defense of his postmodern pragmatist philosophy.[12] More recently, William Connolly again demonstrated that "pluralism is the not the same as cultural relativism, 'absolute tolerance,' or the 'abandonment of all standards.'"[13] For how could a belief about which I feel passionately and for which I am willing to engage others—how could such a belief possibly be "relative" or "equal" to others in my view? It cannot—at least not on the visceral level of my own physical existence as a human being.

The specter of Relativism exists only in the disembodied ether of abstract thought. It is itself relative, not absolute—a fact that professional intellectuals tend to forget due to their preoccupation with "pure" ideas and cognitive language. As human beings, however, we always already find ourselves situated in specific historical contexts and traditions that make us prone to certain beliefs at the expense of others. Hence, Ernesto Laclau and Chantal Mouffe fully agree with Rorty that Relativism is a "false problem," because nobody, not even Marxists, can possibly discern the "objectivity" of these various traditions or the degree to which they render a "truthful" representation of the real.[14]

> So the question: "If the decision is contingent, what are the grounds for choosing this option rather than a different one?," is not relevant. If decisions are contingent displacements within contextual communitarian orders, they

can show their verisimilitude to people living inside those orders, but not to somebody conceived as pure mind outside *any* order.[15]

The crucial point is that nobody lives "as pure mind outside *any* order"— except, of course, analytical philosophers' beloved "Brain in a Vat." Yet to ponder a language-analytical question such as "Is Relativism absolutely true?" simply leads to the same conundrum of self-reference as other semantic paradoxes. Their only solution lies in distinguishing between different levels or types of reference, as Bertrand Russell and Alfred North Whitehead have demonstrated. It follows that strongly held personal beliefs are absolutely true on the visceral level and relatively arbitrary on the cognitive level. And because cognition (still) requires a body, neither part of this statement is true and yet both are. No logic will dissolve this paradox. We can only hope to live with it as best as possible.

THE ONTOLOGICAL TERRAIN OF POLITICAL PHILOSOPHY

A leftist ontology need not fear the philosophical charge of Relativism nor the Marxist critique of foundationalism. It remains suspended in between these two poles. In fact, the tension it exhibits between (subjective, historical) beliefs on the one hand and (objective, timeless) truth on the other testifies to the essential "conflict between politics and philosophy"—a conflict that pervades the entire history of political philosophy.[16] Hannah Arendt pursues the origins of this conflict back to the Greek polis and Aristotelian philosophy. Because philosophy is defined by its search for the origin and the true nature of Being, it disregards the heterogeneity of everyday phenomena in favor of their alleged essence. Philosophy, so Arendt argues, searches for the human (singular) instead of coming to terms with how humans (plural) actually live and act together, a question at the heart of political thinking. Because "*the* human is a-political. Politics emerges only *in-between-humans* and thus outside of *the* human."[17] According to Arendt, this active involvement in the mundane world of everyday phenomena distinguishes political thinkers from both Greek philosophers and modern scientists alike, both of whom study the world from the outside rather than acting within it. They look for the singular essence of things rather than the multiple relations between them. "After all, we are living in a phenomenological world. Would it thus not make more sense to look for the relevant and meaningful on the surface of things?"[18] Political philosophy comes to an end once it dissolves the constitutive—albeit conflict-laden—bind between theoretical knowledge and human practice. For Arendt, thinking and talking are inextricably linked to action.[19]

Although Leo Strauss in "What is Political Philosophy?" identified more with the elitist position of the philosopher than that of the public intellectual, he nonetheless emphasized the same visceral nature of political philosophy:

> [T]here are things which can only be seen as what they are if they are seen with the unarmed eye; or, more precisely, if they are seen in the perspective of the citizen, as distinguished from the perspective of the scientific observer.[20]

Whereas the social sciences seek to provide a value-free and objective description of society, political philosophy, in Strauss's view, recognizes the impossibility "to study social phenomena. . . . without making value judgments" (16). For Strauss, basic ontological and anthropological issues are always at stake in political philosophy, and his relentless critique of modern historicism and positivism—exemplified, he claimed, in the works of Max Weber—is directed against Weber's disavowal of his personal biases and beliefs that inevitably influence his "scientific" studies.

And yet, although the endorsement of such beliefs is crucial for political philosophy to survive—because, without them, it would further degenerate into a mere academic discipline like political theory or political science— Strauss nonetheless defines political philosophy as "the attempt to replace opinion about the nature of political things by knowledge of the nature of political things" (5). Strauss thus situates the specific "knowledge" sought by political philosophy somewhere in between personal opinions and scientific facts, meaning that it is neither purely objective nor merely subjective. It is, rather, a philosophical and thus value-oriented "truth." It is this embodied knowledge or visceral truth about the good life that Strauss calls wisdom, a wisdom he found expressed most poignantly in the teachings of Socrates and Plato.

A leftist ontology need not return to Greek philosophy to recognize the importance of embodied knowledge for politics. But it must let go of the scientific aspirations of nineteenth-century Marxism and recognize that politics involves "tactical work on that affective register of being which flows into the higher intellect but is not highly amenable to direct regulation by it."[21] No leftist ontology can afford to disregard the fact that "the human" is not alive. Only humans are, and they are not entirely rational beings. Their actions are based as much on beliefs as they are on knowledge, and the Left must take a more constructivist, positive, affirmative position toward human beliefs instead of just trying to dissect them scientifically, or, worse still, dismiss them as mere ideology. The ontological terrain called Being or the world is not just there, awaiting intellectual analysis. Its essence is performed and its nature constructed.

No ontology is objectively true in a scientific or logical sense. Such insights into the essence of Being remain God's prerogative, if you wish. As Strauss keeps reminding his readers, the modern endorsement of objectivity itself constitutes a value judgment that exists side by side with other moral, religious, or political values and not above them. Indeed, it was precisely Carl Schmitt's insistence on the ontological primacy of the political that prompted Strauss's eminent critique of Schmitt's work.[22] By contrast, Strauss, at his best moments, recognizes the fundamental contestability of a philosophical truth statement while at the same time he keeps defending the validity of its insights. As this interior tension demonstrates, a given ontology is neither true nor relative, but normative. It expresses a coherent system of beliefs about the world and calls for a particular course of action commensurate with these beliefs. This is not to deny that a particular ontology may try to become absolute by reacting hostilely to criticism directed against its fundamental premises. But this suppression of dissent does not make that ontology more true than others. It simply renders its borders more rigid.

A leftist ontology pursues the exact opposite approach. Although it employs a secular–materialist perspective to construct its ontological–normative terrain, it acknowledges and welcomes the existence of interior tensions within its system.[23] What sets it apart from other constructions is precisely the way in which it engages these tensions among its midst: it neither suppresses them (as do totalitarian systems) nor engages them in a reasonable and neutral dialogue (as do liberal systems). Rather, it immediately elevates these conflicts onto the ontological level. Hence, every conflict *within* the system inevitably becomes a conflict *about* the system, thus calling into question the historical validity of the normative foundations that constitute it. What is commonly called the "ontology of the political" thus ceases to be the neutral ground upon which "leftist," "centrist," or "rightist" perspectives meet and try to come to terms with each other. Instead, political struggle is ontological in the sense that it constructs the very nature of this allegedly neutral ground. There is no political ontology beyond this construction. Politics always engages—and seeks to define—the parameters and rules of the sociopolitical terrain where different beliefs encounter each other. A leftist ontology therefore recognizes that every-day political practice—and not just "the political"—is defined by this daily struggle about the very nature of our world and its lines of communication, about who possesses the right and the power to delineate its borders and enforce its rules.

THREE PREMISES

A contemporary leftist ontology must be based on three interrelated prem-ises. First, it must recognize that politics today has (once again) reached a point of radical distinction, and that any attempt to examine the space of the political must begin by drawing fundamental boundaries at the ontologi-cal level. However, at stake is not just any ontology, but one that acknowl-edges and thinks through its paradoxical, antifoundational horizon. This is why paradoxical formulations loom large in Alain Badiou's mathematical ontology of set theory, or in Michael Hardt and Antonio Negri's economic ontology of biopower, or in Ernesto Laclau's political ontology of social antagonism, or in Slavoj Žižek's psychoanalytical ontology of the real, or in Giorgio Agamben's ontology of bare life, or in Jacques Derrida's attempt to replace ontology with hauntology.

What renders these various models "leftist" is the shared belief in the historical malleability of the (paradoxical) ontological terrain they investi-gate. Contrary to Heidegger, Schmitt, Strauss, Habermas, or Rawls, what I call the neoleft does not seek to uncover the timeless ground of the sociopolitical, be that ground conceived as the pre-Socratic mindfulness of Being (Heidegger), or the Socratic wisdom about the good life (Strauss), or the modern (that is, nationalist) friend–enemy distinction (Schmitt), or today's sovereignty of liberal–democratic procedures (Habermas, Rawls).[24] Unlike Rawls and Habermas, leftists do not simply stipulate the sover-eignty of liberal reason as it exists today, but recognize its contentious past and uncertain future. And contrary to conservatives such as Leo Strauss, they do not seek to "go back" to classical philosophy and the "most ele-mentary premises of the Bible for reconstructing the essential character of 'the natural world'" either.[25] There is nothing natural about the social order at all, which is to say that this order cannot be reconstructed, but must always be reinvented anew. Although political philosophy necessarily takes place within an already given terrain of established norms, it also cultivates a discussion and conflict about these norms and this very terrain as such. This effort to invent a new ontological space within the ever-changing hori-zon of our sociopolitical field characterizes *A Leftist Ontology*.

It follows—second premise—that although time continues to remain an important concept for political philosophy, questions about space become primary.[26] This spatial turn in the humanities is linked to both geographical aspects of globalization and topological inquires about the paradoxical nature of (social) space. Indeed, the effort to think the outside as a constitutive and malleable part of the inside has been crucial for post-Marxist theory over the last two decades. Insisting on the possibility of historical change and hegemonic interventions, Laclau and Mouffe refer to the social field as an ontological horizon rather than an ontological ground. Whereas *ground* is a foundationalist term that reintroduces the surface–depth distinction, *horizon* implies an ever-receding, historically shifting borderline that remains internal to the social and defies the internal/external distinction:

> This irresoluble interiority/exteriority tension is the condition of any social practice: necessity only exists as a partial limitation of the field of contingency. It is in this terrain, where neither a total interiority nor a total exteriority is possible, that the social is constituted.[27]

The terrain of the social thus constitutes a self-subversive totality that, although it can never become total, nonetheless confronts no limit outside itself. Similar to Heidegger's ontological difference or Lacan's definition of the real as that which cannot be symbolized, Laclau and Mouffe define the outside of the social as an outside within an inside.[28] Still an advocate of post-Marxism in 1994, Žižek described this "*undecidable* alternative Inside/Outside" as a "paradoxical topology" in which surfaces absorb depth and ideology becomes "more real that reality itself."[29]

The task at hand, then, is not simply to draw up new and different boundaries of the sociopolitical field. Rather, we must try to rethink the very notions of boundaries or limits as such and examine the political repercussions of this effort. Is it possible to conceive of the political in such a way as to absorb or internalize its constitutive outside? Answering "yes" to this question is not to deny that there will always be a "them" (Mouffe, Rorty), a "void" (Badiou), or a "part of no part" (Rancière) that defines "us" or our present situation. But these are internal rather than external divisions whose contingent nature escapes the prestructured terrain of liberal reason, conservative values, or historical materialism. Today's borders are less ordered and more fluid than these traditions would have us believe, and the traditional inside/outside distinction seems far less useful today than even twenty years ago.

At the same time, it seems not only legitimate but mandatory to ask about the geopolitical consequences of these abstract topological reflections. The claim that the outside has been relocated on the inside appears questionable in light of the continued exploitation of third world countries by first world global economies. Although Hardt and Negri's *Empire* sought to demonstrate the inevitability of capitalism's immanent demise, their theory was met with incredulity by many on the Left. The Right just shrugged its shoulders and went back to business as usual. And although there is no shortage of other attempts to translate today's topological insights about the nature of space into concrete geopolitical action—Alain Badiou, Jacques Rancière, Ernesto Laclau, and Chantal Mouffe are some names that come to mind—I doubt that any of them will be able to convince the 68'ers who marched in the streets of Paris or today's WTO protesters of the political viability of their philosophical ideas. Personally, I find it difficult to blame social activists for their skepticism vis-à-vis theory. Faced with the complexity of contemporary political philosophy and the obvious need for socioeconomic change on the ground, it certainly seems plausible to disregard the latter and focus on the former. Insofar as theory is needed, historical materialism will do just fine.

Still, I think it would be a mistake to dismiss a leftist ontology as nothing but abstract speculation. To do so would imply that the discussion of (academic) ideas impedes rather than propels real (material) change on the ground. But such a crude separation between thought and matter is yet another remnant of nineteenth-century scientific positivism, which conceived of thought and action as oppositional terms, when, in fact, they supplement and constitute each other. At this point in history, most of us will agree that the current global economic crisis that started in 2007 is the direct result of the neoliberal belief in unfettered markets, financial deregulation, and global capitalist expansion. Alan Greenspan's assumption that productivity always grows and the stock market always rises—in the long run, of course, and only if everybody is left to fend for themselves!—constitutes the basic economic premise of neoliberal/conservative politics. This premise had material effects that are impossible to dissociate from the ideas and actions informed by that premise.

Thus, the third and final premise of this anthology is to insist on the process of thinking as an embodied process, meaning that thought actively interacts with (rather than passively represents) the world. Indeed, the horizon of this interaction constitutes the field of political philosophy. Although there continues to be an intense debate about the (allegedly) rival ontologies of Gilles Deleuze and Alain Badiou—a debate that pits "abundance" against "lack" and the "univocity of being" against the "multiplicity of names"[30]— both thinkers agree on this vital point: "To think is to create—there is no other creation," Deleuze contends, while Badiou argues that "politics is an active thought," which is why he defines his own "Metapolitics" as "real instances of politics as thought."[31] This interdependency of thinking and doing is also acknowledged by disciplines other than political philosophy. It is embraced by pragmatists such as C. S. Peirce and John Dewey, and proponents of constructivism and cybernetics like Heinz von Foerster, Humberto Maturana, Bruno Latour, and Ian Hacking have likewise insisted on the perviousness of the classical frontier that separates matter from thought.[32] Whether in the realm of politics, science, or culture, thought must always be grounded in social contexts. It must always matter. Otherwise, thinking would not be equal to its name.

THE LEGACY OF CARL SCHMITT

Before introducing the various essays of this anthology, I want to bring the above-mentioned premises of leftist ontology into focus. I suggest to return to the legacy of Carl Schmitt and the issue of Left versus Right with which I began. Schmitt is important today not simply because he bequeathed to us the concept of the political, but because his insight into the irreducible moment of decision goes right to the heart of political ontology. To repeat, our task will be to conceive of its constitutive borders (between inside and outside, friends and enemies) in other than Schmittian terms. A brief overview of the various critiques of Schmitt—from the democratic left, the center, and the right—will delineate the horizon of possible responses to what Chantal Mouffe calls "The Challenge of Carl Schmitt."

Habermas's antipathy to Schmitt is well known. For him, the "really problematic move that Carl Schmitt makes . . . is the separation of democracy from liberalism."[33] Schmitt's separation of democracy (that is, the question of political identity) and liberalism (that is, the question of political consensus) is meant to guarantee "an ethically homogeneous substratum of the population" by "reducing it to argument-free acclamation by immature masses," Habermas argues in "The Horrors of Autonomy" (139). Schmitt's goal is to create a homogeneous inside (the friends) by banishing all foreign elements (the enemy) to the outside. In order to achieve this goal, Schmitt embraces an "aesthetics of violence" and advocates a "life-and-death struggle for self-assertion" against all enemies both inside and outside the state (134). On the international level, this "metaphysical" politics leads to war. On the national level, it culminates in "the violent destruction of the normative as such" (137), because the state reserves the right to consider anybody an enemy to its people. Thus, Habermas concludes, Schmitt pursued an antiliberal, fascist form of decisionism that led straight to the Führer principle of Nazi Germany.

The problem with Habermas's critique of Schmitt is that it deflects from the major task of liberal–democratic (that is, consensus-oriented) systems, namely to come to terms with the inexorable moment of decision and the potential violence it includes. Thus, when John Rawls opposes the "well ordered people" living in lawful states with the "burdened people" living in "outlaw states," he explicitly acknowledges the right of the former to wage a "just war" against the latter.[34] In an earlier book, Rawls refers to this necessity as "the fact of oppression," meaning that any "moral doctrine can be maintained only by the oppressive use of state power."[35] Somewhat more cautiously, Habermas refers to the "gentle coercion" *(sanfte Nötigung)* required to bring to "reason" those who refuse to join the communicative process of Western liberal democracies.[36] In the wake of 9/11, Habermas explicitly recognizes the constitutive paradox of liberal tolerance: "since [tolerance] can only be practiced within a boundary beyond which it would cease, it possesses itself a kernel of intolerance."[37] Intolerance, then, is not some threatening force coming from the outside, but one that haunts tolerance from within. Yet Habermas shies away from thinking through this crucial insight of an internal outside, an outside that operates from within the realm of communicative action and democratic principles. Instead, he immediately externalizes the danger and reestablishes the traditional inside/outside model, which, topologically speaking, it not at all different from Schmitt's:

> A democratic constitution can thus tolerate resistance from dissidents who, after exhausting all legal avenues, nonetheless oppose legitimately reached decisions. It *only* imposes the condition that this rule-breaking resistance be *plausibly justified* in the spirit and the wording of the constitution and conducted by *symbolic* means that lend the fight the character of a *nonviolent* appeal to the majority.[38]

In other words, once resistance becomes "implausibly justified" and is conducted by "violent" rather than "symbolic" means, liberal tolerance must cease and democracy will be forced to defend itself.

This sounds reasonable. However, if intolerance indeed constitutes an irreducible kernel within tolerance itself, as Habermas suggested earlier, then democracy's purported self-defense is also an act of self-aggression, an act of violence against its-self that changes the nature of the very democracy it seeks to defend. Although Habermas recognizes this disturbing dynamic, he pushes it from the center to the periphery and finally beyond the boundary of reason. Because it is unreasonable to insist on the paradoxical nature of democracy, it apparently makes more sense to Habermas to externalize the threat and to purge reason and democracy from its internal other. What remains after this operation, however, is some idealized and preconceived notion of rational forms of communication that cannot and must not become a matter of debate in its own right. For if it did, we would circle back to the original question of who delineates the borders of reason and democracy to begin with. Who will make the final decision about when it is time for democracy to defend itself, and who will enforce this decision over and against the allegedly unreasonable objections of others? These questions define the threshold where Habermas's communicative action ends and Schmitt's decisionism begins. It is only a small step that separates the two.

Leo Strauss was the first to comment on this hidden analogy between modern liberalism and Schmitt's conservatism. Strauss's seminal review of *The Concept of the Political* argued that Schmitt still remained a prisoner of the liberalist tradition he sought to overcome, because "the affirmation of the political as such proves to be a liberalism with the opposite polarity."[39] Whereas liberals condemn those who refuse to enter the "neutral" ground of rational deliberation so as to avoid fighting, Schmitt simply values "the affirmation of fighting as such, wholly irrespective of what is being fought for. In other words: he who affirms the political as such comports himself neutrally toward all groupings into friends and enemies."[40] According to Strauss, both liberals and Schmitt endorse a neutral position with respect to specific values. Both are abstract moralists that focus on formal rather than content-related principles. This moral relativism—the fact that modern man "no longer knows what he wants" because "he no longer believes that he can know what is good and bad, what is right and wrong"[41]—remains inextricably linked to the liberal–positivist neutralization of values that, in Strauss's view, characterizes the decay of the modern era.

Against the background of Strauss's conservative critique, we are now able to appreciate the reception of Schmitt from the leftist side of the political spectrum. Contrary to Strauss, Chantal Mouffe charges Schmitt with too little rather than too much neutrality toward the other—a seemingly liberal claim. Hence, in order to define her own position, Mouffe needs to engage in a two-front struggle against both (Habermasian) liberalism and (Schmittian) decisionism. Against the former, Mouffe insists on the irreducibility of social antagonism, because "democratic consensus can be envisaged only as a *conflictual consensus*."[42] There can never be "a rational consensus without exclusion" because there never was an "impartial" or neutral rationality to begin with.[43] This belief constitutes Mouffe's ontological commitment to the constitutive role of conflict in human society.

On the other hand, however, she also criticizes Schmitt's central thesis that social homogeneity is the sine qua non of democracy: "According to Schmitt, there is no possibility of pluralism—that is, legitimate dissent among friends—and conflictuality is relegated to the exterior of the democratic unity."[44] Unlike Schmitt, Mouffe seeks to pull this outside into the democratic community. Her goal is to transform Schmitt's (mutually exclusive) "antagonism" between enemies into a (collaborative) kind of "agonism" among friends. Whereas Schmitt's model pits (internal) homogeneity against (external) heterogeneity and thus presupposes static and always already given (national, cultural, racial) borders, Mouffe acknowledges the historical flexibility of these borders in light of sociopolitical change. "There is no hegemonic articulation without the determination of a frontier, the definition of a 'them,'" Mouffe concedes. However, "in the case of liberal–democratic politics this frontier is an *internal* one, and the 'them' is not a permanent outsider."[45] Although social conflict is inevitable, the identity of those we oppose varies historically. "They" are always already a part of "us."

Mouffe's radical democratic position coincides with the premises of a leftist ontology outlined above. It is crucial to note that Mouffe's defense of democratic principles also includes an ethical imperative to support radical democracy, which, she argues, "is a conquest that needs to be protected as well as deepened."[46] Ernesto Laclau differs from Mouffe on this point. Although both believe in the "ontological primacy of politics," Laclau vehemently argues "against contemporary currents which tend to an 'ethicization' of ontological levels."[47] Why? Because

> from the fact that there is the impossibility of ultimate closure and presence, it does not follow that there is an ethical imperative to "cultivate" that openness or even less to be necessarily committed to a democratic society.[48]

Laclau's argument—namely that the ethical imperative to cultivate openness "does not follow" logically from the impossibility of social closure—

is correct. Logically speaking, Mouffe's ethical denunciation of political acts that seek to establish social closure falls prey to the same critique she herself levels against liberals such as Habermas and Rawls. Whereas Mouffe appeals to democracy and the political as the highest principles worthy of protection, they appeal to reason and morality instead. On the abstract level of philosophical reflection, however, neither of these terms is more than an empty signifier in Laclau's sense. They are all just rhetorical constructions. This is why Laclau has "concentrated on the ontological dimension of social theory rather than on ontical research."[49] This approach finally led him to embrace populism, because populism does not have a particular referent requiring ethical protection: "Populism is, quite simply, a way of constructing the political."[50] It reveals "something about the ontological constitution of the political as such" without endorsing a specific political program on the ontic level.[51]

But Laclau's analysis misses the point that ethics is not solely a question of logic. Quite the contrary, ethics operates mainly on the visceral level of embodied living. Questions of right and wrong behavior are contextual and gain their significance in specific historical situations. They are not just abstract, logical principles in the mind—never mind that analytical philosophers like to treat them as such. So yes, from a logical point of view, Mouffe's politico-ethical intervention "in the name of democracy" is just as good or bad, reasonable or unreasonable, as Rawls's intervention in the name of morality or Habermas's defense of communicative reason.[52] These are political choices, not philosophical ones. But that is precisely the reason why the Left should feel free to embrace them. For if we assume, like Bobbio, that "men are more equal than unequal," then we should embrace openness and radical democracy as the most promising venues to achieve equality.

Still, for some political philosophers on the left today, the political differences between Mouffe's radical democracy, Habermas's liberalism, or Schmitt's conservatism are too limited to warrant their continued support for the ongoing project of Western democracy. They regard democracy's ontological terrain as too confined and too neutral to be of much use today. Alain Badiou in particular considers liberal–democratic systems the reason rather than the solution for many of the world's lingering problems. Others advocate a democracy to come (Derrida) or a return to the Leninist–Stalinist form of socialism (Žižek). While it has become increasingly difficult to keep track of these different interventions in political philosophy today, there have only been a few anthologies or comparative studies that provide a broad overview without focusing exclusively on single authors or specific issues.[53]

Essays and Themes

This was the main reason that led me to propose a seminar on the topic of "A Leftist Ontology?"—still with a question mark at the time—for a national conference at Penn State in April 2005. As is often the case, the responses from the invited conference participants and those joining us later for this publication were far more mixed than I had expected. There were some who liked the topic and others who did not. There were philosophers, social scientists, cultural theorists, and literary scholars, deconstructionists and Marxists as well as Foucauldians, Habermasians, Lacanians, Deleuzeans, Badiouians, and all possible crossovers and combinations in between. Having reread the essays in this volume many times, I think it is fair to say that most contributors agree with at least some of the ideas mentioned in this introduction, but that hardly anybody would want to endorse all of them. That is, of course, how it should be in a good discussion, and I am very grateful for the different viewpoints that came together in this volume. They are, I believe, indicative of the vitality and the importance of our topic. But the heterogeneity of the essays also made it more difficult to subdivide them into appropriate categories. After much internal debate, I chose to divide the eleven papers into four distinct clusters in spite of various other thematic bonds that exist among them. The book's structure should thus be understood as offering just one conceptual map among others, and readers are invited to chart their own course through this intellectual territory generated in response to the question of "A Leftist Ontology."

The first section is called "Agamben, Violence, and Redemption." The title pays tribute to the tremendous influence of Agamben's work not only for contemporary political philosophy, but across academic disciplines both in Europe and the United States. The two essays in this group focus in particular on Agamben's *Homo Sacer* series as a pivot for engaging other seminal figures in the history of political philosophy, including Max Weber, Carl Schmitt, and Walter Benjamin. The overall goal of this section is to (de)limit the space of the political.

The introductory essay aptly demonstrates the contentious nature of our topic: "There is no Leftist ontology" is the opening statement of William Rasch's reflections on "The Structure of the Political vs. the Politics of Hope." Rasch calls for an end to the philosophical self-scrutiny that has preoccupied the Left ever since it lost political ground during the conservative shift in the United States and Europe in the 1980s. His point is certainly not to oppose intellectual debates about politics or to reject one particular leftist program in favor of another. Rather, his critique aims at what he considers the futility of these abstract discussions for everyday life. However sophisticated they may be philosophically, these debates become sterile politically unless they turn toward the practical realm of lived relations where decisions are made, implemented, and enforced. This emphasis on the irreducibility of enforceable decisions in human society lies at the center of Rasch's defense of the political. Contrary to previous and recent forms of leftist Schmittianism (exemplified in Walter Benjamin's "Critique of Violence" and Giorgio Agamben's *Homo Sacer*), Rasch does not believe it possible to transcend the realm of sovereign power toward some postpolitical paradise. By denouncing sovereignty tout court instead of trying to limit its negative effects, the utopian "politics of hope" paralyzes rather than encourages the Left because it abandons the political in favor of theological or metaphysical principles.

Eva Geulen's essay, "The Function of Ambivalence in Agamben's Reontologization of Politics," is more sympathetic to Agamben's project. Geulen concentrates on Agamben's central effort to overcome the dilemma of sovereignty that, in his view, has dominated Western philosophy from its beginning and continues to haunt first world political systems today more than ever. Agamben's solution, according to Geulen, is to resurrect the nineteenth-century concept of *Lebensform*. Intimately related to Heidegger's Dasein, *Lebensform* denotes a form of life whose primordial unity does not allow for the moment of decision that constitutes political sovereignty. *Lebensform* does not feature differentiation at all. Hence, instead of offering apologies for Heidegger's sympathy for the Nazis, Agamben pursues the opposite tactic: he argues that precisely because of its entanglement with dictatorial sovereignty, Heideggerian Dasein can carry the promise of a nondivisional form of life. Agamben thus relies on what Geulen calls the "power of ambivalence": "Ambivalence seals, as it were, the promise that the highest point of suffering announces salvation and that salvation can only be expected by way of the passage through the low point." Geulen's explicit critique of Agamben focuses on precisely this point. She argues that Agamben short-circuits his politico-philosophical theorem of ambivalence with the historical life of prisoners in the camps. Thus, the constitutive tension between philosophy and politics collapses. By identifying the *Muselmann* with the archaic figure of the *homo sacer*,

"Auschwitz becomes the zero point that alone can bring salvation." This is unacceptable, Geulen concludes. In spite of its numerous merits, Agamben's political ontology ultimately "discredits itself."

Our second section is called "The Persistence of Marxism." The juxtaposition of Agamben, discussed in part I, and Jameson, discussed in part II, not only highlights their different approaches toward politics and the political. It also brings to mind the fact that neither, so far, has sought substantially to engage the ideas of the other. Agamben's rejection of classical Marxism is as unrelenting as Jameson's defense of it. Trying to move beyond this static opposition, the essays in this section examine various possibilities of modifying Marxist theory in light of the contemporary world in which we live. Contrary to the philosophical–historical studies of the first part, this section focuses in particular on the relation between the global economy and contemporary culture.

Nicholas Brown and Imre Szemán's essay "Twenty-five Theses on Philosophy in the Age of Finance Capital," endorses one of the anthology's major premises, namely that "any intervention in history's course has to take place at the level of thought." The major difference to several other essays is the authors' belief that "old concepts [might prove] more productive than new ones" in the present context. Thus, against the current trend to dismiss Marxist terms like "dialectics," "totality," or "the universal" as outdated philosophical remnants of a bygone era, Brown and Szemán recognize them as indispensable tools for the critique of today's finance capital. In their view, Capital still remains the driving force of history, and it would be disastrous for the Left to mistake other, merely heuristic terms (such as "the West" or "modernity") to possess the same incisive quality. Likewise, concepts such as "difference" or "multiculturalism" produce little or no insight into the workings of capitalism at best. At worst, they might even serve to support capitalist functions and practices. Brown and Szemán, as skillful dialecticians, recognize that a similar critique might be leveled against their own ideas. But this only goes to prove, they argue, that the dialectical method of self-refutation still offers the best protection against the *hybris* of self-righteous intellectualism.

Jeffrey T. Nealon takes another approach toward Jameson. Instead of reconnecting Marxism with its Hegelian roots, Nealon's "Periodizing the 80s: The Cultural Logic of Economic Privatization in the United States" seeks to uncover "a certain positive Jamesonian itinerary" and a much less discussed "affirmative critique practiced by Jameson." Nealon detects this affirmative dimension in the performative contradictions of Jameson's seminal essay on postmodernism, which, he claims, rhetorically performs the postmodern confusion of signification it critiques. Writing during the 1980s, the "affirmative" Jameson thus implicitly challenges his readers to productively engage the then-new modes of perception and cognition that had already vanquished the historical consciousness of the 1960s—in spite of Jameson's reluctance to acknowledge this fact. With Jameson's essay "Periodizing the 60s" used as a conceptual guide, Nealon then develops a similar critique of the conservative spirit of the 80s—a period that just came to a close at the beginning of the new millennium. Just like leftist intellectuals in the 80s could not let go of the corpse of negative critique they inherited from the 60s, liberals and conservatives today cannot let go of their idealist version of capitalism they were taught to embrace during the 80s and 90s. But today's capitalism has morphed into something new entirely, and Nealon provides a detailed account of the economic and cultural shift toward total privatization that characterizes today's financial markets. What if, he asks provocatively toward the end of his essay, the "recent American cultural production isn't so much a retreat from the world of politics and engagement, but precisely an attempt to render the personal as the new frame of reference for public discourse—the thing that we all have in common"? If so, then our goal must be to understand exactly how finance capitalism works and what it renders (im)possible in the sociocultural realm. Otherwise, any push against or beyond capitalism will prove ineffective in the end.

Economic and cultural issues also lie at the center of the remaining two essays in this section. Philip Goldstein's essay, "Marxist Theory: From Aesthetic Critique to Cultural Politics," provides a comprehensive overview of deconstructionist and/or postmodernist philosophy in the context of both Frankfurt School and contemporary Marxist theory. Critical of Eagleton's and Jameson's call for a return to Adorno's aesthetics as the most promising venue to take on the cultural logic of late capitalism, Goldstein revisits the philosophico-historical roots of Adorno's cultural pessimism by means of a detailed discussion of Lukács and Heidegger as well as Derrida's comments on their works. His survey leads him to deny the political relevance of Frankfurt School's aesthetic critique for us today. Instead, he advocates a Foucauldian-based institutional politics exemplified in the recent work of Pierre Macherey: "Macherey shows that a Foucauldian theory . . . frees the critic to take local action," Goldstein contends. By contrast, Adorno's focus on negativity and his totalizing critique of instrumental reason leads to the politically disabling conclusion "that writing/art, not political action, overcomes the oppressive influence of equipmental or instrumental reason." Goldstein concludes that Adorno's mode of aesthetic critique cannot accommodate the "diverse feminist, black, gay, ethnic, or postcolonial programs and movements" that contribute to leftist politics today.

Benjamin Robinson pursues the question "Is Socialism the Index of a Leftist Ontology?" His premise contends that the abundance of different ontological theories on the Left leave us with only two choices: either to return to a kind of Heideggerian being-in-the-world as the smallest common denominator among all of them, or to deny the relevance of ontology for politics altogether. Either choice, however, further erodes the Left/Right distinction and ultimately plays into the hands of conservatism, Robinson claims. His solution is to move away from a political ontology toward a socialist or systems ontology. Entirely relational and thus economic in nature, a systems ontology maps out the various relationships that exist between fundamental and mutually incompatible ontological orders. It also features an index that indicates whether or not these orders can be brought into some kind of equilibrium, which, Robinson argues, is the ultimate goal of any leftist- or socialist-oriented ontology. "The ontological problem for leftism comes down to whether and in what way the specifically socialist index—a distinct equilibrium between otherwise incompatible orders— exists." The bulk of Robinson's essay responds to this question by providing a comprehensive analysis of socialist vs. free-market economic theory.

The third section of this anthology, entitled "Deconstruction/Politics," concerns the relationship between these two terms. Derrida's claim, in 1994, that "Deconstruction had never any sense or interest . . . except as a radicalization, which is to say also *in the tradition* of a certain Marxism, in a certain *spirit of Marxism*," irritated many Marxists and led them to denounce what they perceived as the apolitical, if not conservative, nature of deconstruction.[54] Similarly, other critics have dismissed the deconstructive brand of post-Marxism advocated by Laclau and Mouffe as antimaterialist, relativistic, or even idealist, claiming that it is of no use for the formulation of a leftist politics.[55] The writers in this section disagree with this assessment and try to account for the ontological function of language and rhetoric as the basis of the political.

Roland Végső's essay, "Deconstruction and Experience: The Politics of the Undeconstructable," begins with a concise summary of Negri and Hardt's, Žižek's, and Laclau's critiques of the political impetus of Derrida's philosophy. Although in conflict with each other, these three leftist per-spectives coincide in their critique of "the limits of deconstruction" as they call for a "more precise articulation of the position of the undeconstruct-able within deconstruction," Végső concludes. In response, he provides a detailed discussion of Derrida's notion of experience in order to strengthen the phenomenological roots of deconstruction. For Derrida, Végső argues, "the subject of politics is constituted by an undeconstructable experience." Although "impossible," this experience still exists precisely as an experi-ence of the impossible. Végső draws two interdependent conclusions from this insight: first, that a "deconstructionist ontology (or hauntology) cannot be inherently leftist," because there is "no logical move from radical unde-cidability to a leftist politics"; and second, that it is precisely Derrida's "political (and not philosophical) attempt to identify the undeconstructable with emancipation" that situates him squarely within the leftist political tradition.

Sorin Radu-Cucu's "Politics and the Fiction of the Political" provides a historical account of how the distinction between politics *(la politique)* and the political *(le politique)* established itself in the 1980s in the context of deconstructive and post-Marxist French philosophy. After tracing the implications of this distinction in contemporary theory, Radu-Cucu pres-ents a series of close readings comparing Laclau's recent work with that of Alain Badiou and Claude Lefort. What distinguishes Laclau from the latter two, Radu-Cucu argues, is his effort to provide an ontology of the social that is exclusively grounded on rhetorical modes of representation. For Laclau, what ultimately matters in politics is the promise of establishing any order rather than the specific content of a particular order. With refer-ence to Laclau rather than Derrida, Radu-Cucu comes to a similar two-pronged conclusion, as did Végső in the previous essay. Although "there is no Leftist ontology" as such, ontology nonetheless "becomes indispen-sable to Leftist politics, inasmuch as it leads to the possibility of hegemonic relations" and thus to the social implementation of leftist political demands.

The last contribution in this section, Alberto Moreiras's "The Last God: María Zambrano's Life without Texture," introduces a thinker whose work still remains largely unknown in English-speaking countries. Moreiras demonstrates the relevance of María Zambrano's political philosophy by reading it in the context of Heidegger's post-*Kehre* reflections on Being. He argues that Zambrano radicalizes Heidegger's attempts to move be-yond subjectivity as the transcendental ground for thinking and politics. Because subjectivity, sovereignty, and militancy are inextricably linked and coconstitutive of the ontotheological history of Western thought, Zambrano thus develops an understanding of the political that abandons this history—the identity of thinking and being—in favor of thinking nothingness or nonbeing as the prerequisite for redemption and a return of the sacred. According to Moreiras, this active dismantling (and not just forgetting) of Being "requires a renunciation to the renunciation of the excess of being. . . . Only in that renunciation to renunciation, in that double renunciation and double distance, will the totality of thought open up." While Zambrano's "promise of an altogether different politics" places her work in close proximity to Derridean deconstruction, her insistence on this double process (that is, the active undoing of Being in favor of embracing nothingness as redemption) moves into an altogether different direction that is neither phenomenology, nor existentialism, nor (Christian) theology and whose precise contours are difficult to delineate today, Moreiras concludes.

The last part of the anthology, headed "Psychoanalysis and the Political," concerns efforts to base leftist politics on a nonessentialist ontology of the body. The two essays in this section are critical of traditional political philosophy and its demand for rational conflict resolution, which, they argue, has failed to offer effective remedies against human aggression and irrational desires that are part of the human psyche. Hence, these writers agree with Lacan and others that the political cannot be conceived of as a question of the good or the rational. Rather, it must confront the force of desire, the compulsion of the drives, and the physicality of the flesh.

Christopher Breu, in his essay, "Signification and Substance: Toward a Leftist Ontology of the Present," argues that Lacanian psychoanalysis, with its attention to the tripartite relationship among language, desire, and materiality, is able to overcome the current deadlock between the two most important theoretical developments of the last decades: the metaepistemological critique of nature, biology, and language proffered by poststructuralism on the one hand, and the critique of late capitalist economic inequality advanced by neo-Marxist and globalization theories on the other. Breu negotiates this dyadic tension between discourse and materiality via the tripartite categories of the imaginary, the symbolic, and the real. Thus, his Marxo-Lacanian ethics is able to address the fundamental role of fantasy in contemporary politics, which proclaims our powerlessness vis-à-vis the symbolic structure and economic power of global capitalism: "Breaking with this fundamental fantasy would also mean. . . . letting go of our fantasies of social class, cultural capital, and hierarchical racial, gendered, and sexual difference along with the bourgeois ethics that justifies them . . . in order to fully recognize the randomness and arbitrary qualities of the market and our position in it," Breu concludes.

"A Politics of Melancholia" by Klaus Mladek and George Edmondson, examines why "the left . . . continued to mistrust, even to despise, not just the melancholic alone but its own melancholic tendencies." Whereas Rasch's introductory essay categorically rejects leftist melancholia as detrimental to the achievement of progressive political goals, Mladek and Edmondson recognize the "political thrust" of the melancholic's "unerring fidelity to the object, his unconditional commitment beyond all considerations of the pleasure principle, his noninstrumental resistance." Via a close reading of Judith Butler's and Antonio Negri's theories of subjectivity in the context of Freudo-Lacanian psychoanalysis, Mladek and Edmondson conceptualize a nonreactionary politics of melancholia that affirms the right to refuse action and to expand the traumatic moment of inertia indefinitely. The leftist melancholic knows that although we cannot redeem the past, we cannot just let go of it either. This rejection of a forward and goal-oriented politics distinguishes the politics of melancholy from Alain Badiou's endorsement of subjectivity as seized by the event. With Badiou, "One is enjoined to maintain fidelity to that which has seized and shattered her, but never to the instance of seizing and shattering itself." The melancholic, by contrast, affirms a "pure loss without reciprocity" and holds onto the "lost cause of neighborhood and community" in spite of it all.

Our final contribution is Bruno Bosteels's afterword, entitled "Thinking, Being, Acting; or, On the Uses and Disadvantages of Ontology for Politics." Rather than offering isolated remarks on the various essays in this book, Bosteels's conclusion addresses some of the underlying threads and questions that run through the entire collection as a whole. Is ontology the right term to address the anthropological assumptions advocated by Bobbie and others? Does the postmetaphysical ontology espoused by most contributors not lead to the hypostasization of clichéd ontological principles at the expense of pragmatic social action? Should we therefore not turn our attention to the possibility of a leftist theory of the subject to avoid this impasse? The theory of the subject, Bosteels argues, "turns out to be barred or blocked, put under erasure, or kept at the level of virtuality or potentiality without actuality, by some of the most radical arguments for a leftist ontology in this volume." Inspired most notably by the philosophy of Alain Badiou, Bosteels implies that there can be no progressive sociopolitical change without thinking through the emergence of subjectivity and the subject of politics. He also argues for a revalidation of the philosophical and political dimension of actuality over and against the current infatuation with potentiality, multiplicity, and becomings. Bosteels's cautious evaluation of the relationship of ontology and politics thus complements—or counterpoints—the more affirmative vision expressed in William E. Connolly's foreword. To some degree, then, our debate about a leftist ontology is framed by the philosophical terrain opened up in Deleuze's and Badiou's work, although I do not believe that the diverse essays in this book are reducible to either pole. Instead, they aspire to open up new venues for political thought in the hope of breaking new pathways for social action. Whether or not they succeed will be determined by our readers and their response to the ideas presented in this book.

NOTES

1. Jorge Raventos, "From the New Left to Postmodern Populism: An Interview with Paul Piccone," *Telos* 122 (2002): 137–38.

2. Hans Ulrich Gumbrecht, *Production of Presence: What Meaning Cannot Convey* (Stanford: Stanford University Press, 2004), 160, n. 2.

3. Anthony Giddens, *Beyond Left and Right: The Future of Radical Politics* (Stanford: Stanford University Press, 1994). For a detailed critique of Giddens's position, see Chantal Mouffe, *On the Political* (London: Routledge, 2005), 35–63.

4. Norberto Bobbio, *Left and Right: The Significance of a Political Distinction*, trans. Allan Cameron (Cambridge: Polity Press, 1996), 67.

5. Ibid, 60, 63. Allan Cameron, in his introductory notes to the book, rightly insists that "Left and Right do not represent two sets of fixed ideas, but rather an axis which shifts considerably from one generation to the next" (ix).

6. Bobbio, *Left and Right*, 72.

7. Perry Anderson, *Spectrum* (New York: Verso, 2005), 131. All further references to this book will appear parenthetically in the text.

8. Anderson led the charge against post-Marxist theory in general, claiming it reduces history to an utterly random and indeterminate process. See his *In the Tracks of Historical Materialism* (London: Verso, 1984). Referring to Anderson, Terry Eagleton detected in Laclau and Mouffe "a familiar idealist move" that refuses to recognize the ontological primacy of materialist history. Terry Eagleton, *Ideology. An Introduction* (London: Verso, 1991), 219. Similarly, Norman Geras protested against a perspective that inevitably leads to a "bottomless, relativist gloom, in which opposed discourses or paradigms are left with no common reference point." Norman Geras, "Post-Marxism?" *New Left Review* 163 (May–June 1987): 67.

9. The idea of never-dying Marxism was introduced even before Jacques Derrida published his *Specters of Marx* in 1994. See Fredric Jameson, "Actually Existing Marxism," *Polygraph* 6/7 (1993): 170–95, and Arif Dirlik, "Post Socialism/Flexible Production: Marxism in Contemporary Radicalism," *Polygraph* 6/7 (1993): 133–69.

10. The charge of "performative contradiction" was first raised by Karl-Otto Apel not against Marxism, but against French deconstruction. Karl-Otto Apel, *Towards*

a *Transformation of Philosophy*, trans. Glyn Adey and David Frisby (London: Routledge, 1980), 225ff. Jürgen Habermas has been the most reliant advocate of this
critique over the last two decades, for example in *The Philosophical Discourse of
Modernity: Twelve Lectures*, trans. Frederick G. Lawrence (Cambridge: MIT Press,
1987), 185ff. Boris Groys's *Das Kommunistische Postskriptum* (Frankfurt: Suhrkamp,
2005) specifically focuses on the role of paradox in classical and orthodox Marxist
theory. For a comprehensive overview of the discursive role of performative contradictions, see Barbara Herrnstein Smith, *Belief and Resistance: Dynamics of Contemporary Intellectual Controversy* (Cambridge: Harvard University Press, 1997).

11. Carl Schmitt, *Der Begriff des Politischen* (Berlin: Duncker & Humblot, 1932).
More recently, the term has been used in both Claude Lefort's "The Question of
Democracy," in *Democracy and Political Theory* (Minneapolis: University of Minnesota Press, 1988), and in Philippe Lacou-Labarthe's and Jean-Luc Nancy's *Retreating
the Political*, ed. Simon Sparks (New York: Routledge, 1997). The latter in particular refers to the distinction between the abstract system of social relations (i.e., "the
political," or, in French, *le politique*) and the empirical filling of this system with a
particular content ("politics," or, in French, *la politique*). Andrew Norris, however,
rightly emphasizes the vagueness of this distinction in today's critical discourse.
Andrew Norris, "Introduction: Giorgio Agamben and the Politics of the Living
Dead," in *Politics, Metaphysics, and Death: Essays on Giorgio Agamben's "Homo Sacer,"*
ed. Andrew Norris (Durham: Duke University Press, 2005), 28, n. 50.

12. Richard Rorty, *Objectivity, Relativism, and Truth* (Cambridge: Cambridge University Press, 1991), 100.

13. William E. Connolly, *Pluralism* (Durham: Duke University Press, 2005), 41.

14. Ernesto Laclau and Chantal Mouffe, "Post-Marxism Without Apologies," in
Ernesto Laclau, *New Reflections on the Revolution of Our Time* (London, New York:
Verso, 1991), 104.

15. Ernesto Laclau, *Emancipations* (London: Verso, 2000), 85.

16. Hannah Arendt and Karl Jaspers, *Briefwechsel, 1926–1969*, ed. L. Köhler and
H. Saner (Munich: Piper, 1985), 325; my translation.

17. Hannah Arendt, *Was ist Politik? Fragmente aus dem Nachlaß*, ed. Ursula
Ludz (Munich: Piper, 2003), 11; my translation.

18. Hannah Arendt, *Vom Leben des Geistes I. Das Denken* (Munich: Piper, 1979),
37; my translation.

19. See Arendt, *Was ist Politik?* 48, 102ff.; Hannah Arendt, *Zwischen Vergangen-
heit und Zukunft. Übungen im Politischen Denken I*, ed. Ursula Ludz (Munich: Piper,
1994), 314ff.

20. Leo Strauss, "What is Political Philosophy?" in *Political Philosophy: Six Essays
by Leo Strauss*, ed. Hilail Gildin (Indianapolis: Bobbs-Merrill, 1975), 21. All further
references to this book will appear parenthetically in the text.

21. Connolly, *Pluralism*, 126.

22. In his critique of *The Concept of the Political*, Strauss rightly notes that
Schmitt oscillates between denying and admitting the possibility of ever moving
beyond the political. In those passages where Schmitt admits of this possibility, he
links the fate of the political with that of humanity in general. According to Strauss,
Schmitt believes that "The political is . . . not only possible but also real; and not

only real but also necessary. It is necessary because it is given in human nature. . . . Accordingly, the thesis of man's dangerousness is the ultimate presupposition of the position of the political." Leo Strauss, "Notes on Carl Schmitt, *The Concept of the Political*," in Carl Schmitt, *The Concept of the Political,* trans. and ed. George Schwab (Chicago: University of Chicago Press, 1996), 95. Strauss's main critique of Schmitt then focuses on the fact that Schmitt's belief in the inherently dangerous nature of man cannot be deduced logically from his own concept of the political. In fact, Strauss argues, it is the other way around: Schmitt's anthropological premise about man's dangerousness serves as the foundation for his embrace of the political. Hence, as soon as we challenge this anthropological premise, Schmitt's contention that the political is ontologically primary or more important than other social fields falters.

23. The term *secularism* is ambivalent and mobilizes a variety of different concepts, as William E. Connolly has reminded us. Our version of it would be one that does not suppress the political relevance of religious beliefs or other "visceral aptitudes." William E. Connolly, *Why I Am Not a Secularist* (Minneapolis: University of Minnesota Press, 1999).

24. With regard to the term *neoleft,* see Carsten Strathausen, "A Critique of Neo-Left Ontology," *Postmodern Culture* 16, no. 3 (Fall 2006).

25. Leo Strauss, *Natural Right and History* (Chicago: University of Chicago Press, 1953), 80.

26. See Doreen Massey, *For Space* (London: Sage, 2005).

27. Ernesto Laclau and Chantal Mouffe, *Hegemony and Socialist Strategy: Towards a Radical Democratic Politics* (New York: Verso, 1985), 111.

28. Slavoj Žižek was among the first to forge a connection between Laclau and Mouffe's claim about the impossibility of the social and Lacanian terminology. Slavoj Žižek, "Beyond Discourse-Analysis," afterword to Ernesto Laclau, *New Reflections on the Revolution of Our Time* (London, New York: Verso, 1991), 254. Laclau himself has explicitly acknowledged that his understanding of (an empty) universality is closely tied to Lacan's notion of the Real and/or the *objet petit a.* See, for example, Laclau, *New Reflections,* 235. With regard to Laclau's relation to Heidegger, see Ernesto Laclau, "A Reply," in *Laclau: A Critical Reader,* ed. Simon Critchley and Oliver Marchart (London: Routledge, 2004), 288ff.

29. Slavoj Žižek, "Introduction: The Spectre of Ideology," in *Mapping Ideology,* ed. Slavoj Žižek (New York: Verso, 1994), 17, 30.

30. See Alain Badiou, *Deleuze: The Clamour of Being,* trans. Louise Burchill (Minneapolis: University of Minnesota Press, 2000), and the excellent collection of essays edited by Lars Tonder and Lasse Tomassen, *Radical Democracy: Politics between Abundance and Lack* (Manchester: Manchester University Press, 2006).

31. Gilles Deleuze, *Difference and Repetition,* trans. Paul Patton (New York: Columbia University Press, 1994), 147; Alain Badiou, *Metapolitics,* trans. Jason Baker (London: Verso, 2005), 77, xxxix. There is no space here to engage Peter Hallward's objection that Deleuze's work, unlike Badiou's, "is essentially indifferent to the politics of this world" because it "disables action in favor of contemplation." Peter Hallward, *Out of this World: Deleuze and the Philosophy of Creation* (New York: Verso, 2005), 162–63. Suffice it to say that Hallward examines Deleuze's legacy exclusively in

philosophical terms. His intriguing study, however, does not comment on Deleuze's influence among artists, critics, and other public figures over the last decades.

32. See, for example, Ian Hacking, "Soziale Konstruktion beim Wort genommen," in *Wissen zwischen Entdeckung und Konstruktion,* ed. Matthias Vogel and Lutz Wingert (Frankfurt: Suhrkamp, 2003).

33. Jürgen Habermas, "The Horrors of Autonomy: Carl Schmitt in English," in *The New Conservatism: Cultural Criticism and the Historians' Debate,* ed. and trans. Shierry Weber Nicholsen (Cambridge: MIT Press, 1989), 139. All further references to this essay will appear in the text. For Chantal Mouffe, of course, this separation between liberalism and democracy is absolutely crucial, and she fully supports Schmitt on this point. See Chantal Mouffe, *The Democratic Paradox* (New York: Verso, 2000).

34. John Rawls, *The Law of Peoples, with The Idea of Public Reason Revisited* (Cambridge: Harvard University Press, 2001), 4.

35. John Rawls, *Political Liberalism* (New York: Columbia University Press, 1993), 37.

36. Jürgen Habermas, *Die Einbeziehung des Anderen: Studien zur Politischen Theorie* (Frankfurt: Suhrkamp, 1996), 217; my translation. It is interesting to note the similarity between Habermas's formulation and that of Leo Strauss, who likewise contends that "in fact, it is not altogether wrong to describe justice as a kind of *benevolent coercion*" (Strauss, *Natural Right and History,* 133; my emphasis).

37. Giovanna Borradori, *Philosophy in a Time of Terror: Dialogues with Jürgen Habermas and Jacques Derrida* (Chicago: University of Chicago Press, 2003), 34.

38. Ibid., 41ff.; my emphasis.

39. Strauss, "Notes on Carl Schmitt," 105.

40. Ibid. Let us recall that Strauss also mobilizes this charge of relativism against modernity in general and scientific positivism in particular. Hence his critique of Max Weber, who similarly embraces formalist principles that remain without specific content: "Thou shalt have ideals," Strauss paraphrases Weber's overall position, "be that good or bad" (Strauss, *Natural Right and History,* 4ff.). According to Strauss, Weber's "theoretical attitude implies equal respect for all causes, but such respect is possible only for him who is not devoted to any cause" (46).

41. Leo Strauss, "The Three Waves of Modernity," in Gildin, *Political Philosophy,* 81.

42. Chantal Mouffe, "Introduction: Schmitt's Challenge," in *The Challenge of Carl Schmitt,* ed. Chantal Mouffe (New York: Verso, 1999), 4. See also Laclau and Mouffe, *Hegemony of Socialist Strategy,* xvii.

43. Chantal Mouffe, "Carl Schmitt and the Paradox of Liberal Democracy," in Mouffe, *Challenge of Carl Schmitt,* 44.

44. Mouffe, "Introduction: Schmitt's Challenge," 5.

45. Mouffe, "Carl Schmitt and the Paradox of Liberal Democracy," 51; my emphasis. Similarly, Slavoj Žižek claims that Schmitt illegitimately "displaces the *inherent* antagonism constitutive of the political on to the *external* relationship between Us and Them." Slavoj Žižek, "Carl Schmitt in the Age of Post-Politics," in Mouffe, *Challenge of Carl Schmitt,* 27.

46. Chantal Mouffe, *The Return of the Political* (London: Verso, 1993), 145.

47. Laclau in Chantal Mouffe, ed., *Deconstruction and Pragmatism: Simon Critchley, Jacques Derrida, Ernesto Laclau, and Richard Rorty,* ed. Chantal Mouffe (London: Routledge, 1996), 60, 58.

48. Ibid., 77.

49. Laclau, "A Reply," 321.

50. Ernesto Laclau, *On Populist Reason* (London: Verso, 2005), xi.

51. Ibid., 67.

52. A similar critique is advanced by Bill Rasch, *Niklas Luhmann's Modernity: The Paradoxes of Differentiation* (Stanford: Stanford University Press, 2000), 166ff.

53. A notable exception is Tonder and Thomassen, *Radical Democracy.*

54. Jacques Derrida, *Specters of Marx: The State of the Debt, the Work of Mourning and the New International* (London: Routledge, 1994), 92.

55. See Michael Sprinker, ed., *Ghostly Demarcations: A Symposium on Jacques Derrida's "Specters of Marx"* (London: Verso, 1999).

I

AGAMBEN, VIOLENCE, AND REDEMPTION

1

The Structure of the Political vs. the Politics of Hope

WILLIAM RASCH

There is no Leftist ontology. Let me phrase this less ontologically. There *ought not* be a *Leftist* ontology. To think one hears the music of the spheres and recognize in it the tune to "La Marseillaise" is a sign of desperation, a sign that the political game is being lost and therefore ought to be rigged. No matter how bruised, dazed, bloodied, and confused it may be, the Left must quit its search for subjects of history or any other deus ex machina and fight its fight in the only realm fit to fight in—the political. So if the Left wishes to construe its mission ontologically, if it wishes to articulate the ontological commitments inherent in a position or the ontological presuppositions of an argument, then the political ought to be the domain (or language game, form of communication, operative distinction, or whatever else one's other ontological commitments dictate) of scrutiny; and the Left must recognize that the shape of the political accommodates the entire seating chart of the French National Assembly, not just its left half. So good at denaturalizing natural law and secularizing the divine, the Left should resist, finally, the temptation to reenchant politics with visions of a postpolitical paradise, whether achieved by violence or moral and normative hectoring. The multitude will no more rise spontaneously with a uniform voice than did, despite cinematic fantasies, the World War I dead out of their graves to accuse the living. The Left, then, should not compete with liberal obfuscations about perpetual peace but should concentrate on the little and big wars that accompany our days on earth. Individuals will bitch and moan, kick and scream, and it is to the bitching and kicking we must attend, little by little, and be open to the moaning and screaming of even those who hate us. Even those whom we exclude from the political when

3

we have power remain in the ontological frame. Even they remain potentially political and will still fight for the privilege of having power. And even
we—that is, the Left—have to recognize this fact.

So what commitment underlies the list of imperatives in the previous
paragraph? I presuppose an ontological priority of violence, though my use
of the term *ontological* is conventional and not necessarily based on any
specific definition of what ontology might mean in the Western tradition
in the twentieth or twenty-first centuries. I see the political as a means of
limiting but never eliminating violence (and its varied sublimated forms)
in social life. The stress on limitation rather than elimination (limited war
rather than perpetual peace, for example) is based on pragmatic rather
than ontological, anthropological, or psychological considerations, though
these cannot be completely avoided. It assumes that theories of ultimate
pacification are either unrealizable (no matter how ideal the speech situation in a global public sphere may be), or, worse, lead, by way of a violence
to end all violence, to total wars (and totalitarian suppression). The inflex-
ibility of goals dictates a terrifying flexibility of means. The political should
be the realm (institutional and communicative) in which and by which
violence is reduced and managed in all forms of social life. By assuming
the impossibility of complete pacification, one need not explain the presence
of violence as a moral or political aberration; thus, dealing with violence
need not derive its legitimacy from moral, religious, or scientific discourse.
Indeed, because the eruption of violence is always expected, its successful
avoidance is a gratifying blessing.

All Leftist (and Rightist, Centrist, human, [other] animal, vegetable, and
mineral) politics ought to start from this premise. It is the premise that
informs the following reflections.

The Form of the Political

Whatever other merits Walter Benjamin's 1921 essay "Critique of Violence"
may or may not have, and whatever other aims he may have pursued in it,
the operative distinctions he draws there give clear shape to arguments,
then and now, about the nature of the political. I refer to the fundamental
(and fundamentally evaluative) distinction he makes between mythic and
divine violence on the one hand, and then, within the realm of mythic violence, the distinction between law-preserving and law-positing violence on
the other. Much has been written on this essay and on the nature of divine
violence, its messianic qualities and apparent promise for a longed-for but
unknown and unknowable future. I do not propose to add substantially to

this discussion. That is, my focus is not on the essay as such, but rather on the schema his distinctions provide. That schema may be sketched as follows:

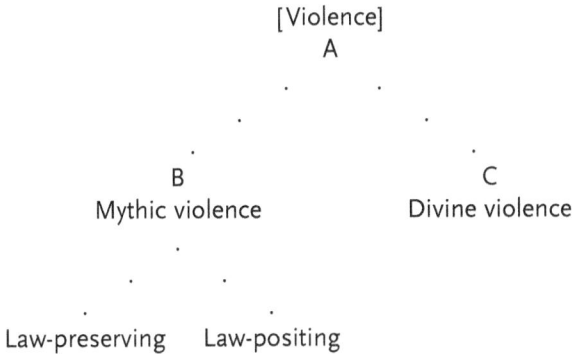

[Violence]
A

B
Mythic violence

C
Divine violence

Law-preserving   Law-positing

Mythic violence, with its legal functions, is easily recognizable as the modern manifestation of political life as state violence. In the terms bequeathed to us by Emmanuel Sieyès, law-preserving and law-positing violence can be equated with constituted and constituent power. At the time of the French Revolution, Sieyès identified the "nation"—more specifically, the Third Estate—as the true constituent power of the state and hence as the source of all law. He conceded that at this stage of history, the nation no longer manifests itself immediately as a common will, but works through representatives to whom it delegates power by way of a constitution. Nevertheless: "The nation exists prior to everything; it is the origin of everything. Its will is always legal. It is the law itself. . . . The national will . . . simply needs the reality of its existence to be legal. It is the origin of all legality."[1] On this view, the nation serves as an immanent god, as the formless source of all form. "A nation never leaves the state of nature and, amidst so many perils, it can never have too many possible ways of expressing its will. . . . [A] nation is independent of all forms and, however it may will, it is enough for its will to be made known for all positive law to fall silent in its presence, because it is the source and supreme master of all positive law."[2] As the source of constituted power (law), the constituent power sets limits but remains itself unlimited.

Benjamin has nothing but contempt for this view of the political, as a quick glance at the final paragraph of the essay will show us. Were one to direct one's gaze, he writes, "only at what is close at hand," one would notice a dialectic of decay in operation, as every act of law-preserving violence "indirectly weakens the lawmaking violence it represents, by suppressing hostile counterviolence. . . . This lasts until either new forces or those earlier suppressed triumph over the hitherto lawmaking violence and thus found a new law, destined in its turn to decay."[3] Whatever these new or old forces may be, they remained locked in the merely political struggles of mythic violence. One might therefore read in this passage the history of European revolutions in which the state apparatus is passed on from one constituent power to the next, namely from the privileged castes to the Third Estate in 1789 and from the bourgeoisie to the dictatorship of the proletariat in 1917. In each case, a purported revolutionary violence reveals itself to have been simply a means used for the acquisition of political power and thus for the maintenance of state power. Were, however, "the existence of violence outside the law" possible, were it possible to feel the effects of a "pure immediate violence," a true "revolutionary violence" that is the "highest manifestation of unalloyed violence," a "divine violence" that is the "divine judgment" of a "true war," then we would witness the founding of a "new historical epoch" that suspends all law and abolishes the power of the state.[4] This crescendo of apocalyptic imaginings culminates in the poetically beautiful and rhetorically devastating indictment of the political contained in the final three sentences: "But all mythic, lawmaking violence, which we may call 'executive,' is pernicious. Pernicious, too, is the law-preserving, 'administrative' violence that serves it. Divine violence, which is the sign and seal but never the means of sacred dispatch, may be called 'sovereign' violence."[5]

The powerful, prophetic tone of Benjamin's evocation of divine destruction marks a radical intensification of the distinctions Georges Sorel develops in *Reflections on Violence*—so much so, in fact, that it remains unclear how the two sets correlate with one another. If one takes Sieyès's distinction between constituted and constituent power as the background against which Sorel casts his reflections, then one can imagine that both Sorel's political and his proletarian general strike take place within the realm of Benjamin's mythic violence, that is, within the realm of clearly defined political activity. On this reading, a political general strike, in which acquisition of state power, not its overthrow, is at stake, is merely the attempt of the socialist parliamentary parties, upon which Sorel heaped mountains of scorn, to seize the administrative apparatus of the state, its law-preserving function, while leaving the state otherwise as it is. The constituent power— whatever or whoever that may be—remains undisturbed. The proletarian general strike, on the other hand, which has nothing immediately at stake but the strike itself, could be seen as the unmediated manifestation of a new constituent power positing a new law and thus a whole new political structure whose shape remains unknown and unknowable. "The syndicalists," Sorel assures us, "do not propose to reform the State, as the men of the eighteenth century did; they want to destroy it."[6] Thus, while force "aims at authority, endeavoring to bring about an automatic obedience," violence "would smash that authority."[7] The distinction between a political and a proletarian general strike, if contained within Benjamin's mythic violence, marks an implosion of the state, an immanent destruction and putative renewal.

At the same time, however, Sorel wishes to make a qualitative distinction between a negatively marked *force,* whose object it is "to impose a certain social order in which the minority governs," and a positively valued *violence* that "tends to the destruction of that order."[8] This distinction can be translated into German only with the help of adjectival qualifiers, and thus *force* seems clearly recoded by Benjamin as the mythic violence *(mythische Gewalt)* of the state and *violence* as the divine violence *(göttliche Gewalt)* that stands outside all law. Accordingly, if *violence* is associated with the general proletarian strike, then that form of revolutionary activity cannot be thought of in political terms, for, as divine violence, it must stand outside the realm of the political altogether. As the manifestation of divine violence, the proletarian general strike no longer functions simply as a new constituent power or law-positing violence, but as the violence that destroys all law. By radicalizing Sorel's distinctions, Benjamin removes Sorel's proletarian general strike from the dialectic of law's renewal and decay and thus fully and unabashedly returns to it the messianic quality that has been at the heart of leftist revolutionary longing since long before Marx made messianic hope scientific.

Mischievously, Benjamin uses another pregnant Sorelian term to mark the denigrated realm of the political, namely *myth,* while elevating the theologically inflected *divine* (again: *göttlich*) to the status of a Sorelian myth. Sorel, you will recall, distinguishes the myth of the general strike from the intellectual projects of utopia. "Whilst contemporary myths," Sorel writes, "lead men to prepare themselves for combat which will destroy the existing state of things, the effect of utopias has always been to direct men's minds towards reforms." Furthermore, a "myth cannot be refuted because it is, at bottom, identical to the convictions of a group" and thus "unanalysable into parts that could be placed on the plane of historical descriptions." Utopias, on the other hand, "can be discussed like any other social constitution."[9] It seems, then, that Benjamin's relatively insubstantial description of divine violence as the "antithesis" of state violence "in all respects" follows from the necessarily nonrational, nondiscursive nature of political myth. Thus Benjamin is limited by the "unanalysability" of divine violence to the following series of negations: "If mythic violence is lawmaking, divine violence is law-destroying; if the former sets boundaries, the latter boundlessly destroys them, if mythic violence brings at once guilt and retribution, divine power only expiates; if the former threatens, the latter strikes; if the former is bloody, the latter is lethal without spilling blood."[10]

One might do well to pause here and ask whether it makes sense to treat Benjamin's essay as a political tract. Most recent receptions of Benjamin consider his writings to be more on the order of revelations—of the nature of literature, of language, indeed, of being as such. Thus his "Critique of Violence," with its theological elevation of Sorelian language, could be said to be not a political critique but rather a critique of the political per se. This, of course, is its danger, for the temptation becomes one of thinking the political precisely in theological, which is to say, in messianic and redemptive terms. This temptation is one that Giorgio Agamben has found impossible to resist.

At stake for Agamben, as it was for Benjamin, is the uncoupling of law and violence. Pure violence correlates with pure being before it is captured in the meshes of logos. It is parallel to the pure communicability of language rather than the communication facilitated by language when it is used as a means. Violence *pur* is not a means, but pure mediality as such. Referring then to the closing lines of Benjamin's essay, Agamben can conclude that "pure violence exposes and severs the nexus between law and violence and can thus appear in the end not as violence that governs or executes *(die schaltende)* but as violence that purely acts and manifests *(die waltende)*."[11] On this view, the political as presently constituted, as law and violence, can only be thought of as the epitome of nihilism. As Agamben states in *Homo Sacer*, the emblem of the political within modernity is the camp; its product is the degradation of human existence that the term *bare life* is meant to convey. To engage in the political as presently constituted is to become contaminated, infected with the guilt imposed by law. Agamben quotes Benjamin's assertion: "If violence is also assured a reality outside the law, as pure immediate violence, this furnishes proof that revolutionary violence—which is the name of the highest manifestation of pure violence by man—is also possible."[12] Revolution is here thought of not as the political revolutions of old, not as 1789, which must inexorably lead to 1793, not as a revolution of political power against political power, but a revolt against the political as such. Accordingly, the revolutionary violence that both Benjamin and Agamben advance here is not the law-positing constituent power that forms part of the mythic violence of the state; it is not a constituent power of a discrete political collective with particular interests. Instead, it is thought of as a pure constituent power that constitutes a radically new order and thus a radically new historical epoch simply by way of its absolute destructive capacity. This new order is something other than a political order, for it issues no law and exerts no violence.

According to Agamben, upon reading Benjamin's essay, Carl Schmitt instantly recognized the very real threat its subversive categories posed to the regime of guilt, law, and violence that Schmitt purportedly fought to uphold. It is as if a seam in the fabric of the heavens had torn open to reveal God in all his anger and glory, and Schmitt felt himself called upon to repair the damage before anyone noticed. Thus Agamben constructs an "esoteric dossier," a hidden call and response between Benjamin and Schmitt, in which the former plays the provocateur and the latter the state's agent of repression.[13] On Agamben's reading, Schmitt's *Political Theology* is only understandable as a fighting retreat in the face of Benjamin's onslaught. Thus, because Benjamin correctly identifies constituent power with the promised revolutionary catastrophe of divine violence, Schmitt is forced to give up the distinction between constituent and constituting power that he developed in his *Die Diktatur* (originally published in 1921), and replace it with the notion of sovereign decision. In Agamben's view,

> [I]t is in order to neutralize this new figure of a pure violence removed from the dialectic between constituent power and constituted power that Schmitt develops his theory of sovereignty. The sovereign violence in *Political Theology* responds to the pure violence of Benjamin's essay with the figure of a power that neither makes nor preserves law, but suspends it. Similarly, it is in response to Benjamin's idea of an ultimate undecidability of all legal problems that Schmitt affirms sovereignty as the place of the extreme decision.[14]

In other words, faced with the threat of redemption, Schmitt secures the condition of possibility for the camps.

I find this claim to be odd. Not only does it entail the assumption that in *Political Theology* all the discussion of and debate with Anschütz, Bodin, Bonald, Donoso Cortés, Gierke, Hegel, Hobbes, Jellinek, Kant, Kelsen,

Krabbe, Leibniz, Locke, de Maistre, Marx, Proudhon, Rousseau, Schelling, Stahl, Stein, Weber, and others must be seen as a mere exoteric smoke screen to hide from view the much more explosive and dangerous Benjamin; but it also asserts that "decision" replaces rather than complements the distinction between constituent and constituting power, or that it somehow marks the opposite of undecidability. I concede, however, the assertion's attraction and note that it may not be altogether without merit— though I reject the values Agamben assigns to the protagonists of this drama. Schmitt may indeed have recognized in Benjamin's text both a theological heresy and a political danger, for Schmitt knew that attempts to establish the Kingdom of Heaven on Earth are blasphemy—religious and political blasphemy. He may have recognized in Benjamin a true political theologian, not in the sense Schmitt meant when he used the term to outline a research methodology, but in an emphatically and dangerously religious sense. Neither Benjamin nor Agamben use secularized theological concepts just to dissect what lies before them; rather, they describe the political in an aestheticized theological idiom that invests it with a redemptive meaning and importance that political discourse can never bear. Even when redemption is explicitly denied, it is evoked, and we respond, or are meant to respond, with longing. Referring to Benjamin's views on baroque eschatology, Agamben writes that this "'white eschatology' . . . does not lead the earth to a redeemed hereafter, but consigns it to an absolutely empty sky," that "this white eschatology . . . shatters the correspondence between sovereignty and transcendence" that Schmitt purportedly advances, and that it instantiates a "zone of absolute indeterminacy between anomie and law, in which the sphere of creatures and the juridical order are caught up in a single catastrophe."[15] There is a cavalier indifference to human suffering in this sanitized scene of catastrophe. There is no hint here of a Schopenhauer-like resignation of the will as the world executes its revenge on the human species, perhaps one day by way of a truly "divine" environmental catastrophe. Thus Agamben's invocation of catastrophe must be comforted by the very foreknowledge it forswears. That is, it peeks around the corner to see what the new historical epoch will look like. Not surprisingly, it always finds what it looks for. "What becomes of the law after its messianic fulfillment?" Agamben asks. Law's "deactivation," he answers, its "inactivity," its being put out of work. What awaits us, then, is the following:

> One day humanity will play with law just as children play with disused objects, not in order to restore them to their canonical use but to free them

from it for good. What is found after the law is not a more proper and original use value that precedes the law, but a new use that is born only after it. And use, which has been contaminated by law, must also be freed from its own value. This liberation is the task of study, or play.[16]

Heaven on earth as a Victorian nursery, without the nanny; or perhaps an academic office, located in a building only Kafka could design, where neither students nor administrators will ever find it.

Pure violence stands outside the realm of the social altogether. It imagines itself, to be sure, as the purification of politics, as the pure politics of a purified world, for Agamben is repulsed by the dirty, messy, sticky, smelly world of the political every bit as much as St. Paul was by the dirty, messy, sticky, smelly world of sex. But what about the rest of us, those who are content to see messiahs crucified whenever and wherever they make their appearance? What about those of us who inescapably inhabit the world of the political and are apparently so blinkered and blinded by state power that we deny the reality of redemptive politics? To those who have their doubts about redemption, I suggest we crawl directly into the belly of the beast of mythic violence to see what we may find.

WEBER AND VIOLENCE

In his famous lecture, *Politics as a Vocation,* delivered in January 1919, during a time of rebellious upheavals after World War I, Max Weber could claim, with reasonable assurance of being understood, that the "decisive means of politics is the use of violence" and again that "politics operates with . . . power, backed up by the use of *violence.*"[17] This assertion to be sure was subject to qualification. The political, he said, makes use of "specific means of *legitimate violence per se,*" a distinction he emphasized in his famous posthumously published definition of the state as a "compulsory political organization with continuous operations" (364) whose "administrative staff successfully upholds the claim to the *monopoly* of the *legitimate* use of physical force in the enforcement of its order."[18] The political, then, is a subset of violence—or rather, the one arena of human sociality in which legitimacy is bestowed upon the use of violence. As such, politics distances itself, sometimes antagonistically so, from seemingly universal ethical injunctions against violence. The Sermon on the Mount, with its turning of other cheeks, is Weber's favorite example. With explicit reference to Machiavelli, Weber distinguished between political and personal ethics, between pragmatic reasoning for the good of the collective on the one hand and the concern for the salvation of one's soul on the other. There is no universal, categorical imperative that can paper over the differences, no ethic that "could establish substantially *identical* commandments applicable to all relationships, whether erotic, business, family or official, to one's relation with one's wife, greengrocer, son, competitor, with a friend or an accused man" (357). System rationalities demand specific system ethics, and the ethics of the political cannot do without recourse to the threat of violence.

Weber, of course, was not advocating violence for violence sake or extolling its supposed sublime, manly virtues; he was just noting its ever-present possibility and thus the necessity for transforming the bastard war of all against all into its domesticated, controlled, and legitimated doppelgänger. Weber, in other words, not only embraced what Benjamin would later call "mythic violence" as the realm of the political, but also made no apology for employing it as a means to ensure social order. Thus Weber—and all those like him, from Hobbes to the present, who concede to violence utilitarian political purposes—can be seen as the explicit target of Benjamin's wrath. Especially concerning divine violence, the hope for the ultimate catastrophe and the new era to follow, Weber was profoundly skeptical. Revolutionary violence, he noted, promises purgation by way of "one *last* act of force to create the situation in which *all* violence will have been destroyed for ever" (361). When invoked by erstwhile pacifists, revolutionary violence became the chiliastic call of prophets who say they see the promised land of perpetual peace just beyond the horizon. Weber disputed their vision.

When Weber spoke of revolution, he not only referred to the Bolsheviks and Sparticists of January 1919, but also and quite explicitly to the syndicalists of the previous decades. He had occasion to rehearse his objections to the faith in revolution in June 1918, when he lectured officers of the Austro-Hungarian army on the nature of socialism, on revolution, reform, democracy, the bourgeoisie and proletariat. One would have liked to have been in Vienna when Weber tried to reassure these officers of the propaganda unit. They had reason to be alarmed. Would revolutionary discontent spread from Russia to the empire and sap the fighting spirit of the troops? Would transnational worker solidarity that had collapsed so quickly under the weight of patriotic fervor in 1914 become a reality four years later and undermine the war effort? To these and similar questions, Weber replied, the "old revolutionary hope of catastrophe, which lent the *Communist Manifesto* its emotive power" and that filled the masses with "faith in the sudden dawning of a blissful future, a faith which had been given to them by a gospel which proclaimed, like the Christians of old: 'Salvation may come this very night,'" had given way to the more moderate belief in an evolutionary process of gradual reform. Massed now in parliamentary parties, these new social democrats sought power legally as the first step toward realizing a socialist society in which "men will no longer rule over men" (294). Whether this reassurance calmed the officers' fears is doubtful, for Weber also sounded a new alarm. The old midcentury revolutionary hope had been rekindled of late by the radical trade union movement, the syndicalists. The catalyst for catastrophe is now the notion of the general strike. Through "terror," he explained, and the "sudden paralysis of all production," it was thought that those in control, especially entrepreneurs, would be compelled to "renounce the management of the factories and place it in the hands of committees to be formed by the trade unions" (297). Here Weber asked a crucial, and for him a typical, question: When this happens, who will actually run industry? Workers are just that—workers! And "since the management of all modern factories is based entirely on calculation, knowledge of the products, knowledge of demand and technical schooling"—in other words, on the increased rationalization of society at large—specialists will still be required, namely "*non*-workers," "ideologues from the intellectual strata." Here he shrewdly, if not cynically, noted that the syndicalist movement in France and Italy was dominated by intellectuals, thinking no doubt of Georges Sorel and of his old friend, Robert Michels. "What are they looking for in syndicalism?" he asked. His answer? "It is the *romanticism* of the general strike and the *romanticism* of the hope of revolution as such which enchants *(bezaubert)* these intellectuals." Then, turning the screw one more time, he added: "If one looks at them, one can see that they are romantics, emotionally unfit for everyday life or averse to it and its demands, and who therefore hunger and thirst after the great revolutionary miracle" (298).

With his castigation of what he deemed to be the irresponsible fantasy of intellectuals, Weber was of course not only exercising his own hardheaded realism, but also playing to the pragmatic sensibilities of his audience and indulging in tropes we have become accustomed to in contemporary conservative rants. Nevertheless, one reads his invective with a type of discomfort that comes from recognition. By using the verb "to enchant" *(bezaubern)* and the noun "miracle" *(Wunder)*, he pointed to a grand desire that would animate Benjamin and that, as we saw with Agamben, still animates similar intellectuals a century later: the desire to step wholly and completely out of the rationalized, disenchanted modern world that has come into being not just as a result of the development of technology, bureaucracy, and other modes of administering the modern subject, but is, as we often hear, the direct result of all Western metaphysics.

Weber is not altogether unsympathetic to this desire. His decade-long correspondence with Robert Michels attests to the profound respect Weber had for the convictions that animated passionate believers in revolutionary catastrophe. And as is well known, he was similarly concerned with the deadening effects of increased rationalization of society and bureaucratization of politics—so much so that he theorized the necessity of charismatic political leaders and the desirability of plebiscitary democracy to reinvigorate the body politic. Nevertheless, all of this was to take place within the political realm and was to proceed cautiously and with a sense of sober responsibility. He simply could not make the leap of faith required of one to accept the premise upon which eschatological violence was founded. Weber's frustration with such a theologically inflected resurrection of revolutionary hope, then, is the frustration of one who has a decidedly more secular view of the political. A political ethics that recognizes the ever-present possibility of violence, rather than its glorious self-immolation, is the ethics of the human being in an unredeemed, and unredeemable, fallen state. Civil peace, not civil perfection, is the goal of such politics. Perhaps Craig L. Carr's eloquent description of the early modern natural law theorist Samuel Pufendorf as one "who labored to demonstrate how it is possible to live with political authority, and why it is not possible to live well without it" best approximates the tradition Weber represents.[19] It is not a neutral articulation of the nature of the political but a fittingly modest one, for it presupposes that if one deigns to live on this earth at all, "living well" is the best one can hope for. Accordingly, this description does not fear the term *authority*, does not assume its sudden overcoming or gradual withering away, and thus brings with it not only the pledge to preserve civil peace but also uncomfortable yet unavoidable associations of rule, dominion, coercion, and obedience. The civil peace that is promised is always a truce, never a perpetual peace, and always paid for with concessions.

That it is not possible to live *well* without political authority implies that it is possible, but only possible, to live well *with* it. It seems to follow, then, that though political authority is conditionally necessary (if we wish to live well), the various forms of political authority are not. Some may be better than others, but none is ordained. In other words, the political as an autonomous operation in modern society is necessary precisely because there is no single necessary way that human affairs can be ordered. On this view, the political does not found the just society, the redeemed society in which "men will no longer rule over men." Rather, in the necessary absence of the just society, the political puts into effect a livable space, a place in which living well, but only living well, can be achieved.

THE SOVEREIGNTY OF CONTINGENCY

If this is the case—and of course such a view of the political can no more be demonstrated than can the belief in the efficacy of revolutionary catastrophe—does divine violence have any function at all? For my answer (which may seem banal, but I hope not altogether unimportant), I will return to Carl Schmitt.

In *Die Diktatur*, Schmitt defines the sovereign dictator as one who does not preserve an existing constitution but rather attempts to create the conditions, ex nihilo as it were, that would allow for a new constitution. It seems that Schmitt thinks Cromwell's to have been a pure form of such a dictatorship, for Cromwell found the source of his power in God and never claimed to represent the people. Indeed, according to Schmitt's account, Cromwell believed that to cede power to the people or its representatives before the conditions for a new order had been established would be a sin. Accordingly, Cromwell could and did dissolve parliament with no appeal to the will of the people. On the contrary, with the dissolution of parliament for the third time in 1658, Cromwell merely claimed that God should judge. Such a dictatorship, Schmitt writes, appears as a miracle *(Wunder)*—one is tempted to say as the manifestation of divine violence—for, in analogy with the suspension of the laws of physical nature, the legal order is rent asunder.[20]

Now, Cromwell is neither my hero nor Schmitt's, but it is worth asking what kind of God Cromwell served so singularly. Hans Blumenberg has traced in the most economical terms both the appearance and disappearance of this God and has named Him contingency. We think of contingency in opposition to necessity—the order of things is not fixed, it could be other than it is. This opposition, which did not exist in antiquity, is, Blumenberg maintains, the invention of Christianity and the consequence of the belief in a creator who is imagined standing above and outside His creation. Aristotle's God, Blumenberg tells us, was conceived as pure actuality, the Christian God as omnipotent will. Because of the latter, reality becomes a potentially infinite series of possibilities, only one of which can be actualized at any one time. The world does not contain its ground within itself;

it is not an emanation of a substance but the result of an act of will by an all-powerful Creator who could, at any time, act other than He does. The world is not a given; it is a gift. Pose the question: Why did God create the world? If God is omnipotent, one can only answer: Not because He followed the unfolding of a law or design, or because it was His destiny to do so, but simply because He wanted to. His was a willful, arbitrary act that could always be retracted and always be exercised anew. With the disappearance of God, all we have left is the trace of His will, namely the contingent formation of the world that could always have been and could always still be other than it is. No longer a gift, it becomes an accident, a series of coordinated coincidences, the surprise of unintended consequences.

Benjamin wished to have violence—divine violence, please note—outside the law to preserve the possibility of revolution, to preserve the possibility of having the political be other than it is. Taken alone, this desire would accord with—indeed, would record—the necessity of thinking contingency in an accidental universe. Divine violence would then be the marker, the sign, the point within the scheme of violence that lay purely outside legal violence to remind us that though the political can never be simply negated, it can always be destroyed and fashioned anew. But to say that a given order can always be other than it is, is to say nothing about the quality of possible change, or rather, to postulate no quality at all for it. A catastrophe leaves a vacuum that needs to be filled, but it comes with no instructions saying how or with what. Benjamin had no desire to provide such instructions, yet seemed not to be content to let it rest there either. For he also wrote that the political—mythic violence—is reprehensible, despicable, indecent, to be condemned. These are some of the possible readings of the word *verwerflich,* and if one looks at the root of the word, one might conclude that one ought simply to reject the political altogether, to eject it completely out of the world by subjecting it to a final dispensation, a final violence that would extinguish all violence and with it all contingency, in order to introduce an ultimate unalterable necessity. One might come to believe that catastrophes are always miracles, that the willful God might be a predictable one. Even if no pictures are painted of paradise, the apocalyptic force evoked by Benjamin's language cannot help, I submit, but lead one into the temptation of thinking redemption. Indeed, Agamben is so led into that temptation that he cannot resist making the occasional sketch of the garden for us to contemplate. Who can blame him? Is not the *heilige Vollstreckung* of Benjamin's last sentence literally meant to be the execution of the political, the final solution to its problem?

This, of course, explains Benjamin's and Agamben's appeal. The world of the political *is* dirty, messy, sticky, and smelly. The world we wish to live in *is* the world at play, the world of the study, the world whose obligations are not worldly. And one can have that world—on occasion, though one can only capture it—and, yes, "capture" necessarily evokes a violent image—one can only realize it willfully, through acts of sovereign decision. These unavoidable decisions are necessary because the order of the world, any order of the world, is not. What Agamben wishes to separate, namely Schmitt's attempts "to reinscribe violence within a juridical context" and Benjamin's desire to "assure it—as pure violence—an existence outside of the law," cannot be so neatly kept apart.[21] The contingency of the political is dependent upon its various actualizations, just as the pure communicability of language is not hidden but made visible by its various acts of communication. The grafting together of violence and law creates the condition of possibility for the imperfect sociability of the political, just as the latter's imperfection creates the condition of possibility for change, a possible change for which "revolution," "catastrophe," perhaps even the "miracle" of "divine violence" may serve as suitable signs.

The form of the political, if it can be said to have a form, can only be stated as the paradoxical necessity of contingency. One might therefore plausibly speak of the form of its necessity and the contingency of its forms. Because everything except necessity is possible, living well is the best we can hope for. Really, when you think of it, who could ask for anything more?

NOTES

1. Emmanuel Joseph Sieyès, *Political Writings*, ed. and trans. Michael Sonenscher (Indianapolis: Hackett, 2003), 136, 137.

2. Ibid., 138.

3. Walter Benjamin, *Selected Writings*, ed. Marcus Bullock and Michael Jennings, trans. Edmund Jephcott (Cambridge, Mass.: Harvard University Press, 1996), 1:251.

4. Ibid., 1:251–52.

5. Ibid., 1:252. The original German is far more evocative: "Verwerflich aber ist alle mythische Gewalt, die rechtsetzende, welche die schaltende genannt werden darf. Verwerflich auch die rechtserhaltende, die verwaltete Gewalt, dir ihr dient. Die göttliche Gewalt, welche Insignium und Siegel, niemals Mittel heiliger Vollstreckung ist, mag die waltende heißen." Walter Benjamin, *Gesammelte Schriften*, ed. Rolf Tiedemann and Hermann Schweppenhäuser (Frankfurt: Suhrkamp, 1980), 2:203. Given that this text is crucial to Giorgio Agamben's assault on the notion of sovereignty, the English translation of *waltende* as "sovereign" is particularly unfortunate.

6. Georges Sorel, *Reflections on Violence,* ed. Jeremy Jennings (Cambridge: Cambridge University Press, 1999), 107.

7. Ibid., 170.

8. Ibid., 165–66.

9. Ibid., 28–29.

10. Benjamin, *Selected Writings,* 1:249–50.

11. Giorgio Agamben, *State of Exception,* trans. Kevin Attell (Chicago: Chicago University Press, 2005), 62.

12. Benjamin, *Selected Writings,* 1:252; Agamben, *State of Exception,* 53.

13. Agamben, *State of Exception,* 52.

14. Ibid., 54.

15. Ibid., 57.

16. Ibid., 64.

17. Max Weber, *Weber: Political Writings,* ed. Peter Lassman, trans. Ronald Speirs (Cambridge: Cambridge University Press, 1994), 360, 357. References to this work will henceforth be provided in the body of the text.

18. Max Weber, *Economy and Society: An Outline of Interpretive Sociology,* 2 vols., ed. and trans. Guenter Roth and Claus Wittich (Berkeley: California University Press, 1978), 1:54.

19. Craig L. Carr, "Editor's Introduction," in *The Political Writings of Samuel Pufendorf,* ed. Craig L. Carr, trans. Michael J. Seidler (Oxford: Oxford University Press, 1994), 3.

20. Carl Schmitt, *Die Diktatur* (Berlin: Duncker & Humblot, 1994), 127–31.

21. Agamben, *State of Exception,* 59.

2

The Function of Ambivalence in Agamben's Reontologization of Politics

EVA GEULEN

Translated by Roland Végső

Ontology has never been a great concern for the German Left. Since Adorno's *The Jargon of Authenticity* at the very latest, critical theory's fearful distance from ontology has turned into open hostility. With the exception of Hannah Arendt and Leo Strauss (who in this regard must be considered Americans), it has always been French and Italian authors like Gilles Deleuze, Jean-Luc Nancy, and Alain Badiou who found themselves interested in the ontological premises of politics. One possible explanation for this discrepancy is the fact that in Germany, Martin Heidegger's engagement with National Socialism remains the test case for any attempt to link politics and ontology under the conditions of modernity. Whether and how Agamben passes this test remains to be seen.

Certainly no one has argued more forcefully over the past couple of decades for founding or refounding politics on ontology than Giorgio Agamben. According to him, this alone could redeem us from the harmful paradigms of sovereignty. It is precisely this claim that irritates his German critics.[1] Regardless of whether Agamben, like Arendt before him, is accused of writing a history of decline *(Verfallsgeschichte)* (modeled on Heidegger's history of the forgetting of being) or whether he is charged with insufficiently differentiating between the historical reconstruction of individual cases and a transhistorical structure with quasi-transcendental properties a certain (understandably) deep-seated skepticism regarding Agamben's tendencies to fuse politics and ontology regularly emerges. Whether such skepticism is justified is best determined at the point where ontological and political claims converge most directly: Agamben's proposed solutions for leaving the dilemma of sovereignty behind, the transformations of which he traces between the historical emblems of the *homo sacer* on the one hand, and the concentration camp on the other.

Agamben's contribution to the theorization of sovereignty emerges indirectly from his rejection of the Leftist critique of the state. He strongly
criticizes all antistatist efforts of Marxist and anarchistic provenance, which
reduced the state to an ideological construction of the ruling powers that
would simply disappear upon the demystification of those powers. Because
Agamben believes that this amounts to a dangerous underestimation of
the problem of sovereignty, he turns instead to Hobbes's and Schmitt's
theories of sovereignty, which were suspected by the Left to be nothing
more than pseudolegitimizations of those in power. His reformulation
of the theory of sovereignty comprises two contrary movements. On the
one hand, his idiosyncratic rereadings of different theories of sovereignty
seek to expand the semantic horizon of this problematic beyond its traditional limits to such an extent that sovereignty reveals itself to be the matrix
or an a priori of Western politics from antiquity to today. On the other
hand, he focuses exclusively on one specific aspect of sovereignty, namely
the relation that the state and the legal order entertain with the bare life
(the creaturely existence) of human beings. Agamben analyzes how the
law and the state first establish this relationship and then govern it. Traditionally, theoreticians of sovereignty were primarily concerned with the life
of human beings in their capacity as citizens of a state and not as living
beings. Agamben sets out to prove that this distinction between political
existence and mere life has always constitutively belonged to the *arcana
imperii,* regardless of whether we are dealing with monarchies, democracies, or the totalitarian systems of the twentieth century. For Agamben, the
essence of Western politics lies in the exclusion of life from politics.

However, the logic of sovereignty developed on the basis of these presuppositions is characterized by the additional paradox that life and law,
bare life and political life (*zoe* and *bios* in Aristotelian terms) are on the one
hand divided, while on the other hand they overlap and can even collapse
entirely into each other so as to produce what Agamben likes to call a *zone
of indistinction.* What is being excluded is thus not without a relation to
that which excludes. This is why it became possible for the presumably
excluded life at some point in history to move to the center of politics. As
Foucault put it: "modern man is an animal in whose politics his own existence as a living being is at stake."[2] The way this politicization of life came
about is a matter of historical chance, but the fact that such a development
could come about at all is due, Agamben believes, to the aporetic structure
of the inclusive exclusion and exclusive inclusion at the heart of sovereignty. Agamben also calls this fatal dialectics the "sovereign ban" to which

the *homo sacer* is exposed. Traditionally, *homo sacer* had been defined as someone who is simultaneously excluded from the sacred and the profane law and is therefore entirely exposed to the ultimate power of the law to kill him with impunity. According to the ancient definitions Agamben has consulted, everybody may kill without fear of persecution, but no one may sacrifice a *homo sacer*. Unlike Foucault, who emphasizes the power of biopolitics to "make live," Agamben wants to disclose the older and more sinister motif of the death threat. Still unlike Foucault, Agamben also believes that sovereign power has been biopolitics all along.

For Agamben, the sovereign ban can only be broken by a "new," yet-to-emerge form of politics. His double critique of Arendt and Foucault (who previously diagnosed the decline and the transformation of traditional politics in modernity) proves that the new politics he envisions would be neither restorative nor utopian. To Arendt's, or incidentally also Leo Strauss's, attempts to rehabilitate the classical distinction between *polis* and *oikos* (between the political and the private) in response to their mutual collapse in modernity, he concedes (quite realistically) no chance. Similarly, he distances himself from Foucault's occasional mumbles of a completely other body and another economy of desires.[3] Instead, Agamben relies on a principle that his critics occasionally apostrophize as messianism or apocalypse. However, it seems advisable to describe this structure in a less preemptive fashion and without recourse to such labels.

At the beginning of the first *homo sacer* book, Agamben claims in a peculiarly ambiguous way that our problems "will be solved only on the terrain—biopolitics—on which they were formed."[4] In other places too, Agamben suggests that this fatal biopolitics is also the predestined site for redemption from sovereignty, whose originary act was the production of a biopolitical body. At the end of his study, he reiterates these provocative claims: "This biopolitical body that is bare life must itself instead be transformed into the site for the constitution and installation of a form of life that is wholly exhausted in bare life and a *bios* that is only its own *zoē*" (188). The decisive concept that regularly appears in the vicinity of such enunciations but remains unexplained in the first book, *Homo Sacer: Sovereign Power and Bare Life,* is "form-of-life." As a philosophical concept, form-of-life gained currency in the nineteenth century in Dilthey, Spranger, and later in Wittgenstein and Cavell. It usually designates the threshold at which individual lives border on forms of communal life. However, by form-of-life, Agamben clearly does not mean contemporary identity politics of minorities. Such an interpretation can be excluded on the basis of a short text entitled "Form-of-Life," in which Agamben argues that this type of politics remains caught within the limits of the old model of sovereign politics. Identity politics would only add more distinctions to the original distinction between bare life and citizen, such as "the voter, the worker, the journalist, the student, but also the HIV-positive, the transvestite, the porno star, the elderly, the parent, the woman."[5] Hence, form-of-life must signify something very different from "life styles," which are turned into juridically and politically codified identities separated "from their coherence in a form-of-life."[6]

Rather, by form-of-life, Agamben understands a life in which no bare life can be isolated at all. Thus, the concept of form-of-life suggests an inseparable unity that in the course of history has always been separated into forms of law and mere, formless or bare life. However, if the expression form-of-life designates an originary unity of life and its form, then there is sufficient reason to suspect this concept and Agamben's new politics of social romanticism.[7]

As indicated above, the test case for Agamben's notion of a new politics is how he deals with Heidegger's link to National Socialist biopolitics. Agamben himself leaves little doubt that his notion of form-of-life is immediately akin to Heidegger's Dasein,[8] which is characterized by facticity—that is to say, by our everyday experience of being unable to distinguish Being from modes of being because as living beings, we always find ourselves already in a situation from which we cannot abstract. The credibility of Agamben's claim that biopolitics ought to be transformed into a form-of-life hinges in part on whether he can successfully differentiate Heidegger's philosophy from National Socialism. This attempt occurs in two places: once in his book on the *homo sacer,* and then once more in his later book on Auschwitz and the witness. In both cases, Agamben pursues a very peculiar strategy. Unlike most Heidegger apologists, and contrary to what one might expect, Agamben highlights and even intensifies the affinities between Heidegger's philosophy and National Socialism. In a daring argumentative maneuver, he approximates the characteristics of Dasein to the indistinguishability of law and fact in the concentration camps. All his efforts are directed at multiplying the analogies between Heidegger and National Socialist biopolitics, only to suddenly turn the entire argument on its head by marking the point where Nazism and Heidegger are said to radically diverge. Nazism, claims Agamben, turned biological life into the site of permanent decisions about the value of this or that life. For Heidegger, on the other hand, who rejected all philosophies of value, Agamben notes that *homo sacer* became "the inseparable unity of Being and ways of being, of subject and qualities, life and world" (153). Opposite the Nazis' emphasis on decisive differences, we find Heidegger's Dasein as the transformation of life into a unity "in which it is impossible to isolate something like a bare life" (153). This unity, which Agamben designates as form-of-life and that Heidegger calls "Dasein," withdraws from every external decision, and with this, Agamben suggests, escapes the fatal logic of the sovereign ban. Although the transformation of biopolitics into a form-of-life cannot be accomplished from the outside with the help of evaluating measures, Agamben believes that it "itself has the form of an irrevocable decision" (153). Whether this argument concerning the difference between Heidegger and National Socialism is sufficiently convincing and whether Agamben has thereby also definitively clarified his own confusing claim that biopolitics must become form-of-life, is open to debate. What warrants closer inspection here are his methods and techniques of argumentation.

The reversal occurs only at the very point where it no longer seems possible to disentangle Heidegger from the Nazis. That the point of no return should be the turning point recalls a figure of thought, also favored by Heidegger himself, which occurs throughout the twentieth century in different variations. In his 1950s essay devoted to the threat posed by modern technology to humanity, Heidegger employed this figure by invoking a verse from Hölderlin that meanwhile has become proverbial: "Wo aber Gefahr ist, wächst das Rettende auch" ("But where danger is, grows/The saving power also").[9] According to this logic, the moment of greatest danger at the same time also represents the greatest chance for change. This assumption could perhaps explain why Agamben's alternatives to the sovereign ban and biopolitics are so notoriously ambivalent. Ambivalence seals, as it were, the promise that the highest point of suffering announces salvation and that salvation can only be expected by way of the passage through the low point. One can call this figure eschatological or dialectical, but where such terms are staunchly avoided (as in the case of Heidegger and Agamben), the coincidence of danger and salvation is perhaps best described as the power of ambivalence.

The figure of thought at issue is much older than the twentieth century. It refers back to the ancient formula according to which the spear that inflicted the wound can also heal it. But what has remained from this certainty in modernity is but a dim hope. Nevertheless, Derrida draws on this motif, and Adorno's negative dialectics is inconceivable without it. In the concluding piece of *Minima Moralia*, one reads that "consummate negativity, once squarely faced, delineates the mirror image of its opposite."[10] Agamben's alternatives to the sovereign ban undoubtedly belong to this tradition precisely because they are ambiguously tied to what they want to get rid of. Yet there are significant differences between Agamben's use of the figure and Derrida's or Adorno's: In his book on Auschwitz, he tests the redemptive potential of ambivalence on the murder of Jews in concentration camps. This categorically distinguishes him from Heidegger, Adorno, and most of all Derrida, who emphatically warned against linking the Holocaust to figures of salvation.[11]

Auschwitz names for Agamben the highest point of the sinister entanglement of biopolitics and sovereign power, because with the concentration camps, something that had always been and still remains possible in extralegal spaces of exception (the *zones d'attentes* of places like airports and refugee camps) did pass over into fact. Not every refugee in a refugee camp is a *homo sacer,* but every one of them is virtually exposed to the possibility of becoming one. Whether or not he is murdered does not depend on the law but on the civility of those temporarily endowed with sovereign power. The institution of camps, which began long before Auschwitz, marks for Agamben a paradigm change because in them, the temporally limited state of exception (whose proclamation defines the sovereign) was for the first time institutionalized and made permanent. The camp fixes the wandering figure of the outlawed *homo sacer* in time and space. Camps are spatialized states of exception on the grounds of a national territory whose legal order does not apply to them. This is why in a contrafactual allusion to Carl Schmitt's *Nomos of the Earth,* Agamben calls the camp the "nomos of modernity" (166–80).

The significance of the particular case of National Socialist extermination camps lies in the fact that the potential to be killed (represented by the figure of the *homo sacer*) was there factually realized. And precisely this is the reason why Agamben chooses Auschwitz as the beginning for a new, no longer juridically predisposed ethics in his book *Remnants of Auschwitz.*[12] As a realized possibility, Auschwitz marks for him the point of no return from which we may expect change. Hence the figure known in the language of the concentration camps as the *Muselmann* designates "the threshold of a new ethics."[13]

The *Muselmann* appears as the modern incarnation of the archaic figure of Roman law, the *homo sacer,* while the camp appears as the materialization of the state of exception. However, once Agamben identifies the camp inmate as the historical fulfillment of a *figura* whose shadow has been with us since ancient Rome, his project becomes highly problematic and questionable.

The new paradigm of sovereignty (the camp as the new *nomos*) and a specific historical event (Auschwitz) coincide. By virtue of being both paradigm and example, Auschwitz becomes the zero point that alone can bring salvation. Agamben instrumentalizes the pseudoeschatological figure of thought in a way that neither Adorno nor Heidegger were familiar with. In the few places where Heidegger, who remained notoriously silent after 1945, addressed the extermination camps (which also happens to be the place where he called the camps places for the "fabrication of corpses"), he concluded that the once possible experience of death had turned into its own opposite.[14] But he did not envision a new ethics. Adorno, on the other hand, whose ethics is epitomized by the dictum "never again Auschwitz!" certainly never suggested that Auschwitz would be the place of the consummate negativity that delineates "the mirror-image of its opposite." Quite to the contrary, he always called attention to the fact that the world does not present itself as the catastrophe that it really is, which is why intensified and exaggerated constructions are necessary. In the concluding piece of *Minima Moralia* quoted above, he writes:

> The only philosophy which can be responsibly practised in face of despair is the attempt to contemplate all things as they would present themselves from the standpoint of redemption. [. . .] Perspectives must be fashioned that displace and estrange the world, reveal it to be, with its rifts and crevices, as indigent and distorted as it will appear one day in messianic light.[15]

The hyperbolic magnification of such details has the advantage of explicitly marking its own subjective status as a construction. In contrast to Adorno, Agamben directly assumes the standpoint of salvation without a detour, when he defines Auschwitz as the place of a new ethics and designates the *Muselmann* as its protagonist. The highly problematic ambiguity of this undertaking is due to the figure for which Hölderlin's verse "Wo aber Gefahr ist, wächst das Rettende" stands. An ontologization of politics which justifies itself in reference to the camp inmate's form-of-life discredits itself. Although Agamben's reflections on ethics contain many interesting propositions, especially regarding the necessity of analyzing the juridical origins of ethical concepts such as "guilt" and "responsibility," his attempt to found a new ethics on Auschwitz and the *Muselmann* remains both problematic and conceptually unnecessary. Nietzsche's *Genealogy of*

Morals testifies to the possibility of critiquing the juridical dimension of traditional ethics without recourse to any determining instance.

While Agamben's exercises in ontologization qua ambivalence are problematic, he has also offered a critique of the category of ambivalence that cannot be ignored. It can be found in his discussion of Jacques Derrida and the topos of undecidability in the latter's reading of Kafka's "Before the Law." As is well known, Derrida did not read the parable as most of its interpreters have done, namely as the failure of the man from the country before the law. Rather, he considered the deferral that condemns the man again and again to waiting for an event that happens by not happening: The elusiveness of what is yet to come is sustained by this persistence. Agamben, on the other hand, proposes another reading, according to which the closure of the law by the doorman constitutes an actual event, even though nothing at all appears to happen. He interprets the man from the country as an agent provocateur whose waiting amounts to a complex but eventually successful strategy to achieve the closure and fulfillment of the law. At this point, Agamben's polemics against Derrida quickly move beyond the limits of a mere disagreement between interpretations and become a question of principles as well as something personal. Inasmuch as deconstruction posits "undecidables that are infinitely in excess of every possibility of signification," Agamben believes that it intentionally prolongs the fatal state of waiting.[16] Hence deconstruction merely repeats the paradox and the ambivalence of sovereignty: "What threatens thinking here is the possibility that thinking might find itself condemned to infinite negotiations with the doorkeeper."[17]

Agamben even claims that Derrida and deconstruction, with their insistence on deferral and their persistent emphasis on ambiguity and ambivalence, actually block or at least infinitely delay the closure and fulfillment of the law and sovereignty. Derrida is indirectly alluded to in Agamben's paraphrase of a biblical passage: "Woe to you, who have not wanted to enter into the door of the Law but have not permitted it to be closed either."[18] Whether Agamben's discussions of form-of-life or his emphatic notion of witnessing can achieve the closure of the law prevented by the Pharisees of deconstruction is doubtful. But Agamben's acute aversions against insisting on ambivalence are sufficiently clear.

Perhaps even more significant than Agamben's critique of ambivalence in his discussion of Derrida is an analysis of ambivalence in his book on *homo sacer*, where he reviews different scholarly attempts to reconcile the dual attributes of the *homo sacer*: that he can be killed but cannot be sacrificed.

Two contradictory attributes are condensed in the adjective *sacer,* whose link remained hidden from ancient as well as modern commentators because they were unable to reconcile their knowledge of the characteristics of the sacred with the paradoxical definition of the *homo sacer.* Although they knew about the ambivalent semantics of *sacer,* which can mean "sacred" as well as "cursed," this knowledge hardly clarifies the mysterious figure. Everyone could kill the *homo sacer* without committing murder; but the one who sacrificed him to the gods was guilty of sacrilege. These two attributes (the impossibility of sacrifice and the possibility of unpunishable murder) render the description of such a man as sacred rather puzzling. Because sacralization *(consecratio)* usually denotes the passage from the profane to the divine order of law, the ban on sacrifice appears to be inexplicable. But if one assumes (as the myth scholar Karl Kerényi did) that the *homo sacer* was sacred in the sense that he belonged to the gods of the underworld, then it remains inexplicable why anyone could kill him without committing a sacrilege.

Ethnologists and myth scholars tried to solve the contradictory attributes of this enigmatic figure by invoking the concept of taboo, which, since the nineteenth century and even in psychoanalysis (as in Freud's *Totem and Taboo*), was generously applied to explain ambivalent phenomena such as the dual meaning of sacredness. Whatever is declared taboo is simultaneously sacred and cursed, equally the object of veneration and of fear. But the appeal to ambivalence as the final ground and irreducible originary quality of everything sacred not only does not explain anything in this case, but it also actually disfigures the problem. At this point of his survey, Agamben sketches a brief history of "The Ambivalence of the Sacred" since the nineteenth century. These few pages in *Homo Sacer* amount to one of Agamben's most convincing achievements. The significance of his courageous exposure of ambivalence as a "scientific mythologeme" (75) cannot be overestimated for any attempt to understand the relationship of religion and law in modernity. Agamben's critique of the ambivalence theorem pertains directly to the recently rekindled debate over secularization in general and to the problems of modern political theology in particular.

According to Agamben, not religion but law was in the beginning. This is the lesson to be drawn from his critical analysis of all attempts to explain the notion of sacredness by resorting to the category of ambivalence. Ever since the nineteenth century (up to and including René Girard), scholars in the thrall of the secularization thesis were looking for the origins of the ambivalence of the sacred in primitive societies. In search of lost religious phenomena, they remained blind to the juridical origins of the sacred. The Roman legal figure of the *homo sacer*, the emblem of the differentiation of sacred and profane law, is Agamben's strongest argument in support of his demand for the illumination of the legal origins of a supposedly originary, forgotten, repressed, or otherwise latently present religiosity. In this regard, Agamben's main concern (the analysis of the systemic connections between the increasing juridification of life worlds and the growing number of people living outside any legal order), is no longer a problem of ambivalence (that Adorno and Horkheimer could only recognize and theorize in the form of a *Dialectic of Enlightenment*). In Agamben, this growing tension becomes transparent as a structure that one can describe, analyze, criticize, and change. If the price for grounding politics in ontology is the perpetuation of the very kind of ambivalences that Agamben's own critical account of ambivalence helps to analyze and dispel, then one ought to resist the temptation to ontologize. It is quite possible to separate Agamben's ethical speculations in the Auschwitz book from his sober analyses of the sacred and his critique of the ambivalence theorem. There is no theoretical, not to mention any political or ethical, reason to connect the two. We can enlighten ourselves about the legal origins of our thought and our politics without any reference to a new ethics or politics.

Notes

1. Eva Geulen, *Giorigo Agamben zur Einführung* (Hamburg: Junius, 2005).

2. Michel Foucault, *The History of Sexuality, Vol. I: An Introduction*, trans. Robert Hurley (New York: Vintage, 1990), 143.

3. Michel Foucault, *The Care of the Self: The History of Sexuality, Volume III*, trans. Robert Hurley (New York: Vintage, 1988).

4. Giorgio Agamben, *Homo Sacer: Sovereign Power and Bare Life*, trans. Daniel Heller-Roazen (Stanford: Stanford University Press, 1998), 4. Subsequent references to this essay will appear in the text.

5. Giorgio Agamben, "Form-of-Life," in *Means without End: Notes on Politics*, trans. Vincenzo Binetti and Cesare Casarino (Minneapolis: University of Minnesota Press, 2000), 6–7.

6. Ibid., 6.

7. Susanne Lüdemann, "Geltung ohne Bedeutung: Zur Architektonik des Gesetzes bei Franz Kafka und Giorgio Agamben," *Zeitschrift für die Philosophie* 124 (2005): 499–519.

8. In "Form-of-Life," Agamben borrows some passages word for word from the ninth paragraph of Heidegger's *Being and Time* without any indication, which also suggests that this might be a common practice in Agamben's texts.

9. Martin Heidegger, *The Question Concerning Technology and Other Essays*, trans. William Lovitt (New York: Harper, 1977), 34.

10. Theodor Adorno, *Minima Moralia: Reflections from a Damaged Life*, trans. E. F. N. Jephcott (London: Verso, 1996), 247.

11. Jacques Derrida, "Force of Law: The 'Mystical Foundation of Authority,'" in *Deconstruction and the Possibility of Justice*, ed. Drucilla Cornell, Michael Rosenfeld, and David Gray Carlson (New York: Routledge, 1992), 3–67.

12. Giorgio Agamben, *Remnants of Auschwitz: The Witness and the Archive*, trans. Daniel Heller-Roazen (New York: Zone Books, 1999).

13. Ibid., 69.

14. Martin Heidegger, "Die Gefahr," in *Bremer und Freiburger Vorträge, Gesamtausgabe* (Frankfurt am Main: Klostermann, 1994), 79:56ff.

15. Adorno, *Minima Moralia*, 247.

16. Agamben, *Homo Sacer*, 25.

17. Ibid., 54.

18. Ibid.

II

THE PERSISTENCE OF MARXISM

Twenty-five Theses on Philosophy in the Age of Finance Capital

NICHOLAS BROWN and IMRE SZEMÁN

> Repudiation of the present cultural morass presupposes sufficient involvement in it to feel itching in one's finger tips, so to speak, but at the same time the strength, drawn from this involvement, to dismiss it.
>
> —THEODOR ADORNO, *Minima Moralia*

> . . . shooting off with the speed of a rocket from A (where one is anyhow) to B (where everything is just the same) . . .
>
> —MAX HORKHEIMER and THEODOR ADORNO, "The Culture Industry"

PHILOSOPHY TODAY

"During long periods of history," Walter Benjamin wrote, "the mode of human sense perception changes with humanity's entire mode of existence."[1] One would expect no less of thought itself. It should come as no surprise to assert today that philosophy is historical through and through. This recognition of philosophy's historicity is one of the great legacies of Marx's thought. Once consciousness is linked to social being and the "ruling ideas" of an epoch are characterized as "nothing more than the ideal expression of the dominant material relations, the dominant material relations grasped as ideas,"[2] it is only a willful bad faith that could lead one back into the slumber of ontology and metaphysics—taxonomic practices that mortal beings use to tally up the categories of immortality. A century and a half after *The German Ideology*, it is tempting to imagine that philosophy is no longer in need of such a stern reminder about the necessary material limits of its activity. Historical consciousness now reigns supreme in the academy in inverse proportion to the infertile toxic brownfields that characterize the postmodern mental landscape outside it. Bristling with endless qualifications and equipped with a map to the minefields of reductive thinking, critical philosophy today actively acknowledges its own contingency and highlights its limits as proof of its active confrontation with categories that will always prove to be inadequate to their objects. What more could one want or expect? What other form could it take on the ruins of those grand theories diligently elaborated in multiple volumes of tortured prose? In light of the disappointments and general squalor of mental life in the age of finance capitalism, should we not see in the vanguard of contemporary theory evidence that for once thought has run ahead of its historical moment, preserving within it the kind of utopian possibilities once connected with art and the aesthetic?

Of course, such imagined ends betray their own bad faith. It is not hard to see how this vision of the philosophical enterprise reenacts its own version of historical development, one that is essentially the same as Kant's vision of the Enlightenment. The final dismantling of the great master narratives is itself a grand narrative—why else would people get excited about it? This kind of story of growth and development, of the unfolding of life from seed to oak tree, cannot help but reactivate the suspicions of critical theory, which, understanding itself to be a relentless critical nomad, expresses a permanent suspicion about beginnings (childhood) and endpoints (maturity), as well as of the established pathways by which one travels from one to other. Indeed, critical philosophies of all stripes—those wildly variegated and interpenetrated sets of concepts collectively referred to as "theory"—have assumed much of their identity from their suspicion of fixed categories and meditations on the eternal.

Philosophy today faces two challenges: first, it is not critical enough of its own processes and concepts; second, it is inadequate to the present.

The first claim can be grasped more easily than the second. Reading theory today, it is remarkable how many concepts have been transformed into entities that one can imagine snatching with tweezers and dropping in a jar for further study back in the lab. Too often theory challenges the equation between concepts and objects only to dead-end in the reassertion of some primal category like "desire," "the subject," "the political," and so on. It is perhaps impossible to do otherwise; but in that case we should be aware of the limits of what we parade about as critical theory. As Nietzsche reminds us, there is nothing especially impressive about hiding something behind a bush only later to trumpet its discovery.

The question of the adequacy of thought to its age is a more difficult one to make sense of. "The ideas of the ruling class are in every epoch the ruling ideas."[3] If this is the case, why should we imagine that this is any different today? If philosophy even considers this question, it does so ambivalently. On the one hand, Marx and Engels's famous formulation has been seen, especially in the case of contemporary societies, as far too reductive. As Raymond Williams has pointed out, "the body of intellectual and imaginative work which each generation receives as its traditional culture is always, and necessarily, something more than the product of a single class."[4] Nor can dominant thought be thought of as uniformly of the moment; ideology is perpetually disturbed by residual and emergent forms that are inevitably mixed into the stew. As Adorno expressed it so beautifully in *Negative Dialectics,* "Philosophy, which once seemed obsolete, lives on because the moment to realize it was missed."[5] The emergent, having failed to merge into the dominant, persists as residual. But if almost no one has taken up Adorno's challenge—to inhabit the residual as a critique of the actual—it is because genuinely critical possibilities of theoretical thinking are often assumed to be engendered automatically by the intimate epistemological interference imposed by the heterogeneity that characterizes modernity. It is as though the acknowledgment that there is no pure, homogenous, monolithic ideology necessarily implied that ideology contained its own critique.

On the other hand, the professoriate is fond of pointing out that critical thought today is pretty much an accident waiting to happen, not only in the "culture at large" but within the academy itself. For instance, Masao Miyoshi has claimed that "the current academic preoccupation with 'postcoloniality' and multiculturalism looks suspiciously like another alibi to conceal the actuality of global politics."[6] He is hardly alone in making such claims. Gayatri Spivak opens her appraisal of contemporary thought by stating straight out that "Postcolonial studies, unwittingly commemorating a lost object, can become an alibi unless it is placed within a general frame."[7] There is no point in rehearsing the same kinds of criticisms that have been leveled at postmodernism, deconstruction, Western Marxism, and so on. At one point or another, all of them have been accused of collaborating unwittingly with the Man. In this case, "critical" thought is in fact precisely adequate to its moment, just not in the way it imagines itself to be. It reiterates, no doubt in sublimated or misrecognized form, accepted social structures and political presumptions—effectively canceling out real critical reflection. As Michael Hardt and Antonio Negri have pointed out in *Empire*—Alain Badiou has made this point more acerbically—"the postmodernist politics of difference not only is ineffective against but can even coincide with and support the functions and practices" of global capitalism as it exists today.[8]

But if academic "critical theory" appears on this perspective as little more than a highly elaborated version of contemporary capitalism's spontaneous philosophy, at the very most its vanguard wing, then the former proposition—that an adequate theory of the present can be discovered in the culture at large, reconstructed from the sheer heterogeneity of agendas and the interference of the residual and the emergent—is an even less satisfactory position to adopt. Philosophy's critical power exists because it is, in fact, inadequate to, not the same as the main substance of the age. Generally, as Hegel was pleased to remind us, philosophy belongs to the residual, always lagging behind—even if contemporary theory has always been more likely to claim for itself a position in the emergent. In this context it is useful to remember that odd moment of self-reflection in *Dialectic of Enlightenment* where Horkheimer and Adorno pause to claim that their critique of the total system can emerge only because they just happen to occupy the interstice between the end of classical German philosophy and the burgeoning of American mass culture. It is only because the former is radically incommensurate with the latter that Horkheimer and Adorno could hate both of them properly. But what this tends to mean is that philosophy is in fact unable to take up the present adequately. We might, then, possess a critical philosophy after all (or even a whole slew of them, each with its array of anthologies and journals), but it is a philosophy of the city, the pedestrian, and urban public space, and not of the freeway, the drive-through and the swirl of suburban crescents. (The old urban downtown revived as a simulacrum of its former self does not bring the social world back in line with this thought, but instead leaves it yet a further step behind.) This is why this critical philosophy retains a romantic fascination with Benjamin's arcades and can treat Las Vegas or pseudourban enclave only with horror.

The question that we want to pose here is: what would be a philosophy adequate to the age of globalization, an age dominated by finance capital? But instead of indulging in the kind of definitional exercise that might now be expected (as if anyone wants to read yet another survey of the modalities of globalization—local and global, the end of the nation and its continuation, the production of antinomies out of every one of the concepts that social scientists have mistaken for the structure of life itself in Western modernity), we want to throw out another possibility. The task facing philosophy today is to examine its filiations to its most hallowed concepts and to consider anew their productivity within a new frame of reference— one, for instance, in which Europe is no longer the leading edge of world history. Easy to say, harder to think.

Unexpectedly, the result of this task might be to see old concepts as more productive than new ones, which suffer not merely from the fact that they are inevitably expressions of the general conditions of possibility of the present moment, but also because of the way in which the eternal production of the new is linked more strongly than ever to the basic drive of capitalism. The concrete meaning of any concept—what it is able to do as opposed to what it can be said to signify—depends decisively on the world in which it finds itself. And indeed, the last twenty years have seen the political significance of whole fields of concepts silently switch valences— often unnoticed by those who use them—as though an unexplained flip-flop of the earth's magnetic field had taken place at the level of the concept. Whatever its utopian origins, the idea of the State has seemed since Marx to be a repressive one, fundamentally the tool and right hand of Capital. But now, with post–cold war mutations in the global market, the State is suddenly seen by many on the Left as a potential bulwark against the predations of multinational capital. Transgression has long been transformed into a shock value whose primary purpose is to move units, not to disturb social limits. The Universal, in the name of which an oppressive particularity came to dominate the globe, suddenly seems the last bastion against a neoliberal world order that is happy enough to maintain differences (if only of wages, working conditions, and marketing parameters) as long as they are subsumed without resistance within the global market. A notion of subjective authenticity that had seemed to justify the worst sort of complacent self-privilege—not to mention the scabrous possibilities of ethnic and racial authenticity—tempts us once again with the offer of protection against the most corrosive and cynical ironies of commodity culture. The aesthetic, which was so plainly the property and instrument of an elite defending its prerogatives, may yet turn out to be the last subjective vestige of utopian possibility. Totality, which was surely an alibi for a will to power, may be our only tool for grasping the new functioning of global Capital. And History itself, which had been exposed as the master trope of nineteenth-century racist ideology, now seems to be a powerful weapon against an ideology of the continual present.

All of these statements could of course be taken as profoundly conservative ones; to utter any of them without irony would invite a swift rap on the knuckles with the ruler of critical–theoretical thought. (It is good to remember that all genuinely historical thinking is ironic through and through, setting up truth only to turn it on its head the next moment.) In a lapsarian mode, this would be globalization as imagined by John Gray or

Samuel Huntington—the decline and necessary return of tradition and of "values," an essentially conservative stance. In a triumphalist pose, some of these formulations could take on the aspect of globalization as imagined by Francis Fukuyama or Thomas Friedman—global Americanism without apologies or tears. And, insofar as the philosophical categories invoked are those of Western modernity, this pose is repeated on the left in the kinder, gentler ideas of cosmopolitan governance elaborated variously by David Held, Richard Falk, and Ulrich Beck. In light of these positions, it might seem that taking a genuinely critical view of globalization necessitates the adoption of a narrative of cultural, social, or political apocalypse: super-consumerism, globally dispersed; hypercapitalism, more theoretically innovative than anything coming out of the factories of conceptual innovation called graduate schools; monstrous pleasures (leading to social banality) made possible only by monstrous exploitation (leading to social collapse)—all of which can be sketched in minute detail, with great epistemological care not to simplify things for the sake of polemics, but about which, alas, nothing can be done. (Or almost nothing. One can say: Obama gave me hope and confidence that the right gesture has been made.)

Instead of adopting the comfortable (and, as Derrida reminded us, ultimately conservative) space of apocalypse, we propose to recapture conceptual territory lost to both conservative and cosmopolitan narratives of globalization, to develop a way of thinking about the actual without resorting to ambivalence or despair. In doing so, one always flirts with danger. Jean Comaroff and John L. Comaroff point to the troubling resurgence of the concept of "civil society" at the present moment. "During inhospitable times," they claim, civil society "reanimates the optimistic spirit of modernity, providing scholars, public figures, poets, and ordinary people alike a language with which to talk about democracy, moral community, justice, and populist politics."[9] So who could object to its appearance at this profoundly asocial moment? As Comaroff and Comaroff point out, civil society assumes in its reappearance much the same ideological function it played when it first emerged in the late eighteenth century:

> Amidst populist moral panics, mass-mediated alienation, crises of representation, and scholarly perplexity, Civil Society, in its Second Coming, once more becomes especially "good to think," to signify with, to act upon. The less substance it has, the emptier its referents, the more this is so; which is why its very polyvalence, its ineluctable unfixability, is intrinsic to its power as panacea. It is the ultimate magic bullet in the Age of Millennial Capitalism.

For it promises to conjure up the most fundamental thing of all: a meaningful social existence.[10]

A meaningful social existence: this is the goal, after all. It could be a long march.

Twenty-five Theses on Philosophy in the Age of Finance Capitalism

Nothing human is alien to me. Everything should be doubted.

—KARL MARX

We present here a set of theses that might help to imagine the role and scope of philosophy in the age of finance capitalism. The sources of these theses are as eclectic as a music collection: they bear with them the traces of broken relationships, misdirected enthusiasms, the inevitable, short-lived fascination with the new, the enduring influence of old favorites that one cannot get past (about a final category—"things that sounded good drunk"—we'll say no more). These theses should not be taken as prescriptive. They might be read in the light of Friedrich Schlegel's conception of his philosophical fragments, as scraps or remnants of a total system that could never really exist.

Fredric Jameson has described his own critical practice as a "translation mechanism," a theoretical machine that makes it possible to convert other discourses into the central political problematic that animates Marxism.[11] We conceive these theses in much the same spirit: as grasping toward a mediating code rather than presenting a set of truth-claims. The utility of these theses will thus be determined by their ability to help produce a philosophy politically rather than conceptually adequate to finance capitalism—a philosophy that takes up the political challenge of the present without thereby failing to become anything more than an expression of (an adequation of) the dynamism of finance capitalism itself.

1

A theft.—Relativism is the dialectic for idiots.

2

Hegel is dead.—One is always coming up against reminders that we have "moved beyond" teleological, Eurocentric Hegel. Sometimes these reminders come in the imperative. But how do we know something is beyond something else, rather than behind it or beside it, above it or below it, without reference to a vanishing point? And isn't the presumption of a vanishing point in time what we call teleology? Never mind: teleology and Eurocentrism—the dominion of the Same—are bad ideas and they should be avoided. Hegel, bless his eighteenth-century soul, didn't always manage to do so. But why this fixation on Hegel? Let us rather say that the method he invented, but which even he did not always fully understand, has nothing to do with these. Anyone who can muster the strength to read Hegel with both sympathy and skepticism—in other words, to read Hegel like we read everyone else—can see that teleology is the thinnest veneer, even if diligently applied, a last-ditch attempt to save the dialectic from its own deepest implication: the perpetual deferral of utopia, the impossibility of recuperating contradiction once and for all. Far from being a philosophy of the Same, the dialectic elevates antagonism into an ontology, and in so doing turns the very fiber of being into a tissue of fissures, contradictions, frustration, and carnage. The violence of this gesture—visible, above all, in Hegel's brutal contempt for Kant and the often deadpan irony brought to bear on anything that resembles a unitary conception of Being—is lost on us today, due in no small part to Hegel's own rhetoric. But like those Victorian novels where social upheaval is prevented how? by staging a marriage!—the flimsiness of the ultimate reconciliation gives the clue to its falsity. As with the "cosmological constant"—which Einstein briefly introduced into general relativity to silence what his own theory said about the history of the universe—so with teleology: the dialectic gets along better without it. It has been said that every competent student of physics today knows far more about general relativity than Einstein ever did. Perhaps we are in a position to understand the dialectic better than Hegel.

3

American Hegelians.—Critical common sense in North America still gets itself worked up into a lather about the evils of the dialectic. But even during the heyday of the most recent orthodoxy, it wasn't always easy to see what it was fighting against. Once upon a time, in a land far, far away, the dialectic meant Kojève, or Sartre, or Stalinist pseudophilosophy. Enemies worth fighting! But we literal-minded North Americans largely missed the point and developed a hatred for a Hegelian orthodoxy that we never really experienced. Who were the American Hegelians? There were some—not in the last century, but in the one before that. One ran a shoe factory and lived for a time with the Creek in Oklahoma. Another was a superintendent of schools and believed the dialectic could be used to show that history would end in St. Louis, Missouri. These were the American Hegelians. And then there's Francis Fukuyama—another Midwesterner, by the way. So what's the panic? See thesis #2.

4

A bad penny for your thoughts.—The best critics of the dialectic are practical dialecticians. As for the rest of us, we must beware lest we find ourselves, in our relation to thought, in the position of Milton's Abdiel, rushing to God with his discovery, only to find "Already known what he for news had thought/To have reported."[12]

5

As easy as 1, 2, 3.—The thought of the One goes around creating an awful mess, but it's not terribly common among metropolitan intellectuals. Call it fundamentalism, call it narrow nationalism, call it ethnic chauvinism—or call it the philosophy of Being: the idea is that totality should conform to a single rule. The thought of the Three effectively means the thought of infinity; it is always perfectly correct—and perfectly banal. Multiplicity is easy to find, Difference is indeed everywhere—and very useful, too, for playing whack-a-mole with the thought of the One. But a concept as universal as Difference necessarily lacks all specificity. It is empty as to content. How, then, without content, can there be any difference? Are we not back to the thought of the One? This is not mere logic chopping. The point is not that there is no difference between the Same and the Different; that would be absurd. Rather, it is that they share a Ground—that every mere difference exists by virtue of a field that stamps it with the imprint of the Same. The most innovative thinker of the Three is Alain Badiou, who adds it to the thought of the Zero, and in so doing produces, in the antagonism between Situation and Void, a brilliant version of the thought of the Two.

So what is the thought of the Two, the structuring antagonism? Here's an ontological version of it. We all know that the subject's object doesn't coincide with that same object in itself because if it did, the subject would be God. In other words, knowledge is imperfect. But here's the part that's easy to forget: the subject is not a fool, and knows this. The "object in itself," then, is also the subject's object. Both are real; the object is not, so to speak, simultaneous with itself. It is split, not between what is known of it and what is beyond knowledge, but between the object that exists for us and the object that exists (for us) independently of us. But if the subject knows the same object in two different and incompatible ways, then neither is the subject simultaneous with itself. This should make it clear that the subject–object split is misnamed. The split is within the object itself—or if you prefer, within the subject. This restlessness within the object (or the subject) is called History.

The choice among these three options—or is it two?—is not trivial.

6

Three classes or two?—The existence of classes in our age is not a factual question but a political one. Nobody will deny that wealth is distributed unevenly. Those who want to do something about this live in a world that consists of two strata, the poorer and larger of which must struggle against the domination of the richer and smaller. Those who benefit, or think they benefit, from the status quo live in a world with three classes or, what is the same thing, with none, because the notion of the "middle class" can encompass everyone who does not belong purely to Labor or Capital in the classical sense—which is to say virtually everyone. The question is not whether, empirically, there are two classes or three or a thousand or none. The question is rather: is there class antagonism, or isn't there? Here, the distinction between the descriptive and the political—perhaps always a spurious distinction—disappears.

7

More haste, less speed.—Though it belongs to a different era, *Minima Moralia* is a handbook for conducting philosophy in the age of finance capitalism. One cannot avoid reflecting on the temptations and limitations of bourgeois intellectual thought, and indeed, of the temptations of reflecting on these temptations. The concept of "reflexive modernity" lately championed in the social scientists by Ulrich Beck and the architect of the Third Way, Anthony Giddens, seems to represent an advance over a modernity that has no prefacing adjective. But just as being against capitalism doesn't imply that one is a socialist, so being reflexive doesn't mean the problems of modernity are magically solved. Adorno reminds us again and again of the institutional settings out of which thought grows, and the constraints and expectations these settings produce. "Since there are no longer, for the intellectual, any given categories, even cultural, and bustle endangers concentration with a thousand claims, the effort of producing something in some measure worthwhile is now so great as to be beyond almost everybody."[13]

Is it possible that Totality has been rejected not because it is specious or Eurocentric, but because we think it takes too much time? It might as well be admitted: far from having been slowly co-opted by a shift from a university of culture to a university of excellence, as Bill Readings suggests, intellectual labor is the very model for production in the age of finance capital. Long before high-tech firms plopped pool tables down in the middle of their high-ceilinged, reconverted factory buildings, the professoriate was working twelve-hour flex-time days on gothic campuses and hanging out at the faculty club.

As for us: guilty as charged. The lesson here is to leave behind even the lingering idea of intellectual purity vis-à-vis the contaminated state of the rest of the world. And to think with less speed, but more urgency.

8

Aura after aura.—There is no longer anything threatening or dangerous about Walter Benjamin's reflections on the significance of mechanical reproduction for "a number of outmoded concepts, such as creativity and genius, eternal value and mystery."[14] It is often forgotten that Benjamin positions his reflections as coming at the end of a fifty-year process of social transformation that was only beginning to be expressed symptomatically in culture in the 1920s and 1930s. Benjamin's work on mechanical reproduction is thus belated; indeed, Benjamin was writing at the dawn of the age of electronic circulation, an age that Debord (also belatedly) sketched in *Society of the Spectacle*.

What kinds of things are born in and destroyed by electronic circulation? It would be wrong to suggest that this is a question that no one has yet taken up. However, it seems to us that when it has been addressed, the question is taken too literally. The attempt to think about the social significance of images and visuality at the present time seems to be stuck in the to-and-fro of the epistemologies of idealism. The problem of mediation has not got beyond certain very basic notions in Hegel, perhaps because Hegel is not to be got beyond. Whatever the case, contemporary thought has tended to conceive the history of representation as a very undialectical intensification of a more or less eternal dynamic.

Ours is an age that imagines the visual to have a specific and exceptional force and power. The idea of American cultural imperialism (itself a stand-in for globalization) is often imagined as synonymous with the spread of the visual signs emanating from the United States: advertising, the design of consumer packaging, Hollywood. Nevertheless, our theories of electronic circulation amount to undertheorized ideas about cultural diffusion (any visual image will expand to fill the existing global space), osmosis (it seeps into you), and contamination (it poisons you). More needs to be said.

9

The world is not legible, but audible.—As for the other side of global culture, the flow of musical form across the surface of the globe, things look even less promising. Both disciplinary musicology and cultural studies approaches to music are—somebody has to say it—stupidly empirical in the absence of any sort of remotely adequate theory of the object. But music is an activity by means of which bodies are synchronized into a social body, and a genuine theory of music may one day be able to do more to explain the modalities of global culture than any theory of the image. The global trajectory of musical forms, subterranean and unpredictable compared with the colonization of the world by the Image, may be the very substance in which new social relationships are registered. The job of theory, in that case, would be to cognize (*interpret* does not seem quite the right word) the noncognitive (*unconscious* does not seem quite the right word) performance of musical being-in-the-world. Could it be, as Jacques Attali proposed, that "the world . . . is not legible, but audible"?[15] Unfortunately, Attali's thesis remains in the realm of science fiction: Music predicts the future! The missing term that would make this intelligible is desire. Can we say more reasonably that music embodies a social desire? Sometimes this desire dies and nothing is born. But if the desire is realized in social form, the musical form that nurtured it appears prescient.

10

Nobody knows, everyone is in the know.—Simultaneously, two contradictory theses about that most alien of creatures, the mass, have been emerging in globalization. On the one hand, there is a sense that globalization institutes an era in which, belatedly, mass culture critiques hit their mark. Now that global media monopolies have anxiously consolidated their hold on every aspect of leisure, we can safely skip over the more optimistic pronouncements of some theorists of mass culture and go straight to Horkheimer and Adorno: "Fun is a medicinal bath."[16] On the other hand, globalization is also the era of the end of ideology and of the universality of cynical reason (in Žižek's famous formulation, "they know very well what they are doing, but still, they are doing it").[17] What philosophy in the age of finance capitalism needs to explain is how both of these phenomena can not only occur together, but are in fact also produced out of the same historical conditions of possibility (and contradiction). Elsewhere Žižek writes that "a direct reference to extra-ideological coercion (of the market, for example) is an ideological gesture *par excellence:* the market and (mass) media are dialectically interconnected."[18] In other words, whatever explanation one produces must come from the inside rather than the outside. It is not only, as Hardt and Negri suggest, that the outside has disappeared: for philosophy, it was always a mistake to conceive of an outside. But that's history for you.

11

The eclipse of so-called tradition.—For Gramsci, "traditional" intellectuals are connected to one another across time. Because "traditional intellectuals experience through an *'esprit de corps'* their uninterrupted historical continuity and their special qualification, they put themselves forward as autonomous and independent of the dominant social group."[19] It is this simultaneous autonomy vis-à-vis the present and filiation to the past that still fires the imagination of critical theorists, even though we are now suspicious of both this separation and this connection. But what if we imagined ourselves first and foremost as "organic" intellectuals? Shouldn't we more properly see ourselves as part of that strata of intellectuals that, especially in the age of finance capitalism, give contemporary capital "homogeneity and an awareness of its function not only in the economic but also in the social and political fields?"[20] The exemplary organic intellectual in the age of factories and production is the engineer. Like it or not, the exemplary organic intellectuals in the age of finance capitalism are intellectuals and cultural workers—otherwise known as "content providers."

12

Ex nihilo.—You can't start from scratch. If the unruly spirit of Adorno must energize one part of philosophy in the age of finance capitalism, the caution of Raymond Williams should animate the other. The technological euphoria that pervades the official discourses of finance capitalism all too often finds its equivalent in the enthusiasm of theory for all manner of technotheories (from Debord's spectacle to Haraway's cyborgs) that contemplate a present that has made an absolute break with the past. Williams reminds us that things are far messier than that. Every social formation is the product of more than a single class, and the product of more than a single age. Academics who theorize the present in the manner of science fiction films (the ones that imagine the future as so absolutely future that not even the practice of eating real food remains) have a predilection for nineteenth-century houses.

It is an open question whether futurity can be positively conceived at all. The future is no more than a lack in the present. As the Mozambiquan writer Mia Couto puts it in his story "Os mastros do Paralém" ("The Flags of Beyondward"), "o destino de um sol é nunca ser olhado": the destiny of a sun is never to be beheld.[21] Positive visions of the future like the cyberutopias of our own very recent past or the popular futurisms of the 1950s—or for that matter Plato's *Republic*—cannot think the future; they can only rearticulate the actual in futuristic form.

13

Without a base.—The base/superstructure model has had a rough ride since it was taken all too literally by those Marxists who followed Marx. By now, everyone agrees that what is fundamentally missing from this model is, as Williams has said, "any adequate recognition of the indissoluble connections between material production, political and cultural institutions and activity, and consciousness."[22] Paulin Hountondji and others have described the ways in which the cultural is finally collapsed into the economic, and the economic into the cultural, in such a manner that one must go beyond what is implied in Williams's criticism. There needs to be a whole new model of causality in the age of finance capitalism because one of the things that distinguishes this period from all others is that it no longer makes sense to comprehend the social totality through the lens of even a highly developed and complicated idea of base/superstructure. John Tomlinson writes that

> the complexity of the linkages established by globalization extends to phenomena which social scientists have labored to separate out into the categories in which we now, familiarly, break down human life: the economic, the political, the social, the interpersonal, the technological, the environmental, the cultural and so forth. Globalization arguably confounds such taxonomy.[23]

What this means is that we have to take seriously the fact that material explanations may require increasing reference to immaterial forces and entities.

At any rate, one need not be ashamed to maintain that, precisely to the extent—not necessarily great—that humanity controls its own destiny, any intervention in history's course has to take place at the level of thought. This is not the same as idealism. No doubt an infinity of determinations come before thought; no doubt, even, the truth of thought lies outside itself. But if nothing can happen until it becomes possible, possibility cannot be understood in a purely materialist way. Conception, too, is a condition of possibility.

14

We refute us thus.—Every materialism is vulgar, ripe with unexamined presuppositions to be sneered at by any philosopher who happens to pass by. Every philosophy is an idealism susceptible to some version of Johnson's boot. What if both these statements are true? Perhaps then the only way out is to occupy the antagonism between them: not by refuting one to champion the other, but rather by engaging in the intimate and perpetual struggle against one's own idealism. How many people have tried this? We can think of one, anyway.

15

Worstward ho!—Words like *We* and *Ours* embolden polemics such as these. Fear not: we imagine neither a universal subject nor a unitary community. But we also refuse to imagine a "West" that has long founded not only the unreflective "we"s and "our"s of the Eurocentric academy, but also their critique. Indeed, we assert that there is no West, there is no Westernization; for that matter, there is no modernity or modernization. There is Capital, and there is its limit, as expressed both in its internal contradictions and in active resistance to it (which is also, in a different way, internal). There is therefore no such thing as multiculturalism. The instant something becomes a culture—the moment that it ceases to be a world—it belongs to Capital or, what is more rare, resistance to Capital. What we call the "West" names this culturalizing machine, an aspect of Capital. Perhaps especially, of capitalism now.

16

Capitalism always comes from elsewhere.—It is well known that the disequilibrium intrinsic to the function of capital can be kept under control only by the expansion of capital itself: as Marx put it in the *Grundrisse*, "the tendency to create the world market is directly given in the concept of capital itself. Every limit appears as a barrier to be overcome."[24] This is from the perspective of Capital. But it should not be thought that any place is originally capitalist and therefore free from the encroachment of capital. From any human perspective, Capital is always encroaching. The privatization of government, the corporatization of the arts, of higher education, of sports, of heretofore unrationalized industries like cattle ranching, continues in the dominant countries today a process that has gone by many names, among them *colonialism* yesterday, and *enclosure* before that.

17

Capitalism is indigenous everywhere.—Marx's pages in the *Grundrisse* on "precapitalist" modes of production, problematic though they are in so many respects, are important for suggesting that every social formation tends to produce inequalities that can easily give rise to a pool of free labor—a suggestion, it should be noted, that is corroborated by any number of fictional narratives of the colonial encounter. Capitalism is not simply another, particularly voracious, social formation, but rather, as Deleuze and Guattari claimed in *Anti-Oedipus* (1983), the specific nightmare of every social formation, the secret possibility, always repressed, of recoding existing social inequalities as the capital–labor relation. To confuse "Capitalism" with the "West" is to elevate the latter, a merely heuristic category, to a causal level where it has no place.

18

Ex hybridis, libertinis servisque conscripserat.—It is finally recognized that hybridity, one of the dominant terms of the end of the last century, presupposed its opposite. This incoherence cannot be removed simply by asserting, as the most advanced thinkers of hybridity did, that hybridity goes "all the way down," that the essence that inheres in the concept can be deferred infinitely, any more than the fable to which this phrase refers can explain the suspension of the earth in space by resting it on an infinite series of turtles. At some point both theories presuppose a ground. If hybridity really went all the way down, it would annihilate itself as a concept. This is not to argue for authenticity; indeed, if by *hybridity* one means simply "lack of essence," it does indeed go all the way down. But in order to maintain its distinctness as a concept, hybridity must also mean a "combination of essences." There is no way out of this contradiction except to return the word to its origins in a class distinction. In Latin, *hibrida* refers to the child of slave and freeborn. *Hybridity*, then, would come to refer to something like the complicity of homologous class fractions in dominant and dominated regions of the globe. But no doubt we have better words for this.

19

Same difference.—It is becoming clear that the hegemonic concept of Difference is at one and the same time the most universal and (therefore) the most empty concept, virtually synonymous with Being because both name the very medium of experience. In fact it is Difference (as slogan and as concept), not Totality, that reduces the complexity of the world to the monotonous Same, because the truly different (that is, what refuses to be seen as merely different—what goes, for example, by ideological names such as *totalitarianism, fundamentalism, communism,* and *tribalism*) is excluded from the field of difference. The primacy of "difference" in fact outlines an identity—the unacknowledged frame of the monoculture, global capitalism.

20

Fear of error or fear of truth?—A position of permanent critique can itself become yet another kind of metaphysics. Suspicion about the strategic function of the signified, for example, is a powerful demystifying tool, but in its chronic form, it produces a delimitation of the domain of truth more crippling than any naïveté.

21

The good, the bad, and the ugly; or, the baby and the bathwater.—It has been said that the essence of liberalism is a facile separation of the good from the bad, as though systems—economic, philosophical, whatever—could be simply carved up and the undesirable elements discarded: Competition is good but poverty is bad, so let's just get rid of poverty (while retaining the dynamic that sustains it); Marx is good but revolution is bad, so let's forget about revolution (while educating undergraduates in the poetry of *Capital*). Totality, incidentally, is the name for the rejection of this tendency, which is as common as ever—it is virtually the editorial policy of the *New York Times*—but a seemingly contrary tendency is equally insidious. This is to conflate a philosophical concept not with its dialectically necessary other but with an ideological cognate. Utopia is a case in point: the construction of utopias is a transparently ideological operation, but the notion of utopia— that is, the reservation within thought of an horizon that is not merely the present—is essential to any genuine politics. Indeed, the failure to think utopia in the strong sense leads directly to utopia in the first sense—in particular, to the utopia (never called that) of a market without poverty.

This corresponds to Hegel's "bad infinity" of infinite approximation as opposed to the properly infinite judgment. The same goes for Totality, the denigration of which in current thought serves to discredit the dialectic by associating it with the thematics of the eradication of difference, with which it has nothing in common.

22

And the truth shall set you free.—"In any case, the death of metaphysics or the overcoming of philosophy has never been a problem for us: it is just tiresome, idle chatter. Today it is said that systems are bankrupt, but it is only the concept of system that has changed. So long as there is a time and a place for creating concepts, the operation that undertakes this will always be called philosophy, or will be indistinguishable from philosophy, even if it is called something else."[25] This is true, and yet Deleuze and Guattari's description of this ceaseless activity of invention called philosophy can't help but send the wrong message in an age that has grown accustomed to the language of invention—inventing communities, inventing identities, inventing ideas . . . hey, no problem! But the generation of concepts does not occur willy-nilly. If philosophy's truth originates outside itself (as Lenin taught us), so does it finally reside. The real truth of all thinking, its effective truth, is of a fundamentally different order than the truth it claims for itself. In Christian allegory, the anagogic Truth that it seeks is only an alibi for its real truth, which is the production of faith and a community of believers. So too with thought. If the intellectual wants to change the world, so much the better. But here there are no shortcuts; Saint Augustine could not just order his congregation to believe. There are other, perhaps better, ways to change the world. But for the intellectual, however naive it may seem, the only path is responsibility to Truth.

23

What is to be done?—This is the question that is not being asked today. Let us call one possible position the politics of immanence. Better yet, let us call it Michael Hardt and Antonio Negri. There is to be no revolution, certainly no Party; the world to come will arrive through a plurality of struggles that, taken as a whole, express the desire of the multitude. What desire? The desire that was so effortlessly co-opted during the cold war by high wages in the first world and (relatively) generous development aid in the third? Or the desire that, after the disintegration of actually existing socialism, exists only to be brutally crushed in the name of the Market? For the secret of the story of the immanent desire of the multitude is that it qui-etly relied on a prior transcendent revolution. Once the revolution (or at least its vestige) disappears as Capital's threat and horizon, the desire of the multitude has no recourse. And surely we do not need to be reminded that in the wrong circumstances the utopian desire of the multitude can be channeled toward the most obscene ends. The other position might be called the politics of transcendence; or better yet Slavoj Žižek and Alain Badiou. There is to be a revolution, even a revolutionary party, but revolu-tion is fundamentally a decision, a risky experiment never guaranteed to succeed, and therefore an untheorizable particularity. Yes, yes, yes—and a resounding no. Lenin had a theory of revolution, a very precise under-standing of the historical conjuncture in which revolution was a possible decision. But our situation, in which no merely national revolution will have much significance (the dilemmas faced by the few national govern-ments genuinely on the Left are evidence enough of this), is immeasurably more complex than Lenin's. We remember Lenin because his revolution succeeded. How many failed? The potential cost of not asking what is to be done is a period of bloody and ineffective rebellions, some of them deeply reactionary. Neither is invoking something like Seattle much help; the protests against our current mode of globalization are a sign and a slogan, but not an organizing principle. And waiting for a messiah will only waste time. What we face instead is the hard work, the collective work, of theo-rizing the possibilities that inhere in our current conjuncture and possible ways to proceed. The only thing worse than picking the wrong moment would be missing the right one, and it may come sooner than we think.

24

What is the multitude? Since the moment of its appearance, we have been enchanted with the poetry of the multitude. But before we get too carried away, it's worth asking what it is. How can it both resolutely refuse being reduced to a unity and at the same time explode in a political project? Isn't a positive political project—as opposed to political drift, the average of all political projects, or to "the multitude against," a unity imposed negatively from without—a concrete unity? Hardt and Negri invoke neuroscience to explain the apparent contradiction. The brain doesn't have a center of com-mand, but it manages to make decisions without ever being a real unity. What feels in our daily life like a subjective decision is just the outcome of innumerable parallel processes. So far so good; in some sense, this is no more than obvious. But allow us to ask the dialectical question of the reality of the appearance: What if the illusion were taken away? Isn't the illusion of a subject itself a necessary part of the functioning of this decentered system that is not a subject? But in this case, the illusion is not simply an illusion but also real. Can we then read Hardt and Negri's analogy back again into political subjecthood? Is the illusion of transcendent unity essential to the functioning of a real immanent multiplicity? Does someone have to come up with a project and sell everyone else on it? Does the political subjectivity of the multitude require—gasp!—a political vanguard to bring it into being? Somehow, we're not too keen on that idea, either.

25

Project(ions).—Writing philosophy in the age of finance capitalism is neither the most self-indulgent (and thus useless) practice possible, nor is it the sole space in which it is possible to fan the flames of aesthetic–utopian imaginings. As Fredric Jameson reminds us, "Capitalism itself has no social goals."[26] It is through philosophy that such goals can be imagined.

NOTES

1. Walter Benjamin, "The Work of Art in the Age of Mechanical Reproduction," in *Illuminations,* ed. Hannah Arendt, trans. Harry Zohn (New York: Shocken Books, 1968), 222.

2. Karl Marx, "The German Ideology," in *The Marx–Engels Reader,* ed. Robert C. Tucker (New York: Norton, 1978), 172–73.

3. Ibid., 172.

4. Raymond Williams, *Culture and Society, 1780–1950* (New York: Columbia University Press, 1983), 320.

5. Theodor W. Adorno, *Negative Dialectics,* trans. E. B. Ashton (London: Routledge, 1973), 3.

6. Masao Miyoshi, "A Borderless World? From Colonialism to Transnationalism to the Decline of the Nation-State," in *Global/Local: Cultural Production and the Transnational Imaginary,* ed. Rob Wilson and Wimal Dissanayake (Durham, N.C.: Duke University Press, 1996), 79.

7. Gayatri Chakravorty Spivak, *A Critique of Postcolonial Reason* (Cambridge, Mass.: Harvard University Press, 1999), 1.

8. Michael Hardt and Antonio Negri, *Empire* (Cambridge, Mass.: Harvard University Press, 2000), 142.

9. Jean Comaroff and John L. Comaroff, "Millennial Capitalism: First Thoughts on a Second Coming," *Public Culture* 12, no. 2 (2000): 331.

10. Ibid., 334.

11. Xudong Zhang, "Marxism and the Historicity of Theory: An Interview with Fredric Jameson," *New Literary History* 29, no. 3 (1998): 365–66.

12. John Milton, *Paradise Lost,* Book VI, 20–21.

13. Adorno, *Minima Moralia: Reflections from a Damaged Life,* trans. E. F. N. Jephcott (London: New Left Books, 1974), 29.

14. Benjamin, "Work of Art," 218.

15. Jacques Attali, *Noise: The Political Economy of Music,* trans. Brian Massumi (Minneapolis: University of Minnesota Press, 1985), 3.

16. Max Horkheimer and Theodor W. Adorno, *Dialectic of Enlightenment,* trans. John Cumming (New York: Continuum 1996), 140.

17. Slavoj Žižek, *The Sublime Object of Ideology* (London: Verso, 1989), 29.

18. Slavoj Žižek, "Introduction: The Spectre of Ideology," in *Mapping Ideology,* ed. Slavoj Žižek (New York: Verso, 1994), 15.

19. Antonio Gramsci, *Selections from the Prison Notebooks,* ed. and trans. Quintin Hoare and Geoffrey Nowell Smith (New York: International Publishers, 1971), 7.

20. Ibid., 5.

21. Mia Couto, *Cada homem é uma raça* (Rio de Janeiro: Nova Fronteira, 1998), 185.

22. Raymond Williams, *Marxism and Literature* (Oxford: Oxford University Press, 1977), 80.

23. John Tomlinson, *Globalization and Culture* (Chicago: University of Chicago Press, 1999), 13.

24. Karl Marx, *Grundrisse,* trans. Martin Nicolaus (New York: Vintage, 1973), 408.

25. Gilles Deleuze and Félix Guattari, *What Is Philosophy?,* trans. Hugh Tomlinson and Graham Burchill (New York: Verso, 1994), 9.

26. Fredric Jameson, "Globalization and Political Strategy," *New Left Review* 4 (2000): 62.

4 Periodizing the 80s: The Cultural Logic of Economic Privatization in the United States

JEFFREY T. NEALON

> Any political philosophy must turn on the analysis of capitalism and the ways it has developed.
>
> —GILLES DELEUZE, *Negotiations*

How Soon Is Now?

After the economic meltdown of fall 2008, it may seem like the era of unbridled faith in free-market or neoliberal capitalism is waning in the United States. With the federal government busy orchestrating huge bailouts of the private sector, it would seem that the slick era of "small government and big business," born in the Reagan 1980s and intensified through the Clinton 90s, is definitively over, and that we're on the verge of a retooled era of mid-twentieth-century Keyneseanism. However, I think this would be a hasty conclusion. Let's recall that the last similar global market crash was not in the 1920s but in 1987, constituting a minor blip before returning to the full-on charge of the neoliberal revolution. And there were of course similar calls in the late 1980s to regulate and get the government further involved in financial markets, with various "reforms" implemented in the banking and investment industries (especially for savings and loans and their risky mortgage and investment practices—sound familiar?). But we all know what happened to those hand-wringing reforms: they were completely forgotten by the mid-1990s. Likewise, what we saw in the fall of 2008 was not really a change of course or swerve away from market dictates at all. What you see when you see a government bailout of private industries is not so much the beginning of a brave new socialism, but simply the other shoe dropping: with the privatization of wealth on a massive scale comes the socialization of risk on an almost unthinkable scale, well over a trillion dollars of what amounts to "success insurance" paid out to private companies in public, taxpayer funds. At the end of the day, these bailouts are not the abandonment of free market ideology, but simply the other face of the privatized, free-market coin we've become so familiar with since the 1980s.

Indeed, it feels a lot like 1987 both economically and culturally these days. Even the fashion and entertainment segments of CNN (the impatient "get to the point" news network) are 80s saturated: the hottest new radio format is all 80s, with several stations going from the ratings cellar to number 1 in about the time it takes to play the extended dance remix of "Tainted Love." On the fashion front, runways and malls are filled with 80s-style fashions; I recently saw a designer-ripped T-shirt that said, somewhat confusedly, "Kiss Me, I'm Punk." But, as always, the real confirmation of the thesis comes in the commercials: 80s new wave and punk play over Isuzu ads, while Iggy Pop urges on a new generation of *Love Boat* patrons in their hedonistic "Lust for Life." I swear not long ago I heard The Smiths, whose myopic 80s anthems to frustration were perhaps second only to American Music Club for their sheer misery quotient, playing over an upbeat commercial for an SUV.

Although the return of the 80s is hardly surprising—how long could the nostalgia industry keep recycling 70s hip-huggers?—it remains a decade with something of a PR problem. Put most bluntly or economically, the 80s are haunted by the specter of Gordon Gekko's "greed is good" speech in the 1987 film *Wall Street*. It's difficult for the 80s to shake its reputation as the decade in which self-interested capitalism went utterly mad; indeed, it's hard to imagine the 80s without conjuring up pictures of cocaine-addled yuppie scum with slicked-back hair and suspenders, floating worthless junk bonds to finance leveraged buyouts (LBOs) that callously ravaged what was left of good jobs in industrial America. Mary Harron's 2000 film version of Bret Easton Ellis's 1991 *American Psycho* cannily tries to replay some of the madness of the 1980s—the kind of madness thoroughly documented in Bryan Burrough and John Helyar's *Barbarians at the Gate*, about the mother of all LBOs, 1988's KKR hostile takeover of RJR-Nabisco.

The 80s, in short, was the decade where the dictates of the market became a kind of secular monotheism in the United States, thereby opening the door to the now-ubiquitous corporatization of large sectors of American life: welfare, media, public works, prisons, and education. In fact, such a market dictatorship, honed in the many palace coups that were the 80s LBOs, has become the dominant logic not only of the U.S. economy, but also of the fast-moving phenomenon known as globalization. Downsize, outsource, keep the stock price high—those are the dictates of the new global version of corporate *Survivor*. Indeed, it seems clear that American TV hit *Survivor* and its clone shows can be dubbed "reality" television only if we're willing to admit that reality has become nothing other than a series of outtakes from an endless corporate training exercise, with the dictates of 80s management theory (individualism, excellence, downsizing) having somehow become "the real." In fact, the exotic, "primitive" physical locations of *Survivor* argue none too subtly for the naturalization and universalization of these corporate strategies. Watching *Survivor*, it seems as if GE's corporate template for the 80s—"eliminating 104,000 of its 402,000-person workforce (through layoffs or sales of divisions) in the period 1980–90"—had somehow become the way of nature.[1] In the end, *Survivor's* tribal council functions simply as a corporate board, demanding regular trimming of the workforce, until finally the board gets to award a huge executive bonus of $1 million, with all decisions along the way having been made according to an economist's notion of subjectivity— what Michael Jensen has dubbed the "resourceful, evaluative, maximizing models of human behavior" (194). On further reflection, then, maybe it's not so much that the 80s are back culturally, but that they never went anywhere economically: the downsizing and layoff mania of the 80s— designed to drive up stock prices and impose market discipline on corporate managers—has now simply become business and cultural orthodoxy, standard operating procedure. Following *Survivor's* lead, one might call it reality, a state of affairs as tailor-made for the boom cycles as it is explanatory of the bust cycles that inevitably follow them. Less dramatically, one could say that the economic truisms of the 80s remain a kind of soundtrack for today, the relentless beat playing behind the eye candy of our new corporate world, a world that's been shocked by the downturns of 2008, but one that has hardly abandoned the monotheistic faith that markets are the base line of freedom, justice, and all things good in the world, for so-called liberals and conservatives alike. For a concise version of this mantra, one need look no further than Barack Obama's remarks in the summer of 2008: "I am a pro-growth, free market guy. I love the market. I think it is the best invention to allocate resources and produce enormous prosperity for America or the world that's ever been designed."[2]

This across-the-board and continuing acceptance of 80s-style market principles is one of the primary reasons why one might want to periodize the 80s, to steal a phrase from Fredric Jameson. To periodize the recent past is, of course, simultaneously to periodize the present: to begin figuring out how the cultural, political, and economic axioms of today (mandates only beginning to take shadowy shape) are related the axioms of yesterday (mandates on which we should presumably have a better theoretical handle). Indeed, if there is such a thing as "a leftist ontology" (and I'm tempted to think that there isn't, or at least that there's more than one), Jameson's work may offer less an ontological proof of its existence than an initial direction for further inquiry into the topic: his axiom, "always historicize," which mobilizes ontology ("always") transversally and necessarily linked to materialism ("historicize"). It is, at least, in that materialist or genealogical sense, importantly imbricated with the axiomatic thrust of something that one might call ontology, that this essay will proceed.

At this point, the reader might wonder how, why, or even if Jameson's work offers us a privileged path forward, insofar as today's postmodern materialists of the neo-Deleuzean variety tend to think of Jameson as someone dedicated to an old-fashioned—been there, done that—leftist ontology, namely dialectics. Well, like Foucault's nagging historical questions concerning power and exploitation (it took the entire nineteenth century for us to get a handle on what "exploitation" was, he reminds us, and surely it will have taken the twentieth and some chunk of the twenty-first before we have any workable sense of what "power" is),[3] I wonder whether the Jamesonian dialectic has really been exhausted of its critical potentials. To put it more precisely, I wonder whether a certain positive Jamesonian itinerary surrounding the work of historicization or periodization remains unexplored or underexploited. In short, we all know about dialectical method's attachment to the work of the negative; but surely any such work of negation must, in a dialectical system, be compensated for by an equally robust movement of affirmation. What about this less-discussed affirmative critique practiced by Jameson?

For a sense of that neglected Jameson, we need look no further than his most (in)famous essay, "Postmodernism; or, The Cultural Logic of Late Capitalism." Holding at bay for a moment the many constative things we know or think we know about what the essay means or what it wants (a new totalization, a negation of consumer culture, a cognitive map, a return to this or that style of modernist subjectivity), I'd like to suggest that we concentrate instead on the essay's performative aspects—looking quite simply at how the essay does its work. For me, rereading this essay highlights a contradiction of the sort that we can only assume is intentional—antinomy being precisely the kind of shifting quicksand of an *Abgrund* on which dialectical thinkers influenced by Adorno often build their homes. In short, if Jameson is indeed a thinker of dialectical, progressive totalization (of the kind familiar from an old-fashioned reading of Hegel), then he certainly doesn't practice what he preaches. The style, range, and sheer volume of reference in the essay is anything but restricted or developmental in a recognizable sense; there's certainly no Hegelian movement from sense certainty, to unhappy consciousness, to the heights of knowledge, absolute or otherwise. Instead, from the opening paragraphs and their mishmashing of punk music and the minimalist song stylings of "Phil" Glass, through discussions of Nam June Paik, Andy Warhol, Heidegger and Derrida, E. L. Doctorow, Bob Perelman, the Bonaventure Hotel, Duane Hanson, Brian De Palma, and so on, we get less an analytical snapshot or critical dissection of postmodernism than a jump-cut-laden video starring it. We are presented, in other words, with many, many modes of postmodern cultural production, but hardly any sense of postmodernism's sublated meaning. And the hasty list of examples provided above doesn't even try to account for the heavy volume of seemingly passing reference which is so characteristic of Jameson's style on the whole: in the Austinean sense, he "uses" Doctorow or Warhol in/as "Postmodernism"; but he in addition mentions a truly dizzying array of postmodern cultural productions that would seem to have very little or nothing in common: Ishmael Reed, Godard, John Cage, *Reader's Digest,* Foucault, John Ashbery, Stanley Kubrick, Chinatown (both the Polanski movie and the San Francisco neighborhood referenced in Bob Perelman's poem "China"), Robert Wilson, David Bowie, the architecture firm Skidmore, Owings & Merrill, and William Gibson—not to mention what must be the only extant reference to B-list movie actor William Hurt within the canon of poststructuralist theory.

On what's become the standard reading of this essay, the wide range of Jamesonian reference does indeed harbor a performative point, but it's largely a negative one: we, as readers, are meant to experience the dizzying array of centerless intensity produced by this laundry list of cultural productions; and as we try and deploy our outmoded categories to "read" or make sense of this puzzling, affectless flat surface, we're led inexorably to Jameson's conclusion: we need a new cognitive map. Without it, we're stuck with a meaningless and monotonous march of shiny, contextless consumer images. On this reading, the very intensity of the Jamesonian barrage—so much postmodern cultural production, so many examples—is meant to highlight not so much the positive (if sinister) force of postmodern cultural production, but instead to solicit our (modernist, all too modernist) inability to respond.

Fair enough, and—mea culpa—I've advanced just such a reading of Jameson elsewhere.[4] But here I'd like to highlight the fact that there's another Jameson, one lurking beside (or maybe even in dialectical opposition to) the negative, stony, finger-wagging one we think we know. In classical dialectical fashion, Jameson insists that this negative inability can also provoke "a more positive conception of relationship":

> This new mode of relationship through difference may sometimes be an achieved new and original way of thinking and perceiving; more often it takes the form of an impossible imperative to achieve that new mutation in what can perhaps no longer be called consciousness. I believe that the most striking emblem of this new mode of thinking relationships can be found in the work of Nam June Paik, whose stacked or scattered television screens, positioned at intervals within lush vegetation, or winking down at us from a ceiling of strange new video stars, recapitulate over and over again prearranged sequences or loops of images which return at dyssynchronous moments on the various screens. The older aesthetic is then practiced by the viewers, who, bewildered by this discontinuous variety, decided to concentrate on a single screen, as though the relatively worthless image sequence to be followed there had some organic value in its own right. The postmodernist viewer, however, is called upon to do the impossible, namely, to see all the screens at once, in their radical and random difference; such a viewer is asked to follow the evolutionary mutation of David Bowie in *The Man Who Fell to Earth* (who watches fifty-seven television screens simultaneously) and to rise somehow to a new level at which the vivid perception of radical difference is in and of itself a new mode of grasping what used to be called relationship.[5]

There's of course a lot going on here, in one of Jameson's most overt statements concerning "a more positive conception" of "what used to be called relationship" in and around postmodern cultural production. Most striking in this passage is Jameson's neo-Deleuzean (though he'd undoubtedly prefer the adjective "utopian") call for "a new mutation in what can perhaps no longer be called consciousness." Not a lot of nostalgia or mourning here.

Perhaps less obviously, this paragraph also comprises the essay's most overt moment of reflexive self-thematization. We readers of Jameson are positioned as the hapless viewers of Paik's rapid-fire video installations: "bewildered by this discontinuous variety" of cultural stuff that Jameson so quickly offers us, we tend "to concentrate on a single screen"—this or that specific example—"as though the relatively worthless image sequence to be followed there had some organic value in its own right." However, this critical failure, far from being the negative and inevitable point of Jameson's essay, is overtly thematized as the trap to be avoided in reading it: "The postmodernist viewer, however, is called upon to do the impossible, namely, to see all the screens at once, in their radical and random difference; such a viewer [who is also Jameson's reader—*mon semblable, mon frère et soeur*] is asked to follow the evolutionary mutation of David Bowie in *The Man Who Fell to Earth* (who watches fifty-seven television screens simultaneously) and to rise somehow to a new level at which the vivid perception of radical difference is in and of itself a new mode of grasping what used to be called relationship." Rather than primarily constituting a requiem for the nonschizo, somehow-still-centered mediating functions of modernist subjectivity, Jameson's essay is a call for revolution in this thing that can no longer be named by its quaint, old-fashioned handle: consciousness. On a performative reading—which will only allow itself to speculate concerning constative meaning by first taking into account performative form— Jameson's work is far more schizo than it is centered, more postmodern than it is modern. And this ambitious formal agenda should hardly surprise us, because Jameson is certainly a thinker who's had more than his share of things to say about the political and theoretical implications of "style."[6]

So in this essay I'll be taking up and intensifying both Jameson's call for a revolution in historical consciousness, and the immanent, experimental, well-nigh mishmashing style in which that call is announced.

THESE THINGS TAKE TIME

Jameson's essay "Periodizing the 60s" argues that the 1960s—or more precisely, the cultural, economic, and social upheavals that we commonly lump together and refer to as "the 60s"—actually began with the global decolonization movements of the mid-1950s and ended sometime in the early to mid-1970s. In other words, Jameson suggests that the 60s is not so much a calendar decade bounded by the years 1960 and 1970, but instead a period of transversally linked revolutionary historical developments that lasted nearly twenty years.

One might flesh out Jameson's claim by venturing that the 60s began politically sometime around the events of Dien Bien Phu in 1954, followed by the Algerian uprising starting on its heels, the Bandung conference in 1955, the strengthening of Indian independence in south Asia, and continuing struggles for decolonization in Africa in the 50s. Economically speaking, the postwar suburbanization of the United States and Western Europe led to a sharp intensification of consumption-based capitalism in the so-called first world. Concomitantly, the second world of Soviet influence was solidified in the mid-50s, with satellite nations becoming important players in the increasingly hot cold war. The rapidly decolonizing, nonaligned third world may have freed itself from direct political control by the former imperialist nations, but it quickly became sutured into a severe and controlling debtor relation with international capitalism: economics, in short, was already becoming the primary means of recolonizing the nonaligned nations, a movement that only intensified through the 60s and into the massive debt crises of the 1970s (with the increasing activism of the Bretton Woods institutions, the World Bank, and the International Monetary Fund). Culturally, the mid-50s in the West saw a wide range of disparate global responses to the intensifying cold war: from the postcolonial theorizing of Fanon and C. L. R. James, to the increasing exhaustion of international modernism in the face of mutually assured destruction (one thinks of Beckett especially here, but also the films of the French auteurs and the dreams of liberation and mobility connected to everything from abstract expressionist painting to Beat literature). In any case, the revolutions we characterize as part and parcel of the 60s can be seen to have had their roots in the 50s, or at least it's a provocative and useful intervention to begin with that historicizing, periodizing premise.

On the other side of the 60s, the fall of Saigon in 1974 or the Watergate scandals of the early to mid-70s are perhaps the most dramatic political markers of the end of the 60s, at least in the United States. Economically, the most convenient break on the other side of the 60s is probably 1971's Smithsonian Agreement, which officially took the U.S. dollar off the gold standard, allowing worldwide currency values to float, their value determined by markets of supply and demand rather than by reference, however tenuous, to the real value of gold reserves in Fort Knox. Culturally, the overdose deaths of 60s icons Jimi Hendrix, Jim Morrison, and Janis Joplin—all in the early 70s—are often pointed out as definitive breaks with the joyful, experimental ethos of the culturally liberated 1960s.

Of course, what counts as a key cultural, political, and economic reference could be multiplied, refined, and argued exponentially; this is part of the gambit and provocation of Jameson's periodizing hypothesis. But I'd like to mine two relatively uncontroversial premises from Jameson's "Periodizing the 60s": first, calendar markers are not the be-all and end-all of grappling with historical periods; and, second, insofar as Jameson's "Periodizing the 60s" was published in 1984, it suggests that only from after the end of an epoch can one begin to size the era up historically or begin to periodize it—following, perhaps, Derrida's famous remarks on deconstruction and its relation to modernist philosophies of the subject: it is precisely from the boundary of a historical period, from inside its continuing end or closure, that one might hold out some retroactive or retrospective hope of naming what happened there.

In following up Jameson's periodizing thesis a few decades later and focusing it narrowly on the United States, I am tempted to say that whenever the 60s finally ended in the United States, the period that emerged in its wake was not so much the 70s as it was the 80s: the conservative, "down with big government" period of backlash that fueled the Reagan revolution; and the intensification of that pro-business, market-take-all ethos in the 1990s. One might say that the 80s, that period of market-mad privatization, began in the mid- to late 70s, with the global reorganization of production. Fueled by the evisceration of government regulation and protections, the beginning of the LBO years in the United States, and the unprecedented run-up of the equity markets, the Reagan 80s had quite a run through the Clinton go-go 90s. Indeed, if in the United States "the 60s" functions politically as a kind of shorthand for resistance and revolution of all kinds, "the 80s" most immediately signifies the increasing power and ubiquity of markets and privatized corporatization in everyday life. And the 90s were the clearly the period of full bloom for the conservative fiscal agenda that was hatched in the 80s. The market-tested Reagan truisms of the 80s were intensified to fever pitch throughout the 1990s (you remember: the government can't do anything right, we're not in the business of nation building abroad, social security should be wholly privatized, the wealthy getting wealthier is actually good for the rest of us, the Dow will run at 36,000).

And though it's a little hard to say exactly when the economic, political, and cultural regime we call "the 80s" began in earnest in the United States (Reagan's election in 1980? the Iran hostage crisis of 1979? the Talking Heads' first album in 1977?), one might say a bit more definitively when the 80s ended: if not with the bursting of the NASDAQ dot-com bubble in fall 2000, then certainly with the wave of corporate scandals (Enron, WorldCom, Arthur Andersen) that followed. And perhaps most definitively, the events of September 11, 2001 ended an era of antigovernment sentiment in the United States. In the present social and political climate, where people in airports happily take their shoes off at the behest of government flunkies, it's hard to remember how omnipresent the tirades against big government were in the 80s and 90s. (Think about Waco, Randy Weaver,

Timothy McVeigh, and Oklahoma City: when these days merely to question the government's actions in the war on terror is labeled "treason," right-wing pundit Ann Coulter's catchy term, it's difficult to recall the hardcore intensity and ubiquity of antigovernment hatred during the 80s and 90s, especially among conservatives.) In terms of foreign policy, the U.S. government's forays into nation crushing/building in Afghanistan and Iraq seem possible only in a world that's very different from the isolationist corporatism that ruled the 80s and 90s (remember the conservative outrage against nation building in Somalia). There were a few cries of "socialism" during the bailout discussions of 2008, but adding several hundred billion dollars of taxpayers' money to the various packages somehow silenced the critics of big government. In short, the nation-state, which had looked like it was becoming an anachronism in the world of triumphant global corporatization, is back—and in a big way. But none of the things that progressives might like about the nation-state, like entitlement programs for the poor, seem to have much chance of returning with it.

On the affective level of everyday life in the United States, it's pretty clear that whatever happened culturally and economically in the 1980s and 90s, we're living in a different period. We're still living that legacy, but many of the dominant economic, cultural, and political rules of the game have changed dramatically.

That being the case, I want to engage here in a kind of periodizing thought experiment, one that takes some of its inspiration from Jameson's "Periodizing the 60s." I want to suggest that, like Jameson's more global thesis about the 60s, the 80s in the United States were a period—an era with a loose cultural, economic, and political affinity—that lasted roughly twenty years, from, say, Reagan's election in 1980 to the summer of 2000 or the fall of 2001. If that period is or feels like it is over today, we may be at a point where we can begin to describe and grapple with what happened there, and to speculate concerning what's likely to come about in its wake. If the culture wars of the 80s are to be remade for a new millennium by a new moral majority, I think it pays for us to think through the substantial economic and cultural differences between the fire last time, and the fire this time—that is to say, it may pay to think through what has disappeared since the 80s, what has intensified, and what, if anything, has remained the same. In short, and in anticipation, I'll try to suggest that over the past twenty years in the United States, the major shift in economic and cultural terrain is within capitalism itself—which is no longer exactly the same thing it was in 1980s. Less dramatically, one could say

that the privatizing economic mandates of the 80s remained and intensified throughout the 1990s. And this perhaps is the most obvious way
that the economic truisms of the 80s linger on today, even after the bubble burst. As Thomas Frank writes, "the free-market faith is still with us.
What's gone is the optimism."[7]

STILL ILL

Jameson's "Periodizing the 60s" was published in 1984, the same year as
his epoch-making "Postmodernism; or, The Cultural Logic of Late Capitalism." The two essays have much in common, each illuminating aspects
of the other. One can, for example, more clearly understand Jameson's
skepticism about the "cultural dominant" of 80s-style postmodernism by
recalling one of the central themes of "Periodizing the 60s," namely, that
the 1980s are or were a period of cultural containment in the United States,
a dialectical inversion of the artistic, political, and economic energies unleashed in the 60s. Artistically, the experimental avant-gardism of the
60s—pop art, performance art, Black Arts—is met in the 80s by the culture wars and the increasing corporatization of artistic production; politically, antiwar and civil rights movements of the 60s are countered by the
"moral majority" Reagan backlash of the 80s—the revenge of white sub-
urbanites; economically, the global decolonizations of the 60s and the
United States' abandonment of the gold standard in the early 70s are met by
the massive global debt crises and inflationary spirals of the 1980s (and the
concomitant rise in power of finance institutions like the Federal Reserve,
World Bank, and International Monetary Fund). If, as Jameson writes, "the
60s were . . . an immense and inflationary issuing of superstructural credit;
a universal abandonment of the universal gold standard; an extraordinary
printing up of ever more devalued signifiers," then the bills unfortunately
come due in the 80s: "the dreary realities of exploitation, extraction of surplus value, proletarianization and . . . class struggle, all slowly reassert themselves on a new and expanded world scale."[8] (And, needless to say, this
description of the early to mid-80s also has some considerable resonance
with the present situation in the United States, where we'll soon have to
reckon with the staggering debts—human, environmental, and monetary—
accrued by the United States' go-it-alone style of global imperialism.)

Reading Jameson's 60s essay next to his postmodernism essay also
suggests that he harbors very little hope for nostalgia as a mode of critical
engagement—that is to say, he argues that the political and artistic strategies of resistance born in the 1960s aren't likely to be effective in the very

different social and political climate of the 1980s. In diagnosing and con-
testing economic and social realities from the vantage point of 1984, Jameson notes that "the older methods [of the 60s] do not necessarily work":
"nostalgic commemoration of the glories of the 60s," he notes in the essay's
opening line, is the first "error" to be avoided in any kind of historicist
thinking about the present.[9] Finally, "Periodizing the 60s" shows us that
the historical transition from the 60s to the 80s is very poorly understood
if we thematize that transition solely within the preferred terms of 60s-
style narratives—as the unleashing of subversive social energy (the 60s)
that's overcome by the repressive backlash of the 80s; 60s authenticity vs.
80s co-optation; 60s resistance vs. 80s normalization. In other words, the
narratives by which we characterize that period called "the 60s"—narratives
of unprecedented rebellion, resistance, and liberation—don't necessarily
do much useful work in explaining or intervening within a very different
historical situation. Taking a good deal of the wind out of the "wasn't that
a time" ethos, Jameson rather soberly suggests that the economic narratives
of the 60s—rather than the artistic or political ones—may be most useful
in thinking historically about the present. The social revolutions of the 60s,
he writes, "may perhaps best be explained in terms of the superstructural
movement and play enabled by the transition from one infrastructural or
systematic stage of capitalism to another."[10] Leave it to Jameson to bring
the wet blanket of economics to a 60s beach party.

Here, I want to follow Jameson insofar as he suggests we need to do a
genealogy of the recent economic past, not so that we can nostalgically
recall and celebrate the gains and losses, but finally so we don't delude
ourselves into thinking that the oppositional strategies of the past can unproblematically and effectively be imported into the present. (As I suggest
above, I take this to be the force of the Jamesonian slogan, "always historicize.") If Jameson's two 1984 essays suggest—however subtly—that many
left-leaning academics in the mid-80s were still stuck in the outmoded
mind-set of the 1960s, and that an economic analysis was the clearest way
to show this, I want to fast-forward that hypothesis another twenty years. To
put my concern baldly, it seems to me that much North American humanities theory of the present moment is essentially stuck in and around the
80s; perhaps the easiest and most effective way of breaking that spell is
to try and think economically as well as culturally about the differences
between the two periods.

To take only the most obvious example of such present-day theoretical
anachronism, Jameson's "Postmodernism" itself remains a touchstone for

cultural studies work on the present. It's a perennial syllabus favorite, and it continues to function as a term-setter for debates about economics and culture today. This, it seems to me, is quite odd (and quite un-Jamesonian). Remember that when Jameson's "Postmodernism" was published in 1984, the Berlin Wall was still firmly in place; the cold war was in fact heating up again, with Reagan's new morning in America still dawning; the Dow Jones was struggling to run at 1200; Paul Volcker's inflation-worried Fed had U.S. interest rates sky high; Japan, it seemed, was the economic power to be reckoned with and feared in the next century (recall that in the industrial midwest of the mid-80s, people would routinely vandalize Japanese cars and motorcycles); in 1984, Americans were just beginning to talk about AIDS; the first Mac computer—with 286 stunning K of RAM—debuted in North America in January 1984, introduced in a splashy, Orwellian Super Bowl commercial; and the Internet—at least as we know it—was still the stuff of science fiction.

We live, in other words, in a very different world from the early to mid-80s. Though we still live with the fallout of the 80s, it's clear that the economic component of our "cultural dominant" is no longer that particular brand of "postmodernism, or late capitalism." In fact, the neo-Marxist hope inscribed in the phrase "late" capitalism seems a kind of cruel joke in the world of globalization (late for what?). So among the tasks of periodizing the present, a collective molecular project that we might call *postpostmodernism,* is to construct a vocabulary to talk about the new economies (such as post-Fordism, globalization, the centrality of market economics, the new surveillance techniques of the war on terrorism) and their complex relations to cultural production in the present moment, where capitalism seems nowhere near the point of its exhaustion. Although the hopes contained in the phrase "the new economy" have all but dried up in recent years, the dreary realities of its market dictates remain very much with us—one hesitates to say permanently, but as far as the eye can see at the present moment. Also, I should note that I take mine to be a diagnostic project: any kind of tentative *pre*scription for treating current ills would have to follow from a thick *de*scription of the symptoms and their genealogical development over time. So it's to that descriptive or diagnostic project that I now turn.

HAND IN GLOVE

So how does or did this thing called economic privatization work? What exactly is the relationship of the 80s LBO craze, for example, and today's more seemingly sedate corporate orthodoxy? Not surprisingly, most economists—right and left—point to a fairly straight line of economic development from the 80s to today, from the death of the old economy to the triumph of the new. As Michael Jensen, Harvard economist and leading theorist of the new market-take-all economy, writes in his 2000 *Theory of the Firm,* LBOs or "LBO associations and venture capital funds provide a blueprint for managers and boards who wish to revamp their top-level control systems to make them more efficient" (56). Rather than issue an apology for the excesses of the 80s, Jensen's work constitutes a cheerleading tribute to "LBOs and their role in the restoration of competitiveness in the American corporation" (64). Indeed, if you want to ask why the Dow Jones Industrial Average shot up more than 10,000 points between 1985 and 2000, when it had managed only about 1,000 points of total growth in the half-century between the 1929 crash and 1980, one need look no further than Jensen and his vision of "unlocking shareholder value."

Among all the other things that sprang onto the economic scene in the 80s, the most central throughout the 1990s was this Jensenite notion of shareholder value, which translated into an almost total corporate emphasis on maintaining a high stock price. For the better part of the twentieth century, American businesses didn't worry too much about their stock price, and the financial sector of the economy was certainly nowhere near the center. Production was king, with an economic and corporate structure dedicated to the Fordist courses of expansion, production, and liberal spending originally mapped by J. M. Keynes and tailored for the postwar megacorporation by J. K. Galbraith. And Jensen is very much aware of the historical reasons for the triumph of production-based economics; the finance-based model lost considerable luster in the 1929 U.S. stock market crash and subsequent worldwide depression. Through the depression and war years to the baby boom generation, the crash of 1929 resonated louder than bombs within the collective memory of American business. And as a result, the financial sector of a midcentury corporation was hardly in any position to call the corporate shots.

Under a Keynesean or Galbraithean theory of the firm, shareholders and others in the private finance sector are a low priority—not exactly an afterthought, but certainly not the enterprise's primary reason for being. "Slow and steady growth" was the mantra of American business from the 50s through the 70s, and disgorging large amounts of public corporate cash to private stockholders is not a good way to manage such growth. Servicing the stockholder is, in fact, destabilizing for those who actually work at the firm—so-called stakeholders. Keeping the stock price and dividends high commits everyone at the firm to an uncertain, quarter-by-quarter, what-have-you-done-for-me-lately mind-set, rather than a long-term pattern of steady growth.

Doug Henwood usefully sums up the orthodoxy of midcentury corporate America in *Wall Street:*

> Galbraith dismissed profit maximization as the goal of a giant firm in favor of the growth in sales and prestige. To thrive, it needed not maximum profits, but "a secure minimum of earnings" that would keep it from having to tap troublesome capital markets or cope with demanding outside stockholders. . . . The technostructure had little to gain from high profits, which would only be passed along to shareholders, and might even entail higher risk.[11]

In such a Galbraithean scenario, it's more or less admitted that shareholder profits could always be greater; but the corporate management and workforce have little incentive to take the risks necessary to squeeze out every last little bit of profit—especially because such profit would, in the end, not help anyone *in* the corporation. Rather, such profits would be paid *out* to private individuals who don't work at the company, but rather hold its stock. So goes the wisdom of corporate technocracy, the thinking attributed to "the man in the gray flannel suit": Why risk your job, your public reputation, and the jobs and of your colleagues to secure higher profit for private shareholders, who have no stake in the everyday running of the corporation, no knowledge about the intricacies of the product line, no expertise in the industry? This corporate orthodoxy helps explain why, for example, the Dow Jones Industrial Average didn't break the 1,000 mark until 1972; and even then, it didn't top 1,100 until more than a decade later, in 1983. During the period from 1990 to 2000, by contrast, rarely did three months go by without a hundred-point gain in the Dow. From 1995 to 1999, thousand-point yearly gains were the norm.

Indeed, the LBO era of the 1980s constituted nothing less than an assault on the Galbraithean corporation, the giant company and its truism that steady and predictable growth is good for all. For Jensen, this seemingly rosy picture of slow growth brings with it a horrible cost: inefficiency. Who's running these corporations, Jensen asks? The answer, in Jensen's view, is middle managers—glorified production supervisors and half-wit business administration majors in cheap suits. And who are they loyal to?

The people who work for them and their immediate bosses; the private shareholder is nowhere to be seen in the equation. In short, Jensen was outraged that businesses were not being run according to the interests of their ostensible owners, the shareholders. Jensen sums up the woeful rise of managerialism this way: "As financial institution monitors left the scene in the post-1940 period, managers commonly came to believe companies belonged to them and that stockholders were merely one of the many stakeholders the firm had to serve" (65–66).

The LBO movement of the 80s, fueled as it was by the mantra of "unlocking shareholder value," was nothing less than a civil war within American business, with shareholders (buoyed by the rise of the large institutional investor, the almighty mutual fund) demanding their piece of the corporate pie. And Jensen makes crystal clear the stakes of this internecine war: "The mergers, acquisitions, leveraged buyouts (LBOs), and other leveraged restructurings of the 1980s constituted an assault on entrenched authority that was long overdue" (9). True to his market orthodoxy, Jensen prefers to talk about the 80s LBO craze as a market itself, the "corporate control market" (3). And Jensen very much articulates the orthodox line in contemporary business—the history written by the winners—which understands the 80s as a kind of massive market correction: individual stockholders stepped in to discipline the lazy and unproductive practices of the old-line corporation. As Jensen smugly sums up, the 80s meant curtains for "those we used to call 'entrenched' management" (4). We all know the story: tens of thousands would "lose their jobs as the inefficient and bloated corporate staffs are replaced by LBO partnership headquarters units" (78). Ah, efficiency.

What was enshrined through the notion of "unlocking shareholder value" is a new-fashioned kind of class warfare, the revolt of the rich. Simply put, Jensen asserts that the people who put up the money should get the profits: "For control to rest in any other group would be equivalent to allowing the group to play poker with someone else's money and would create inefficiencies that lead to the possibility of failure" (2). Because rich people are so obviously and voraciously greedy, Jensen implies, they can be counted on to do anything necessary to maximize profits, which are hiding here behind the code word *efficiency*. As Jensen baldly states, "In the private corporation, stockholders and bondholders, who bear the wealth effects of changes in firm value, have incentives to monitor managers to prevent them from making transfers of corporate assets to workers or permit workers from making such transfers" (194). This, the upward distribution of wealth to CEOs and shareholders while management and workers are ground under finance's heel is the real agenda and effect of 80s-style corporate privatization.

With the recent high-profile crackdowns on corporate malfeasance in the United States, we might be tempted to say that the new barbarians are finally getting theirs. Note, however, that precious few Harvard MBAs or Wharton grads took the perp walk for the cameras: the two CEOs actually led off in high-profile chains were Tyco's Dennis Kozlowski, an alum of Seton Hall, and the hapless John Rigas of Adelphia, a Rensselaer Polytechnic graduate. Of the other infamous CEOs, note that WorldCom's Bernie Ebbers was a working-class kid from Alberta, Canada, and an unlikely alum of Mississippi Baptist College, which he attended on a basketball scholarship; Enron's Ken Lay was a graduate of the University of Missouri. The folks taking the heat are, in other words, aggressively not old-money, Ivy League WASPs, and it's no coincidence that these upstarts are served up as scapegoats while everyone else repeats the line they learned from the frat-house scandals of their college days: it's just a few bad apples, not a systematic problem.

Note also that the investigations that have produced this crackdown, such as it is, were instigated and fueled not by the outrage of unions, employees, the Securities and Exchange Commission, the Justice Department, or the general public, but by the shareholders of these corporations. Although there's a nice populist feel to watching CEOs and CFOs being humiliated, their falls from grace owe virtually nothing to old-fashioned public outrage at the excesses of big business. They were taken down by the power and influence of Enron, Qwest, Adelphia, and WorldCom stockholders—which is to say that recent corporate scandals don't necessarily contradict the privatizing, shareholder-take-all logic of the 80s; they in fact confirm and intensify this logic. Since the 80s, CEOs have been paid lavish salaries to do what the shareholders hired them to do: drive the stock price sky-high, by any means necessary. But when the proverbial shit hit the fan, the shareholders turned on their flunkies in a New York minute. So what you're seeing when you see a CEO in handcuffs is largely the continuation of an internecine war among the superrich and a concomitant extension and consolidation of the shareholders' power in corporate America. It's most assuredly not the result of a populist revolt against corporate fat cats. Likewise, it's these same mega-wealthy shareholders (not regular folks with 401k programs) who pulled out of the stock market completely in 2008, worsening the crash.

WHAT DIFFERENCE DOES IT MAKE?

At some level, this is a familiar story: in the move from Fordism to post-Fordism and beyond, capital has become increasingly deterritorialized, floating flexibly free from production processes, and coming to rest more centrally in the orbit of symbolic exchange and information technologies. In addition, private notions of finance assert themselves over more public modalities of production in the corporation and in the public sphere at large. Lean and mean financial efficiency becomes the mantra; and in a nutshell, efficiency means privatization. That having been said, however, perhaps we need to follow those 80s masters of masochism, The Smiths, and ask, "What difference does it make?" Why rehearse this story, which tends only to make people on the left feel hopeless and resentful? Aside from bemoaning the state of advanced finance capital, what can we do with this genealogy of the recent past?

First, when it comes to the present state of theory in the humanities and the possibilities for mobilizing response to the logic of privatization, this genealogy suggests that it's no longer very productive to think in the terms of theoretical drama familiar from the 1980s. As Jameson notes, those terms themselves are already a hangover from the 60s: that is to say, it's becoming increasingly unhelpful to replay the drama that posits a repressive, normative stasis or essentialism that can only be outflanked by some form of more or less liberating, socially constructed fluid openness. At this point, we'd have to admit that privatized finance capital has all but obliterated the usefulness of this distinction: to insist on the hyridity and fluidness of x or y is the mantra of transnational capital—whose normative state is the constant reconstitution of value—so it can hardly function unproblematically as a bulwark against that logic. Think of the war on terrorism, for example: in order to be patriotic in this war, we in the United States are being asked not to repress or downsize our desires: no collective, public efforts like wholesale rationing or conserving to enhance the war effort. Rather, in a 180-degree turnabout from the austere rhetoric of the Reagan 80s, Uncle Sam now wants us to liberate our individual desires in the face of the axis of evil (defined primarily as anti-desire, anti-individual, fundamentalist repression), so we're asked to consume, travel, refinance our mortgages, buy durable household goods. Follow your personal desires! That'll stick it to Al-Qaeda.

Indeed, when Led Zeppelin plays over Cadillac commercials and the Rolling Stones 2005 tour is sponsored quite literally by the housing bubble (its official sponsor was AmeriQuest Mortgage), you have to assume that the cultural rebellion narratives of the 60s, which often revolved around the liberation of an individual's or group's desire in the face of the various social repressions, can now officially be pronounced dead. Under an economic logic that is in fact dedicated to the unleashing of multifarious individual desires and floating values (broadly speaking, a corporate–nation-state model), rather than desire's dampening or repressive territorialization on a gold standard of univocal value (broadly speaking, the traditional nation-state model), the role of social normalization (previously the purview of the nation-state and its ideological apparatuses) needs to be rethought from the ground up. Put simply, a repressive notion of normalization is not the primary danger lurking within contemporary capitalism. There are myriad social and political dangers latent in the neoliberal truisms of finance capital, but the rigid normalization of cultural options isn't paramount among them. (To take only the most obvious example, it's not corporate capitalism that's at the forefront of discrimination against gays and lesbians—Disney offers same-sex partner benefits; my blue-state university only recently started offering them, over the continuing objections of the state legislature.)

A bit more abstractly, I'd suggest that contemporary capitalism marks a transmutation in the very notion and function of value itself. The privatization of *economic* value has been easy enough to point out: over the past twenty years, public assets have been increasingly handed over to private corporations in the name of market efficiency, and the disparities of wealth distribution in the United States have grown to nearly unbelievable proportion. These are well known but still shocking versions of the more and the less: more than 75 percent of the wealth in the United States is held by less than 10 percent of the population; the richest 1 percent of individuals own about 40 percent of the country's wealth.[12]

But what, I wonder, do we make of the equally intense, though much less commented on, *cultural* privatization of value that's happening across artistic and educational realms as well? Consider, for example, the following trends in recent American cultural production:[13]

- The memoir, with its emphasis on private experience, is clearly *the* literary form of our time, intensifying the almost complete triumph of the personal voice in contemporary American poetry. And if personal voice and experience has triumphed at the high cultural end of the literary spectrum, it's even more ubiquitously on display in the more popular segments of the book market. Indeed, if you've trolled the bookstore or the best-seller lists lately, you'll see that an emphasis on revealing personal narrative has become integral to everything from managing corporations to coaching basketball. These days, even something as legendarily mundane as military service is packaged as a self-actualization technique ("Become an Army of One"). Likewise, American politics is saturated with this confessional tone on both sides of the aisle: Bill Clinton's constant confessions set a tone for a political style that was intensified by George W. Bush (the confessed alcoholic) and his intensely "personal" political style ("I'm a decider. I decide."). Indeed, a "deeply personal vision" of some kind seems to be a prerequisite for any kind of public success these days.

- The body (that site of negotiation between public and private, inside and outside) has become the most important academic topic of our generation. In a related vein, the hottest topic on the literary and cultural theory futures market these days seems to be affect (or, even more straightforward, a renewed emphasis on feeling).

- The home is the new work and play space of our time, leading to an unprecedented privatization of the culture and entertainment industries: high-speed Internet, digital cable and satellite TV, home theater systems, and pay-per-view movies. And when one leaves home, one steps into a home on wheels, an SUV or a minivan that's built specifically to mirror the womblike, privatized comfort of home. Even strolling the streets is a privatized proposition these days, with the personalized soundtrack of an iPod (remember when pods were just for body snatchers?) or the constant chatter of cell phone conversations.

- In popular music, think of the rise of grunge and rap in the 1990s. Both of those (very different) forms are or were absolutely dedicated to some notion of subjective authenticity and the revelation of personal experience. In contrast to the collective, angry punk music of the 1970s, think of the fragile, wounded subjectivity that haunts 1990s Nirvana or Pearl Jam songs—not to mention the hyperinteriorized affect of contemporary American indie rock figures like Elliot Smith, Will Oldham or Chan Marshall. And one might note that virtually every successful rapper or neorapper raps largely about him- or herself: Snoop Dogg raps about Snoop Dogg, Eminem about Eminem.

- The discourse surrounding the planning and building of the World Trade Center memorial reminds us of the more or less permanent innovation in public monuments and public memory put forth in Maya Lin's 1982 design for the Vietnam war memorial in Washington: our public memorials are no longer the heavy, hulking statues and phallic structures of the past, but serial invocations of individual heroism. In terms of public memorialization of the past, these days it's all about the names, the people. The stunning popular success of Ken Burns–style historiography in the United States is yet another instance of this tendency: Burns's wildly successful visual and narrative histories of the Civil War, not to mention professional baseball and jazz, all point out one simple cultural truth: history isn't real to the public in the contemporary United States until and unless it's run through the wringer of individual subjects and their interior, private experiences. (One suspects this phenomenon also has some bearing on the huge success of Mel Gibson's *The Passion of the Christ*. Presumably everybody knows the plot, so it's not suspense that brings them to the cineplex; both proponents and detractors of the film point to its highly charged, affective focus on Christ's personal, private suffering.)

- Major sporting events, such as the Olympics or even the Kentucky Derby, have become orgies of personal revelation, at least as far as the American TV coverage of them is concerned. Whether we know anything at all about the ins and outs of speed skating, pole vaulting, or horse racing, we're all familiar with the endless stories of speed skaters or pole vaulters whose heroic recovery from Some Terrible Disease fuels their drive for Olympic Gold, or the horse trainer who saved a bunch of kids from a plane crash, and brings that same fierce dedication to his work at the track.

- In the university over the past twenty years, we've seen the triumph of student-centered process pedagogies of various kinds—peer learning, portfolio grading, reader-response criticisms—making education personally relevant to the students. Specifically within English departments, where I live, one need only look at the nationwide boom in creative writing majors and classes for confirmation of personal experience's return to centrality.

- The great public debates of the American present are largely debates about privacy. From abortion to virtual surveillance (credit reports, Internet trackers, cameras in public spaces), from gay marriage to the security concerns raised by the Patriot Act and the so-called war on terror, it seems that shape and scope of the private sphere is one of the primary fronts where the public debates of the near future will fought.

All of these things are, it seems to me, a part of this smear of privatized value across the social and economic spectrum. Oddly enough, though, the artistic or cultural forms of the privatization of value are seldom discussed as further lamentable symptoms of neoliberal economics, but rather as bulwarks against that very logic. An emphasis on the small, private, intimate, noncommodified, seemingly self-empowering moments of everyday life is usually thought to offer us a kind of swerve around the logics of the market and its inhuman profit motive. Think globally, resist locally, as they say, which, if nothing else, presents us with an interesting problem: just as the subject seems definitively to have disappeared into a virtual ether (we are all posthuman, we are all cyborgs), something like an individual voice is back on the cultural landscape, and in a big way.

This odd relation between economic privatization the cultural privatization leaves us with a series of pressing questions: is there a way to understand this cultural turn to privatization, other than ideologically (that is, as a kind of compensation or wish fulfillment: at a historical moment when the interior feelings of any particular private individual count for close to nothing on the national economic and political stage, these feelings come back with an ideological vengeance, displaced and contained in the cultural arena)? Are celebrations of individuals and their intimate experiences merely cultural compensation for an economic system that renders the individual's private feelings and desires almost completely moot? To return to the Jamesonian vein in which the essay began, one might ask whether the turn to privatized interiority as the privileged locus of *cultural* value is merely a regressive symptom of privatization's triumph in the *economic* realm?

This, I think, is a most tempting conclusion for this analysis—and I'm not sure that I disagree with it. But as much as I'm attracted to this conclusion, in the end, I want to question it. Surely there are other ways of understanding this cultural turn to interiority or the private, and no doubt I'm overemphasizing its complete triumph. And one might point out that privatization in the cultural realm doesn't necessarily lead to the same consequences as privatization in the economic realm. Finally, to return once again to Jameson, one might wonder whether my own resistance to categories of the "private" or the "individual" are themselves holdovers of the 60s and its dreams of collectivity?

In conclusion, let me attempt to turn the screw yet another notch. Maybe what we're seeing in the turn to the private in recent American cultural production isn't so much a retreat from the world of politics and engagement, but precisely an attempt to render the personal as the new frame of reference for public discourse—the thing that we all have in common.

If since the 80s we've seen an unprecedented invasion of the personal and the private by the dictates of the market (the unmediated impingement of the economic on our formerly personal lives), perhaps this turn to reconsidering the personal is not so much a quietistic desire to get back behind the complexities of contemporary life and find the "real me" as much as it is a direct artistic response to the current economic situation, where capitalism has already worked its way into every fiber of our "private" lives. To take that colonization of the private seriously, one would almost have to turn to an examination of private experience—precisely to see where it might be able to take us, or where it might trap us.

The economic logic of financial privatization has its cultural upshot in the complete triumph of what Michel Foucault famously calls "biopower": unlike Foucauldian discipline, whose work on bodies is primarily realized through institutional training, biopower is a more intense and saturated form of power that works throughout entire populations and takes on its target, life, quite directly (as opposed to discipline's necessarily mediated, institutional character). To use a Foucauldian economic metaphor, the sovereign power of the king was a very inefficient, wholesale mode of power's distribution to the socius: early modern spectacles of execution and torture were expensive and not particularly effective in keeping royal order. Discipline, on the other hand, discovered and deployed a much more economical and effective "retail" power over individual bodies at particular, transversally linked sites of training (the family, the school, the clinic, the factory, the army). According to Foucault, biopower goes one step further in the lightening of power, in making it more effective, working on individuals "really and directly" (*réellement et directement*, not words Foucault throws around lightly). For Foucault, biopower is the primary type of power at work in modern societies—a very efficient mode of power that infuses each individual at a nearly ubiquitous number of sites ("everyday life"), rather than touching specific subjects at particular sites of training. Take sexuality, Foucault's primary example of biopower: not everyone has a shared disciplinary identity (soldier, mother, or student), but everyone does have something like a sexuality. In Foucault's words, such an ascendent and ubiquitous biopower has "acted by multiplication of singular sexualities. It did not set boundaries for sexuality; it extended the various forms of sexuality, pursuing them according to lines of indefinite penetration. It did not exclude sexuality, but included it in the body as a mode of specification of individuals."[14] Biopower, then, is what one might call the operating system of contemporary American economic and cultural life.

Oddly enough, such a genealogy of modern power would suggest that what Americans have in common is not our public lives (our fragmented disciplinary roles as citizen, teacher, activist, consumer), but our private lives (our continuous construction of a lifestyle, a sexuality, an identity). If there is something that we might call the realm of the contemporary American "common," that vector that directly connects the cultural to the economic in the contemporary United States, for better or worse, it's the private realm, not the public sphere. As Paolo Virno writes, contemporary conceptual personae like the infamous multitude have to be understood in terms of the private—which is to say, that version of a commonweal which is opposed to and unlike the modernist notion of the citizen, the public, or the people of the nation-state. For Virno- and Deleuze-inspired autonomist Marxism on the whole, there is an odd linkage between privatization (the complete triumph of biopower, economically and culturally) and the power of the multitude. It is, in fact, only under the condition of one that the other can takes its proper place on the historical stage.

In Virno's *Grammar of the Multitude,* the link between the multitude and the everyday common is made not so much in the Spinozistic sense (as it is for fellow autonomist Antonio Negri), but in Aristotle's sense of "common places" in the *Rhetoric:* "Such places are 'common' because no one can do without them (from the refined orator to the drunkard who mumbles words hard to understand, from the business person to the politician). Aristotle points out three of those places: the connection between more and less, the opposition of opposites, and the category of reciprocity."[15] The Aristotelian common places that Virno cites here are nothing other than modes of intense exchange—a cramped, local negotiation within a closed system, rather than a universalizing public appeal to some kind of unifying outside. These are, then, questions about the distribution and redistribution of what we might call life. As Virno writes, "The multitude is a mode of being, the prevalent mode of being today,"[16] and it may be that for the near future, the ubiquitous private sphere, rather than the increasingly rare public sphere, will harbor the intense action in American cultural production. And a new modality of cultural resistance to capital will have to be born along with it.

In any case, the real question this leaves us with is the question of today. Given the intensifications of privatized capitalism since the 1980s, what cultural, political, and economic routes of becoming and of escape are opened up for us today? And what ones are gone forever? Is something like personal voice being reinvented or remediated in everything from local music scenes to Internet protest movements? Or is the turn to the private in cultural production the final ruse and completion of the privatization of economic value—does postpostmodernism merely close the trap set for us by postmodern capitalism? Will the crash of 2008 really change the playing field of multinational capitalism, or will it simply rearrange the dominant players? Of course, it's a little too early to tell what will happen with the multiple cultural legacies of a shift in economic production, because such response is ongoing, multifarious, and largely experimental. Which is to say that the work of critique, as Jameson reminds us, moves and gains foothold through an immanent and positive engagement with a present that is not a hole or a trap, but is "rather to be imagined in terms of an explosion: a prodigious expansion of culture throughout the social realm, to the point at which everything in our social life—from economic value and state power to practices and to the very structure of the psyche itself—can be said to have become 'cultural' in some original and yet untheorized sense."[17]

Notes

1. Michael C. Jensen, *A Theory of the Firm* (Cambridge, Mass.: Harvard University Press, 2000), 38. Subsequent references appear parenthetically in the text.

2. See Obama's CNBC interview, June 10, 2008; transcript available at http://thepage.time.com/obama-interview-on-cnbc/.

3. See Foucault's exchange with Deleuze, "Intellectuals and Power," in Deleuze's *Desert Islands*, ed. David Lapoujade, trans Michael Taormina (New York: Semiotexte, 2004), 206–13.

4. Jeffrey T. Nealon, *Double Reading: Postmodernism after Deconstruction* (Ithaca, N.Y.: Cornell University Press, 1993), 144–52.

5. Fredric Jameson, *Postmodernism; or, The Cultural Logic of Late Capitalism* (Durham, N.C.: Duke University Press, 1991), 31.

6. See especially Jameson's *Sartre: The Origins of a Style* (New Haven: Yale University Press, 1961) and his *Late Marxism: Adorno; or, The Persistence of the Dialectic* (London: Verso, 1990).

7. Thomas Frank, *One Market Under God: Extreme Capitalism, Market Populism, and the End of Economic Democracy* (New York: Anchor, 2001), 3.

8. Fredric Jameson, "Periodizing the 60s," in *The 60s without Apology*, ed. Sohnya Sayres et al. (Minneapolis: University of Minnesota Press, 1984), 208–9.

9. Ibid., 208.

10. Ibid.

11. Doug Henwood, *Wall Street: How It Works, and for Whom* (New York: Verso, 1998), 259.

12. Doug Henwood, "Wealth News" (http://www.leftbusinessobserver.com/Wealth_distrib.html).

13. This list is adapted from chapter 4 of my *Foucault Beyond Foucault: Power and Its Intensifications since 1984* (Stanford, Calif.: Stanford University Press, 2007).

14. Michel Foucault, *The History of Sexuality, Volume 1,* trans. Robert Hurley (New York: Vintage, 1978), 47.

15. Paolo Virno, *A Grammar of the Multitude,* trans. Isabella Bertoletti et al. (New York: Semiotexte, 2004), 36.

16. Ibid., 26.

17. Jameson, *Postmodernism,* 48.

5 Marxist Theory: From Aesthetic Critique to Cultural Politics

PHILIP GOLDSTEIN

Since the 1990s, Terry Eagleton, Fredric Jameson, and others have revived the aesthetic theory of Theodor Adorno on the grounds that, unlike Michel Foucault, Jacques Derrida, and other poststructuralists, who accommodate the social system, Adorno's aesthetics subverts its foundations.[1] As Jameson notes in *Late Marxism*, "Adorno's Marxism, which was no great help in the previous periods, may turn out to be just what we need today" (5). I grant that poststructuralists like Derrida and Foucault do not accept Marxist realism, by which I mean its ontological commitment to and systematic description of a reality independent of the observer's beliefs and feelings.[2] I will argue, however, that Adorno's notion of instrumental reason and Foucault's concept of "power/knowledge" parallel Martin Heidegger's and Jacques Derrida's notions of ontotheology,[3] what in later work Heidegger calls "equipmental" thinking in order to describe the customs, practices, or "being" dominating social life. Adorno critiques instrumental reason more radically than Foucault does, but his critique reduces it to repressive political domination and grants subversive force only to speculative theory or high art. In contrast, Foucault rejects the instrumental reason of Adorno and the equipmentality or ontotheology of both Heidegger and Jacques Derrida and describes the positive import and historical development of these practices or technologies. He shows, moreover, that they enable the subject to engage in a local politics, what he terms "self-fashioning." As Pierre Macherey argues, Foucault's work implies that critics can reform these practices by opening texts and discourses to their local schools and movements.

THE AESTHETICS OF THEODOR ADORNO AND MARTIN HEIDEGGER

It is well known that in the *Dialectic of Enlightenment,* Adorno and Horkheimer critique what they call "instrumental reason," a notion they derive

80

from the Hegelian Marxist Georg Lukács but explain in a Heideggerian manner. They argue that in the Enlightenment's fashion, this rationality opposes mythological outlooks at the same time that it imposes an equally mythological faith in modern science. As they say, "Just as myths already entail enlightenment, with every step enlightenment entangles itself more deeply in mythology."[4] Contrary to mythology, science maintains that humanity, not the gods, rules nature, yet "myths already entail enlightenment" because both mythology and science presuppose that knowledge enables the knower to dominate nature and people. In the name of facts and laws, the enlightenment dismisses the magic and fantasy of myth but enlightenment "entangles itself in mythology" in that it endows established social structures with a mythical inevitability (27).

Adorno and Horkheimer's influential account of the culture industry illustrates this view of instrumental rationality. They argue that it governs the industry's technology, language, and institutions, ensuring that the industry does not achieve its own ends. It promises to grant wishes, fulfill hopes, and realize desires, but it actually preserves the status quo. While new works advertise their originality and uniqueness, they adhere to rigid, mechanical formula and remain within predetermined forms or generalities, duplicating other products and affirming industrial life. As they say, "The constant pressure to produce new effects (which must conform to the old pattern) serves merely as another rule to increase the power of conventions" (128). The culture industry offers creativity, independence, originality, success, and happiness, yet by increasing "the power of conventions," the industry destroys the individuality, thoughtfulness, and resistance of the artist and the consumer, both of whom learn quickly enough that they are just like everyone else and could easily be replaced.

This critique of the culture industry shows how terribly oppressive Adorno and Horkheimer consider instrumental reason to be. Their negative view of it derives from Georg Lukács, who in turn revises and extends Karl Marx's account of commodity production.[5] According to Marx, capitalist production imbues commodities with the mystical powers that tribal societies reserve for their totemic gods. Instead of using commodities, people worship them. People have diverse ends and purposes, but commodity production destroys the ability of individuals to define themselves; their products—cars, machines, theories—impose definition, self, and purpose upon them. As Marx says, "[T]he social character of men's labour . . . assumes, in their eyes, the fantastic form of a relation between things. . . . This I call . . . Fetishism."[6] Fetishized in this way, commodities displace and conceal the social relations organizing society and acquire the rationality and the value that capitalism denies humanity.

Lukács argues that capitalism extends the commodity's domination to all social institutions. He shows that as a result, an instrumental rationality—which calculates means and not ends, evaluates techniques and not values, and seeks autonomy and not community—governs the social and the economic institutions of bourgeois society. As J. M. Bernstein points out, Lukács says that once economic institutions gain their independence, capitalism imposes this rationality on all realms, including the intellectual. The sciences, the humanities, and the other disciplines functioning within this context examine the internal relations of their discipline and ignore its social relations. The "exchange value" of their works matters more than their use "value." Like commodities, these "reified" disciplines consider themselves autonomous and ignore their underlying social conditions.

To overcome this domination of instrumental reason, Lukács adopts the Kantian ideal of the autonomous ethical subject, what Kant termed the "kingdom of ends," but accepts Hegel's systematizing account of sociohistorical experience rather than Kant's unknowable "thing-in-self." Because Hegel's faith in Spirit's absolute knowledge produces an alienating and vitiating self-consciousness, Lukács also adopts Marx's historical totalities not because they are scientific but because they relieve this Hegelian self-consciousness and justify a radical, working-class politics. For example, in the influential essay "Reification and the Consciousness of the Proletariat," Lukács argues that the autonomous ethical subject can oppose but cannot destroy modern society's reified forms of commodity production because the subject's ethical norms do not provide a sufficiently critical perspective. In addition, the oppositional theorist must adopt the historical terrain of the working class, whose practical activity can overcome the divisions and the conflicts of social life. In 1921, when the Soviet revolution was flowering and Western revolutions looked possible, an optimistic Lukács moved to the USSR because he believed that the working class is "the identical subject–object of the social and historical processes of evolution."[7]

Adorno and Horkheimer also assume that instrumental rationality dominates bourgeois social life and that Hegelian theory undermines it; with fascism recently defeated, the cold war underway, and the capitalist economy booming, they maintain, however, that instrumental rationality assimilates the working class too. Moreover, Lukács defends communism, which, he claims, will evolve beyond Stalinist tyranny, whereas, like Herbert Marcuse, who says that Soviet Marxism perpetuates what he calls "technical progress as the instrument of domination," Adorno and Horkheimer claim that the scientific Marxism of the communists also imposes the oppressive domination of Enlightenment rationality.[8] They accommodate cold war anticommunism because they say that the communist countries have become totalitarian, destroying their opponents in the name of objective history (41).

Not only do they consider the communist countries totalitarian, they also claim that instrumental rationality does not begin with the capitalist system, as Lukács says; it begins with the classical Greeks. They show, for example, that Homer's *Odyssey* shows Ulysses resisting the sirens in order to underline the Greek mastery of nature: "Measures like those taken on Odysseus's ship in face of the Sirens are a prescient allegory of the dialectic of Enlightenment" (27). The mastery of nature, along with opposition to mythology, characterize the propositional logic and conceptual discourse of both the Greeks and the modern Enlightenment.

Contrary to Lukács, Adorno and Horkheimer take the modern instrumental rationality to begin with the ancient Greeks, not with capitalism, to co-opt the working class and to render communism totalitarian. In addition, they reject Lukács's belief that the distinct periods of history will eventually culminate in full communism, which unites and reconciles the fragmented subject with itself. He maintained that as the typical characters of the realist novel show, the subject passes through distinct historical stages, with the subject's alienation and fragmentation coming to an end only in the communist era. By contrast, Adorno denies that at history's end, the fragmented subject will be reconciled with itself. He claims that on the contrary, the dialectical Hegelian reconciliation of subject and object itself represents the domination of Enlightenment reason. This purely conceptual reconciliation imposes an abstract identity that denies the subject's concrete particularity. Contrary to Hegel and Lukács, he considers the nonidentity of subject and object liberating. As he says of Hegel, "Nowhere does he define the experience of the non-identical as the *telos* of the aesthetic subject or as its emancipation."[9]

Adorno's view of instrumental reason derives from Lukács's view but differs from it substantially. These differences suggest, moreover, that his view parallels those of Heidegger and Derrida. As I will show, Heidegger and Derrida also establish an intimate relationship between theory and social life, what Heidegger initially terms the "ontotheological" tradition but later calls "equipmental" thinking or "the essence of technology." As Eagleton points out, Adorno appreciates nonidentity, multiplicity, and difference

as fully as Derrida and other poststructuralists do. Eagleton argues, nonetheless, that in the realist fashion, Adorno also recognizes the positive identity and human values in art.[10] In Late Marxism, a more negative Fredric
Jameson, in *Late Marxism,* says that unlike the poststructuralist theory of
Derrida or Foucault, who accept liberal ideals and reject any representation
of the real, Adorno's "revolutionary" theories emphasize "the presence of
late capitalism as a totality within the very forms of our concepts or of the
works of art themselves" (9, 31). What I will show is that although Foucault
rejects the ontotheological tradition of Heidegger and fosters local action,
despite many differences, both Derrida and Adorno accept this tradition,
which denies the possibility of meaningful action or reduces it to reformist
liberalism.

What are the parallels of Adorno and Heidegger? In *Being and Time,*
Heidegger's major work, Heidegger says that the tradition conceals the
ontological truth of what, like Aristotle, he calls Being or what is and that
the philosophical analysis of human experience uncovers that forgotten
truth. This view of human truth, or "Dasein," rejects the transcendental
ideals of Edmund Husserl, who was Heidegger's teacher, on the grounds
that in the Cartesian manner, it ignores the concrete human experience of
time and space. Similarly, Adorno, whose dissertation examined the phenomenology of Husserl, points out that he rigorously restricts interpretation to what the bare, intuitive data show and to what they logically imply,
and ignores the terms and the categories mediating between them and
the world. Heidegger also rejects Kant's and Husserl's belief that we can
know things as they affect our sensibility, not things as they are in themselves, on the grounds that this view reduces the theorist to his or her subjective constitution. Similarly, Adorno claims that bracketing the natural
standpoint makes the resulting knowledge of essences subjective, a matter
of individual consciousness and not of systematic truth.[11] Heidegger also
rejects the positivist or analytic view whereby only empirical experience
can justify or falsify assertions, on the grounds that this view amounts
to little more than the clarification of what is already known. Similarly,
Adorno suggests that a form of conceptual "identity-thinking"—analytic
philosophy's correspondence theory of truth, which seeks in the proper
name the equivalence of thing and concept—reduces language to the literal imitation of given experience.

More importantly, Heidegger says that since the classical Greek era, Western society has "darkened," losing the capacity to experience the poetic
"shining of truth." The Western tradition's propositional and equipmental

or technological modes of understanding dominate, producing the presence of beings but not of Being itself. Similarly, Adorno and Horkheimer, claim, contrary to Lukács, that instrumental rationality began with the classical Greeks, not with the capitalist system, and dominates modern social life. As Richard Bernstein says, "In Heidegger's fateful, strong reading of the 'history of being' . . . we find a thematic affinity with Adorno's claim that the seeds of 'identity logic' with its hidden will-to-mastery are to be found in the very origins of Western rationality."[12]

After World War II, disillusioned with fascism, communism, and the capitalist West, Heidegger finds that on the basis of mathematical calculation and the systematic ordering of physical science, the essence of technology is to construe or "enframe" what exists exclusively exists as useful stock, or "standing-reserve." Humanity "postures as the lord of the earth," but, failing to grasp "this enframing as a claim," it stands "in subservience to it."[13] In *Late Marxism*, Jameson objects that "[e]rror, what is called metaphysics or identity, is in Adorno the effect of an increasingly powerful social system, while in Heidegger it is that of an increasing distance from some original truth" (10).[14] The later work, which expresses Heidegger's disillusion with (but not a repudiation of) German fascism, maintains, however, that "the essence of modern technology" is to deny humans their sense of self or identity. Adorno and Horkheimer also say that instrumental rationality dominates society, but they claim that it assimilates all opposition, including the working class. Enlightenment science, which denigrates nature and reifies logic, aesthetics, information, and the status quo, ensures the conformity and the repression of the masses.

On literary issues, Adorno argues that great texts can emancipate the reader if they undermine conventional modes of understanding and thus the practices of instrumental reason. He claims that great art resists the conventions of the reader as well as the reifying effects of instrumental reason and the rigid concepts of science.[15] Unlike *Being and Time* (1927), which argues that the hermeneutics of the human sciences reveals the truths of Being hidden or forgotten by Western ontotheology, *Language, Poetry, Thought* and Heidegger's other later work also claim that art, rather than hermeneutics, reveals those truths. Heidegger says that genuine understanding, which is circular or temporal, projecting a before and an after, requires openness or letting be. That is, truth or Being can reveal itself if it is let be, but it can be let be only if the subject participates, setting aside its preconceptions of itself and its world and experiencing the object fully.

Heidegger thus argues that to let truth be, the artistic text reveals and conceals Being, disclosing and hiding truth. In this conflicted text, what Heidegger terms "earth," which denotes both the work's concrete materials and a perspective that puts them into place, resists "world," which is not only the meaning of the work but also the coherence and totality achieved by it. To appear or be "open," Being comes into the "clearing" established in the work, yet Being also remains hidden, for earth "juts" into world, setting world into itself. Because the work cannot disclose Being without concealing it, neither earth nor world achieve mastery.[16] What's more, this strife of earth and world has political import: as Bernstein says, "The strife . . . becomes a general characterization for the relation of elements in a totality which can then be projected onto a community."[17] Adorno condemns Heidegger's notion of Being because he attributes what he terms its "authenticity" to the jargon resulting from German fascism.[18] Adorno also claims, nonetheless, that instead of affirming political or theological truth, texts betray unresolved conflicts and oppositions that implicitly describe society's hidden totality. Moreover, Heidegger distinguishes between art that "shuts its eyes" to its status as useful stock or "standing reserve" and art that resists that status. As he says, "[E]ssential reflection upon technology and confrontation with it" can happen in such a "realm" as "art," but only if it "does not shut its eyes to the constellation of truth, concerning which we are *questioning*."[19] Horkheimer and Adorno also divide art into the self-conscious high and the unreflective mass or popular. As they suggest, high art accepts and subverts established aesthetic practices and ruling ideologies; unlike popular or mass art, it resists its commodified character and reaffirms the totality as a negative moment projecting a utopian vision.

In general, Adorno adopts the Hegelian Marxism of Lukács, not Heidegger's philosophical notion of being, but dismisses political resistance because he shares Heidegger's views of art and reason, not Lukács's view of them. In *Late Marxism,* Jameson maintains, however, that Adorno's pessimistic dismissal of political opposition, and hence the parallels of his theory and Heidegger's, do not matter because political events, class struggle, and sequential social formations represent three distinct "frameworks." Because Adorno's Marxism has to do with the third framework, social formations, not with the first, political events, these frameworks preclude criticism of Adorno's pessimistic view: "This recognition [of the frameworks] was meant, if not to solve, at least to neutralize, what seemed to me false problems and meaningless polemics . . . where proponents of an active, shaping role of working people seemed to confront those for whom disembodied forces and logic of capital were somehow at work" (8). To oppose postmodern skepticism, he adopts, just the same, the contrary view: that totalizing practices are real and political. As he says, "without books," young leftists will draw "the entire web of interrelated social levels together into a totality, which then demands the invention of a politics of social transformation" (251). The phrase "without books" underlines how strongly Jameson believes in totalizing Marxism's ontological truth; "in its fundamental reality," capitalism is, as he says, "one and indivisible, a seamless web, a single inconceivable and transindividual process."[20] Thanks to this faith, he minimizes the parallels of Adorno and Heidegger and lapses into a contradiction: the framework of the totality cannot neutralize polemics about working-class resistance and still allow the totality of the young leftists a politics of social transformation. If the totality of the young leftists demands this politics, the totality of Adorno also demands it, yet Adorno fails to provide it.

Jacques Derrida also accepts Heidegger's account of Western metaphysics and dismisses political resistance, but he rejects Heidegger's notion of Being as well as Adorno's Hegelian realism. In the influential essay "Différance," Derrida grants, for instance, that as temporizing and differing, *différance* explains Heidegger's distinction between beings and Being, or ontology and theology. Moreover, just as Heidegger argues that the difference of being and Being has been forgotten, so Derrida says that the trace revealing this difference has been erased. Derrida objects, however, that Heidegger defends the privileges of consciousness, including its status as "self-presence." The ontotheological tradition takes language to serve the ends of thought; however, as the inaudible "a" in *différance* suggests, writing lies outside "Being" but generates effects that Heidegger (mis)construes as the venerable presence of "Being." Hence, Heidegger's uncovering the Greek roots of the Western tradition does not escape or overcome the tradition.

In *The Truth in Painting*, Derrida accepts Heidegger's claim that the art work of Van Gogh reveals and at the same time conceals the truth of Being; however, Derrida faults Heidegger, and by implication Adorno, for assuming that art represents a pretextual reality. That is, Derrida objects that Heidegger, who says that the shoes which one of Van Gogh's paintings depict are peasant shoes, and Meyer Shapiro, the art historian who claims that the shoes are Van Gogh's shoes, not peasant shoes, naively assume that the shoes possess a "precritical or pretextual reality," giving them a "character" or making them a "subject."[21] As a step toward an "unveiling" of truth or being, this pretextual reality can, Derrida says, leave one "practically disarmed in the face of the ingenuous, the precritical, the dogmatic, in the face of any 'preinvestment' (be it 'fantasmic,' 'ideological,' etc., or whatever name you call it)" (318). Alluding to Marxist realism, Derrida adds that "on the pretext of delivering you from the chains of writing and reading," those who "hastily lock you up in a supposed outside of the text: the pre-text of perception, of living speech . . . of real history . . . try to intimidate you, to subject you to the oldest, most dogmatic, most sinisterly authoritarian program, to the most massive mediating machines" (326).

Derrida forcefully debunks Heidegger's, and by implication Adorno's, claims that art depicts realities beyond writing or discourse. While Eagleton argues that Adorno, who is responsible to the public, rightly distinguishes between the good artistic and the bad, reified whole, Derrida argues that Marxism does not escape Western reason or ontotheology. In *Specters of Marx*, he shows that in the name of science, Marx critiques ideology, commodity fetishism, and other versions of the spiritual or spectral other whose recurring phantoms derail the communist movement; however, because they are already within Marxism and thus part of Marx's revolutionary spirit or communist movement, he fails to exclude this spectral other, whose presence reasserts itself as the revolution's spirit, or in other ways. Both Derrida and Adorno maintain, however, that communism is a utopian vision, not a practical enterprise. Derrida adopts a "messianic" concept of justice, rather than the subversive negativity of an aesthetic totality; he claims, nonetheless, that the "indestructible condition of any deconstruction" and the vital "legacy" of Marx affirms an absolute hospitality to a religious or messianic other, including the dead.[22] Because Derrida also says that deconstruction undermines "sedimented layers of social practice" and reveals the decisions grounding them, such absolute hospitality subverts institutional or established practices or technologies as fully as Adorno's aesthetic negativity or Heidegger's notion of Being does. In other words, while deconstruction faults the realism or ontological truth of Heidegger's notion of Being and Adorno's speculative dialectics, in the name of writing or the messianic other, deconstruction also opposes the technologies of instrumental or equipmental reason and denies political action any positive import.

THE HISTORIES AND POLITICS OF
MICHEL FOUCAULT AND PIERRE MACHEREY

Foucault, who late in his life called Heidegger "an overwhelming influence" on his work, also develops a Heideggerian account of technological practices,[23] but he justifies a local politics and rejects both the equipmental reason or ontotheology of Heidegger and Derrida and the instrumental reason of Adorno.

Foucault shows that changing historical conditions—not, as Kant claimed, the transcendental forms of human understanding—explain the changing modes of discourse. Following Gaston Bachelard and Georges Canguilhem, he maintains that evolving paradigms explain the historical development of a discourse or science. In *The Order of Things*, he shows that the Renaissance, the classical era, and the modern era constitute historical ontologies or epistemes that established the disciplines that subsequently undermined them. For example, the knowledge and techniques of the Renaissance's episteme serve, he says, to interpret the resemblances suggested by linguistic signs. This interpretation guarantees that hermeneutics, which claims that the microcosm of linguistic signs mirrors the macrocosm of the world, provides knowledge of the world. By contrast, the classical episteme of the seventeenth and eighteenth centuries does not, he claims, construe knowledge as the hermeneutic interpretation of signs uniting microcosm and macrocosm. Rather, this episteme establishes a relation between knowledge and mathesis, a universal science of measure and order. This relationship establishes, in turn, a number of empirical domains, including general grammar, natural history, and analysis of riches.

In turn, the nineteenth century breaks with this eighteenth-century pursuit of order. In place of an order that explains identities and differences, the nineteenth century substitutes a notion of history in which analogy explains the succession and arrangement of distinct organizations. The nineteenth century also substitutes the study of the familiar philology, biology, and political economy for the eighteenth century's strange study of language, riches, and history. In this way too, knowledge, which acquires new figures (production, life, language), has changed. In the twentieth century, Foucault claims that the modern disciplines fracture the unified figure of the human being in terms of which nineteenth-century phenomenology grounds them. The modern episteme divides into the mathematical sciences, the social sciences, and philosophical disciplines and thereby undermines the phenomenological project: to establish the human foundation of the sciences.

Heidegger also rejects the Kantian distinction between transcendental reason and empirical sensibility. As Schwartz says, he too adopts the historical belief that the conventions and norms or "being" of an epoch explain its changing discourses. He does not, however, explain the positive histories of an epoch's disciplines and discourses; rather, he examines the major philosophers so as to show that thanks to the disciplines and sciences, Being has been forgotten.[24]

In later work, Foucault also examines the historical development of a discourse, but he distinguishes between an archaeology, which explains the broad episteme underlying and justifying the norms and procedures of established discourses, and a genealogy, which, unlike a totalizing episteme, reveals the local institutional contexts in which a discourse has evolved and acquired legitimacy. In this genealogical work, he claims that as a strategy with dispositions and techniques, discourse forms a complex of power/knowledge that organizes diverse institutions, including the family. As Han points out, such a genealogy denies the relative autonomy of a discourse or discipline and examines instead its internal conflicts and external authority or social influence as well as the nexus or mutual elaboration of power and knowledge.

Adorno and Heidegger also say that technological or instrumental reason dominate society, but they claim that Being has been forgotten or that modern cultural life produces only ideological conformity and intellectual vacuity. In contrast, Foucault shows that by positively organizing and reorganizing social life, the technologies of power/knowledge constitute the "normal" individual or social subject. Moreover, Foucault's distinction between an archaeology and a genealogy undermines the speculative critique, public or universal intellectual, and ontotheological tradition of Heideggerian theory. Because a genealogy recounts the internal divisions or conflicts of a particular discourse, a genealogy depicts its discontinuous or fragmented history, rather than a monolithic tradition.[25] Moreover, a genealogy allows what in *The Use of Pleasure* Foucault considers an ethics of self-fashioning.[26] That is, a genealogy justifies the political action undertaken by what he calls the "specific intellectual," rather than the ontological truth and speculative, aesthetic, or textual critique defended by Adorno, Heidegger, and Derrida.

THE FOUCAULDIAN CULTURAL THEORY OF PIERRE MACHEREY

Pierre Macherey, Foucault's fellow student and colleague at France's elite École Normale Supérieure, elaborates the cultural import of Foucault's methods. Because Macherey was, he says, "particularly stimulated" by Foucault's notion of an episteme, he develops an archaeological approach in which artistic works elaborate an archive of conventions and norms.[27] He claims, for example, that Hugo's *Les Misérables* describes society as a sea in which, like the night, uncertain characters appear and disappear. He says that this description takes for granted an episteme in which a subterranean man emerges from a tumultuous society. This episteme, created by the press and elaborated from 1840 to 1850, informs the work of the radical Karl Marx and the conservative Alexis de Tocqueville, as well as liberal social theorists. Macherey admits that French society ultimately grants the man below a structural position and that as a result this episteme governs French social relations in this era, but he does not admit that this episteme improves or distorts the era's understanding of social change. He recognizes that to explain society's conditions of existence, a great period of history elaborates such an episteme, yet like Foucault, he considers it a functional necessity, not the improved understanding of Marxist realism nor the distorted representation imposed by ideology.

In addition to this archaeological method, Macherey develops a genealogical approach in which a literary or philosophical text acquires meanings when readers reproduce them in their sociohistorical contexts and at the same time the local, disciplinary contexts constituting the critic or philosopher leave them free to exercise political influence within those contexts.

In the Althusserian *A Theory of Literary Production,* Macherey claims that literature, situated between objective science and humanist ideology, reworks ideological discourses, parodying and deforming them, but that it does not recognize or condemn them. The ordinary reader falls victim to the text's ideology, whose hidden purposes he inadvertently carries out, but the scientific critic, who has objective knowledge of history, discovers the ideological import of the gaps.[28] In his genealogical work, texts acquire reality or existence when readers reproduce them, not when writers produce them. As he says, "works are not at all 'produced' as such, but begin to exist only from the moment they are 'reproduced.'"[29] In his Althusserian work, what enables the scientific critic to grasp a text's ontological truth or objective historical insight is the author's productive activity, not his or her intentions or beliefs, because the gaps and inconsistencies produced by the author stimulate the critic's activity. In the Foucauldian work, the gaps and inconsistencies still matter, but now they free readers to produce their own interpretation. As he adds, the reproduction of texts has "the effect of dividing them within themselves, by tracing the thin line of their discourse in such a way as to make an entire space of gap and play appear in it, into which seeps the indefinite possibility of variations."[30] Heidegger and others also claim that this "space of gap and play" stimulates the readers' activity, but they argue that the gaps and inconsistencies enable readers to grasp the text's revelation of ontological or historical truth. By contrast, the gaps and inconsistencies that Macherey takes to stimulate the readers' activity free readers to deviate not only from the author's perspective, but also from their own.

Moreover, these new realizations may involve misinterpretations and misunderstandings, what he terms "true errors": "what at first regard appear to be of the order of falsification, concerted or involuntary, returns in forms of expression which, for being deviants, are not less authentic in their manner and in any case necessary."[31] These deviant but authentic "forms of expression" result in "true errors" rather than "falsification." Moreover, they may exert significant historical influence. For instance, Macherey shows that Madame de Staël, situated at the borders where German, French, and other cultures meet, effectively imposed on the French the "creative" belief that Immanuel Kant reconciles sentiment and reflection, and thereby defends an obscure and formal, but still vital, kind of philosophical enthusiasm. In this way, she created an influential mythology that described Germans as idealist dreamers asleep in a spiritual fog; as he says, her "mythology of Germany . . . dominated France for more than half a century."[32]

On these grounds, Macherey faults literary criticism that takes the historical context of the author as the work's ontological or realist truth. That is, this method claims that readers can bring an old work to life only if they enter into or recreate the divided historical context of the dead author. Citing Marx, Hegel, and Sartre, he shows that this approach reduces the work to "dead fruit":

> In the very constitution of the work of art in general, and of the literary work in particular, there is something which condemns it to become outdated and no longer to exist except in the form of a relic in the absence of the social content in relation to which it was produced.[33]

Macherey argues that Foucault frees the work from this existence as a relic. Not only does Foucault critique the notion that the work is a mirror in which author and reader construct a relationship, giving the author a "feigned objectivity," but he also suggests that the work is the result of a reproduction resulting from the readers' discourses. As a result, readers open a text to the contexts and conventions by virtue of which readers may produce it and themselves.[34]

Consider, for example, the very different accounts of Hegel and Spinoza that Macherey wrote before and after his Foucauldian turn. In the Althusserian *Hegel ou Spinoza* (1979), he says that Spinoza's material concept of substance is more truthful than Hegel's notion of Spirit because Spinoza's concept of substance acts in diverse modes and does not mediate contradictory moments, whereas the self-conscious spirit of Hegel denies the ambiguity of historical developments and favors a teleological kind of evolution. In the Foucauldian *dinosaure,* Macherey is particularly interested in the different Spinozas constructed by Hegel, not in who is right. For instance, he points out that "[t]he Spinoza of the *Science of Logic,* a primitive, oriental theorist of indeterminate being, is not at all that of the *Lessons of the History of Philosophy* . . . essentially a post-Cartesian philosopher, a 'modern,' marked by the categories of reflection and analysis of what Hegel calls a logic of essence."[35] These different versions of Spinoza are not mistaken; they show the contrary ways in which Hegel elaborated his system.

As these contrary accounts of Hegel's Spinozas suggest, Macherey's Foucauldian work says that what explains a text's import is not its realism or ontological truth but its realizations or misreadings. Jacques Rancière, who like Macherey initially accepted and subsequently repudiated Althusserian Marxism, also adopts a Foucauldian account of cultural history. In his account, a regime of conventions and norms, what he terms a distribution *(partage)* of the sensible, governs the history of art or philosophy.[36] For example, in what he calls a classical or poetic regime, "high genres" were, he says, "devoted to the imitation of noble actions and characters, and low genres devoted to common people and base subject matters. The hierarchy of genres also submitted style to a principle of hierarchical convenience: kings had to act and speak as kings do, and common people as common people do."[37] By contrast, the representative regime rejects the poetic regime's hierarchical schema of classification and describes representative or mimetic ways of organizing ways of doing, seeing, and judging any objects. Lastly, the aesthetic regime identifies art not by its means of creating or representing objects but by a mode of sensibility that is proper to artistic products and that involves a sensibility becoming strange to itself.

Unlike Adorno, Heidegger, and Derrida—who, as I noted, maintain that art or writing critiques the technological practices dominating modern social life—Rancière and Macherey both say that Foucault's notion of an episteme or an archive allows them to explain the history and politics of artistic or philosophical practices. However, Rancière accepts the aesthetics of Adorno, who maintains that art preserves its subversive force, as well as the antiaesthetic theory of Jean-François Lyotard, who denies that art such subversive force on the grounds that they both elaborate the Kantian aesthetic regime, making art an autonomous enterprise or "metapolitics."

In contrast, Macherey accepts the Marxist critique of idealist theory. For instance, in discussing Hegel's idealist dialectics, he grants that its "materialist" core, as Marx and Engels claimed, is "'wrapped' in a teleological discourse of a unitary nature affirming the ineluctable reconciliation of . . . opposites." He maintains, however, that they got his idealism wrong: as Macherey says, "Their blunder corresponds precisely to the illusion of an independent theoretical knowledge, realized in the form of a doctrinaire materialism."[38] The history of philosophy still includes diverse systems in contradiction with each other, as Hegel claimed, but a materialist philosophy does not affirm realist or ontological truth or construct purely speculative theories resisting or transcending "instrumental reason," as Adorno maintained. Rather, this history explains the systems' evolving archives of conventions and the reader's changing reproductions of a text.

Moreover, Rancière argues that because influential regimes construct and reconstruct the political communities that organize the work or labor of society, the political context of a historical regime regulates and justifies its aesthetic conventions. In contrast, Macherey maintains that the reader's realizations or reproductions of a work may rupture with the work's historical context and give the work new import in new contexts. Moreover, like Ernesto Laclau, Chantal Mouffe, and others who deny that hegemonic discourses fully interpellate or constitute the subject, Macherey argues that for Foucault, the discourses of power/knowledge constituting the subject always leave it some room to maneuver.[39] As Macherey says,

> [H]aving lost the faculty of contesting from outside the historical system that conditions it (as if it constituted itself a counter-system), the subject that has understood that the project of liberating itself was illusory, maintains the possibility of contesting it from inside by demonstrating that which reveals its singularity against the grain of its claims to universality.[40]

In other words, even though the subject is constituted by the discourses governing its sociohistorical context, the subject can still resist those discourses and change the context if it grasps its limits and the discourses' conflicts and historical evolution.

CONCLUSION

Scholars object that unlike the critical theory of Adorno or the Frankfurt School, which enables the subject to resist the social system and achieve liberation, Foucault's methods accommodate the conservative policies dominating Western governments.[41] Richard Rorty claims, for example, that the "Foucauldian academic Left in contemporary America is exactly the sort of Left that the oligarchy dreams of: a Left whose members are so busy unmasking the present that they have no time to discuss what laws need to be passed in order to create a better future."[42] Similarly, Timothy Brennan says that since the 1980s, the cultural left has promoted Foucault and other European thinkers in order to discredit left Hegelians like Adorno, whom Brennan considers genuinely oppositional despite his accommodation of cold war anticommunism and the parallels between his views and Heidegger's. Brennan claims that, as a result, the "cultural left" "helped produce . . . forces of self-enrichment, rigged elections, and wars for oil—all operating under the unifying myth of a carefully packaged Christian belief."[43]

I have argued, however, that Adorno, disillusioned with fascism, capitalism, and Soviet communism, adopts Lukács's notion of instrumental reason, but in a pessimistic, Heideggerian fashion, he maintains that instrumental reason, which began in the Greek era, not under capitalism, dominates and represses modern social life, assimilating and defeating its working class and its other opponents. While Derrida says that writing/art undermines a text's revelation of Being's presence or history's reality, Adorno and Heidegger claim that art reveals the ontological truth of Being or of capitalism's repressed totality. They all claim, however, that writing/art, not political action, overcomes the oppressive influence of equipmental or instrumental reason. Although Foucault also develops Heideggerian theory, he interprets it in positive terms whereby its historical ontologies or epistemes enable the subject to assert itself. Moreover, as Macherey maintains, he allows the subject an indeterminacy or self-fashioning that permits progressive action. That is, Macherey shows that a Foucauldian theory that explains the divided historical context of literature or philosophy and the evolution and influence of a literary or philosophical text frees the critic to take local action. It is true that Macherey's Foucauldian materialism does not promote revolution; nonetheless, it fosters a cultural politics that can open (but not reduce) literary and philosophical studies to their diverse feminist, black, gay, ethnic, or postcolonial programs and movements.

NOTES

1. See Terry Eagleton, *The Ideology of the Aesthetic* (Cambridge, Mass.: Basil Blackwell, 1990), 334–35 and 354–55. See also Fredric Jameson, *Late Marxism: Adorno, or The Persistence of the Dialectic* (New York: Verso, 1990), 248–49. Subsequent references to these books will appear in the text.

2. The term *realism* has two significant meanings. First, in ontological terms, *realism* is the belief that reality exists independently of the beliefs and feelings of the observer. Second, the term denotes the Marxist claim that its theories characterize social life objectively—that is, independently of how anyone feels about it.

3. For instance, in "The Origins of the Work of Art," Heidegger says, "It . . . turned out that equipmental being has . . . occupied a peculiar preeminence in the interpretation of beings." Martin Heidegger, *Poetry, Language, Thought*, trans Albert Hofstadter (New York: Harper & Row, 1975), 38. Subsequent references to this text will appear parenthetically

4. Max Horkheimer and Theodor W. Adorno, *Dialectic of Enlightenment*, trans. John Cumming (New York: Continuum Press, 1972), 8. Subsequent references to this text will appear parenthetically.

5. See Andrew Feenberg, who says that "Adorno himself acknowledged that Lukács' concept of reification" led to the Frankfurt School's modern view of capitalism. Andrew Feenberg, *Lukács, Marx and the Sources of Critical Theory* (Totowa, N.J.: Rowman and Littlefield, 1981), 165.

6. Karl Marx, *Capital: A Critical Analysis of Capitalist Production* (Moscow: Progress, 1965), 72.

7. Georg Lukács, *History and Class Consciousness: Studies in Marxist Dialectics*, trans. Rodney Livingstone (Cambridge, Mass.: MIT Press, 1971), 149.

8. Herbert Marcuse, *One-Dimensional Man* (Boston: Beacon Press, 1964), 42–44.

9. Theodor Adorno, *Aesthetic Theory*, trans. C. Lenhardt (New York: Routledge, 1984), 113.

10. See Terry Eagleton, *The Ideology of the Aesthetic* (Cambridge, Mass.: Basil Blackwell, 1990), 353–55. See also Max Pensky, "Editor's Introduction: Adorno's Actuality," in *The Actuality of Adorno: Critical Essays on Adorno and the Postmodern*, ed. Max Pensky (Albany: State University of New York Press, 1997), 6.

11. See Theodor W. Adorno, *Against Epistemology: Metacritical Studies in Husserl and the Phenomenological Antinomies*, trans Willis Domingo (Cambridge, Mass.: MIT Press, 1985), 6, 36–38.

12. Richard J. Bernstein, "The Rage against Reason," *Philosophy and Literature* 10, no. 2 (1986): 198. See also Jürgen Habermas, who says, "As opposed as the intentions behind their respective philosophies of history are, Adorno is in the end very similar to Heidegger as regards his position on the theoretical claims of objectivating thought and reflection." Jürgen Habermas, *The Theory of Communicative Action*, vol. 1, trans. Thomas McCarthy (Boston: Beacon Press, 1981), 385. For thorough discussions of these similarities, see Fred Dallmayr, "Adorno and Heidegger," *Diacritics* 19, no. 3–4 (Fall–Winter 1989): 82–100; David Roberts, "Art and Myth: Adorno and Heidegger," *Thesis Eleven* 58 (August 1999): 19–34; Krzysztof

Ziarek, "Radical Art: Reflections after Adorno and Heidegger," in (*Adorno: A Critical Reader*, ed. Nigel Gibson and Andrew Rubin (Malden, Mass.: Blackwell, 2002), 341–60. For a dismissal of these similarities, see *Late Marxism*, where Fredric Jameson says, "I have been surprised by the increasing frequency of comparisons with his arch-enemy Heidegger, whose philosophy, he once observed, 'is fascist to its innermost core'" (9).

13. Martin Heidegger, "The Question Concerning Technology," in *Martin Heidegger: Basic Writings from "Being and Time" (1927) to "The Task of Thinking" (1964)*, 2nd rev. and expanded ed., ed. David Farrell Krell (New York: Harper Collins, 1993), 332.

14. See also Timothy Brennan, who says that the importance of Heidegger stems from "his self-appointed role as historical foil to the Hegelian left." Timothy Brennan, *Wars of Position: The Cultural Politics of Left and Right* (New York: Columbia University Press, 2006), 16.

15. In *Iconoclasm in Aesthetics* (Cambridge: Cambridge University Press, 2003), Michael Kelly grants that Adorno's and Heidegger's views of art show such similarities, but he claims that in a typically philosophical manner, they characterize art as universal, only to find that art disappoints them. Both argue that art sets the universal and the concrete in opposition, but far from siding with the universal, they claim that art does not resolve the opposition.

16. Heidegger, *Poetry, Language, Thought*, 39–57.

17. J. M. Bernstein, *The Fate of Art: Aesthetic Alienation from Kant to Derrida and Adorno* (University Park: Pennsylvania State University Press, 1992), 124.

18. See Theodor W. Adorno, *The Jargon of Authenticity*, trans. Knut Tarnowski and Frederic Will (Evanston: Northwestern University Press, 1973), 15–30.

19. Heidegger, "Question Concerning Technology," 340.

20. Fredric Jameson, *The Political Unconscious: Narrative as a Socially Symbolic Act* (Ithaca, N.Y.: Cornell University Press, 1981), 40.

21. Jacques Derrida, *The Truth in Painting*, trans. Geoff Bennington and Ian McLeod (Chicago: University of Chicago Press, 1987), 286–87. Subsequent references to this book will appear in the text.

22. Jacques Derrida, *Specters of Marx: The State of the Debt, the Work of Mourning, and the New International*, trans. Peggy Kamuf (New York: Routledge, 1994), 28.

23. Michel Foucault, cited in Michael Schwartz, "Epistemes and the History of Being," in *Foucault and Heidegger: Critical Encounters*, ed. Alan Milchman and Alan Rosenberg (Minneapolis: University of Minnesota Press, 2003), 163. Gilles Deleuze says that Foucault reads Heidegger through Nietzsche: the will to power explains the ability of discourse to bring what is into the open or the clearing, where it becomes visible even as it recedes into darkness. See also Stuart Elden, *Mapping the Present: Heidegger, Foucault and the Project of a Spatial History* (London: Continuum Press, 2001), 2.

24. Schwartz, "Epistemes and the History of Being," 171–72.

25. See Paul Allen Miller, "The Art of Self-Fashioning, or Foucault on Plato and Derrida," *Foucault Studies* 2 (May 2005): 54–74.

26. Michel Foucault, *The Use of Pleasure: The History of Sexuality, Vol. 2*, trans. Robert Hurley (New York: Random House, 1985), 1–33.

27. Pierre Macherey, *Histoires de dinosaure: Faire de la Philosophie, 1965–1997* (Paris: Presses Universitaires de France, 1999), 167–68.

28. Pierre Macherey, *A Theory of Literary Production,* trans. Geoffrey Wall (London: Routledge and Kegan Paul, 1978), 1–14.

29. Pierre Macherey, *In a Materialist Way: Selected Essays by Pierre Macherey,* ed. Warren Montag, trans. Ted Stolze (London: Verso, 1998), 47.

30. Ibid., 47.

31. Macherey, *Histoires de dinosaure,* 173; my translation.

32. Pierre Macherey, *The Object of Literature,* trans. David Macey (Cambridge: Cambridge University Press, 1995), 30.

33. Macherey, *In a Materialist Way,* 42.

34. Warren Montag treats Macherey's later view, in which he considers art capable of many different readings, as a mere "rectification" of his earlier, Althusserian view: "As Macherey has argued in a recent 'rectification' of his earlier work, to consider literature solely from the point of view of production leads to 'insurmountable contradictions.'" Warren Montag, *Louis Althusser* (New York: Palgrave Macmillan, 2003), 67. The trouble is that the later view is based on his Foucauldian critique of the science/ideology opposition, but Montag never mentions that critique or explains Macherey's development.

35. Macherey, *Histoires de dinosaure,* 174.

36. Terry Eagleton also produces and subsequently repudiates an Althusserian account of literary criticism, but he goes on to defend the progressive import of aesthetics: despite its "specious form of universality," it envisions "human energies as radical ends in themselves which is the implacable enemy of all dominative or instrumentalist thought" and seeks to debunk the work of Foucault, whose notion of the body acts "among other things as a convenient displacement of a less immediately corporeal politics, and . . . as an ersatz kind of ethics." Eagleton, *Ideology of the Aesthetic,* 9, 7.

37. Jacques Rancière, *The Politics of Aesthetics: The Distribution of the Sensible* (New York: Continuum, 2004), 13.

38. Macherey, *In a Materialist Way,* 141.

39. See Ernesto Laclau and Chantal Mouffe, *Hegemony and Socialist Strategy* (London: Verso, 1985), 122–33; see also David Cousins Hoy, who in *Critical Resistance* (Cambridge, Mass.: MIT Press, 2004) says that for Foucault critique shows the subject that it has possibilities that were previously unknown or unacknowledged (81–88). Judith Butler also says that Foucault allows the subject to resist the dominant ideals or ideologies constituting it, but she maintains that the subject parodies them and thereby implies new possibilities. See Judith Butler, *Gender Trouble: Feminism and the Subversion of Identity* (New York: Routledge, 1990), 33–34. Daniel O'Hara makes a similar claim in *Radical Parody: American Culture and Critical Agency after Foucault* (New York: Columbia University Press, 1992). In *Foucault and Feminism: Power, Gender, and the Self* (Boston: Northeastern University Press, 1993), Lois McNay argues that Foucault's work on sexuality, by formulating a relational notion of identity, opens the possibility that various subjectivities can form a democratic coalition (111).

40. Macherey, *In a Materialist Way,* 99.

41. Christopher Norris says, for example, that in his last works, Foucault recognizes this fault, for his accounts of the strategies and tactics whereby men of the classical Greek and the Christian eras regulated their bodies and thereby assured the health of their souls reinstates the normative force and rational autonomy of the subject, what he termed its ethical self-fashioning. Nonetheless, Foucault's historical studies for the most part construe the subject as a puppet of the social system, unable to challenge the status quo. As Norris says, "It seems to me that Foucault found himself in the awkward position of one who sought to maintain a strongly oppositional or counter-hegemonic stance, yet whose outlook of extreme epistemological and ethical skepticism left him at the last no ground on which to stand in advancing these claims." Christopher Norris, "What Is Enlightenment? Kant According to Foucault," *Reconstructing Foucault: Essays in the Wake of the 80s*, ed. Silvia Caporate-Bizzini and Ricardo Miguel-Alfonso (Amsterdam: Editions Rodopi, 1994), 84. Similarly, citing Jürgen Habermas, Gerhard Schweppenhäuser says that unlike Adorno, who shows us "how to integrate the ambivalence of fundamental normative ideas into a critical theory of morality," "Foucault's archaeological and genealogical critique of power and rationality . . . reduces 'functionalistically,' 'validity claims . . . to the effects of power' and, 'naturalistically, the "ought" to the "is."'" Gerhard Schweppenhäuser, "Adorno's Negative Moral Philosophy," in *The Cambridge Companion to Adorno*, ed. Tom Huhn (Cambridge: Cambridge University Press, 2004), 330. See also Timothy Brennan, *Wars of Position: The Cultural Politics of Left and Right* (New York: Columbia University Press, 2006), 151; and Eagleton, *Ideology of the Aesthetic*, 378–79.

42. Richard Rorty, *Consequences of Pragmatism: Essays, 1972–1980* (Minneapolis: University of Minnesota Press, 1982), 153.

43. Brennan, *Wars of Position*, 12; See also Todd Gitlin, who says that Foucault became "all the rage" because he insisted that "every sphere of life—every profession, indeed, every field of knowledge—was saturated with power. Knowledge was 'power/knowledge'. . . . In a time of political blockage . . . this was what the enclaves of the academic Left wanted to hear. . . . If the Right held political power, what did it matter?" Todd Gitlin, *The Twilight of Common Dreams: Why America Is Wracked by Culture Wars* (New York: Henry Holt, 1996), 152. See also Walter Benn Michaels, "The University Déclassé," *Journal of the Midwest Modern Language Association* 37, no. 1 (Spring 2004): 19.

6
Is Socialism the Index of a Leftist Ontology?

BENJAMIN ROBINSON

THE EXISTENTIAL INDEX

The more one thinks about the historical socialist experience bounded by the years 1917 and 1990, the years of European state socialism, the more embarrassing a positive intellectual engagement with it might seem. Besides the practical questions posed generally by an amoral raison d'état, and more pointedly by the particular immorality of Eastern Bloc party rule, one is left to ponder real socialism's uninspiring record of functional legitimation and social performance. There is a temptation to move on and be done with it, drawing for political inspiration from an uncontaminated well of leftist virtue that springs from a bedrock more fundamental than state–administrative history: from pure freedom, equality, and solidarity. If it turns out that state socialism, like fascism, was nothing but a failed episode in the history of global liberalism, there will nonetheless remain much to say about it in the context of an archaeology of modernity: the powerful collective affects it evoked, the strategic limitations of liberal popular integration it revealed, and the distinct social–technical limitations its political order represented. There will, however, be nothing to say about a socialist ontology, because really existing socialism will have revealed itself to have been falsely existing—not socialism as a signified with meaningful currency today, but socialism as an empty signifier, a label that has irredeemably (and retrospectively) lost its meaning. Of course, even without a socialist ontology, we could still point to leftist ideals like *liberté, egalité,* and *fraternité* as discursive acts; we could ascribe nominal existence to their pronouncement, simply not systemic existence. I argue here, however, that without a socialist ontology, leftist politics remains a gesture, without reference to either real subjects or a mutually valid world. Leftism, in my view, in fact implies no political ontology as such, for a political ontology grounds a left and right equally without regard to content, but a systems ontology with socialism in it. The corresponding rightist ontology is, reasonably enough, not a political ethics, concerned with disparaging values like liberty, equality, and solidarity per se, but a rival philosophy of existence that holds that no systemic organization of these values, as envisioned in the leftist ontology, exists (in any modality of actuality or possibility). Both ontologies, of course, can hold that human minds and bodies exist and that their pains and pleasures matter, and also that a shared world exists in which these bodies and intentions cooperate and collide. The political distinction, however, concerns what lies in between.

Let me clarify what I mean by ontology, and more specifically by systems ontology. Many philosophical traditions from the sophists, through the nominalists, to the logical empiricists have denied the existence of ideals and universals. They have proposed instead either a promiscuous but never transcendental ontology based on the infinite relativity of situated perspectives, or a very parsimonious ontology based on concrete empirical perception at a point in time. In the case of the sophists, for example, "what is" has more to do with a sense for the right time and place than with any logos or eidos manifesting itself beyond each time and place. In the case of the logical empiricists, careful induction over many observations might lead to the warranted hypostatization of a single object (though even here, without any transcendental certainty); thus, I might reasonably conclude the existence of a leaf after many observations of its persistence, but to infer from one leaf to the existence of a universal (eidetic) category "leaf" (or "leaf-ness") would be unwarranted in all instances. I choose these examples of skeptical and strict ontologies not because I share their assumptions, which limit the world narrowly to what one can assert of it either occasionally or logically, but because they suggest a useful spirit of ontological discretion. In this spirit, we need to consider whether socialism exists somehow analogously to the punctual empirical perception of an external object ("this leaf") or even of my internal states ("my pain," "my pleasure"); or whether it exists more functionally in the way that we generalize from discrete acts of floating in water to a hypostatization of "buoyancy"; or whether yet it exists in the way that "ghosts" and "specters" are said to exist, discursively, as suggestive metaphors for, say, past events or future projects.[1]

In the following, I make the case that despite leftist critiques of "the administered world" (Adorno), we do well to start our inquiry into socialist ontology with those twentieth-century socioeconomic administrations in which communist parties held sway. The argument is that by analyzing to what extent socialism existed as a distinct social system after the 1917 revolution, one clarifies what it means for a leftist politics to commit to socialism as something that exists as a valid project of future political decision. Rudolf Carnap has reflected on the question of whether one can meaningfully discuss the reality or validity of a system, noting that "to be real in the scientific sense means to be an element of the system; hence this concept cannot be meaningfully applied to the system itself."[2] When one speaks of the real existence of the system itself, one makes a more or less deliberate choice, but a choice that, if it is to be tenable, must yield elements of compelling reality in an empirical sense. "Those who raise the question of the reality of the thing world itself have perhaps in mind not a theoretical question as their formulation seems to suggest, but rather a practical question, a matter of a practical decision concerning the structure of our language."[3] Carnap here emphasizes that the choice of systems is a practical one, qualifying that practicality with regard to semantics, as a choice concerning "the structure of our language." I will argue, as does W. V. O. Quine, that a semantic system implies an ontology, a way the world *is*.[4] In other words, a leftist ontology (or leftist semantics, if one follows Carnap in this) concerns neither the whole world in an exclusive final sense, nor punctual elements within a given world, but the practicality of a system that gives us a world of stable elements and relations we might call socialist. The problem, or antinomy, is this: one cannot empirically commit to one "thing world" over another (say, socialism, whatever that might be, over liberalism) if there is no shared index of reality to decide between them. At the same time, a purely theoretical or normative commitment is empty as long as the choice is not proved on the practical level where the things in a chosen system have a self-evidence—what I will call apodictic force—that lets them serve as their own index of validity. Related to the two sides of this objective antinomy, furthermore, there are on the subjective side likewise two contrary affective stances. I emphasize affect, rather than rational orientation, because of the murky epistemology involved with validating what is real. Thus, in the former case, where an "ontological commitment" (Quine) transpires without facts in the realm of decisionistic values, the subjective pathos is sublime or ecstatic. In the latter case, where the ontological commitment is less a matter of discretion and more a matter of the sensual authority of facts, the corresponding pathos has the cool affect of behaviorism: the things of the world speak for us. "It is easy to imagine a thoroughly empirical 'felicitology' on a behavorialistic foundation," the logical empiricist Otto Neurath claimed without a hint of irony in the otherwise roaring 1920s, "which could take the place of traditional ethics."[5]

By considering especially the economic realm in which socialism asserts itself, I aim to make clear why socialism's reality is an ontological issue, not a semantic one. As my reference to Quine already hints, however, I do not wish to separate the ontological and semantic (the real and the meaningful) as though they were two independent realms. Rather, I want to emphasize how economically meaningful facts depend on the system's own material reference. As a framework for ordering the production, distribution, and consumption of goods, an economic system coordinates psychic intentions in a physical world of facts, and its success or failure reveals itself with an empirical authority distinct from that of bookkeeping's arithmetic; that is, a firm might calculate the price of its products exactly right to earn it a healthy return, but unless the products actually sell to someone, the paper balance is a meaningless figure. At the same time, in any system, there has to be some meaningful reference point for coordinating the actions of its various elements, and it is this key notion of a correlating index bridging the meaningful and the factual that ties together the various strands of my argument. An index is a type of sign that, in C. S. Peirce's definition, signifies with a minimum of interpretation and a maximum of self-evident (or apodictic) force.[6] It stands between the realms of banal facticity (minimal interpretation) and ecstatic resolution (maximal force), pointing like a medical thermometer to an objective bodily state on the one hand and a crisis of intervention on the other. Going beyond the temperature of single body, the utilitarian Jeremy Bentham dreamed of a "political thermometer" for adding up, with the simple compulsion of a sum, "the greatest happiness of the greatest number" in the body politic, and the later utilitarian F. Y. Edgeworth dreamed of a similar device he called a "hedonimeter." Interest in indexes, however, was hardly restricted to Anglo-American utilitarians and pragmatists; we find the same plain-sounding term in the anything but plain phenomenology and existentialism of thinkers as different as Edmund Husserl and Walter Benjamin, for whom the index is a sign that, in an act of overwhelming perception, literally links everybody with everything—and points politically divided subjects toward their common task. It is to this more passionate index that I will turn first as a way of gauging the content of leftist ontology in the era surrounding World War I and the Russian Revolution. I then turn to a series of twentieth-century economic debates about real socialism and general equilibrium theory, and finally I return to some positive indexes like those described by Peirce.

POLITICAL ONTOLOGY VERSUS SOCIALIST ONTOLOGY

A glance at modern intellectual history makes it immediately apparent that recognizable leftists in fact suppose ontologies of all sorts, suggesting the futility of specifying leftist ontology in the singular. The Marx of 1844, for instance, grounds his critique of alienated labor on the postulate of "species being." Communitarian thought more generally opposes liberalism by postulating the existence of the community prior to the individual. Proudhon, by contrast, holds individuals of uncorrupted instinct to be the basis of civil association, which must defend itself against the depredations of the sovereign state. Over and against the false hypostatization of both the constituted state and contracted civil society, Hardt and Negri behold the anarchic immanence of a multitude as the stuff of "a new ontological reality."[7] And even for a thinker like Ernesto Laclau, for whom social order goes no deeper than a "chain of equivalents" linking otherwise incomparable values into a political bloc as tenuous as a Freudian cathexis, his ontology (or antiontology, because the negative predominates) follows the situational one proposed by the ancient sophists.[8] We might sum up such ontologies conjunctively to one encyclopedic leftist ontology, or exclude disjunctively all elements not common to each. My guess is that neither operation would take us very far. Alternatively, we might move from this multiplicity to a deeper apprehension of their common world horizon, in which all special ontologies share one "Being-in-the-world." This Heideggerian move, as we know from Heidegger's controversial legacy, compels us to ask whether "the ontological," in the emphatic existentialist sense, wouldn't transform serviceable ontologies of leftist praxis, however mutually incompatible, into a political nihilism, the sort of latent fascism briefly revealed in Heidegger's notorious *Rektoratsrede* of 1933. If we resist this imputation of rightism and conclude that the ontological doesn't imply a distinct politics, then fine— but our inquiry, along with a substantive meaning for leftism, ends in a great big pre-Socratic whoosh: "the source of coming-to-be for existing things is that into which destruction, too, happens."[9]

At the same time, rejecting an ontological container altogether for the abyss of groundless antagonism only leads to a similar problem of indistinction between left and right, where they are reduced simply to rivalry with no further substantial determination. In Carl Schmitt's famous agonistic argument for the priority of politics over the state and civil society,

politics is fate because the existence of an enemy is ontologically fundamental, and so, therefore, is coexistence among political rivals—there are
no moral, aesthetic, or rational determinants to political rivalry, only the
ad hoc intensity of solidarity and separation.[10] Because it gives us a world
only in the negative sense of sharing a destiny to compete over values
among which there is no objective basis for deciding, the ontology least
capable of being political for our purposes is a political ontology. What
exists is articulated by the sheer "this-ness" (irreducibility, or hecceity) of
each decision struck between disparate values, and politics comes down to
initiating and naming the differences we fight over. Like the strict positivist's leaf, whose properties do not exist as independent universal substrates
but coincide only with *this* leaf, so too is taking sides in such a political
ontology an instance of nothing but itself—what, in its negativity, initially
passes as a critique of fin-de-siècle positivisms finally ends up in the purely
immanent positivism of decision.[11] To put as sharp a point on it as possible, where positivism holds a punctual ontology of objects, decisionism
holds a punctual ontology of subjects. In both cases, the punctuality excludes those larger ontological frameworks (that in Carnap's words hold
"abstract entities like properties, classes, relations, numbers, propositions,
etc."[12]) in which leftism is situated.

As my brief references to modern intellectual history suggest, my argument for a socialist ontology historicizes the act of ontological commitment,
but in a way that is less concerned with singular events than with the relational systems that straddle or issue from them. Thus, I consider the two
early twentieth-century thinkers, Husserl and Benjamin, as responses to
the "crisis of classical modernity," the set of tensions and reversals growing
out of the nineteenth-century modernization process.[13] In the time of political uncertainty leading up to and following the Great War and the Russian Revolution, their thoughts represent two situated attempts to conceive
subject/object correlations. What I claim is that as different as their ontologies are, both philosophers need a correlation to exist as an index that
itself stands ecstatically outside the era's subject/object divide. The importance of such an index is not unique to their thought; rather, the common
concern of two such contrasting thinkers suggests how central indexicality
was to the time. The ecstatic index responds to the loss of transcendental orientation announced so influentially in the sociology of Max Weber,
who postulated a world of irreducibly distinct value spheres—a world without a world, so to speak. He held that our practical orientations, instead
of drawing on a common ground, came from an arbitrary choice among

rationalized guidelines that then, in retrospect, commanded our highest respect. While the external guidance of rational professions coordinated individuals, there was no further legitimacy for the various institutions of reason themselves; the "disenchanted world" lacked any standpoint on its own relentless processes.[14]

Husserl's response to an apparently sundered modernity took him in an opposite direction from Weber's stoic persistence in abjection. Although Husserl is known as a transcendental philosopher, his phenomenology of the life world—the reassembled world of modernity—is not an ahistorical rationalism. He bases his ontology on an infinite series of embodied historical actors and an infinite series of abstract validating acts. It is both a horizon (without a singular determination, or arché) and a ground (without senseless multiplicity, or chaos). In a pair of striking formulations, Husserl writes that the subject of historical infinity is the "everyone" who is "the subject of all groundings ever to be accomplished,"[15] and that the object of logical infinity is the "world," which is "the totality of what is taken for granted as verifiable."[16] Between *everyone* and the *world*, Husserl places an ontologically primordial index, which he calls the "life world," that correlates historical infinity with logical infinity. "The intersubjectively identical life-world-for-all serves as an intentional 'index' for the multiplicities of appearance . . . through which all ego-subjects . . . are oriented toward a common world and the things in it."[17] This index reveals itself only upon the strenuous bracketing out (epoché) of the natural attitude toward things, and with the apperception of the intentional mind-set as such. The very condition of the life world's revelation is the suspension of a practical—and political—attitude to the world.

Benjamin held an ontology that at first couldn't seem more different from the elder philosopher's enveloping life world.[18] Where Husserl recoiled from Weimar's nihilism, Benjamin heralded the era's fragmentation as the decisive loss of any order-conserving aura of authenticity, and conceived his task as exploding the most punctual sense perceptions out of the life worlds of Dilthey and Husserl, "indeed seeing in the analysis of the small individual moment the crystallization of the total event."[19] Torn from a received network of affinities, these "intensified perceptions" are for Benjamin an index revealed in the "now time" that correlates the isolated fragments of historical past with a messianic whole beyond the conventions of history, law, and progress.[20] Like the wormhole of a gravitational singularity, space-time collapses for Benjamin into a singular dialectical image of unique ontological privilege (the present, in both senses of the word, of the now time). This ontology sharply foregrounds an index that maps a suffering, fragmented history into a complete messianic domain.[21] It is a surprising ontology because although it seems so different from Husserl's in elevating the singular punctual perception over the apperception of totality, the same thing stands at the center of both: an index.

Benjamin resists Husserl's phenomenological a priori by emphasizing the historicity of his dialectical images, asserting that "what distinguishes these images from the 'essences' of phenomenology is their historical index."[22] It is not a very thoroughgoing distinction, however, especially coming from the antihistoricist Benjamin and directed at transcendental–historical phenomenology. For both Husserl and Benjamin, chaos is the empty separateness of positivism and order the security of a vigorous perception beyond the fossilized protocols of positive science. What such divergent thinkers both require ontologically is some sort of vivid index to map the way out of a world of contingency and meaninglessness. For them, historically, that was the world of Weimar-era instability and its proliferating and incompatible rules. Through his emphasis on the "apodictic" and "self-evident," Husserl highlights the meaningful but noninterpretive aspect of an index, while Benjamin's idea of figural legibility likewise goes beyond interpretation to the sudden intuition of connection beheld in a dialectical image.[23] The disciplined ecstasy of the phenomenological epoché contrasts with the theological ecstasy of Benjamin's dialectical image, yet in both cases, the index is an ecstatic sign. It is a sign that stands outside of the everyday instrumental order of subject and object and by virtue of its transcendence serves as the measure of action beyond the discordant roles of isolated existence.

At this point, I want to turn my ontological discussion to an index of a very different sort, a prosaic index drawn like Bentham's and Edgeworth's from the dismal science, in order to locate the leftist index among the more practical objects and subjects of economics. I emphasize these distinct discourses of indexicality for two reasons. First, it might seem that the ecstatic index I have described simply stands above history—whether in rationalist or mythical fashion—and guides us in moments of crisis without reference to historical time. Second, it might seem that the affect evoked by the index is compatible only with acts of revolution or conversion and cannot serve as a standard for patiently building a new order. Both these impressions are misleading. The economic index—the "leading indicator" of real socialism—is to be sought neither in the order of ecstatically transcendental subjects of rationalist or romantic variety, nor in the order of transcendental objects of physical or ideal consistency. The new figure I introduce into the discussion at this juncture (the last element of the socialist ontological equation) is equilibrium. I argue, using the example of modern economics, that an index emerges as a potential equilibrium among the previously inchoate orders that it aspires to regulate. It is thus a supremely circuitous sign, for the subject observing the index is itself among the orders being regulated by it, as are of course the objects. Subjects and objects alike thus both find their most prosaic (but binding) measure in the oscillations and tendencies of the index itself. The ontological problem for leftism comes down to whether and in what way the specifically socialist index—a distinct equilibrium between otherwise incompatible orders—exists. Like Husserl's life world, the socialist index points to a series of historical actors rather than a closed identity; unlike it, it does not transcend the subject/object distinction required for the practical will. While this leftist index universally coordinates subjects with objects, it is also an entity that practically verifies itself against a rival index (the free market) that holds similarly universalistic claims. If socialism exists as the index of leftist intentions, it has to exist in a way that puts its capitalist rival out of business; but not in a way that, like Benjamin's dialectical image, settles every coming ontological score.

Four Economic Ontologies

> The movements of society are spontaneous and not artificial, and the desire
> for joy which manifests itself in all its activities unwittingly drives it
> towards the realization of the ideal type of State.
>
> —PAUL PIERRE LE MERCIER DE LA RIVIÈRE, 1767

As Ernst Kantorowicz famously describes it, sovereignty issues from the mystical union of the king's two bodies, the royal body, which dies, and the body politic, in which the dignity of political incorporation lives on through succession.[24] What, however, can we say about the essence of socialism that, I contend, survives not only Lenin's bodily death, but the disintegration of the political body of the Soviet Union and its Comintern allies? This essence surely isn't the sovereignty of medieval political theology, nor has it turned out to be the effect of political decisionism or discursive constructivism. Socialism's essence, homely as the proletariat, lives on in an economic index, one whose innermost mysteries need to be distinguished from the great reigning economic index of General Equilibrium. I am not invoking the economic index as a "final instance" where the whole cosmic superstructure of being is determined; rather, like any index, the economic index has minimum depth and displays maximum evidence right on its surface, even as the ultimate direction in which it points remains uncertain: if the Dow Jones is climbing, we need not anguish over interpreting the indubitable rise in market value, although we might wonder when or if it will fall again. An economic index is neither a first nor a last instance, but lies plainly in the middle between the personal desires ("intentional states") of *homo oeconomicus,* and the extrapersonal state in which the economy hangs together as a material order of production and distribution. Although it doesn't point from here to eternity, this index is the measure of leftist political commitment, and as such is the enduring essence of leftist ontology.

Because General Equilibrium theory (GE) remains more uncontested than ever after the fall of European socialism, I take its ontological claims about economic equilibrium as the orienting point of my inquiry into leftist ontology. According to GE, an economy is the unified interrelation of all economic agents through the medium of money. In precapitalist economic formations, money was not yet the sole medium for coordinating distinct parts of the production and exchange process in an articulated whole. It is only with generalized commodity exchange and the universal equivalency of money that a distinct economic system emerges.[25] In eighteenth-century France, the Physiocrats pioneered terminology adequate to the emergence of a national economy as an interrelated whole. Through the movement of prices, they observed how the value of land, for example, rippled through the monarchy to affect things as diverse as urban wages and royal tax receipts that recursively affected the value of land. It was this more or less closed circular causality that demarcated the economic as a system. The Scottish enlightenment around David Hume and Adam Smith shared this insight into the compelling power with which a closed system of causality shaped and articulated distinct but coordinated elements of the world. With Smith, one could for the first time speak persuasively of the sovereign individual, rather than the divine sovereign, because individuals, solely on the basis of self-interest expressed in private property values, could generate from inside out an order that was coherent, comprehensive, and rationally related to one's actions. The monuments of this era remain the sovereign individual (with no necessary intentions beyond self-interest) and the invisible hand of automatic coordination (laissez-faire)—and with their economic testament, Locke's civil contracts assume pride of place before absolute sovereign states.

GE, first elaborated by William Jevons and Leon Walras in the 1870s, came to express these automatic economic processes in rigorous mathematical terms. By using the concept of marginal utility, GE explains the systematic nature by which the equilibrium price of a good is reached on the basis of a differential calculus that determines the additional quantity that a participant in the free market still desires of some good instead of another with each infinitesimal increase in its price. The effective demand of real economic agents could thus be observed through GE prices as an invisibly coordinated regulating force within the autonomous whole of the capital-ist economic system, money serving as the coordinating medium not only for accounting and exchange, but also for the hedonistic calculus of plea-sure optimization under appropriate economic conditions. That logical for-malization, with its underlying assumptions about profit-maximizing firms and utility-maximizing consumers, informs most economic policy today.[26]

This pillar of the political–economic order rests on three fundamental propositions that I want to keep in mind: there is a state of compatibility among diverse economic interests coordinated through an economic sys-tem (that is, equilibrium exists); these interests can assume they are all play-ing the same game (equilibrium is unique); and interests tend to converge on such a compatible state (equilibrium is stable). In each of the three antagonistic economic views I now consider, the reality of these conditions is contested. The third proposition, which requires an inherent economic stability rather than an intentionally directed one, is the most controver-sial. In the orthodox GE espoused by Ludwig von Mises, Friedrich Hayek, and Milton Friedman, the economic as such requires that the third propo-sition apply autonomously, without intervention from the noneconomic sphere.[27] In other words, independent actions must be coordinated by in-herent economic forces—Smith's "invisible hand"—or those actions are not economic. For Smith's force to apply, actors need to be motivated to follow economic interests they can calculate on the basis of common mar-ket prices. Only if someone owns property, even just a day of labor power, will she be interested in meeting the marginal utility maximization criteria necessary for the economy to balance supply and demand at equilibrium prices. And only if prices are left free to find their own equilibrium can property owners choose rationally among available alternatives for satis-fying their desires. When considering whether socialism can meet these criteria, Mises writes in 1920 that "without economic calculation there can be no economy. Hence, in a socialist state wherein the pursuit of economic calculation is impossible, there can be—in our sense of the term—no econ-omy whatsoever."[28]

If we accept GE—and there are compelling empirical reasons to do so—then we cannot countenance socialism in our economic ontology. If we persist, however, in trying to understand whether seventy years of social-ism really existed—and there are also compelling empirical reasons to do so—then we need another paraphrase of the economic order. In the 1930s, partly in response to Mises's philosophical interdiction of socialism, the Polish economist Oscar Lange began to address the problem of how eco-nomic calculation might be possible in a system that politically, rather than economically, decided on its equilibrium states, where *homo oeconomicus* converged with *homo suffragans*.[29] This politically steered equilibrium gives us our first alternative economic ontology. For Lange, socialism did exist because a stable equilibrium existed that was called into being not by mar-ket prices, but by a material balance reached through controlled trial and error. "Any mistake made by the Central Planning Board in fixing prices would announce itself in a very objective way—by a physical shortage or surplus of the quantity of the commodity or resources in question—and would have to be corrected in order to keep production running smoothly."[30] The announcement of economic mistakes in a physically objective manner is a far more obvious and compelling index than prices whose significance, despite their mathematization in GE theory, is still subject to interpreta-tion. According to Lange, the physical balance of surplus and deficit could in principle be achieved by a democratic planning board with fewer suc-cessive calculations than a market required, a market and its prices being merely a primitive analogue computer that was being superseded by nas-cent digital technology and its direct quantitative inputs.

Although the next view I consider is deeply influenced by Lange's cyber-netics, it sought a more radical reconceptualization of economics than Lange—indeed, one fully outside GE assumptions. The Hungarian econo-mist János Kornai, considered by many "the only scholar who . . . attempted a general theory of the socialist economy," does not aim to extend the world of the economic on the orthodox terms of either GE or Marxism.[31] Rather, Kornai develops a theory of the economic based on information and values not strictly mediated by money, thereby mooting GE's preemptive disqual-ification of socialism from the realm of the economic. He characterizes socialist economies as "economies of shortage"—in other words, nonequi-librium economies—suggesting an economic ontology that does not require the first postulate of GE theory: that equilibrium exists. In a work pointedly titled *Anti-Equilibrium,* Kornai argues not only that socialist economies are nonequilibrium economies, but that there are in fact no equilibrium econ-omies anywhere, and that GE's discrimination between the formalizable market economies of the West and the administrative (non)economies of the East is untenable. Again, the distinction is untenable not because, as Lange hoped, planned economies can be guided by GE, but because even market economies cannot.[32]

Because there is no significant private ownership, socialist economies cannot rely on prices to generate the information they need, raising the problem of understanding how socialist economic reproduction is systematically mediated. Goods and services are exchanged and accounts formally balanced, but money does not serve as a reliable measure of value. Firms, for example, do not have to attract scarce investment capital on a competitive stock exchange but have state-subsidized budgets that prohibit bankruptcy. They thus do not buy inputs according to a marginal utility calculus; a central planner must instead assume that each firm's demand for any available input is infinite.[33] In fact, because prices are nowhere determined at a level that balances demand with supply, serving simply as conventional markers for accounting, it is not only firms but all economic actors who have potentially infinite demand. The ensuing generalized shortage of goods lends the socialist economy its typical phenomenological forms: hoarding and queuing. The planner's task should thus not be conceived as chasing a GE fantasy of the perfect set of market-balancing prices, but as rationing a general shortage of producer inputs and consumer goods.

The planner's task is complicated by another factor besides the lack of monetary valuation; without private property, it is not clear what subjectively motivates individual economic actors. As a consequence of collective ownership, legal property agents ("the People") are not equivalent to economic property agents. As Jadwiga Staniszkis argues,

> of the three moments of material reproduction—work, capital, and material assets—[the latter two] have ceased to be identified with anyone's actual interest and have at the most become "theoretical interests" resulting from knowledge concerning the requirements of the production process. As such, they have little motivational power. This rift between the requirements of material production and the map of actual interests, together with the systemic absence of a wide range of information which can only be generated by the market, represents the main barrier to the state and the party having real control over the economy.[34]

Although Kornai agrees that socialist economic actors have few motivations as unambiguous as monetary incentives, he recognizes that "there exist some deeper-lying motives, which have a stronger and more lasting influence on management's behavior. Of these I stress that most people *identify themselves with their job*."[35] The Nobel Prize–winning economist Amartya Sen has likewise addressed this apparently nebulous issue of identification, phrasing it as a dilemma about the proper proportion of reason (as an autonomous rational calculus) and identification (a desire to become unified with something) in economic choices:

> Does a person identify with anyone else in deciding on what objects to pursue and what choices to make? Is the idea of social identity vacuous when it comes to explaining behavioral regularities, since no identification is involved other than with oneself? A good deal of economic theory has tended to proceed as if that is indeed the case.[36]

Kornai is ultimately interested in formalized systems, but by insisting on the importance of identification, he understands socialist economies as controlled by a heterogeneous, but systematic, combination of bureaucratic power, social symbolism, material balances, and, to a lesser extent, money.[37] According to Kornai, these factors can be apprehended and socialism systematically reproduced by using diverse incentives, all of which find a place in a socialist ontology. Ontologically, however, the system is not perfectly consistent and free of contradiction, and therefore there is no single medium through which efficiency can be optimized—that is, through which the socialist economy can come into itself as its own pure form. "The tradition of economics has accustomed us to the concept that everything can and must be 'optimized.' . . . But that is a naïve, wishful day-dream. . . . It seems to me that it is impossible to create a closed and consistent socio-economic normative theory which would assert, without contradiction, a politico-ethical value system and would at the same time provide for the efficiency of the economy."[38]

Kornai's polemic against equilibrium sets forth nonequilibrium terms that include capitalism and socialism as possibilities in one theoretical universe.[39] While Kornai recognizes differences between the two systems, he reduces them to distinctions along a single continuum of economic forms. By contrast, the orthodox socialist view that I now consider maintains a strong ontology of socialist difference, thus sharing the exclusivity of GE ontology, only with the opposite polarity. For tactical reasons, Eastern Bloc Marxists considered the cold war stalemate between two separate but relatively stable worlds a moment of "peaceful coexistence." On an analytical level, however, the outcome of this competition was a foregone conclusion. GE's bourgeois ontology, based on the supposedly efficient mediation of money, was self-contradictory and hence nugatory. In the *Grundrisse,* Marx traces how bourgeois wealth in monetary form—the very index that in GE correlates the emergence of the economic as such—"appears as its own mediator" and subordinates, in its drive to universality, all other economic actors.[40] "Note," Marx observes, "that money becomes an end instead of a means and that capital, as the superior form of mediation, everywhere establishes the inferior form, labor, simply as a source of surplus value."[41] In other words, monetary capital loses its medial character and becomes an absolute end, riding roughshod over all other social considerations and encountering other identities only as limitations to be overcome, until "the universality towards which it is perpetually tending finds limitations in its own nature, which at a certain stage of its development will make it appear as itself the greatest barrier to this tendency, leading thus to its own self-destruction."[42]

The target of the Marxist critique is liberal faith in "capitalist production as the absolute form of production."[43] Marxism concedes to von Mises that the market price index is the most generalized measure of commodity exchange. But the commodity economy is only one form of economy, not the whole of the economic; and this very particularity leads to capitalism's overcoming. In the superseding socialist economy—or better yet, one should now drop the ontologically limited idea of economy and simply say "socialism"—instead of capital serving as "the absolute form of wealth coinciding absolutely with the development productive forces,"[44] labor-time steps in as the new mediator. But the mediation by labor does not mean simply putting labor-money in the place of capital-money and letting the rest of the social transformation follow mechanically. There is an important second element to Marx's view of how socialist productive relations will be mediated, namely, by socialized labor as a conscious historical actor. Ernest Mandel writes that "between the growing economic contradictions of the capitalist mode of production on the one hand, and the collapse of capitalism on the other hand, there is a necessary mediation: the development of the class consciousness, organized strength and capacity for revolutionary action of the working class."[45] The new ontology of socialism thus measures itself by an index more vital and compelling than GE's frugal money—regarding labor both as spatiotemporal quantum for economic calculation and as conscious actor pointing toward collective decisions on the basis of labor-time information. Completing our parallelogram of ontologies, then, Marxian economics holds GE theory to be not only inapplicable to socialism, but, except as ideology, simply inapplicable. Socialism might exist coincidentally at the same moment as capitalism, but systematically, it negates and supersedes capitalism's contradictory laws of development. In this view, GE theory has no place, whether west of the Wall or in Lange's extension of it eastward, and neither does Kornai's theory, which denies GE only to squeeze capitalism and socialism into one neutral language of economic description.

BETWEEN POSITIVISM AND DECISIONISM

> From moment to moment the hedonimeter varies; the delicate index now
> flickering with the flutter of the passions, now steadied by intellectual
> activity, low sunk whole hours in the neighborhood of zero, or momentarily
> springing up toward infinity.
>
> —FRANCIS Y. EDGEWORTH, 1881

At this fourfold ontological impasse, we see the danger of making hasty commitments to one unambiguous index of the real—neither an empiricism, marshaling the facts and figures of Dow Jones and GDP, nor a constructivism, creating a guiding light by virtue of a militant discourse, gives us an obvious sign of discretionary truth. Our problem is this: if the ontological is a matter of commitment, commitment for its part, in order to be anything other than decisionism (that is, to be truly leftist), is a matter of ontology. In a seminal 1951 article, often credited with inaugurating the postanalytical turn away from Carnap's positivism, W. V. O. Quine argued against the supposition that we can fit any signifying system piece by piece to a single reality.[46] Would a word, for example, correspond to a physical state at a point x, y, z in time t? Or would the fit be made between a whole sentence and such a state? Quine suggests that indeed, neither an isolated word nor a statement can be tested against reality: "our statements about the external world face the tribunal of sense experience not individually but only as a corporate body."[47] To make his case—and to help us make ours—Quine introduces considerations of economics and equilibrium. We are tempted to believe, he argues, that we can separate the discursive (or logical) from the factual (or empirical) and, once they are neatly disentangled, bring the two into an economical relationship with each other by means of a univocal index (à la Occam's razor). The hitch, Quine argues, is that there is no one such relationship or economy of referential thrift. "In logical and mathematical systems either of two mutually antagonistic types of economy may be striven for, and each has its peculiar practical utility. On the one hand we may seek economy of practical expression—ease and brevity in the statement of multifarious relations. . . . Second, however, and oppositely, we may seek economy in grammar and vocabulary."[48] The one economy is akin to the expressive richness of Shakespearean diction, the other to the standardizing power of binary code. Even in the most technical language, however, it would be hard to determine strictly to which economy one belonged. Is, for example, the use of *economy* in Quine literal, in the sense of the preceding discussion of marginal utility? The difference in ontological commitments between any such economic axes requires that we recognize a semantics that cannot be resolved into any purely logical or observational system of signs. "[T]otal science is like a field of force whose boundary conditions are experience," he writes. "A conflict with experience at the periphery occasions readjustments in the interior. . . . But the total field is so underdetermined by its boundary conditions, experience, that there is much latitude of choice as to what statements to reevaluate in the light of any single contrary experience. No particular experiences are linked with any particular statements in the interior of the field, except indirectly through considerations of equilibrium affecting the field as a whole."[49]

Quine's figure of a general equilibrium returns us to the equilibrium index as the measure for the ontological realism I am pursuing. Just as a functional system is the existential condition for an equilibrium among objects, so is subjective equilibrium the existential condition for fitting subjects into the order of objects.[50] But can Quine's broadly evoked equilibrium conditions for a "corporate body" of statements add up to the "blindly compelling" index that guides political action out of the wilderness of the everyday? As defined by Peirce, the index reveals to us a cardinal existence, a "one" or a "hecceity." "A sign which denotes a thing by forcing it upon the attention," Peirce writes, "is called an *index*. An index does not describe the qualities of its object. An object, in so far as it is denoted by an index, having *thisness,* and distinguishing itself from other things by its continuous identity and forcefulness, but not by any distinguishing characters, may be called a *hecceity*."[51] The pure index conveys the apodictic force of sheer *thisness;* it marks the ecstatic Event sought by thinkers from Benjamin to Badiou and shares the same provenance as Schmitt's irreducible decisions and Husserl's ultimate ontological horizon. It is the last, incontestable guideline for action. For such an index to be a real standard, however, we need to ask, as GE does in the realm of economic interests, whether such a semantic equilibrium, beyond sheer existence, is unique

and stable. As our consideration of both GE and Quine's theory of reference demonstrates, however, the economic possibilities are multiple, as
are their potential equilibria, and in those circumstances, where each index
qualifies the other, the singular object or event cedes to comparable qualities and general terms: revolution cedes to socialist system. The seman-
tically qualified index is no longer the Red Flag, the General Strike, the
storming of the Bastille or the Winter Palace—the Event that stands ecstatically outside of all systems—but a systemic interaction across a corporate
body of significant facts.

At the height of the cold war, Nobel Prize–winning economist Tjalling
Koopmans and his colleague, John Montias, sought a signifying system beyond interpretation for resolving fundamental economic disputes between
capitalism and socialism, claiming that "for an objective comparison, the
descriptions of the systems being compared should be couched as much
as possible in system-free terms. . . . The ideal is that the *primitive* (unde-
fined) terms entering into these definitions be few in number and universal in applicability and prior meaning."[52] As similar as their aspiration is
to transcend the artificiality of given social institutions—this time those of
the cold war rather than the Weimar Republic—their sensibility couldn't be
more different from that of Husserl and Benjamin. It is postrevolutionary
level-headed, where the others are prerevolutionary ecstatic. What interests
me in conclusion is not any authentic choice between a pathos of artisanal
holism or apocalyptic sublime, but observing how these sensibilities are
intimately tied to each other through the common socialist intention they
reference. If the distinction between subjective states is central here, it is
not in contrast to objective commitments, but precisely as their comple-
ment because the socialist ontology of subject–object correlations, as I have
been arguing, concerns intentional states as much as material references.
In this sense, then, the singularity of Koopmans and Montias's objective
terms is the counterpart to the singularity of political decisionism's subjective events, and between these singularities, and coordinating them, lies
the system we are seeking.

Unsurprisingly, Koopmans was a colleague of Oskar Lange's in the
1940s at the Cowles commission for econometrics, and Montias—an art
historian as well as an economist—has an intellectual genealogy in the
material balance tradition founded by the Vienna School logical positivist
Otto Neurath.[53] Neurath, perhaps the key philosophical figure in this nexus
of economic thought, was for his part a major voice in the "socialist calculation" debate whose research led him to believe that a socialist economy

might outperform capitalism. Neurath sought a moneyless means for optimal planning that balanced "objective properties" of economic inputs directly, without the mediation of prices, by conceiving the inputs as "natural kinds" that might, accordingly, relate to each other naturally, on the principle that, as Shakespeare said, "one touch of nature makes the whole world kin."[54] He put his convictions to the test as the director of central planning in the short-lived Bavarian Soviet of 1919 and was Lenin's first postrevolution mentor for thinking about the practical problems of nonmarket economic organization. Although Neurath's plans came to naught in the White Terror that crushed the Bavarian Soviet, his career continued in a telling way: he developed a pictorial language that he claimed preselected no particular properties but let the things to which it referred speak for themselves without interpretation. In a semiotic sense, he sought to bring together icons and indices. Anticipating user-friendly computer icons, he described his ISOTYPE as a

> picture-text style which should enable anybody to walk through the modern world that is beginning to appear about us and see it as he may see a landscape. . . . The aim is to trace the origin of "modern men" and depict their behavior and achievements, without presenting any social or economic theory. . . . An international picture language is combined with a world language.[55]

Rather than dismissing Neurath's technocratic benevolence and Koopmans and Montias's cosmopolitan banality, I share their embrace of some such forceful index as the measure of the socialist real, just as I share the more heroic pathos of the Weimar revolutionaries. Only I also insist that as all-inclusive as the socialist index must be, it cannot eventually be closed off around the finality of either singular things or sovereign decisions: the rivalry of indices entails a trial of revelations and a plurality of experiences. In a world where prophecy must always be proved, the leftist commitment to the existence of socialism is not a commitment to the sign of redemption per se. Rather it is a commitment to a system that coordinates the holistic leftist pathos—in ecstatic as well as everyday forms—to some vast and robust balance of material goods. Leftists, to be sure, like rightists, will concern themselves passionately with the void of pure antagonism and the revelation of the decisive event. Each round of struggle will dissolve the old thing-world into the dust of Anaximander's plenum. But at the end of the day, after the barricades and red flags, a leftist has to own up to the everyday weight of the socialist burden. At that point, only the real objects a leftist carries can be an expedient against the distortions of capital; and as Dean Swift noted of the Laputans, a people who had foresworn the vagaries of discourse for the certainty of things, "if a man's business be very great, and of various kinds, he must be obliged in proportion to carry a greater bundle of things upon his back."[56] In the past century, this awkward bundle of things made leftists alternately ridiculous and terrible, leaving today's left with a sorely tested dignity and an ambiguous legacy of compassion and violence—one it prefers to forget in its utopian moments. But only by taking a historical leftist ontology seriously as a contemporary challenge will it succeed in doing better.

NOTES

1. See, for example, Jacques Derrida, *Specters of Marx* (New York: Routledge, 1994).

2. Rudolf Carnap, "Empiricism, Semantics and Ontology," supplement, in *Meaning and Necessity: A Study in Semantics and Modal Logic,* enlarged edition (Chicago: University Chicago Press, 1956), 207.

3. Ibid.

4. W. V. O. Quine, "Ontological Relativity," in *Ontological Relativity and Other Essays* (New York: Columbia University Press, 1969), 26–68.

5. Otto Neurath, "Sociology and Physicalism," in *Logical Positivism,* ed. A. S. Ayer (New York: Free Press, 1959), 306.

6. Charles Sanders Peirce, *Collected Papers of Charles Sanders Peirce,* ed. Charles Hartshorne and Paul Weiss (Cambridge, Mass.: Harvard University Press, 1931–58), vol. 2, para. 305.

7. Michael Hardt and Antonio Negri, *Empire* (Cambridge, Mass.: Harvard University Press, 2000), 395.

8. Ernesto Laclau, "Populist Reason," *Umbr(a)* 1 (2004): 23–51.

9. This is the Anaximander fragment famously interpreted by Heidegger. The translation here is by G. S. Kirk, J. E. Raven, and M. Schofield, *The Presocratic Philosophers,* 2nd ed. (Cambridge: Cambridge University Press, 1983), 118.

10. Carl Schmitt, *The Concept of the Political,* trans. George Schwab (New Brunswick, N.J.: Rutgers University Press, 1976), 26–27, 53.

11. I call this Schmittian world "pure immanence" in the sense of Horkheimer and Adorno's critique of positivism, and not in the opposed sense of Gilles Deleuze's *Pure Immanence: Essays on a Life,* trans. Anne Boyman (New York: Zone, 2001). Max Horkheimer and Theodor Adorno, *The Dialectic of Enlightenment,* trans. John Cumming (New York: Continuum, 1972), 16. In Deleuzean terms, Schmitt is a positivist of effects, whereas logical empiricists are positivists of causes.

12. Carnap, "Empiricism," 205.

13. See Detlev J. K. Peukert, *The Weimar Republic: The Crisis of Classical Modernity,* trans. Richard Deveson (New York: Hill and Wang, 1987).

14. For a characterization of interwar German philosophy as a response to Weber's rational disenchantment, see Norbert Bolz, *Ausflug aus der entzauberten Welt: Philosophischer Extremismus zwischen den Weltkriegen* (Munich: Wilhelm Fink, 1989).

15. Edmund Husserl, "The Vienna Lecture," in *The Crisis of European Sciences and Transcendental Phenomenology*, trans. David Carr (Evanston: Northwestern University Press, 1970), 278.

16. Ibid., 176.

17. Ibid., 172.

18. Benjamin calls the explosion of the *Jetzt* "the death of the intentio." Walter Benjamin, *Das Passagen-Werk*, ed. Rolf Tiedemann (Frankfurt am Main: Suhrkamp, 1982), N 3, 1, 578.

19. Ibid., N 2, 6, 575.

20. Ibid., N 2, 6; N 2, 4, 575.

21. The literary dimension of the figural index is described in Erich Auerbach, *Mimesis: The Representation of Reality in Western Literature*, trans. Willard R. Trask (Princeton, N.J.: Princeton University Press, 1953), esp. 73–76.

22. Benjamin, *Passagen-Werk*, N 3, 1, 577.

23. Ibid., N 3, 1, 577–78. Peirce's instruments are echoed in Benjamin's metaphor of historical insight as scale in which the infinite past is balanced with the weight of the present (N 6, 5, 585).

24. Ernst Kantorowicz, *The King's Two Bodies: A Study in Mediaeval Political Theology* (Princeton, N.J.: Princeton University Press, 1957).

25. For Marx's view, see Karl Marx, *Pre-Capitalist Economic Formations*, ed. Eric J. Hobsbawm (New York: International, 1965), 107–20.

26. The discussion of GE is indebted to Bruna Ingrao and Giorgio Israel, *The Invisible Hand: Economic Equilibrium in the History of Science*, trans. Ian McGilvray (Cambridge, Mass.: MIT Press, 1990).

27. Ludwig von Mises, *Socialism* (New Haven, Conn.: Yale University Press, 1951); Friedrich A. von Hayek, *The Road to Serfdom* (London: Routledge, 1944); Milton Friedman, *Essays in Positive Economics* (Chicago: University Chicago Press, 1953).

28. Ludwig von Mises, "Economic Calculation in the Socialist Commonwealth," in *Collectivist Economic Planning*, ed. F. A. Hayek (London: Routledge and Kegan Paul, 1935), 105.

29. Oskar Lange and Fred M. Taylor, *On the Economic Theory of Socialism*, ed. Benjamin E. Lippincott (Minneapolis: University of Minnesota Press, 1938).

30. Ibid., 82.

31. Hans-Jürgen Wagener, "Between Conformity and Reform," in *Economic Thought in Communist and Post-Communist Europe*, ed. Hans-Jürgen Wagener (London: Routledge, 1998), 2.

32. János Kornai, *Anti-Equilibrium: On Economic Systems Theory and the Tasks of Research* (Amsterdam: North-Holland, 1971).

33. János Kornai, "'Hard' and 'Soft' Budget Constraint," in *Contradictions and Dilemmas* (Cambridge, Mass.: MIT Press, 1986), 33–51.

34. Jadwiga Staniszkis, *The Ontology of Socialism*, ed. and trans. Peggy Watson (Oxford: Oxford University Press, 1992), 10–11. Translation slightly modified.

35. Kornai, "Economics and Psychology," in *Contradictions*, 69.

36. Amartya Sen, *Reason before Identity: The Romances Lecture for 1998* (Oxford: Oxford University Press, 1999), 2.

37. János Kornai, *The Socialist System: The Political Economy of Communism* (Princeton, N.J.: Princeton University Press, 1992), 91.

38. Kornai, "Efficiency and the Principles of Socialist Ethics," in *Contradictions*, 137.

39. Kornai, *Anti-Equilibrium*, 312.

40. Karl Marx, *Grundrisse*, in *Karl Marx: Selected Writings*, ed. David McLellan (Oxford: Oxford University Press, 1977), 362.

41. Ibid., 363.

42. Ibid., 364.

43. Marx, *Theories of Surplus Value*, in *Selected Writings*, 412.

44. Marx, *Gundrisse*, in *Selected Writings*, 364.

45. Ernest Mandel, introduction to Karl Marx, *Capital*, vol. 1, trans. Ben Fowkes (New York: Vintage, 1977), 84.

46. John Rajchman and Cornell West, eds., *Post-Analytic Philosophy* (New York: Columbia University Press, 1985).

47. Willard Van Orman Quine, "Two Dogmas of Empiricism," in *From a Logical Point of View*, 2nd ed. (Cambridge, Mass.: Harvard University Press, 1961), 41.

48. Ibid., 26.

49. Ibid., 42–43.

50. John Rawls considers "reflective equilibrium" necessary for good judgment. John Rawls, *Theory of Justice* (Cambridge, Mass.: Harvard University Press, 1971), 48–51; John Rawls, *Political Liberalism* (New York: Columbia University Press, 1996), 8. Meanwhile, Martha Nussbaum supplements "reflective equilibrium" with "perceptive equilibrium," emphasizing empirical observation of particulars rather than logical reflection on categories. Martha Nussbaum, "Perceptive Equilibrium: Literary Theory and Ethical Theory," in *Love's Knowledge* (Oxford: Oxford University Press, 1990), 168–94. In liberal moral philosophy, too, there is no unique equilibrium.

51. Peirce, "The Regenerated Logic," in *Collected Papers*, vol. 3, para. 434.

52. T. C. Koopmans and John M. Montias, "On the Description and Comparison of Economic Systems," in *Comparison of Economic Systems*, ed. Alexander Eckstein (Berkeley: University of California Press, 1971), 28.

53. See John M. Montias, "Planning with Material Balances in Soviet-type Economies," *American Economic Review* 49 (1959): 963–85.

54. William Shakespeare, *Troilus and Cressida*, act 3, scene 3, http://www.gutenberg.org/etext/1790.

55. Otto Neurath, *Modern Man in the Making* (New York: Knopf, 1939), 7–8.

56. Jonathan Swift, *Gulliver's Travels*, part 3, chap. 5, http://www.gutenberg.org/etext/829.

III

DECONSTRUCTION/POLITICS

Deconstruction and Experience: The Politics of the Undeconstructable

ROLAND VÉGSŐ

LEFT OF BEING

The question I want to raise concerns the possibility of a leftist ontology from the perspective of deconstruction. The difficulty of the question, of course, lies in the fact that it is not entirely clear whether such a theoretical object is possible to conceive from this perspective. As an introduction, therefore, let us briefly examine a few leftist critiques of Derrida's philosophy that, in spite of their striking political and philosophical differences, share a concern for a set of recurrent motives. What is common to the criticisms of deconstruction made by Michael Hardt and Antonio Negri, Slavoj Žižek, and Ernesto Laclau is that they all concede a limited usefulness to the deconstruction of sedimented discursive formations but at the same time claim that deconstruction does not go far enough in establishing the theoretical foundations of the subject of politics. From a leftist perspective, it appears that something is missing in the deconstructive critique of metaphysics (and classical ontology) that would allow us to break out of the interminable cycle of political critique to accomplish a genuine political act. Without evaluating the ongoing dialogue among these theoreticians, what I want to do here is briefly examine the way deconstruction appears in their respective systems. This introduction will show that on the one hand, the question of politics needs to be addressed in terms of the relation of phenomenology and ontology, and on the other hand, what appears to be missing in deconstructive thought is a more exhaustive reflection on what remains undeconstructable in every situation.

Antonio Negri concludes his reading of *Specters of Marx* with the claim that Derrida moves from a "correct phenomenology" of spectrality to an "inadequate" (theological) ontology of postindustrial capitalism.[1] Negri asserts that spectrality today is an everyday experience—it is the very reality of global capitalism that does not wait for a philosophical articulation. As a result, Negri speaks of *"a common experience of spectrality as clear as the sun."*[2] Thus, if Negri acknowledges the phenomenological correctness of deconstructive analysis but rejects its ontological conclusions, he accepts the phenomenology of spectrality but criticizes ontology as hauntology. Let us then examine the relation of phenomenology and ontology in Negri's criticism in some more detail:

> Derrida is prisoner of the ontology he critiques. When phenomenology changes, he uses it to criticize the horizon of Marxian ontology, and rightly so—but he does so in an inconsequential manner, refusing to change the ontology itself or to reconstruct it according to the standard set by the phenomenological change. He doesn't want to see its occurrence beginning with the spectral and hybrid figures which today, in the age of postindustrial capitalism, produce wealth and reality (and which Derrida nevertheless defines with great care); he therefore does not want to see a movement of ontological constitution and/or the production of subjectivity.[3]

As we can see, Derrida's alleged philosophical mistake is inscribed in a historical scheme and involves an unjustified reversal. Negri suggests that we can speak of a historical change within the very phenomenality of capital. The problem is that Derrida's analysis of the phenomenological change is not followed by a corresponding reflection on the ontological change that lies at its roots. In other words, Negri claims that Derrida uses a phenomenological change to criticize an outdated Marxist ontology, without an attempt to reconstruct ontology according to the logic of the very same change. For Negri, rather than being an emancipatory excess within closed ontological structures (which is the outdated model of the relation of spectrality to ontology), spectrality is actually the very logic of postindustrial capital (and not that of a resistance to it). But if the latter is true, as Negri argues, we need a "new—post-deconstructive—ontology"[4] that would allow us to move beyond the universal terrain of spectrality.[5]

Derrida remains "prisoner of the ontology he critiques" because for Negri, deconstruction is a transcendental philosophy unable to grasp the full significance of immanence. As is well known, for Hardt and Negri, transcendental thought is the ideological product of modern capitalism and is no longer viable in the postmodern age.[6] To use the terms of the ontology outlined in *Empire*, we could say that Negri's objection is that although Derrida potentially has an ontology of Empire, he does not have an ontology of the multitude. That is, there is no theory of the subject of politics (a theory of the "movement of ontological constitution and/or the production of subjectivity") in deconstruction. As a result, Hardt and Negri acknowledge the limited usefulness of deconstruction for the analysis of the discursive structures of Empire, but they also argue that there is a necessary move beyond deconstruction toward the construction of "an effective social, political alternative [to Empire], a new constituent power."[7]

Already in his first book, *The Sublime Object of Ideology*, Slavoj Žižek criticized Derrida and poststructuralism in similar terms when he argued that there is a necessary move beyond the mere deconstruction of ideology. In effect, he argued that deconstruction cannot go beyond the logic of interpellation because its theory of the subject is trapped within the field of imaginary and symbolic identifications. The critique of ideology, however, has to have two distinct levels of analysis: "one is *discursive*, the 'symptomal reading' of the ideological text bringing about the 'deconstruction' of the spontaneous experience of its meaning."[8] But there is another level beyond the deconstruction of ideology that "aims at extracting the kernel of enjoyment, at articulating the way in which—beyond the field of meaning but at the same time internal to it—an ideology, implies, manipulates, produces a pre-ideological enjoyment structured in fantasy."[9] According to Žižek, this inadequate theory of the subject leads to the Hegelian "bad infinity" of an inconsequential political critique that cannot theoretically found the possibility of a move beyond the logic of infinite deferment (metonymic substitutions) by way of an authentic political act (metaphoric cut). This is why, as Žižek insists, "psychoanalysis as a truth-experience" cannot be dismissed as a mere "metaphysics of presence," because it provides the only possible theoretical ground for political action.[10]

At this point, however, we should also consider Ernesto Laclau's reading of deconstruction, which runs parallel with his simultaneous critique of Hardt and Negri as well as Žižek. In the conclusion of his latest book, *On Populist Reason*, Laclau rejects both the politics of full immanence (Hardt and Negri) and the attempt to found politics on an ontologically transcendent instance of determination (Žižek). In place of these, he proposes the category of "failed transcendence."[11] In the background of this debate, however, we find the impulse to apply a deconstructive ontological insight even more consistently then it was done by Derrida. In this respect, Laclau does reveal some affinity with deconstruction because this theory of "failed transcendence" appears to be an interpretation of the Derridean notion of

"contamination" (in this case, the mutual contamination of the transcendental and the immanent). Laclau has always welcomed the deconstructive
critique of ontology for introducing the idea of radical undecidability,
which significantly expanded the possible terrain of political action. At
the same time, however, he also criticized Derrida for not theorizing the
way decisions are made on this undecidable terrain.[12] Thus, Laclau moves
on to a critique of deconstruction when he insists that there is no necessary move from radical undecidability to an ethical injunction. To put it
differently, in order for deconstruction to remain consistent, hauntology
cannot have a normative ethical content.

As we can see, Laclau also argued that there is no theory of the subject
of politics in Derrida's works, but he categorically rejected the alternative
offered by Hardt and Negri because, for him, full immanence cannot explain the emergence of the political subject. Laclau criticizes Hardt and
Negri because they do not have a theory of articulation that on the one
hand leads to the supposedly spontaneous emergence of the multitude as
the subject of politics, and on the other hand amounts to the disavowal
of the very possibility of politics.[13] This also means that for Laclau, Negri's
critique of deconstruction is based on an illegitimate move from the phenomenology of spectrality to an ontology of subjectivity. On the other hand,
while Laclau accepts Žižek's Lacanian theory of the subject, he criticizes him
for his "eclectic" ontology that inconsistently mixes psychoanalysis with a
Hegelian philosophy of history. As Laclau argues, Žižek reduces political
ontology to an a priori given determination that delimits the possible field
of hegemonic operation and thereby establishes the field of a Hegelian type
of logical immanence.[14] As a result, Žižek cannot account for the emergence of the historical subject of the global anticapitalist struggle.

Although a detailed analysis of these conflicting theoretical positions
would no doubt show us a more refined picture of their disagreements, the
summary outline of this debate at least establishes the fundamental ontological coordinates of a leftist confrontation with deconstruction. We encounter here the three paradigmatic positions from which any ontology
can be taken to task: immanence, transcendence, and their contamination.
(Of course, we should also note that leftist politics is apparently compatible with any of these three fundamental positions.) For a philosophy of full
immanence, then, deconstruction is a phenomenology whose ontological
presuppositions (to the degree that they remain transcendental) cut it off
from the possibility of a practical engagement of objectivity. For a philosophy of transcendence, on the other hand, it appears that deconstruction
gives up precisely that exceptional instance of transcendental determination

that would allow it to break out of the logic of infinite deferral to establish the only possible point of reference for political action. Finally, from the perspective of failed transcendence, deconstruction appears to be based on a correct ontological insight (that of a radical undecidability that inhabits the terrain of the mutual contamination of the immanent and the transcendental), but it tends toward an inconsistent application of this insight because it cannot give it a properly political articulation.

Thus, we can see that the common theme running through these analyses concerns the limits of deconstruction (both in the sense of its limitations and the fundamental presuppositions that render it possible). Regardless of whether we locate it on the level of immanence, transcendence, or failed transcendence, what better name could be given to this limit than the *undeconstructable?* In other words, the leftist critique of the limits of deconstruction calls for a more precise articulation of the position of the undeconstructable within deconstruction. So if one of the major problems with deconstruction is that it does not sufficiently theorize the subject of politics, the problem we need to address here is the possibility of constituting a political subject from the experience of spectrality based on a more consistent articulation of the undeconstructable.

By framing the problem of a leftist ontology in these terms, I want to address the recent critical interest in the category of experience as it functions in Derrida's works.[15] On the one hand, we have to insist that in spite of what Derrida's earlier readers claimed, deconstruction does not amount to a full rejection of experience. Along with the critique of metaphysical definitions of experience, another positive notion of experience also emerged in Derrida's works. On the other hand, still in opposition to earlier definitions, we have to explicate this deconstructed notion of experience as precisely such: as a real experience. A more intensive examination of the role of experience in deconstruction is a quintessential exercise if we want to understand the political and philosophical significance of deconstruction.[16] Otherwise, this elusive concept might prove to be a crucial blind spot for deconstructive thought. My main objection to currently dominant interpretations of the Derridean "impossible experience of aporia" is that they effectively reduce it to a simple lack of experience rather than understand it as a kind of experience.

DECONSTRUCTION AS EXPERIENCE

For Derrida, one of the privileged names of the undeconstructable is "the promise." Therefore, the promise is also one of the key categories for the revaluation of the Derridean notion of experience because it functions simultaneously as a fundamental ontological structure and the basic form of the political.[17] So let us consider the following question: What exactly is the promise for Derrida? As he makes it quite clear, the answer is to be sought *"at the point of intersection"* of two different theoretical traditions, "speech act theory and the onto-phenomenology of temporal or historical existence."[18] Derrida expands the meaning of the promise in both registers through a certain universalization of the promise: as a response to speech act theory, he identifies the promise as a general function of language (rather than one particular speech act), whereas in the case of the ontophenomenology of temporal existence, he calls it "a universal structure of experience."[19] As a result of this expansion of meaning (which evacuates its semantic field in order to turn it into the name or ontic metaphor of something that has no name), the promise is no longer to be understood as a linguistic reference to a future present that, by analogy, relegates historicality to the register of a horizon of expectation. Rather, what is at stake here is the elaboration of a theoretical problem that attempts to grasp the promise as the possibility of language as well as the very temporality and historicality of being.

Thus, the formulaic definition that emerges at this intersection is that for Derrida the promise is the experience of the conditions of experience. Immediately, two observations are necessary. First, this definition clearly demonstrates that the promise is primarily an experience and only secondarily a reference to the speech act we all recognize as a promise. In fact, the interesting point for Derrida is that the experience of the promise is always in excess of the speech act. Second, we must emphasize that the conditions of experience are not to be understood in terms of a transcendental subject. Rather, as Paola Marrati puts it, the point is that "the conditions of possibility of experience do not actually precede it."[20] This is why we can say that the promise is internal to experience: it names the way these conditions manifest themselves on the same level as what they make possible. Furthermore, we can also see how the problem of language appears in this problematic. It is important to emphasize that on this level of Derrida's thought, the category of writing simply names the internal inconsistency of experience. It merely refers to the dark hole at the heart of experience that is prior to language. In this sense, the category of the promise serves to name both the conditions of experience as they appear in experience and the conditions of language as they appear in language.[21] This duplicity, however, explains why the status of the promise in deconstruction oscillates between that of a structure and that of an event: the promise is the event of the manifestation of a structural necessity within the field that this structure renders possible.

I will emphasize here the phenomenological origins of deconstruction because I want to argue that the question of the promise itself must be inscribed in the very same problematic.[22] What should be striking for all readers of Derrida's texts, especially in the case of the later texts, is the insistence of the term that keeps reappearing in what we could consider crucial passages of Derrida's arguments. Whenever these arguments reach a point where a definition, or at least the site of a definition, announces itself, the term *experience* appears to mark the basic register within which the given concepts are to be located. Such is the fate of an increasing number of the central categories of deconstruction. The promise, mourning, freedom, friendship, justice, the messianic, aporia, and even deconstruction itself are defined as experiences. It is so much more interesting that the common horizon of all these terms is a certain thought of experience, given the fact that in these texts, we usually do not get an extensive elaboration (or a definition of the deconstructive usage) of this very term. Rather, this definition is dispersed over the Derridean corpus and should be located in Derrida's critique of phenomenology. But besides the actual content of this definition, what is of utmost importance is the status of the term *experience* in deconstruction. As we can see, it is not simply one concept among others, but rather the common denominator of deconstructive conceptuality. Deconstruction redefines philosophical concepts to the degree that it successfully articulates them as experiences. This move is significant because it shows us how deconstruction relates to its extraphilosophical outside (an experience that is not quite a philosophical concept). In other words, it allows us to start explaining how the deconstruction of experience gently turns into the experience of deconstruction.

Before going any further, we have to point out that the theoretical proximity of *experience* and *aporia* is not just a coincidence. Derrida starts with the etymological connection between the two terms and explains that whereas the word *experience* refers to a "passage, traversal, endurance, and rite of passage, but can be a traversal without line and without indivisible border," *aporia* names the exact opposite, "the difficult or impracticable, here the impossible, passage, the refused, denied, or prohibited passage, indeed the nonpassage."[23] In the passage of experience, the aporia marks the moment when the impossibility of further passage, rather than itself persisting as "a passing, a traversing or a transiting," gives way to a "coming to pass" or an advent that presupposes hospitality and the responsibility of a letting-to-come.[24] This moment of blockage and opening is the impossible experience in which radical alterity announces itself. Thus, the aporia is a figure of negativity, but its negative form has to be distinguished from other such figures of philosophy: "it is neither an 'apparent or illusory' antinomy, not a dialectizable contradiction in the Hegelian or Marxist sense, nor even a 'transcendental illusion in a dialectic of the Kantian type,' but instead *an interminable experience*."[25] The two most significant consequences of this definition are that the aporia is no longer a logical problem but an experience, and as such, it is not completely external to experience. As Derrida explains, this internal negativity of experience that opens it up to radical alterity immediately refers us to the level of conditions: "The affirmation that announced itself through the negative form [of the aporia] was therefore the necessity of *experience* itself, the experience of the aporia (and these two words that tell of the passage and the nonpassage are thereby coupled in an aporetic fashion)."[26]

Let us move now from this internal blockage of experience to the problem of the speech act. It might not be immediately obvious, but Derrida's critique of speech act theory is also essentially a reflection on experience. We have to remember that writing as a central category of deconstruction is first introduced in *Edmund Husserl's Origin of Geometry*, where Derrida analyzes the way the possibility of language (or "language in general" but "not the factuality of languages") serves as the condition of possibility of all ideality in Husserl's text.[27] According to Husserl, the special role of writing is that by delivering sense and truth from all empirical subjectivity or a particular community, it functions as the very condition of transcendental subjectivity.[28] Needless to say, Derrida's point will be that this condition of possibility is also a condition of impossibility. What he will try to show, for example, in *Speech and Phenomena*, is that for phenomenology, "the form of all experience is the present: I know with absolute certainty that the universal form of all experience *(Erlebnis)*, and therefore all life, has always been and will always be the *present*."[29] In other words, Derrida criticized Husserl for anchoring the immediacy of experience, its identity to itself, in the living present without the detour of signification. And this is the problematic behind Derrida's engagement of speech act theory as well. For example, in "Signature, Event, Context," we read:

> This structural possibility of being weaned from the referent or from the signified (hence from communication and from its context) seems to me to make every mark, including those which are oral, a grapheme in general;

which is to say, as we have seen, the nonpresent remainder [restance] of a differential mark cut off from its putative "production" or origin. And I shall even extend this law to all "experience" in general if it is conceded that there is no experience consisting of *pure* presence but only of chains of differential marks.[30]

As we can see, the deconstruction of the phenomenology of lived experience forms the basis of the critique of speech act theory as well because the structure of signification is the very structure of experience. In the quoted passage, the internal failure of experience to constitute itself in the present is identical with the internal failure of the sign to bring together signifier and signified.

In relation to speech act theory, then, Derrida performs a double move: he foregrounds this internal failure of language and elevates the performative to a universal structure of language. Let us note that for Derrida the promise is not just a speech act among many others, but the name of a speech act that at the same time designates a general structure of language. In a certain sense, the promise is the speech act that also bears the burden of having to account for the very possibility of speech acts in general:

> It is not a question of a messianism that one could easily translate in Judaeo-Christian or Islamic terms, *but rather a messianic structure that belongs to all language.* There is no language without the performative dimension of the promise, the minute I open my mouth I am in the dimension of the promise. Even if I say that "I don't believe in truth" or whatever, the minute I open my mouth there is a "believe me" at work. Even when I lie, and perhaps especially when I lie, there is a "believe me" in play. And this "I promise you that I am speaking the truth" is a messianic apriori, a promise which, even if it is not kept, even if one knows that it cannot be kept, takes place and *qua* promise is messianic.[31]

In other words, if the promise names a universal structure of language, the universality of language is represented by one particular speech act. This general structure, however, is that of performativity. At the same time, the universalization of the performative dimension is also a way of indicating the impossibility of maintaining a rigorous distinction between the performative and the constative dimensions of language, because it implies that even in constative statements, a performative force is also at work. In the quoted passage, the promise is identified with the imperative "believe me" that refers us to "truth." As a result, there is no language without the messianic promise of truth. But in this definition, the mode of existence of truth is nothing else than its messianic promise. And last, inasmuch as this promise is referred to as a "messianic apriori," it unavoidably refers us to a transcendental dimension. As an a priori, it functions on the level of condition of possibilities, and besides being just a function of language, it becomes the performative condition of language itself.

The best way to summarize this critique would be to say that speech act theory is based on an insufficient confrontation with the condition of language (which lack can actually amount to the denial of this condition):

> Austin's procedure is rather remarkable and typical of that philosophical tradition with which he would like to have so few ties. It consists in recognizing that the possibility of the negative (in this case, of infelicities) is in fact a structural possibility, that failure is an essential risk of the operations under consideration; then, in a move which is almost *immediately simultaneous,* in the name of a kind of ideal regulation, it excludes that risk as accidental, exterior, one which teaches us nothing about the linguistic phenomenon being considered.[32]

The failure to incorporate the negative possibility into a theory of language means that a structural condition is reduced to an empirical accident alien to the very essence of language. To the degree that speech act theory is only concerned with "normal" uses of language, it cannot account for the whole of language.

The Derridean promise follows the logic of this reinscription of "the possibility of the negative" as the very condition of language. During the 1980s, Derrida continued his work on the promise in his *Mémoirs for Paul de Man* and *Of Spirit,* his readings of Paul de Man and Heidegger. The focal point of these engagements is de Man's parody of the Heideggerian dictum "Die Sprache spricht." De Man concludes the chapter devoted to Rousseau's *Social Contract* in *Allegories of Reading* with the following statement: "Die Sprache verspricht (sich)."[33] The three meanings of this expression exploit the different meanings of the German term *das Versprechen,* which, simply put, simultaneously denotes promise and lapsus: (1) language promises: as soon as language speaks, it cannot escape promising (the universalization of the promise); (2) in this act of originary promising, language promises itself (truth is to be located on the level of the performative); (3) but as a *Ver-sprechen,* the promise of language is by definition a failure (the reinscription of the negative terms as a structural moment).

Thus, the promise is the originary failure that renders language possible in the first place.

The continuation of the same argument in *Of Spirit* demonstrates how the problem of the promise can be transposed to the terrain of ontology. Here, Derrida uses the promise to deconstruct a central category of Heideggerian ontology: essence. As Derrida points out, the historical narrative of Heidegger's ontology is based on an opposition of essence *(Wesen)* and the abandonment of this essence *(Verwesen)*. Here Derrida's reading of the promise *(Versprechen)* as the failure of language *(Ver-sprechen)* achieves the metaleptic reinscription of failure (in the form of *Verwesen*) into the very concept of essence *(Wesen)*. For Heidegger, the promise (as *Zuspruch*) is precisely the essence from which the corrupt generation *(verwesendes Geschlecht)* strays away in a historical process of "degeneration." Derrida, on the other hand, by analyzing the aporia of the promise as something impossible yet inevitable, shows that this degeneration as straying away from the essence of the promise is a repetition of the *Verwesen* that makes the promise possible in the first place as *Ver-sprechen:* there is an originary *Verwesen* that constitutes essence in the first place. The failure of essence, therefore, is revealed to be more primary than essence itself.[34]

The reinscription of the negative term and the universalization of the performative dimension of language, however, redefine the promise in excess of the speech act. As a matter of fact, where the promise exceeds the speech act, it also moves beyond the performative. Speaking of the *arrivant*, Derrida writes: "It even exceeds the order of any *determinable* promise."[35] Or in slightly different terms, we could say that the event cannot be reduced to the domain of the performative: "It is too often said that the performative produces the event of which it speaks. To be sure. One must also realize that, inversely, where there is performative, an event worthy of the name cannot arrive."[36] Therefore, although the promise as performative only brings about its own ordinary event, the quasi-transcendental promise of the true event has to be beyond all determinable promises and the register of the performative. Anything that can be reduced to a determinable content in a speech act is already within the domain of the calculable and of knowledge, and therefore already an inauthentic mode of promising. The originary promise of the *à venir* (to come) is actually in violation of all determinable promises. What it announces will come as a surprise and prove all determinable promises wrong or at least insufficient.

Through this necessary move beyond the performative, we can see why in deconstruction we alternate or, to use Derrida's term, "oscillate" between two registers. The event of the promise consists of a performative bringing about as well as an "awaiting without a horizon" of a pure self-exposure to otherness: "The 'to' of the 'to come' wavers between imperative injunction (call of performative) and the patient *perhaps* of messianicity (nonperformative exposure to what comes, to what can always not come or has already come)."[37] And, Derrida adds, "This undecidability is, like freedom itself, granted by democracy, and it constitutes, I continue to believe, the only radical possibility of deciding and of making come about (performatively), or rather of letting come about (metaperformatively), and thus of thinking *what* comes or happens and *who* happens by, the arriving of whoever arrives. It thus already opens, for whomever, an experience of freedom."[38] Although the affirmative passivity of an awaiting and the performative activity of bringing about are inseparable, in the move beyond the "making come about," the "letting coming about" will triumph as the final condition of the experience of freedom.[39]

The underlying motive of Derrida's engagements of ontophenomenology is therefore the problem of difference and its critique through contamination. Derrida's critique of transcendental phenomenology is essentially a critique of the phenomenological difference that supposedly separates the transcendental and the empirical in an absolute manner. It is very important to locate the promise at this level of analysis because the contamination of the empirical and transcendental is one of the most basic theoretical components of deconstruction.[40] In the case of Heideggerian fundamental ontology, on the other hand, Derrida criticizes the very category of ontological difference, the absolute separation of the ontological and the ontic, and the concomitant philosophical and political project of the recovery of an authentic and originary temporality. Already in his texts elaborating the quasi-concept of *différance*, Derrida made it clear that the critique of ontology will involve a rearticulation of the very thought of difference. Furthermore, even in the case of speech act theory, it is again an absolute difference, the impermeable frontier separating the constative and the performative, that will be submitted to a theoretical reformulation. Thus, the transcendental terrain cannot be imagined as autonomous field founding experience, but neither can the empirical be reduced to that of a full immanence; and the ontological description of order cannot be the source of a logical deduction of an authentic mode of being in the world.

As Paola Marrati has suggested, Derrida's work stages a confrontation between Husserl's phenomenology and Heidegger's ontology: "It is not by chance that Derrida plays the question of ontology off against Husserl and, at the same time, holds onto the question of the transcendental and the empirical in order to demonstrate their irreducible contamination instead of following Heidegger and simply allowing this question to drop."[41] Derrida's primary purpose is to deconstruct the ultimate foundation of Husserlian phenomenology, the self-presence of the transcendental subject in the present. In order to achieve this goal, in his early texts, he criticized Husserl for failing to ground his phenomenology on an ontology of time. For example, just to cite one example, Derrida claims that Husserl failed to recognize that the *eidos* of time itself must have a temporal structure: although Husserl investigates the sense of time, he fails to take into consideration the temporality of sense. Therefore, constituting lived experience on the level of the transcendental subject cannot be easily separated from the constituted experience of the world. On the basis of this temporal dimension of the self-constitution of the subject, Derrida introduces the thought of finitude into the phenomenological project. But as Marrati claims, by simultaneously deconstructing and maintaining the transcendental/empirical distinction, Derrida can formulate a critique of the Heideggerian project as well. The contamination of the transcendental and the empirical translates into the "*contamination* of life and death disallowed by Heidegger's notion of Dasein in its 'ownmost being-toward-death.'"[42] Thus, although Derrida identifies an internal limit within the philosophical project of phenomenology and proves that it cannot be the self-founding science it aspires to be, the reference to ontology as a possible foundation is also rejected because the autonomous closure of the field of fundamental ontology is equally impossible. In a certain sense, the very division between phenomenology and ontology is deconstructed by Derrida.

The problems of experience and the promise, therefore, also raise questions about the possibility of philosophy. To illustrate this problem, I will refer here to Derrida's reading of the role of *khōra* in Plato's *Timaeus*. Derrida identifies in the figure of *khōra* a reflection on the origin that will necessarily remain heterogeneous to the field it institutes. *Khōra* is the third genus that founds the possibility of Platonic ontology, yet remains exterior to the opposition of its basic categories, the intelligible (the idea) and the sensible (the mimemes). Hence its difficult status, because it escapes all ontological domestication: it is a structure without an essence, the very anachronism of being, beyond all determination. Although it is outside the field of ontology (and therefore a nonbeing), it receives all possible determinations without appropriating them in order to give place to these determinations. *Khōra* thus becomes the foundation of spatiality that gives place without taking place. In other words, it is "no longer subject to the law of the very thing which it *situates*."[43] Inasmuch as it raises basic questions about the meaning of Platonic philosophy, it also raises the question of the foundation of philosophy. For the discourse on *khōra* is considered to be a bastardized philosophy that had to leave its proper place and had to go outside itself: "Philosophy cannot speak philosophically of that which looks like its 'mother,' its 'nurse,' its 'receptacle,' or its 'imprint bearer.'"[44] Therefore, Derrida's conclusion is that in Plato, the "discourse on *khōra* plays for philosophy a role analogous to the role which *khōra* 'herself' plays for that which philosophy speaks of, namely the cosmos formed or given form according to the paradigm."[45] The internal distortion of philosophy as it tries to confront the alterity of its own foundation is analogous to the way an extraphilosophical reality is maintained by an origin. Thus, the deconstruction of experience and the deconstruction of philosophy meet here—and this is precisely the point where it becomes possible to thematize the experience of deconstruction.

Although deconstruction as a philosophy and an unending critique is the irreducible insistence on the temporalization of all spatial formations (that is, the insistence on the necessary heteronomy of all discourses), it is very much aware of the fact that it cannot place itself outside this critique. Hence, instead of a general assertion of its universal applicability, it provides reflections on the very limits of deconstruction. This limit, as the moment of heteronomy in deconstructive discourse, is actually the undeconstructable condition of deconstruction: justice as an experience of the promise (deconstruction is limited by what makes it possible). We encounter here an extraphilosophical (and extradeconstructive) experience that remains external to the field it institutes. This is why we have to discover the structure of a speculative infinite judgment in Derrida's claim that "Deconstruction is justice"[46] (which statement now functions as the deconstructive version of the Hegelian judgment "The Spirit is a bone"): the subject and the predicate are separated by a barrier of otherness, a radical heterogeneity, that mediates their identity. But if deconstruction is justice, what makes deconstruction the exceptional case is that it claims to coincide fully with the moment of its very own heteronomy. We are dealing with a philosophy that coincides with (or in an ideal case, at least, becomes) the experience it sets out to theorize. Deconstruction coincides with its very condition, its extraphilosophical outside. This coincidence is a necessary condition for maintaining deconstruction in the register of the impossible as that which cannot be reduced to a set of rules and a reproducible technique. Both on the level of philosophical discourse and "that which philosophy speaks of," the promise of deconstruction is the undeconstructable.

THE PROMISE OF DEMOCRACY AND THE POLITICS OF THE UNDECONSTRUCTABLE

Within the field of politics, the experience of the undeconstructable is theorized by Derrida under the name "democracy to come." For us, the most important thing about this democracy to come is that it is an experience (and not a particular system of social organization). Therefore, it combines three quintessential motives whose relation we need to examine in more detail: an undeconstructable experience, the promise, and democracy. Let us start with the following often-quoted passage from *Specters of Marx:*

> Well, what remains irreducible to any deconstruction, what remains as undeconstructible as the possibility itself of deconstruction is, perhaps, a certain experience of the emancipatory promise; it is perhaps even the formality of a structural messianism, a messianism without religion, even a messianic without messianism, an idea of justice—which we distinguish from law or right and even from human rights—and an idea of democracy—which we distinguish from its current concept and from its determined predicates today.[47]

The problem of democracy, therefore, involves the same logic that we encountered in the case of the promise, according to which one particular element of a field simultaneously names the condition of the field and its principle of transcendence. In the case of the promise, we found the following: first, a negative category is reinscribed as a condition of impossibility (the promise as *Ver-sprechen* is the condition of language); then, this condition is identified with one of the elements of the field it establishes (the promise as a speech act); finally, the promise is redefined in excess of the particular element (the promise as unconditional openness toward alterity). In Derrida's discussions of democracy, this logic is played out in the following terms: first, the lack of foundation is reinscribed as a condition of politics (the aporetic structure of democracy is the very condition of politics); then this foundation is identified with one particular political formation (democracy as a determinate historical system); and finally democracy is redefined in excess of actual democracies (democracy as the name of unconditional hospitality).

Democracy to come, therefore, functions as the very condition of politics. This is why Derrida calls it "the *khôra* of the political."[48] In this sense, it gives place to politics without being identical to what it renders possible. In an interview with Giovanna Borradori, Derrida explains that he is well aware of the fact that unconditional hospitality is an impracticable political program (because "no state can write it into its laws"), but it is nevertheless a necessary philosophical concept: "Unconditional hospitality, which is neither juridical nor political, is nonetheless the condition of the political and the juridical."[49] The ontological opening to radical alterity is thus the necessary but impossible condition of politics. This is why the status of democracy (as a historical formation) is exemplary, since it historically marked the first institutionalization of a constitutive impossibility:

> Democracy is the only system, the only constitutional paradigm, in which, in principle one has or assumes for oneself the right to criticize everything publicly, including the idea of democracy, its concept, its history, and its name. Including the idea of the constitutional paradigm and the absolute authority of law. It is thus the only paradigm that is universalizable, whence its chance and its fragility. But in order for this historicity—unique among all political systems—to be complete, it must be freed not only from the Idea in the Kantian sense but from all teleology, all onto-theo-teleology.[50]

The problem I want to highlight here is that of universalization. Once again, a particular element of a field is universalized and reinscribed as a negative condition. Democracy, as a particular political formation, is the only universalizable paradigm because it is capable of turning its own foundational principle against itself. In other words, it is capable of applying the democratic principle of doubt to democracy itself. This possibility reveals the aporetic structure of democracy: "democracy will never exist, in the sense of a present existence: not because it will be deferred but because it will always remain aporetic in structure."[51] The exemplarity and universality of democracy is therefore paradoxical because it is the universality of the impossibility of society, and thus it is the universality of the impossibility of a stable or final universality.

As a result of this aporetic structure, democracy to come will always be in excess of actual democracies. This is why Derrida is careful to distance the self-deconstruction of democracy from antidemocratic politics. In *Politics of Friendship*, for example, he argues that rather than an antidemocratic attack, democratic self-deconstruction is the very essence of democracy:

one keeps this indefinite right to the question, to criticism, to deconstruction (guaranteed rights, in principle, in any democracy: no deconstruction without democracy, no democracy without deconstruction). One keeps this right strategically to mark what is no longer a strategic affair: the limit between the conditional [. . .] and the unconditional which, from the outset, will have inscribed a self-deconstructive force in the very motif of democracy, the possibility and the duty for democracy itself to de-limit itself. Democracy is the *autos* of deconstructive self-delimitation.[52]

Here, democracy and deconstruction designate each other's limits. Similarly to deconstruction, democracy has to be theorized on the basis of its own internal limit. But the universality of democracy is the universality of deconstruction as self-deconstruction. As a result, deconstruction becomes properly political (and properly democratic) at the moment when it delimits its own operation (and not when it simply gives free rein to this operation). We find that democracy is a condition of deconstruction ("no deconstruction without democracy"), which in turn also marks a structural limit of democracy ("no democracy without deconstruction"). To paraphrase: the self-delimitation of democracy is deconstructive in nature, while the self-delimitation of deconstruction is essentially democratic. It is the articulation of its own internal limit that renders deconstruction possible in the first place.

But Derrida's insistence that this democracy to come must be severed from our fantasies of the future and tied to the here and now also shows that it is to be located on the level of an experience. To call it an "impossible experience," however, is not a simple negation of its relation to experience: "This im-possible is not privative. It is not the inaccessible, and it is not what I can indefinitely defer: it announces itself, sweeps down upon me, precedes me, and seizes me *here and now* in a nonvirtualizable way, in actuality and not potentiality. [. . .] This im-possible is thus not a (regulative) *idea* or *ideal*. It is what is most undeniably *real*. And sensible."[53] Interestingly, these last words locate democracy to come, temporally in the here and now, and ontologically on the side of the real and the sensible. It is given a phenomenal form even if it is without content (as it announces nothing). Derrida actually calls it an "aporia-affect," thereby suggesting that its strange phenomenality is that of an affect.[54] It is in this sense that we can claim that the self-deconstruction of democracy and the self-delimitation of deconstruction supposedly lead to an undeconstructable experience.

The politics of deconstruction, then, is a politics of experience that cannot be reduced either to the celebration of the authenticity of lived experience or to the critical position that experience is always only a construction. Rather, as we have seen, Derrida's point is that in spite of the fact that experience can never be reduced to a presence, there is always something essentially undeconstructable in experience (the experience of justice). This tension between the always deconstructable presence of experience and the undeconstructable experience of justice shows that from an ethicopolitical point of view, a mere deconstruction of experience in itself is not sufficient if it does not lead to another experience. Consequently, the privileged moment for Derrida is the undeconstructable experience and not the mere act of deconstruction. To avoid the pitfalls of a "wild deconstruction" of the text of the world, the politics of deconstruction must be articulated in relation to the undeconstructable.

We could paraphrase this last statement in the following way: by setting its own limits, the fundamental political task of deconstruction is always the primary establishment of the field of its own operation. This reversal of perspective (which involves a shift of emphasis from deconstruction to the undeconstructable) also entails that the crucial problem for deconstruction is not necessarily the question of what can still be deconstructed in a given situation. In fact, the most significant question concerns the impossibility of deconstruction: What is it that need not or cannot be deconstructed anymore? The answer to this question will always be split between two different levels: the structural position of undeconstructability and the particular objects occupying this position. As we can see, there is always a minimal distance between the structural position of undeconstructability and what remains or is declared to be undeconstructable in a particular situation. This minimal distance introduces a crucial political dimension to deconstruction because it functions as the locale of the articulation of deconstruction's internal limit that renders it possible in the first place.

Thus, we have to conclude that for Derrida, the subject of politics is constituted by an undeconstructable experience. But if we take this logic a step further, we can also see that this subject is at the same time constituted by the experience of the limit of deconstruction. As a result, according to the very logic of deconstruction, the subject begins where deconstruction ends because the authentic subject of justice can only emerge where deconstruction is no longer possible. The necessary shift from the subject of deconstruction to the undeconstructable subject also demonstrates the theoretical possibility of a deconstructive theory of the subject that would not be based merely on the infinite possibility of deconstruction but pre-cisely on the interruption of the endless deconstruction of a self-present subject. Even if this theory does not yet exist, its outlines are readable within the Derridean corpus. And what these dim shapes suggest is not only that such a theory is possible, but that it is also necessary.

So what can we conclude about the possibility of a leftist ontology from the perspective of the politics of the undeconstructable? First, a consistent application of deconstruction demands that we question the possibility of a leftist ontology. Because one of the basic insights of deconstruction is that the primary ontological terrain of the constitution of subjectivity is that of radical undecidability, it is impossible to found politics on an ontol-ogy. Here we should remember Laclau's point: "Undecidability should be literally taken as that condition from which no course of action necessarily follows."[55] That is, there is no logical move from radical undecidability to a leftist politics. This is why deconstructionist ontology (or hauntology) can-not be inherently leftist. Of course, it can be used for leftist purposes, but that use must be determined on a normative and not on an ontological level.

Second, as we have seen, a common leftist objection to deconstruction holds that the mere process of deconstruction provides no basis for the emergence of a political subject. But the idea of the undeconstructable is potentially a theoretical site within deconstruction that could be used for such ends. The experience of spectrality can give way to an undeconstruct-able experience that could be the deconstructive foundation of the produc-tion of political subjectivity. Thus, within a deconstructionist framework, the fate of leftist politics depends on a particular articulation of the unde-constructable. Derrida's self-avowed leftism, therefore, makes sense, but not because this politics can be logically deduced from his critique of classical ontology. On the contrary, it makes sense precisely because such a move is impossible and therefore there is no necessary link between the emancipa-tory promise of justice and the structural position of the undeconstructable. What is leftist about Derrida is precisely the political (and not philosophical) attempt to identify the undeconstructable with emancipation.

NOTES

1. Antonio Negri, "The Specter's Smile," in *Ghostly Demarcations: A Symposium on Jacques Derrida's "Specters of Marx,"* ed. Michael Sprinker (London: Verso, 1999), 14.

2. Ibid., 9; emphasis in original.

3. Ibid., 12–13.

4. Ibid., 12.

5. Ibid., 13–14.

6. Michael Hardt and Antonio Negri, *Empire* (Cambridge, Mass.: Harvard University Press, 2000), 353–69.

7. Ibid., 47.

8. Slavoj Žižek, *The Sublime Object of Ideology* (London: Verso, 1989), 125.

9. Ibid.

10. Ibid., 154.

11. Ernesto Laclau, *On Populist Reason* (London: Verso, 2006), 239–44.

12. Ernesto Laclau, "Deconstruction, Pragmatism, Hegemony," in *Deconstruction and Pragmatism,* ed. Chantal Mouffe (London: Routledge, 1996), 47–68. See also Laclau's review of *Specters of Marx:* "Time Is Out of Joint," in *Emancipation(s)* (New York: Verso, 1996), 66–83.

13. Ernesto Laclau, "Can Immanence Explain Social Struggles?" *Diacritics* 31, no. 4 (Winter 2001): 7.

14. Laclau, *On Populist Reason,* 232–39.

15. For discussions of the role of "experience" in Derrida's works, see the following works: Peggy Kamuf, "Deconstruction as Experience," *Angelaki* 4, no. 3 (1999): 3–14; Zeynep Direk, "On the Sources and the Structure of Derrida's Radical Notion of Experience," *Tympanum: A Journal of Comparative Literary Studies* (2005) (http://www.usc.edu/dept/comp-lit/tympanum/4/khora.html); Rei Terada, *Feeling in Theory: Emotion after the "Death of the Subject"* (Cambridge: Cambridge University Press, 2001); David Wood, *Thinking after Heidegger* (Malden, Mass.: Blackwell, 2002). For general overviews, see Elizabeth Bellamy and Artemis Leontis's article, "A Genealogy of Experience: From Epistemology to Politics," *Yale Journal of Criticism* 6 (1993): 163–84; Craig Ireland's *The Subaltern Appeal to Experience: Self-Identity, Late Modernity, and the Politics of Immediacy* (Montreal: McGill-Queen's University Press, 2004); and Martin Jay's *Songs of Experience: Modern American and European Variations on a Universal Theme* (Berkeley: University of California Press, 2005). For other important contemporary discussions of the politics of experience, see also the following works: Giorgio Agamben, *Infancy and History: The Destruction of Experience,* trans. Liz Heron (London: Verso, 1993); Philippe Lacoue-Labarthe, *Poetry as Experience,* trans. Andrea Tarnowski (Stanford: Stanford University Press, 1999); Jean-Luc Nancy, *The Experience of Freedom,* trans. Bridget McDonald (Stanford: Stanford University Press, 1993).

16. Zeynep Direk, for example, opened her 2005 article, "On the Sources," with the following complaint: "So far, no reading of Derrida has privileged, in a philosophical way, the concept of 'experience.' As far as I know, the attempt has not been yet made to raise the question of why Derrida uses the concept of 'experience' so abundantly in his later works."

17. In his book, *Derrida and the Political* (London: Routledge, 1996), Richard Beardsworth also argued that at the heart of Derrida's understanding of politics, we find the category of the promise. Beardsworth points out that Derrida's interests in the promise, as it emerged in the late 1980s, was a "*refinement* of the initial elaboration of *différance* and trace" in his earlier writings (36). This is why he concludes that the promise "should be considered as the very law of contamination" (37). In a similar fashion, Leonard Lawlor argues that the promise is a continuation

of Derrida's early critique of phenomenology within an ethicopolitical register. See Lawlor, *Derrida and Husserl: The Basic Problem of Phenomenology* (Bloomington: Indiana University Press, 2002), 211–25.

18. Derrida, "Marx and Sons," in *Ghostly Demarcations: A Symposium on Jacques Derrida's "Specters of Marx,"* ed. Michael Sprinker (London: Verso, 1999), 251.

19. Ibid., 248.

20. Paola Marrati, *Genesis and Trace: Derrida Reading Husserl and Heidegger,* trans. Simon Sparks (Stanford: Stanford University Press, 2005), 175.

21. As Richard Beardsworth observed, "The event of the promise only takes place in that which it makes possible" (*Derrida and the Political,* 155).

22. The following works address Derrida's relationship to phenomenology: Marrati, *Genesis and Trace;* Leonard Lawlor, *Derrida and Husserl;* David Wood, *Thinking after Heidegger.* In order to illustrate the persistence of the phenomenological problematic in Derrida's works, we should also refer here to one of his last works, *On Touching—Jean-Luc Nancy,* trans. Christine Irizarry (Stanford: Stanford University Press, 2005).

23. Derrida, *Aporias,* trans. Thomas Dutoit (Stanford: Stanford University Press, 1993), 14–15, 8.

24. Ibid., 8.

25. Ibid., 16; emphasis added.

26. Ibid., 19; emphasis in original.

27. Derrida, *Edmund Husserl's Origin of Geometry: An Introduction,* trans. John P. Leavey Jr. (Lincoln: University of Nebraska Press, 1989), 66.

28. Ibid., 87–93.

29. Derrida, *Speech and Phenomena,* trans. David Allison (Evanston: Northwestern University Press, 1973), 53.

30. Derrida, *Limited Inc.,* ed. Gerald Graff, trans. Samuel Weber and Jeffrey Mehlman (Evanston: Northwestern University Press, 1988), 10.

31. Derrida, "Remarks on Deconstruction and Pragmatism," in *Deconstruction and Pragmatism,* ed. Chantal Mouffe (London: Routledge, 1996), 82. Emphasis added.

32. Ibid., 15.

33. Paul de Man, *Allegories of Reading: Figural Language in Rousseau, Nietzsche, Rilke, and Proust* (New Haven: Yale University Press, 1979), 277.

34. Derrida, *Of Spirit,* trans. Geoffrey Bennington and Rachel Bowlby (Chicago: University of Chicago Press, 1991), 94. As we can see here, the promise is also a reflection on historicality. For a more detailed discussion of the promise and history, see Derrida's *The Other Heading,* trans. Pascale-Anne Brault and Michael B. Naas (Bloomington: Indiana University Press, 1992); and "Force of Law: The 'Mystical Foundation of Authority,'" in *Deconstruction and the Possibility of Justice,* ed. Drucilla Cornell, Michael Rosenfeld, and David Gray Carlson (New York: Routledge, 1992), 3–67.

35. Derrida, *Aporias,* 34.

36. Derrida, *Without Alibi,* ed. and trans. Peggy Kamuf (Stanford: Stanford University Press, 2002), 234.

37. Derrida, "The Last of the Rogue States: The 'Democracy to Come,' Opening in Two Turns," *South Atlantic Quarterly* 103, no. 2–3 (2004): 336.

38. Ibid., 337.

39. In other words, the promise can be interpreted here on the three levels of foundation, exclusion, and return of the excluded: (1) the originary empty promise is the possibility of language; (2) the promise as a "normal" speech act is part of the system of exclusions as it excludes now the very condition (the originary promise); and (3) the event as the form of radical alterity is the return within language of the originary promise.

40. In *The Problem of Genesis in Husserl's Philosophy*, trans. Marian Hobson (1953–54; Chicago: University of Chicago Press, 2003), Derrida explains how a transcendental condition can have an empirical crisis and shows that crisis is an internal necessity of history. *Edmund Husserl's Origin of Geometry* (1967) is important for us because here Derrida introduces the problem of writing into his critique of phenomenological difference, and in *Speech and Phenomena* (1967), he explains this critique in terms of the trace.

41. Marrati, *Genesis and Trace*, 17.

42. Ibid., 17.

43. Derrida, *"khôra,"* in *On the Name*, ed. Thomas Dutoit, trans. David Wood, John P. Leavey Jr., and Ian McLeod (Stanford: Stanford University Press, 1995), 90; emphasis in original.

44. Ibid., 126.

45. Ibid.

46. Derrida, "Force of Law," 15.

47. Derrida, *Specters of Marx: The State of Debt, the Work of Mourning, and the New International*, trans. Peggy Kamuf (New York: Routledge, 1994), 59.

48. Derrida, "The Last of the Rogue States," 327.

49. Borradori, *Philosophy in a Time of Terror: Dialogues with Jürgen Habermas and Jacques Derrida* (Chicago: University of Chicago Press, 2003), 129.

50. Ibid., 332.

51. Ibid., 331.

52. Derrida, *Politics of Friendship*, trans. George Collins (New York: Verso, 1997), 105.

53. Ibid., 329.

54. Ibid., 327.

55. Laclau, "Time Is Out of Joint," 78.

8 Politics and the Fiction of the Political

SORIN RADU-CUCU

The main purpose of this essay is to determine the rapport between rhetoric and ontology in contemporary Left political thought and its relevance for a "philosophical questioning of the political."[1] By dealing with the concept of the political and its intersections with philosophy, my research will focus on the distinction between politics *(la politique)* and the political *(le politique)*, the main theoretical innovation of contemporary postfoundational thought.[2] According to Oliver Marchart,

> the difference between the new concept of the political and the conventional concept of politics . . . seems to indicate the crisis of the foundationalist paradigm (represented scientifically by such diverse species as economic determinism, behaviorism, positivism, sociologism).[3]

Thinking the political allows the break with the empiricist and positivist approach of political science and the creation of a theoretical inquiry of politics, either within the spirit of political philosophy (Claude Lefort), in relation to Heidegger's ontology (Jean-Luc Nancy and Philippe Lacoue-Labarthe), or in antagonism to the former (post-Marxist thinkers like Alain Badiou, Jacques Rancière, and, to some extent, Ernesto Laclau). While postfoundationalism is, according to Oliver Marchart and Jason Glynos,[4] a category generous enough to include philosophers or political theorists with radically different projects (most of them located on the Left), it needs to foreground, in my perspective, "the elaboration of a language providing us with metaphoric redescriptions of our social relations."[5] Examining the possible ways in which the political was distinguished from politics, the second part of my essay will present a critical view of Alain Badiou's antidemocratic position, and I argue for a postfoundational formula embedded in Ernesto Laclau and Chantal Mouffe's notion of radical democracy, the "deepening and extending the range of democratic practices through the creation of new subject positions within a democratic matrix."[6] After the end of the cold war and the failure of the real-existing socialism as the legitimating project of modernity, the affirmation of the postpolitical horizon of global capitalism becomes the new horizon for a necessary redefinition of democracy in ontological categories.

The activity of the Center for the Research of the Political organized by Jean-Luc Nancy and Philippe Lacoue-Labarthe (founded in November 1980 at the École Normale Supérieure) is the first intellectual scene to address the "retreat of the political," understood both in the sense of a withdrawal and that of retracing. This specific deconstructive strategy had been at the center of heated debates during an event that took place at Cérisy in the summer of the same year, the philosophical colloquium entitled "The Ends of Man: Spinoffs of the Work of Jacques Derrida." The issues discussed in the political seminar at Cérisy became the topic for the series of meetings organized under the center's umbrella. An introductory statement, published in *Retreating the Political,* clearly delineates the premises for instituting (both in the sense of organizing and of giving an institutional grounding) this place of investigation:

> Such an inquiry, the imperative nature of which needs no commentary, no doubt demands the construction of a new object and should not be confused either with a work of "political studies" or with an undertaking of "political philosophy." Philosophy there finds itself called into question; which, for all that, does not presuppose that one can substitute for it a positive (sociological, economical, technological) or normative (ethical, aesthetic—or "political") discourse. (105)

This *ouverture* does not bring about a program in the classical sense of the word. It rather articulates a necessary demand of a philosophical nature. By responding to this task (that is, the interrogation of the political), "philosophy itself is called into question." *To investigate* (Latin, *investigare*) means "to track" or "to trace out." Qua "free place of investigation," the Center for the Research of the Political is therefore the site instituted by the urgency of the following question: What is at stake, for philosophy or perhaps for deconstruction, at the end of philosophy in tracing out the political?

To formulate their position, Nancy and Lacoue-Labarthe return to Derrida's essay "The Ends of Man," first delivered at a conference in New York in 1968, where the political significance of philosophy was broached by Derrida's own insistence on marking, dating, and making known the "historical circumstances" in which he "prepared this communication."[7] Emphasizing the responsibility of thinking, a signature is added to this text, along with a date, referring to a particular historical moment. Derrida's gesture accounts for the philosophical discourse, right when it is delivered, to the reality of that instance, which no longer is simply *any* date, but a specific mark, with its meaning suspended. This suspension calls for two audiences: the participants to the 1968 philosophical colloquium on anthropology, and all the other readers of Derrida's text. In this respect, by speaking about an *end,* the end of *man,* Derrida also acknowledges the urgency of 1968, a year with such ambivalent historical significations: Vietnam is mentioned in Derrida's text, but one needs to remember the French political situation and also, with the same urgency, the Soviet invasion of Czechoslovakia.

As I have mentioned above, the late effects of the talk entitled "The Ends of Man" was the organization in Cérisy, in the summer of 1980, of the symposium borrowing the title of Derrida's text, "The Ends of Man: Spinoffs of the Work of Jacques Derrida." According to Nancy Fraser's rigorous study "The French Derrideans: Politicizing Deconstruction or Deconstructing the Political?" the political seminar organized at Cérisy was the long-awaited opportunity to address a set of questions about deconstruction and politics, issues to be taken on for discussion in the sessions sponsored by the Center for the Research of the Political (1980–84):

Does deconstruction have any political implications? Does it have any political significance beyond the byzantine and incestuous struggles it has provoked in American academic lit crit departments? Is it possible—and desirable—to articulate a deconstructive politics? Why, despite the revolutionary rhetoric of his *circa* 1968 writings, and despite the widespread, taken-for-granted assumption that he is "on the left," has Derrida so consistently, deliberately and dexterously avoided the subject of politics? [. . .] where does he stand vis-à-vis Marxism? [. . .] Is there a politics *already* implicit in his works? And if so, what is it and is it a tenable one? What problems does Derrida's very complex relation with Heidegger pose for those wishing to politicize deconstruction? What sort of political thought remains possible once one has deconstructed all the traditional bases for political reflection?

Is it possible to rethink the political from a Derridean standpoint and what might such an effort look like?[8]

In this set of questions, one can situate the imperative task to constitute a center for "research of the political." In a public context, a certain form of "retreat" from politics illustrated by Derrida's work until the 1980s became the central trope/figure to understand a possible double bind between deconstruction and politics. In a fundamental gesture to talk about the essence of the political, Nancy and Lacoue-Labarthe invited a number of French intellectuals, some not directly associated with deconstruction, to present papers during the center's sessions.[9] The deconstructive–Heideggerian position is best expressed at Cérisy by Christopher Fynsk's intervention, which emphasized a certain silence or hesitation in Derrida's texts in addressing political issues.[10] Fynsk based his comments on a series of claims made by Derrida in *Positions* and in several other interviews. According to Derrida, "philosophical activity does not require a political practice: it is, in every way, a political practice. Once one has struggled to get that recognized, other struggles begin that are both philosophical and political."[11] As Simon Critchley noticed, the theme of Derrida's own retreat "was taken up by Lacoue-Labarthe in an improvised response to the intervention, in which he concurred with Fynsk that there is indeed a silence or withdrawal with respect to politics *(la politique)* in Derrida's work, although, he added, one can rethink the political *(le politique)* on the basis of deconstruction."[12] In their response to Christopher Fynsk in *Retreating the Political,* Lacoue-Labarthe and Nancy refer to Hannah Arendt's account of the "'total' domination of the political" in the modern world as "a completion of a philosophical programme" (95–96). The claim that everything is political[13]—as Nancy showed in a recent essay—"served as the axiom of an entire modern elaboration."[14] From a historical perspective, Lacoue-Labarthe and Nancy insist that the limit/end of the political has been reached via totalitarianism as it parallels "the movement of philosophy drawing to a close."[15] Accordingly, as Lacoue-Labarthe and Nancy note in *Retreating the Political,* the dissociation with the philosophical (including the figures of the Party State or psychological dictatorship) "can only take the form of a 'retreat' of the political" (96). However, their gesture (that is, formulating the retreat of the political) cannot be understood in simple terms, but as a new form of political activism, which already is part of deconstruction via "necessary mistrust and suspicion."[16]

The distinction between politics *(la politique)* and the political *(le politique)* articulates the strange figure of the retreat: whereas politics still pertains to an empirical structure or form, what Lacoue-Labarthe and Nancy call the politics of "Chinese Emperors, [. . .] of Louis XIV or of German social democracy" (125), the political indicates "the essence of the political [. . .]—what, before Heidegger, one might have referred to as the philosophical interrogation of politics."[17] Split between the movement of the withdrawal and that of retracing, the retreat already formulates a specific deconstructive approach whose ontological path is hard to miss. However, in order to enable the work of deconstruction onto the philosophical kernel of politics, a new term (that is, the political) was needed.

The sources of this terminology are undoubtedly related to the work of the German legal theorist Carl Schmitt and his controversial essay from 1932, *The Concept of the Political (Der Begriff des Politischen)*. The term *le politique* (compare the German term, *Das Politische*) is a neologism with a different meaning than *la politique*, while the usage of this term by Lacoue-Labarthe and Nancy is only partially related to Schmitt's notion. The starting point of *The Concept of the Political* is a notion of retreat, historically illustrated by the collapse of the political–theological structure of authority and the transformation of the modern state by various forms of *"depoliticalizations* characteristic of the liberal nineteenth century."[18] On the one hand, the political as a principle of sovereignty is not the normative order as such, but the function that makes possible the bracketing of that specific order, as in the case of the state of exception—a central topic in Schmitt's *Political Theology*. On the other hand, given the retreat or the dissolution of State authority, the political threatens the neutral domains (religion, culture, education, the economy), which, Schmitt notes, "cease to be neutral" (22). Accordingly, the challenge consists of "discovering [. . .] specifically political categories" (25), and thus the identification of specific criteria that would enable the tracing of "all actions with a specifically political meaning" (26). The solution is the famous friend–enemy distinction that beyond the "proceduralism" of the market model instituted by liberal politics reinstates an existential category: on the political scene, the fight between friends and enemies is not to be taken in a symbolic or metaphorical sense. More specifically, the distinction constituting the "concept of the political" is not a normative category within politics but the concrete form of accounting (in Schmitt's perspective) for an autonomous (that is, uncontaminated) identity of the field of politics: "every religious, moral, economic, ethical, or other antithesis transforms into a political one if it is sufficiently strong to group human beings effectively according to friend and enemy" (37).

These ideas refer to Nancy and Lacoue-Labarthe's philosophical effort to distinguish between the political *(le politique)* and politics *(la politique)* by emphasizing the nonnormative aspect of the former. The political for Schmitt is a concept only insofar as it pertains to the oppositional logic of the antithesis friend–enemy, from which all the possible meanings of politics are derived and insofar as it preserves the centrality of group divisions and group alliances. In contrast, for the French philosophers, the question of the political is a philosophical interrogation that only points toward the essence of the political beyond any attempt of figuration or representation. It should not be surprising, however, to see certain similarities between the so-called withdrawal of the political acknowledged by Schmitt's essay and the philosophical reflection about the completion or closure of the political, forged by Nancy and Lacoue-Labarthe in the powerful thesis, "the retreat of the political is nothing other than a retreat of sovereignty" (131).[19]

As I have argued, for Carl Schmitt, the concept of the political appears as a necessary theoretical consideration the very moment when the equation "state = politics" has become "erroneous and deceptive (22)." The undertone of Schmitt's essays is a nostalgic dream of the past, whereas Lacoue-Labarthe and Nancy claim that the retreat of the political contains in its underside the trace of the politics to come:

> Such a retreat (i.e. the retreat of the political qua retreat of sovereignty) makes something appear or sets something free. At the very least, we sought to question ourselves not according to the rule of a nostalgic lamentation for what would have drawn back (we subscribe to the verdict of "immense failure") but according to the hypothesis that this retreat must allow, or even impose, the tracing anew of the stakes of the political. (131)

What happens in the retreat that allows thinking the new of politics without resting on a philosophical (dialectical) ground? How does the retreat perform "the tracing anew of the stakes of the political"? In an interview with Georges Leyenberger and Jean-Jacques Forti, Lacoue-Labarthe admitted the influence of Derrida's essay "The Retreat of Metaphor" on their approach: "we introduced . . . a certain logic of the retreat that we particularly drew out of Derrida's text on metaphor, in order to know that when something retreats it re-traces itself—the erasure leaves a trace."[20] A central category in Heidegger's late work, the notion of "withdrawal of being" constitutes the background of this discussion. As Derrida puts it "metaphysics as a tropical system and singularity as metaphor detour would correspond to an essential withdrawal of Being."[21] Is it possible to read the retreat of the political through the same Heideggerian key? What is the particularity of the retreat of the political in respect to the metaphysical inquiry, itself, as Derrida noticed, a "tropical system" corresponding to the withdrawal of Being? This means that Being, "unable to reveal itself, to present itself except in dissimulating itself under the 'species' of an epochal determination [. . .], Being would only allow itself to be named in a metaphorico-metonymical divergence *(écart)*."[22] This claim could easily be transposed to the political: unpresentable, though constantly represented, appearing only at this doubling of its own nature, displayed only as it permanently redraws. Thus, the difference between politics and political functions in analogy with the ontological difference, while the displacement caused by the logic of the trait (by *différance*) suggests that nothing is pure—neither politics nor the political—and that these categories exist only to have their identity threatened.[23]

Despite the theoretical effort to withdraw from the obviousness of politics in order to think the political, as it relies on Heidegger's own approach of technology, this deconstructive model (of the retreat) does not fully allow for a complete bracketing of politics or its suspension. This means that the retreat of the political is to be understood in a quasi-metaphorical way. The political is thus *nothing,* in the same sense as, after Bataille, whom Nancy often quotes, "sovereignty itself is nothing." In his seminal text "Being Singular Plural," Nancy partially reveals the larger ontological framework in which the retreat of the political operates: "The retreat of the political does not signify the disappearance of the political. It only signifies the disappearance of the philosophical presupposition of the whole politico-philosophical order, which is always an ontological presupposition. [. . .] The retreat of the political is the uncovering, the ontological laying bare of being-with."[24] This statement clearly emphasizes the unity of Nancy's own philosophical project: the deconstruction of the political can be performed as such only by taking over the thinking of Being where Heidegger left it and by creating, via deconstruction, a fundamental ontology structured around the "being-with."

Although the main theme of Nancy's work, the rethinking of community under an ontological horizon, is central to contemporary post-Marxism, his deconstructive model clashes with specific definitions of politics in Leftist thought. For instance, Nancy has recently written about "the totality of politics" as relating to the following ideas: (1) the experience of being-in-common belongs to politics; (2) politics dominates all the other spheres of contemporary life; and (3) the totality of politics is the only way to designate "the essence of existence as a whole."[25] In the context of the demand made by Western or European thought, this central claim needs to be read in relation to a particular understanding that the Heideggerian statement about the end of metaphysics extends its validity to the general project of modernity as such. The totality of politics is, according to Nancy, the axiom of modernity, traced back to the French Revolution, a nodal point for any theory of politics/political, Marxist or not.

The major problem for Jean-Luc Nancy is to account for the possibility of thinking, at this very moment in our modernity, a politics that is not totalizing, that is, a space of being-in-common that is not already, by definition, political. The radical importance of this question enters into the Heideggerian framework by stipulating the task of thinking, not at the end of philosophy but at the end of politics. As Heidegger showed, the end does not need to be taken in a "negative sense, [. . .] as mere decline and impotence."[26] Thus, the end of politics or the end of the universal, legitimating project of modernity seems to leave place only for ontology. From a post-Marxist perspective, the point where Nancy's position becomes problematic is this very suspension of political action: on the one hand, the radical notion of politics to come *(politique à venir)* tacitly situates him on the Left; on the other hand, any kind of politics *now* is reduced, as Simon Critchley noted, to the political. To push the argument further, leftist politics is replaced by ontology. Now, on the Left, Jean-Luc Nancy may claim in "Is Everything Political?" that no politics is possible, without falling into the modern axiom of the totality of politics, without rearticulating what he himself called an ideology of "self-sufficiency and self-production."[27]

REPRESENTATION AND POLITICAL DIFFERENCE

In response to Nancy and Lacoue-Labarthe's notion of the "retreat of the political" formulated in their interventions during the seminars of the Center for the Research of the Political, Alain Badiou argued for a complete opposition/antithesis between politics *(la politique)* and the political *(le politique)*. In order to emphasize his Leftist radicalism, Badiou's usage of these concepts reverses Nancy and Lacoue-Labarthe's terminology. For him, the political is the category that entails a fiction that presents itself as the "structure of truth": "The fiction of the political *[le politique]* is a ghastly fiction, even more as it organizes the disappearance of *politics [la politique]*. In its center, this fiction is that of the gathering, of the bond, of the rapport."[28]

To escape the deadlock of the political involves, for Badiou, an attack of the philosophical foundations that conceive, in theoretical terms, the articulation of the social bond to its sovereign representation. The preliminary part of Badiou's intervention announces the "retreat of the political" as the central figure operating through this fictional ensemble: communication/opinion, parliamentarianism, democracy, or simply liberalism. Daniel Bensaïd insisted on the significance of Badiou's rejection of modern institutions of *doxa,* a fundamental "Platonic gesture": "Marx had the temerity to declare that philosophy would eventually wither away through the accomplishment of its own strategic development: it was now no longer merely a matter of interpreting the world, but of changing it. Today, by way of contrast, Alain Badiou proposes to reiterate the philosophical gesture *par excellence;* a 'Platonic gesture' in opposition to the tyranny of opinion and the renunciations of anti-philosophy."[29]

In this Platonic vein, the fiction of the political is a motif with dense metaphysical implications. Under the supreme rule of *doxa* or *doxas,* the scene of politics and its actors are caught up by the simulacrum of history. As exposed by the dramatic tone of Badiou's own rhetoric, the theater of the political constitutes the impossibility of breaking out of the boundaries of this world of shadows, or, keeping the narrative in Platonic terms, to liberate oneself from the burden of mere illusion. However, what made possible the captivity in the political is, in fact, both that the fictional possesses the structure of truth and that the actors leave themselves corrupted by the "sovereignty of skepticism." To paraphrase Badiou, the imprisonment in the political refers to the belief that any form of political representation—perhaps the idea of representation in general—can exist without subjectivity.

Badiou's text *(Peut-on penser la politique?)* opens up with a full analysis of the contemporary crisis of politics *(la politique)*: "France has entered, politically in the sovereignty of skepticism" (10). According to this diagnosis, the absence of politics is only simulated, not real. It refers, however, to its incorporation in a concrete situation: elections, parliament, unions, presidency, televised declarations. Because the absence of politics encompasses a whole national scene, the rituals of state power and the inoperative quality of categories designating the choice between the left and the right lead to the "retreat of the political." For Badiou, the retreat is an entirely negative concept. It expresses the modern anxiety of the social automatism, a regime where everything takes place without the need for an experience of the political. More so, "philosophy designates the absence of this experience as . . . retreat in the delocalized haven of administration," that is to say "thinking the essence of the political as retreat edges out in the gap . . . between chance and repetition" (1).

Lacking the subjective dimension of politics, the political is a mere construct, an intellectual formation. What retreats with the political, is its attributes, "the linear, narrative figure of the novel, the fiction of the measure, the idea that the social bond be measurable in the thinking according to the philosophical norm of the good State, or the good Revolution" (12). Badiou's intention is to do away with the representative structure of the political, to suggest the affirmative nature of political subjectivity, freed by the political philosopheme, evoked by ideas like the State or the Revolution. In *Peut-on penser la politique?* inspired by Mallarmé ("the social rapport and its momentary measure, that we hold tight or loose as to govern, is a fiction" [13]), Badiou emphasizes the homogeneity of the political, its consolidation as fiction through the categories of political philosophy that consistently aim at fixing the social bond and its measure. The political thus redraws; this means ultimately the withdrawal of certain literary forms (for instance, the novel) and their projection onto the world. It also means a completion of the politicophilosophical—that is, both the end of Marxism and the need to think anew politics as emancipation. According to Badiou, one needs to distinguish between the "death of Marxism" and its "historical destruction" (52) (the Soviet state model). More so, at the core of this argument is the claim that totalitarianism and democracy (also, only a "form of State") constitute the two figures of the "completion of the political under the double category of bond and representation" (17).

As an alternative, Badiou suggests that one needs to perform theoretically and practically an "un-fixing of politics *[la politique]* as rapport or bond," to liberate politics "from the tyranny of history in order to give it back *[rendre]* to the event" (18). What does Badiou mean by these terms? Can we simply assume that politics can ever liberate us from history? Are we not stuck, according to this theoretical position in a typical Marxist utopianism, derived here not from the horizon of "the end of history," but from some secret subjective potential of politics, narrowly understood as pure militancy? Although the political, in its mediating role between social bond and sovereignty, is a static concept, politics no longer refers to performing according to a philosophical norm, but to the mobility to engage with the gap (hole) it has noticed in knowledge or in being. In terms that are not strange to Derrida, for Badiou in *Peut-on penser la politique?* politics means to take a decision "at the point of the undecidable" (19). However, the untying of the social rapport does not rest on deconstruction to give consistency to this act, but on a notion of political difference that overdetermines the ontic–ontologic distinction. Inspired by Lacan and Marx, for Badiou politics (as militancy) appears in relation to the *excess* produced by an "event" within the ontological situation of the State. He also claims that communism is not simply an ideological program but the very political capacity to designate the unrepresentable (that is, the event and its "excessiveness"). In his attack of radical democracy, Bruno Bosteels, one of the most vocal of Badiou's supporters, explicitly formulates this position:

> In order to register the sequences of an emancipatory politics in the last decades, from the student revolts all the way to the Zapatista rebellion, philosophy must traverse and then exceed the frame of deconstruction, in the name of difference or lack, or the representational scheme of the political. The point of departure to rethink politics today is not just the structural gap that always already determines the democratic order, but also the excess over this empty place itself.[30]

In order to conceive of politics from this perspective, Badiou and Bosteels need to offer more than utopian prescriptions for the struggle for equality. My contention with Badiou's position in *Peut-on penser la politique?* derives from a logic that exclusively relies on his peculiar art of disassociation. Although he is willing to separate ideology from Marxism, he simply dismisses any "consistency of a political subject, of a heterogeneous political capacity" (53) that radical democracy may produce. In my view, democracy should not be restricted to a form of state, and thus to an ontic set of institutions establishing the organization of the social. Rather, it should be considered an ontological category. In this sense, I will show that Ernesto Laclau and Chantal Mouffe's theory of democracy, in its most recent development is able to maintain the possibility of radical left politics without giving away the notion of representation.

My criticism of Badiou's project aims specifically at its reduction of politics to militancy. If politics always occurs in the future perfect *(futur antérieure)*—that is to say, the militant will always have acted—how does this notion of subjectivity relate to a future event which in its radical dimension must take everyone by surprise? In its separation from history, and in its effort to silence out the voice of time, Alain Badiou's notion of politics becomes a purely subjective (that is, ethical) intervention, a symbolic investment in the contingent emergence of truth within a situation. In this context, the main challenge to Badiou's ideas is to think the endurance or the persistence of any particular subjective mode. In concrete terms, this problematic is addressed in his theoretical effort to create a "Marxist subjectivity that inhabits the inhabitable" (55). Badiou's project in *Peut-on penser la politique?* relies on a nonideological *(non programmatique)* recomposition of Marxism, whose single operative category, "intervening fidelity," supposedly creates "political organization," that is, "the collective product of an evenmental consistency beyond its immediate sphere" (77). Without a notion of rapport, Badiou's collective organization risks to remain the sum of faithful subjects, unable to create a whole (that is, a people).

The limitations of Badiou's project become clearer from reading him in relation to the early work of Marx. Badiou returns in fact to the main topic of the *Theses on Feuerbach* (1845), the critique of materialism and the invention of the political subject. According to Étienne Balibar's reading, Marx's aphorisms lead to the following hypothesis: "just as traditional materialism in reality conceals an idealist foundation (representation, contemplation), so modern idealism in reality conceals a materialist orientation in the function it attributes to the acting subject, at least if one accepts that there is a latent conflict between the idea of representation (interpretation, contemplation) and that of activity (labor, practice, transformation, change)."[31] Marx's initial solution to this contradiction is to "dissociate between representation and subjectivity" (25), a theoretical perspective similar to Badiou's strategic point in *Peut-on penser la politique?,* the structural criterion he used to distinguish between the political (the representation of the social bond in various forms of sovereignty) and politics (reduced to the organizational praxis derived from subjective engagement with an event, without the mediation of any ideological element, and without the need for any concept of representation).

In my view, Marx had not fallen into the same trap: the invention of political subjectivity cannot do away with mediation. On the one hand, Balibar notes in *Philosophy of Marx* that "Marx transferred the category of subject from idealism to materialism" (26), and this intervention in the history of German philosophy, from Kant and Fichte to Hegel, is in itself revolutionary. On the other hand, Marx "set up the permanent possibility of *representing the proletariat to itself as a 'subject'* in the idealist sense of the term" (26; italics in original). For Balibar, this reversal leads to an original analysis of Marx's *Theses on Feuerbach* in which the materialism of praxis becomes "the most accomplished form of the idealist tradition . . . precisely because that transposition is closely linked to the attempt to prolong the revolutionary experience and embody it in modern society" (27). Badiou does not simply translate the certainties and dilemmas of the young Marx into his own axiomatic language, but in the end, the question of a permanent, resilient form of political experience articulated by fidelity must deal with the passing of time. To put it in different terms, one needs to find in Badiou's theoretical corpus a supplement through which "*a* collective" can, over time, maintain and permanently reinvent its subjective status.

Despite this criticism, I believe that Badiou has identified the right theoretical issues for the intellectual revitalization of Marxism both in the context of the crisis/collapse of real-existing socialisms and in the aftermath of the cold war. The same set of problems was approached from a different theoretical perspective by Ernesto Laclau.[32] Slavoj Žižek describes the deep homology of these two projects in the following terms:

> Against the Hegelian vision of the "concrete universal," of the reconciliation between Universal and Particular (or between Being and Event), which is still discernible in Marx, they both start by a constitutive and irreducible gap that undermines the self-enclosed consistency of the ontological edifice. . . . [T]he dimension which undermines the closure of ontology has an "ethical" character—it concerns the contingent act of decision against the background of "undecidable" multiplicity of Being.[33]

Laclau's most recent book, *On Populist Reason*, continues to develop these issues, focusing on the constitution of popular identities according to a rhetorical logic, "the part functions as a whole" (80). This idea resonates with the core argument of Laclau's theory: "a certain particularity signifies an unachievable universality" (111). Because the split between the concrete content of a particularity and its underside (the universal) refers directly to the hegemonic rapport, in *On Populist Reason* Laclau's argument specifically refers to "the ontological possibility of such a relationship" (111).

While in *Hegemony and Socialist Strategy*, the book coauthored with Chantal Mouffe, Laclau does not explicitly formulate his project in ontological terms, their definition of hegemony ("any practice establishing relations among elements such that their identity is modified as the result of this articulatory practice" [105]) clearly points to that direction. The distinction between metaphysics and ontology is crucial to understand Laclau's position. "Although the concept of ontology preceded the word 'ontology,'" writes Jose Ferrater Mora, "it can be assumed that only when such a word . . . came into use, could philosophers begin to understand fully all the implications of the concept."[34] Accordingly, Aristotle's *Metaphysics* offers the distinction between "first philosophy" studying "the nature and first principles of *ens qua ens*"[35] (the equivalent of the seventeenth-century term *ontology*) and metaphysics, the science of particular types of beings. From a fundamental interest in the question of ontology ("What is to be?") follows Laclau's definition of the hegemonic logic in *New Reflections on the Revolution of Our Times*. In an interview with the journal *Strategies,* conducted in 1988 and published in this book, the question of political articulation is formulated via its centrality to a post-Marxist ontology of production, the "creation of something new out of a dispersion of elements" (182). More so, Laclau's political vision discovers a world founded on the very limit of objectivity: "there is no objectivity that may constitute an 'origin': the moment of creation is radical . . . and no social practice, not even the most humble acts of our everyday life, are entirely repetitive. 'Articulation,' in that sense, is the primary ontological level of the constitution of the real" (182).

In the model illustrated by Alain Badiou, *the new* occurs via the fidelity to the force of the event—the unpresentable working in the situation able to recreate it ex nihilo. For Laclau, the discursive production of new social relations/identities happens through the work of social agents. The ontological possibility of the hegemonic relation is thus not axiomatic but is constituted conceptually within the deconstructed body of Marxist tradition. In Marx's texts, the transition from praxis to production—in Balibar's terms, "any human activity of formation and transformation of nature" (35)—is linked to the discovery of ideology. In the light of Balibar's analysis, we notice that the ontology of production, seen as a remedy to Marx's theory of praxis, designates "production which shapes *man's being* . . . his own means of existence, an activity at once personal and collective which transforms him at the same time as it irreversibly transforms nature and which, in this way, constitutes 'history'" (35). Against Marx's clearly foundationalist approach whose metaphysical coordinates will lead to a philosophy of history, Laclau poses a postfoundational ontology whose only aim is "the discursive production of emptiness" (according to the fourth chapter of *On Populist Reason*). The deconstructive operation he institutes at the core of the Leftist tradition from Marx to Althusser allows him to shift the theoretical focus from ideology ("regional category of the social whole"[36]) to emphasizing "the necessarily discursive character of any object, and the impossibility of any discourse to implement a final suture."[37]

The classical formulas of political hegemony are the following: the metaphoric–metonymic logic corresponds to equivalence (a set of differential demands enters into an equivalential chain, with one partial/particular "identity" taking over a universal form) and difference (the disrupture of the very possibility of any chains to be formed). By definition, the creation of a "people" (or according to Laclau and Mouffe in *Hegemony and Socialist Strategy*, the formation of new identities) is the task of any type of radical democratic politics. This continuous formation of political identities works against the prospect of philosophies of history, either Marxist or neoliberal, that serve us the utopian teleological notion of the "end." "The people" is not an a priori category but the retroactive effect of naming, the result of a primal baptism, a catachrestical operation. Among rhetorical figures, catachresis directly corresponds to the hegemonic logic: as Laclau notes in *On the Populist Reason,* it "is more than a particular figure: it is the common denominator of rhetoricity as such. [. . .] If the empty signifier arises from the need of naming an object which is both impossible and necessary, from that zero point of signification which is, however, the precondition of any signifying process, in that case the hegemonic operation will be catachrestical through and through" (71). Metaphor, metonymy, and synecdoche also have ontological functions and thus may correspond to the categories of classical ontology. Among these categories, Laclau's text explores the crucial role of the notion of the lack (traditionally, the gap existent between contingent and necessary beings) as conceptualized by psychoanalysis.

The psychoanalytic notion of the Real needs to be seen as a necessary background to Laclau's notion of the political. Although Laclau was not directly involved in the activity of the Center for the Research of the Political, the theory of hegemony addresses the question of political difference in an original way. According to Oliver Marchart, "politics . . . becomes internally split into a dimension which internally belongs to the social ('politics' as a social 'sub-system') on the one hand, and on the other, a more radical dimension ('the political') which grounds and regrounds the social from without, or rather, from an ultimately *impossible* outside. Thus, what is named by the term 'the political' is the moment of the institution/destitution of the social respectively."[38] Lacan's thinking of the internal limit of the symbolic (that is, the category of the Real) corresponds to envisioning the impossibility of society to fully constitute itself.[39] This thesis can be translated into a different lexicon, borrowing its categories from ontotheology: at the core of the social, Laclau notes in *On the Populist Reason,* there is radical contingency, "there is a fullness of the community which is missing" (85). If in a theological context the name of fullness (God) points to a different ontological status, of a higher absolute Being,

Laclau's predicament shows that, for modern social theory, this fullness can only appear as the particular promise that embodies it in its absence.

Although the a-theological character of the image of a perfect society institutes itself as horizon for every group engaged in political practice, we still need to inquire into the very presupposition of situating the social on a terrain dominated by the dialectical reversals of two religious concepts: lack and fullness, that is, present lack (the experience of lack) and absent fullness. Our question needs to be situated in relation to Laclau's discussion of the social logic behind populism. Used by Laclau against all the contemporary prejudices that surround it, this category provides a new conceptual framework to think the role of the political in rapport to regulated social or institutional practices. In his review essay of *On Populist Reason,* Slavoj Žižek presented Laclau's argument in the following terms: "Populism is not a specific political movement, but the political at its purest: the 'inflection' of the social space that can affect any political content. Its elements are purely formal, 'transcendental,' not ontic: populism occurs when a series of particular 'democratic' demands . . . is enchained in a series of equivalences, and this enchainment produces 'people' as the universal political subject."[40] This notion of production refers to a rhetorical recomposition of the social space. These are the premises of a weak ontology, whose aim is not to create the foundational certainty of dialectical ordering of history but to inscribe political desire in the discursive production of emptiness.

The unity of a group composed by a plurality of isolated demands in a heterogeneous social field depends on what Laclau in *On Populist Reason* calls the "social productivity of a name" (108), or according to one of his previous essays, *Emancipation(s),* "the social production of 'empty signifiers'" (36). The inaugural moment of this process is thus the creation of a paradoxical political vision, founded on the canceling out of differential ideological positions that always relies on the agency of the "people" as the universal carrier of a mythical task:

> The construction of a "people" will be the attempt to give a name to that absent fullness. Without this initial breakdown of something in the social order—however minimal that something could initially be—there is no possibility of antagonism, frontier, or, ultimately, "people." This initial experience is not only, however, an experience of lack. Lack, as we have seen, is linked to a demand, which is not met. But this involves bringing into the picture the instance, which has not met the demand. [. . .] So from the very beginning we are confronted with a dichotomic division between unfulfilled

social demands, on the one hand, and an unresponsive power, on the other. We start here seeing why the plebs sees itself as the *populus,* the part as the whole: as the fullness of the community is just the imaginary reverse of a situation lived as a *deficient being,* those responsible for the latter cannot be a legitimate part of the community; the chasm with them is irretrievable. (86)

Through discursive practice, plebs are able to reconfigure their identity and claim they are not only a part of the community, but also represent the community as such. This task shows the ontological function of synecdoche and the double process in which it operates; identification (part = whole) is one, and exclusion is the other. In fact, the identification is possible only insofar the exclusion of certain elements validates the new imaginary horizon on which a new community is constituted. The political experience in postcommunist countries is a possible example that indicates that the failure to exclude from political life leading members of the Communist Party not only maintained the connection with the past (lived as deficient being) but also imposed a difficult constitution of a fictional horizon necessary for reshaping the nation. Thus, lack and fullness are purely operative categories. The assumption that they have a role in the constitution of the social may seem philosophically problematic; however, they prove to be useful in explaining apparent paradoxes of social conflicts and the so-called irrationality of society.

Let us summarize the different aspects in Laclau's work that interested us in this essay: (1) rhetorical figures possess particular ontological functions; (2) the political cannot be reduced to various forms of politics and is thus not situated on purely ideological grounds but on larger ontological categories illustrated by the dialectical pair lack–fullness; (3) the impossibility of a fully constituted society points toward an originary disjuncture at the core of Being—that is, the failure of the regime of presentation, a thesis not unrelated to the Derridean deconstruction of the metaphysics of presence. On numerous occasions, Laclau confessed that his ontology would neither be composed around Badiou's "Being as multiple," nor around the theological or the immanentist Spinozist/Deleuzian notion of "one," but rather around the idea of a failed unity. This disjuncture at the core of Being that could be Laclau's true philosophical project can be accounted for in the production of empty signifiers (or, as Laclau notes in *Emancipation(s),* the emergence of the "the structural impossibility of signification as such" [37]). In an ontology founded on the failure of unity, language in its formal (rhetorical) structure becomes the matrix of Being.

These theoretical considerations become more transparent when observed in analogy with paradigm shifts in other scientific disciplines, linguistics, and psychoanalysis, where a similar change was at work. For instance, in *On Populist Reason,* Laclau notes that "Lacan breaks with the notion of a dyad mother/child by adding a third component, detached from the mother, which is the breast—properly speaking, the object of the drive" (114). According to Laclau, Joan Copjec's reading of sublimation as the "elevation of the external object of the drive [. . .] to the status of the Thing" (114) is structurally identical to the notion of hegemony. Developed by psychoanalysis and political theory, the Lacanian *objet a* and Laclau's empty signifier no longer refer to regional structures but to a general (that is, ontological) field.

It is thus imperative to understand that politics would not be possible outside this conceptual terrain where all the three major Lacanian notions—the symbolic, the real, and the imaginary—operate. In this sense, the substitution of the fiction of the political with pure politics recommended by Badiou would not only be problematic from a social theoretical perspective, but also from a psychoanalytical position. Without a mythical horizon, no imaginary identification makes sense. In that situation, any creation of a "people" would simply be mislabeled as irrational, and any prospect of emancipation would remain pure fantasy.

Despite potential deconstructive criticism against the use of the dialectical pair fullness–emptiness, I believe that the use of the logic of incarnation it presupposes fully resembles structurally Derrida's own political discourse organized around spectrality. As in the case of Derrida, Laclau's own deployment of the logic of incarnation dislocates a religious element and makes it operative in a political (that is, nonmystical) setting. The empty signifier is thus a procedural category in which what is at stake is a notion of the universal that is no longer absolute and no longer relates to God, either as transcendent or immanent figure, but acts as the formal structure for the constitution of the social. Derrida's reading of Marx focuses on the figure of the ghost, to a "paradoxical incorporation,"[41] which, as Laclau himself acknowledged, resonates with the emergence of the hegemonic logic. However, as he notes in *Emancipation(s)*, the "hegemonic logic presupposes two further steps beyond spectrality" (70): competition between various "bodies" to become the incarnating "spirit" and the "autonomization of the latter" (71). Consequently, this incarnating spirit "emerges out of a constitutive impossibility, an absolute limit whose forms of representation will be necessarily inadequate" (71).

Laclau's thinking of a postfoundational ontology is thus not incompatible with Derrida's hauntology. However, the deconstructive logic of the specter is followed, according to Laclau, by another moment, when the ontological element has achieved its autonomy. Order, for instance, is autonomous in regard to "particular order in so far as it is the name of an absent fullness that no concrete social order can achieve" (72). In discussing the question of frontiers that appear in political struggle under the banner of populism, Laclau in *On Populist Reason* points toward "the presence of some privileged signifiers which condense in them the signification of a whole antagonistic camp (the 'regime,' the 'oligarchy,' the 'dominant groups,' etc. for the enemy; 'the people,' the 'nation,' the 'silent majority' etc. for the oppressed underdog—which signifiers acquire this articulating role depending, however, on a contextual history)" (87). The analysis will differentiate between the *ontological* role according to which the political frontier appears in the first place, and the *ontic* content that plays that role in various historical circumstances. "The important point," Laclau claims, "is that . . . the ontic content can exhaust its ability to play the role, while, however, the need for the latter remains; and that—given the indeterminacy of the relation between ontic content and ontological function—the function can be played by signifiers of an entirely opposite political sign" (91).

This argument explains the paradoxical alliances between groups belonging to opposite ideological affiliations. A recent situation, in tone with the examples offered by *On Populist Reason,* is the French vote against the European Union constitution, in which both the Left and the Right, for different reasons, rejected a legislative project fully endorsed by the French government. What is largely considered in the media, a vote of protest, is in fact what Laclau in *On Populist Reason* calls an "ontological need of expressing social division." The conclusion aims to show "a central asymmetry between ontological function and ontic fulfilling in relation to discourses of radical change" (88). Political and ideological frontiers often do not necessarily coincide. Political radicalism is, in that sense, the central mark of this very instability at the heart of social formations. Any situation of crisis/disorder is thus a fertile terrain for the emergence of a multitude of populist discourses. In this case the logic exposed by Laclau is at work: the promise of order acquires an ontological status, and the actual ontic content becomes marginal. The merit of this analysis is that it does not situate itself on a purely homogenous ideological terrain; ontological tools, properly used, show the instability of political divisions and the contingent character of the political spectrum, especially in times of organic crises. On the one hand, ontology cannot be appropriated by a predetermined ideology—or to put it in more direct terms, there is no Leftist ontology. On the other, ontology becomes indispensable to Leftist politics, inasmuch as it leads to the possibility of hegemonic relations. As Laclau notes in *Emancipation(s)*, "Politics is possible because the constitutive impossibility of society can only represent itself through the production of empty signifiers" (44).

The empty signifier constitutes a model of representation through which a part of the community identifies itself with the whole, conditioning the formation of "the people"—that is, a particularity elevates itself to the status of the Universal. In this sense, the constitution of popular identities, as Laclau, in *On Populist Reason* notes, "would be impossible with the operation of mechanisms of representation" (161). Laclau does not simply start from a preexistent notion of representation but uses the ontological framework elaborated in his rethinking of populism to approach the kernel of democratic theory organized on symbolic representation. In my view, the consequences of this argument are twofold: first, no Leftist politics is possible without a notion of representation, which becomes operative the very moment one acknowledges the gap between the ontic fulfillment of social demands and the ontological horizon in which they emerge; and second, the displacement of the notion of representation that derives from the political logic of populism traces out the dimensions of radical democracy.

To further address these issues, we need to look closely at Laclau's own engagement with Lefort's "The Question of Democracy," a text delivered during the seminar sessions of the Center for the Research of the Political. Lefort's own argument is organized around a theory of the disincorporation of power in society that happens with the advent of the democratic revolution. The starting point of Lefort's argument is Ernst Kantorowicz's rationale behind monarchy, in which power is embodied in the person of the king, who is both a secular agency and the representative of God. What is at stake for Laclau, in performing a critique of Lefort in *On Populist Reason*, is not so much where "The Question of Democracy" ends up (that is, the conclusions to this text), but the framework in which Lefort himself situates his analysis: "the symbolic transformation which made possible the advent of modern democracy" (164). In his reading, Laclau privileges the "dissolution of markers of certainty"[42] to the symbolic mutation that leads to the disincorporation of the body politic, the emergence of democracy as what Lefort in "The Question of Democracy" calls "the empty place of power" (19). Laclau is therefore opposed to the restriction of the meaning of *politeia* equated to "regime" and instead suggests in *On Populist Reason* a notion that opens up Lefort's text to "a whole political life of a community, of which constitutional arrangements represent only a formal crystallization" (169). Even if the liberal tradition restricts the notion of power to a hierarchical structure and confines politics to institutional acts, the notion of political subjectivity (that is, the dissipation of power in society) is the condition for the symbolic mutation of society at the center of Lefort's own argument. What seems to be at stake in Laclau's critique is Lefort's conception of a fixed place of power, the defining feature of democratic emptiness. That is precisely why in his response to Rodolphe Gasché, Laclau refuses the idea of "place of emptiness" and suggests instead the use of the term "dimension of emptiness," a category that would allow him to account for the displacement of power, the condition for hegemonic struggle and for a political reconstitution of the social. Accordingly, emptiness is for him "a type of identity, not a structural location."[43] Laclau is thus able to formulate the difference between a post-Marxist ontology of producing emptiness (via the notion of representation imposed by popular identities) and a liberal–democratic ontology, which permanently rests only on the immutability and fixity of its empty place of power.

NOTES

1. Philippe Lacoue-Labarthe and Jean-Luc Nancy, *Retreating the Political,* ed. Simon Sparks (London: Routledge, 1997), 108. Subsequent references to this book are cited parenthetically in the text.

2. This is the main thesis of Oliver Marchart's study. In this text, *Post-foundational Political Thought: Political Difference in Nancy, Lefort, Badiou and Laclau* (Edinburgh: Edinburgh University Press, 2007), postfoundationalism is defined as the "constant interrogation of metaphysical figures of foundation—such as totality, universality, essence and ground" (2) and is distinguished from antifoundationalism (featured in the "anything goes" postmodernism) or nonfoundationalism (present, for instance, in Michael Oakeshott's conservatism) (3).

3. Ibid., 14.

4. See also Jason Glynos's essay, "Thinking the Ethics of the Political in the Context of a Postfoundational World: From an Ethics of Desire to an Ethics of the Drive," *Theory and Event* 4, no. 4 (2000).

5. Chantal Mouffe, *The Return of the Political* (London: Verso, 1993), 57.

6. Ibid., 57.

7. The text of this conference is published in Jacques Derrida, *Margins of Philosophy,* trans. Alan Bass (Chicago: University of Chicago Press, 1982), 111–14. The idea of the colloquium organized in 1980 at Cérisy also came from this text by Derrida.

8. Nancy Frazer, "The French Derrideans: Politicizing Deconstruction or Deconstructing the Political?" *New German Critique* 33 (Fall 1984): 127–54.

9. The two distinct positions that illustrate possible approaches of politics, not committed to Lacoue-Labarthe and Nancy's own deconstructive attempts, are to be found in Claude Lefort and Alain Badiou's texts delivered during sessions of the seminar.

10. Christopher Fynsk, "Political Seminar, Contribution I," in Lacoue-Labarthe and Nancy, *Retreating the Political*, 88.

11. Derrida, qtd. in Fynsk, "Political Seminar, Contribution I," 89.

12. Simon Critchley, *The Ethics of Deconstruction: Derrida and Levinas* (Edinburgh: Edinburgh University Press, 1999), 201.

13. The issue of the completion of the political is addressed by Jean-Luc Nancy, "Is Everything Political?" *CR: The New Centennial Review* 2, no. 3 (Fall 2002): 5–22.

14. Ibid., 15.

15. Lacoue-Labarthe and Nancy, *Retreating the Political*, 96. In "Is Everything Political?" in Nancy's words, the phrase "everything is political" "served as a maxim or slogan as much for the various forms of fascism or for those of communism: it was even most likely, notwithstanding all their differences, their true point of contact" (15).

16. Ibid.

17. Critchley, *Ethics of Deconstruction*, 201.

18. Carl Schmitt, *The Concept of the Political* (Chicago: University of Chicago Press, 1996), 23. Subsequent references to this book appear parenthetically in the text.

19. See, for instance, Jean-Luc Nancy, *La creation du monde ou la mondalisation* (Paris: Editions Galilée, 2002).

20. Interview with Lacoue-Labarthe in Georges Leyenberger and Jean-Jacques Forti, eds., *Politique et modernité* (Paris: Editions Osiris, 1992), 200; my translation.

21. See Derrida, "The Retreat of Metaphor," in *Derrida Reader*, ed. Julian Wolfreys (Omaha: University of Nebraska Press, 1998), 116. Rodolphe Gasché has shown that the structure of re-mark in Derrida or the logic of the trait occurs as a response to the thinking of Being in the later Heidegger: "in the same way as the trait of Being is at once the retreat *(retrait)* of Being, the mark that is folded upon itself, the re-marked trace, also retreats in its being." Rodolphe Gasché, *The Tain of the Mirror: Derrida and the Philosophy of Reflection* (Cambridge, Mass.: Harvard University Press, 1986), 292.

22. Derrida, "Retreat of Metaphor," 116.

23. Oliver Marchart, in *Politics and the Political*, also insists on the signification of political difference. His approach more closely follows Heidegger's notion of abandonment of being than Derrida's reading of this notion: "Nancy and Lacoue-Labarthe set out to answer to Heidegger's injunction that Seinsverlassenheit—as 'Politikverlassenheit'—be recollected in its self-concealing history" (65).

24. Jean-Luc Nancy, *Being Singular Plural* (Stanford: Stanford University Press, 2000), 37.

25. Nancy, "Is Everything Political?" 15.

26. Martin Heidegger, "The End of Philosophy and the Task of Thinking," *Basic Writings* (New York: Harper & Row, 1977), 374.

27. Nancy, "Is Everything Political?" 18.

28. Alain Badiou, *Peut-on penser la politique?* (Paris: Éditions du Seuil, 1985), 15, my translation. Subsequent references to this book appear parenthetically in the

text; the translations are my own. See also the recent article by Bruno Bosteels, "For the Lack of Politics: Theses on the Political Philosophy of Radical Democracy," *Theory@buffalo* 10 (2005): 54–81.

29. Daniel Bensaïd, "Alain Badiou and the Miracle of the Event," in *Think Again: Alain Badiou and the Future of Philosophy*, ed. Peter Hallward (London: Continuum, 2004), 94.

30. Bosteels, "For the Lack of Politics," 74–75.

31. Étienne Balibar, *The Philosophy of Marx* (London: Verso, 1995), 25. Subsequent references to this book appear parenthetically in the text.

32. I will be quoting from the following texts in the remaining part of my essay: Ernesto Laclau and Chantal Mouffe, *Hegemony and Socialist Strategy: Towards a Radical Democratic Politics* (London: Verso, 1985); Ernesto Laclau, *New Reflections on the Revolutions of Our Time* (London: Verso, 1990); Ernesto Laclau, *Emancipation(s)* (London: Verso, 1996); and Ernesto Laclau, *On Populist Reason* (London: Verso, 2005).

33. Slavoj Žižek, *The Ticklish Subject* (London: Verso, 1999), 173.

34. Jose Ferrater Mora, "On the Early History of Ontology," *Philosophy and Phenomenological Research* 24, no. 1 (1963): 36.

35. Ibid., 37.

36. Laclau, *New Reflections*, 185.

37. Laclau and Mouffe, *Hegemony and Socialist Strategy*, 111.

38. Marchart, *Politics and the Political*, 249.

39. Laclau and Mouffe, *Hegemony and Socialist Strategy*, 125.

40. Slavoj Žižek, "Against Populist Temptations," *Critical Inquiry* 32 (Spring 2006): 553.

41. Jacques Derrida, *Spectres of Marx: The State of the Debt, the Work of Mourning, and the New International* (New York: Routledge, 1994), 126.

42. Claude Lefort, "The Question of Democracy," in *Democracy and Political Theory* (Minneapolis: University of Minnesota Press, 1988), 19.

43. Ernesto Laclau, "Glimpsing the Future: A Reply," in *Laclau, A Critical Reader*, ed. Simon Critchley and Oliver Marchart (New York: Routledge, 2004).

The Last God: María Zambrano's Life without Texture

ALBERTO MOREIRAS

María Zambrano (1904–91) studied with José Ortega y Gasset at the University of Madrid in the 1920s and was intimately connected to the intellectual events surrounding the Second Spanish Republic. She was at the time something like a radical liberal, in the complicated Spanish tradition, a deep thinker whose early writings already contain hints of the poetic and the religious veins that would mark her later work. She was forced into exile during the Spanish Civil War and initiated a pilgrimage through various countries in Latin America (Cuba, Mexico), then Europe (Italy, France), until her return to Spain in the 1980s. During those long years of defeat, poverty, and intense commitment to the tasks of thinking as she saw them, she produced an idiosyncratic oeuvre that is perhaps one of the most important instances of Spanish thought or Spanish philosophy. Her efforts to be commensurate to the extraordinary circumstances of her life, and of her position as an intellectual, have received renewed attention through the celebrations that marked the one hundredth year of her birth in 2004.

This essay is an attempt to read María Zambrano's major book, *El hombre y lo divino* (1955), as a subdued and almost ghostly but significant critical engagement with the thought of Martin Heidegger—or rather, with the political implications of Heidegger's work.[1] I am particularly interested in examining two of the conceptual structures that Zambrano offers in *El hombre y lo divino*. The first she calls *relación abismada*, which I translate, clumsily enough, as "degrounded relation," and the second, *vida sin textura*, or "life without texture." Those notions should be traced against the background of Zambrano's definition of democracy in her 1958 book *Persona y democracia. La historia sacrificial* (for Zambrano any democratic regime must tend toward the abandonment or refusal of the sacrificial structuration of history); but also against the background of what *El hombre y lo divino* establishes as the epochal or historical dissolution of the identity between being and thinking.

For Zambrano, a democratic politics is bound to the precise determination of the abandonment of "sacrificial history." If the abandonment of the sacrificial structuration of history defines democratic politics, by the same token, the practice of democracy defines an antisacrificial perspective on action. A democratic politics, regardless of what politics could be in itself, is always bent on the suppression of the divide between what Zambrano called "idols" on the one hand, and "victims" on the other.[2] Beyond the search for power or the search for recognition, if politics is understood as the practice of abandonment of the sacrificial structuration of history, then politics appears as specifically democratic politics. This is what Zambrano proposes. But there can be no abandonment of the sacrificial structuration of history insofar as there is no abandonment of the understanding of the political as subjective militancy. If subjective militancy is at the same time a condition and a result of ontology, to go beyond ontology—and that means beyond the subjectivity of the subject as the current horizon of political thinking—is also a condition and a result of an ethical position where every possibility of a nonsacrificial politics is sheltered.

In the identity of thinking and being (doubtless an old notion of philosophy, one of its very first words in the poem of Parmenides), the very principle of sovereign subjectivity that has marked modernity itself is ciphered. There is in effect no sovereignty without subjectivity, in the same way that there is no subjectivity without sovereignty. To paraphrase Juan Donoso Cortés or Carl Schmitt, every relevant concept of political thought in modernity is anchored in transcendental subjectivity, which turns subjectivity into the matrix of everything that is thinkable on the basis of the identification between subject and substance. Zambrano, in her sustained meditation on the necessary deidentification of thinking and being, is already pointing toward an alternative, nonmodern conception of the political. Only from that alternative conceptualization it is possible to formulate a project for political life that is based on the abandonment of the sacrificial structuration of history.

But to abandon the sacrificial structuration of history is also to abandon every attempt at a politics of sovereignty, every attempt at establishing the political on the basis and ground of an experience or practice of sovereignty. As a thinker of the political, María Zambrano thinks the possibility of politics beyond subjectivity and beyond sovereignty. The concepts of degrounded relationship and life without texture are essential to this endeavor.

The Nonprimacy of Politics in Democratic Politics

In terms of the political as the practice of sovereignty, could any possible primacy of politics over history (including economic history) be considered absolute or relative? If relative, then politics would still be subordinate to history in the last instance. If absolute, then politics would be the norm of action. But an absolutely primary politics, that is, an absolutely sovereign politics, would have to rely on the total immanence of its own conditions, and would in fact be normless: that is, it would provide something like a normless norm for action. A politics without a norm, that is, a politics that would itself be the normative standard, without recourse to alterity or to a heterogeneous grounding, can only be a politics of force, and it would have become an ontology (as in the Nietzschean case, where the will to power is the ontological principle of Nietzsche's "grand politics").

Or is it possible that a norm for politics can be found outside history itself, and thus also outside force? That norm would not be an ontology, but it would register at some infraontological level, at the level of desire perhaps, a normative affect regulating something like the Benjaminian hatred of mythic violence, what Derrida refers to as justice, or Alain Badiou's communist invariant. If something like that transhistorical or transpolitical norm were to exist, if politics can emerge through it as heteronormative, that is, always dependent on an affect that would be exterior to itself, then it would be necessary to conclude that politics is always a partisan politics precisely to the very extent that it won't let itself be reduced to force or to an ontology of force. Can politics be thought without partisanship? Is partisanship an unconditional, irreducible determinant of any theory of the political?

Zambrano, as mentioned, states that a democratic politics is bound to the abandonment of sacrificial history. If the abandonment of the sacrificial structuration of history defines democratic politics, then the practice of democracy defines an antisacrificial perspective on action. A democratic politics is always bent on the suppression of the divide between idols on the one hand and victims on the other; it is based on the refusal of the fact that the existence of idols must always feed off the existence of victims. Only democracy, Zambrano says, among all the political systems, can shelter the possibility of marching toward an abandonment of sacrificial history. I am taking it for granted that there is no possibility of social justice without an abandonment of sacrificial history. The abandonment of sac-rifice and social justice are then the goals of democracy. This cuts across other divisions of the political field, such as the Schmittian friend/enemy division, or the division of the social between the part of the whole and the part of no-part proposed by Jacques Rancière.

If politics is exhaustively contained in the friend/enemy division, then politics is defined by power: politics seeks power—its acquisition or its con-tinued possession—as the power of one group over other groups, and it is therefore always already partisan politics. If politics marks the fundamen-tal act of appearance of a claim to existence by the part of no-part, that is, of those who are negated by the ideological articulation of social totality, then politics is defined by recognition: the part of no-part wants to be rec-ognized as such by the social totality, or it wants to be recognized as the social totality (the proletariat as universal class, or the people as general will). If politics is understood as the practice of abandonment of the sacri-ficial structuration of history, then politics appears as specifically demo-cratic politics. Through each of those determinations, there emerges the thought that the only possible nonpartisan understanding of the political is precisely the understanding of the political as always already partisan.

How can we link those three definitions of the political? We can imag-ine a complex interaction between demands for power, demands for recog-nition, and demands for the end of sacrifice in any concrete situation. At their limit, however, the three definitions are incompatible. The demand for power must subordinate one group to another group because its limit is the existence of the enemy, and the enemy must be kept in check, which reveals this practice of the political as profoundly sacrificial and thus anti-democratic. The demand for a democratic end of sacrificial history must give up power insofar as it can only absorb the radical power of the non-application of power, and the demand for recognition is never just either a demand for power, or a demand for democracy and social justice. So the three definitions exceed each other, and in their mutual excess, they orga-nize something like an aporia of the political. Politics would finally be the infinite negotiation between those three demands: for power, for recogni-tion, and for an end to social sacrifice.

But if so, then only democracy can organize, even if aporetically, the simultaneous pursuit of the three demands, because no other system can countenance the end of the sacrificial structuration of history. Democracy can, however, authorize unconditional demands for power and recogni-tion—not any demands for power and recognition, of course, just some:

the absolute power of the people, for instance; or the total recognition of the proletariat as class, which is the political abolition of class; or the total recognition of gender, which is the political abolition of gender. Only in the horizon of democracy is it possible to think of the total subsumption of power, recognition, and the end of sacrifice. But this would be the end of the political, and thus necessarily also the end of democracy, and the end of the end of sacrifice: hence the aporetic character of democratic politics, and, a fortiori, of any politics. As aporetic, the political instance appears as always already heteronormative, never sovereign, not self-contained. Zambrano will make it depend on an experience of the "pure sacred," of the *fondo oscuro*, of a contact with a last god that is to be understood as the very void of any compact fullness.

Zambrano and Heidegger on Forgetting

Zambrano thinks of subalternity as a possibility of an understanding of the political beyond transcendental subjectivity, beyond sovereignty, beyond the conditions under which we have thought of the political in modernity and throughout modernity. Zambrano's notion of democratic politics as the abandonment of the sacrificial structuration of history shows that such an understanding forces us to determine the heteronormativity of the political in favor of a partisan stance, that is, in favor of an always already previous ethical engagement. I would now like to move toward the exposition of the two conceptual structures that I mentioned at the beginning as particularly relevant to understand Zambrano's contribution to political thinking, namely degrounded relation and life without texture, as presented in *El hombre y lo divino*. The latter book can be comprehensively understood as wanting to narrate, impossibly, a history of forgetting—or rather, the history of a forgetting.

In twentieth-century philosophy, the thematization of forgetting is intimately linked to Heidegger's *Being and Time* (1927). But for Heidegger, what is at stake in the history of philosophy is the history of the forgetting of being. Zambrano, roughly thirty years later, does not concern herself with the forgetting of being. What she is interested in is the forgetting of God, and with it the forgetting of the dimension of the sacred, the forgetting of the dimension of the divine as such. For Zambrano, as for Levinas, God is beyond being. God, the sacred, the divine—such is for Zambrano the constellation of an epochal forgetting, the register of a radical insufficiency in the philosophical and spiritual experience of her historical time. Zambrano writes her book, or finishes it, during the years she spent in Rome.

The repeated mention in her book of a white Pythagorean chapel, then re-cently excavated by archaeologists in a neighborhood close to her place of residence, is far from being incidental, just as her references to the Roman Empire's universalism are also not incidental. Zambrano wonders whether the "fortunes of the [Pythagorean] white chapel" are ready to declare, in 1955, their "*oculto sentido,*" or "hidden sense."³ Would it be a counterim-perial sense? What is the secret that Rome preserves, on the side of the vanquished? And why thematize the forgetting of God in order to think, not even democracy, but the possibility of a radically antisovereign, anti-sacrificial politics? Hasn't God been precisely the ultimate guarantor of ontotheology? Hence the very ground of sovereignty? Is there something like a god without sovereignty?

How does one deal with forgetting? To the very extent that the forgetting is such, that is, that it is a true forgetting, it is inaccessible to the memory of the thinker. At most one could rescue traces, if there remains a memory of the forgetting itself, rather than a memory of its object. From that per-spective, is one to think theologically or to think philosophically the forget-ting of the divine, not as forgetting of the *divine* but as *forgetting* as such? What could be the point of a treatise on the forgetting of the divine histor-ically and politically? In 1955, in Rome, at the heart of Latin, Christian, Catholic Europe? To think about the forgetting of the divine is a task dif-ferent from the task Heidegger had indicated as essential: to think through the forgetting of being.

In his 1942–43 lectures on Parmenides, Heidegger came to link the thought of the forgetting of being with the destruction of an imperial thinking of the political, which for him exhausted the European thinking of the political, and which he associated with the curialization of the Greek legacy through the Latin translation of the fundamental concepts of the first beginning of philosophy in Greece (*Parmenides* 43; 46). Western pol-itics are for Heidegger predetermined by the ecclesiastical internalization of the Roman concept of imperial hegemony. For Heidegger, in 1942–43, as the battle of Stalingrad is coming to an end, and with it the might of the Wehrmacht and of Nazi power, the by now for him tragic enterprise of thinking about the forgetting of being has become the enterprise of think-ing through a nonimperial configuration of the political. Zambrano, a few years later, may be attempting something similar from the thought of the forgetting of God. For that nonimperial possibility, which for Zambrano has a name that remained alien to Heideggerian thought, namely democ-racy, the fundamental category is the category of degrounded relation: for

Zambrano, the forgetting of God can only be thought starting from the historical understanding of a degrounded relation to the divine.

El hombre y lo divino contains some hidden references to Heidegger's 1947 *Letter on Humanism*. As is well known, *Letter on Humanism* attempts an account of the present—not just any present, because the essay was written in 1946—through "a thinking that abandons subjectivity."[4] This might sound faintly ridiculous today, when everywhere subjectivity rules as the unthought in our presuppositions. In contemporary political thinking, subjectivity rules explicitly as the posited horizon of any possible thinking of the political, and it is no exaggeration to say that against Heidegger, most contemporary thinking thinks of subjectivity as the true house of being, as the home where contemporary humanity might find refuge against the onset of homelessness, understood as that which is "coming to be the destiny of the world" (219). But subjectivity is for Heidegger homelessness itself. Take, for instance, nationalism, still fundamentally important in 1946: "Every nationalism is metaphysically an anthropologism, and as such subjectivism. Nationalism is not overcome through mere internationalism; it is rather expanded and elevated thereby into a system. Nationalism is as little brought and raised to *humanitas* by internationalism as individualism is by an ahistorical collectivism. The latter is the subjectivity of man in totality. It completes subjectivity's unconditioned self-assertion, which refuses to yield" (221). Man, the human, conceived from subjectivity, remains caught up in "essential homelessness" (221). Is that true also for Zambrano? It certainly is true. But Zambrano takes her path in divergence from Heidegger's.

In *The Question Concerning Technology* (1954), a text therefore strictly contemporary of *El hombre y lo divino*, Heidegger quotes Friedrich Nietzsche on the political importance of philosophy: "The time is coming when the struggle for dominion over the earth will be carried on. It will be carried on in the name of fundamental philosophical doctrines."[5] And Heidegger adds: "'Fundamental philosophical doctrines' does not mean the doctrines of scholars but the language of the truth of what is as such, which truth metaphysics itself is in the form of the metaphysics of the unconditional subjectness of the will to power."[6] Both the Nietzschean will to power and the Hegelian–Marxist kind of transcendental subjectivity ("The essence of materialism [consists] . . . in a metaphysical determination according to which every being appears as the material of labor. The modern metaphysical essence of labor is anticipated in Hegel . . . as the self-establishing process of unconditioned production, which is the objectification of the actual through man experienced as subjectivity" [220]) are what Heidegger has in mind as fundamental doctrines when he says, "the danger into which Europe as it has hitherto existed is ever more clearly forced consists presumably in the fact above all that its thinking—once its glory—is falling behind in the essential course of a dawning world destiny which nevertheless in the basic traits of its essential provenance remains European by definition" (220–21).

What is this dawning world destiny in 1946? Because Nazi Germany has been destroyed, what is present as world-historical can only be conceived in terms of either communism or Americanism. Heidegger's recollective thinking of the history of Being aims at something else, but it must be reached in what he calls a "productive dialogue" with both communism and Americanism, understood as world-historical options that are themselves produced by the history of metaphysics: "Whoever takes 'communism' only as a 'party' or a *'Weltanschauung'* is thinking too shallowly, just as those who by the term 'Americanism' mean, and mean derogatorily, nothing more than a particular lifestyle," as "an elemental experience of what is world-historical speaks out in" them (220). The lag in European thinking, the lag of European thinking with itself, as it makes Europe unable to confront the pincer of Americanism and Sovietism, asks for Europe to assume the guilt of a world conflagration. Europe cannot think its own epoch, and it is because of that that Europe seems to be moving toward a hecatomb that will be presumably larger than the one that was still smoldering in South Germany around 1947. In 1947 Heidegger is still anticipating disaster, never mind his claim that there is a saving power in thinking, in his thinking, that might perhaps avert its consummation.

Is Zambrano, during her Rome years, searching for the establishment of an option for thinking that would be simultaneously anti-Nietzschean, antimaterialist, and endowed with saving power? Yes, without a doubt. Zambrano is, in a sense, repeating the Heideggerian project. Her thematization of the God—of God, of the sacred, of the divine—attempts to offer such an alternative to European thinking. There is a specific will in Zambrano to think an other beginning, and that will is consubstantial to the establishment of a historicopolitical project for Europe. To think of Europe, from Rome, even from the white Pythagorean chapel, and from her condition as a Spanish Republican exile, from her condition as a political victim of a world conflagration, to think of Europe from mourning, and from the mourning for the forgetting of the god, is certainly to think of the future of the world in its degrounded relation with the unknown god, with the last god—with a god, presumably, no longer ontotheological. Ontotheology is for Zambrano, as it was for Heidegger, the very name of the forgetting of the god.

AUTHENTIC HISTORICITY AND THE
REPETITION OF A (NON-)HERITAGE

In paragraph 74 of *Being and Time,* which finally brings the work's entire ontological analytic to rest on the notion of authentic historicity, Heidegger had notoriously sustained that

> the resoluteness in which Da-sein comes back to itself discloses the actual factical possibilities of authentic existing in terms of the heritage which that resoluteness takes over as thrown. Resolute coming back to thrownness involves handing oneself over to traditional possibilities, although not necessarily as traditional ones. If everything good is a matter of heritage and if the character of goodness lies in making authentic existence possible, then handing down a heritage is always constituted in resoluteness.[7]

That heritage is very specifically the German heritage, precisely to the extent that, for Heidegger, the Germanic constitutes the periphery of imperial Rome and therefore preserves the possibility of an other beginning—other than the thinking of a corrupt legacy. The thought of that communitarian heritage or legacy, which later work will make it possible to understand as an anti-Roman legacy, is perhaps the most explicitly political contribution of *Being and Time.* But the hypostasis of this legacy as the instrument of a new politics ruins the possibility of a genuinely alternative understanding of the political in Zambrano's sense.

The simplicity of historical destiny, assumed in resolution, in the anticipation of death, and in the repetition of a legacy, where the establishment of the possibility of an authentic historicopolitical community lies for Heidegger, ignores the terrible facticity of what we would have to call disheritage, disinheritance, or unlegacy. Regarding a historical legacy, the denial of legacy constitutes the outside. In the forgetting of the facticity of unlegacy, the Heideggerian critique of subjectivity cannot avoid falling into the repetition of a subjectivizing communitarianism because it is based on the response to the interpellation of a historical memory. The repetition of a legacy, whether intact or corrupted, excludes unlegacy, unlearns it, hides it. The disinherited is the one who cannot repeat a legacy and falls into forgetting. The abandonment of subjectivity, the accomplishment of a thinking

that abandons subjectivity, is not possible in the wake of the resolute acceptance of a historical legacy. Rather, it fundamentally presupposes a thought
of unlegacy, a thought of disinheritance, of disheritage, a thinking of the
forgetting of that which will not be remembered.

But there is a different possibility: what if repetition could repeat the
disheritage as such? If repetition, in the name of historicopolitical action,
could repeat the nameless as such? Isn't this the only possible form of
thinking about a forgetting? This open search for the nameless and the un-
nameable is the most relevant and poignant tension in Zambrano's text. In
El hombre y lo divino, Zambrano turns the conditions that regulate the difference between theology and philosophy around to the extent that if philosophy were to remain as ontological knowledge, knowledge of being as
such, the knowledge Zambrano seeks is not any kind of positive knowledge of a being, even if that being were to be the being of beings, or the
maximum being. Rather, the science of the divine and the sacred, the science of God or of the last god, is in Zambrano a science of nonbeing, and
thus not a theological science, but rather an a-theology whose emphasis on
the ontological excess, in what is beyond philosophical vision, reaches the
rank of political a-theology.

Is *El hombre y lo divino* a political a-theology? Does it at least give us a formal indication of a possible political a-theology? Zambrano's word is always
at the margins or in excess of any attempt to name representationally or
calculatively regional being. It moves in a region that could be considered
arregional because it is beyond any ontological horizon: the arregional region of the god, of the last god. Zambrano's text on the forgetting of the god,
on the disheritage, unlegacy of the thought of the god in our times, can
offer the possibility of both a political and an a-theological thinking beyond
subjectivity. Perhaps that unknown possibility of thinking finds its source
in what Zambrano calls "the historical reserve that the vanquished always
already form," and as such the site of "whatever is imperceptible in whole
epochs, what was defeated, what never made it to reason or what went
beyond reason, the seed of future reason" (115). That unknown possibility
is then the possibility of subalternity, of subaltern thought.

The notion of degrounded relation appears in Zambrano's text at the
beginning of the chapter called "God Is Dead," which is of course a sustained reflection on Nietzsche's doctrine. For Zambrano, "contemporary
man" embodies, as contemporary, "all the condensed religious history of
humanity, . . . all the conflicts that have occurred in the decisive moments of
history" (127). Thus, "God is dead" is not the announcement of a liberation,

is not the announcement of the beginning of an other history, but rather marks for Zambrano precisely the moment of the degrounding or *abismamiento* of the history of the present: the moment when the forgetting of the god becomes official, to put it that way, and is forgotten as forgetting. Zambrano says: "One could divide things in life into two categories: those that disappear when we disavow them and those of a mysterious reality that, even disavowed, leave our relation to them intact. The latter is the case with that which is hidden in what is today the almost unutterable word, God" (126). She goes on: "The more the object remains outside our horizon, the larger and deeper our relation to it, until it invades the entire area of our life, until it stops being a relation in the strict sense of the term. . . . When one of the two [terms of a relation] . . . disappears, the relation becomes de-grounded. And then it simply happens that the other term, the one that cannot disappear—in this case, us, our human life—is thrown into an indefinable situation, is, in turn, de-grounded" (126).

Contemporary man lives in a degrounded relation; god has disappeared, is dead, or has been disavowed, but in such a way that our relationship to it has come, through its very forgetting, to occupy the entire area of our life. To live in a degrounded relation means to live in the forgetting of forgetting, in degrounded memory. If we embody every conflict in history, the entire history of religious humanity, that is, the entire history of the relation of the human to the divine, and if we do it abysmally, degroundedly, our heritage is disinheritance itself, but to the precise extent that there is no disinheritance without a legacy. Disinheritance, the lot of the subaltern, of the defeated, degrounds the heritage. Disinheritance is the abyss of our time—something the Spanish Republican exiles were in a much better position to understand than Heidegger ever could.

But if disinheritance degrounds the heritage, how are we to extract political relevance from this strange Zambranian figure, which amounts to a radical rereading of the concept of authentic historicity in *Being and Time*? What concept of the political can attend to the impossible memory of unlegacy?

Nothingness beyond Being, and the Last God

I set out to do two things: the first one was to elucidate Zambrano's understanding of democratic politics as the pull toward the abandonment of the sacrificial structuration of history. On this issue, it seemed important to proceed to establish how Zambrano's *El hombre y lo divino* radicalizes the Heideggerian project for "a thought that abandons subjectivity" and through a silent critique of *Being and Time*'s notion of authentic historicity based on the notion of *relación abismada* ("degrounded relation") sets the ground for the democratic repetition of subalternity, for the endless repetition of a legacy of unlegacy upon which the very possibility of the abandonment of sacrifice rests. This is in itself a major accomplishment, perhaps still unequaled in post-Heideggerian political philosophy.

But the second thing was to articulate Zambrano's conception of the political beyond subjectivity and sovereignty and beyond the identification of subjectivity and sovereignty that has produced political modernity as such. The identity of thinking and being, an old Parmenidean word that marks perhaps the beginning of historical metaphysics, forms at the end of metaphysics the thought of transcendental subjectivity in both Hegelian and Husserlian philosophy. But transcendental subjectivity also marks the triumph of the totalitarian state form in the twentieth century. Zambrano, who fought for the Spanish Republic, who became an expatriate and an exile for many years at deep personal cost, produces in the notion of *vida sin textura*, "life without texture," the very possibility of a radically democratic, antisacrificial conception of the political against subjective militancy.

Subjective militancy is ontotheological militancy. There are two primary ways of it in modernity. In the first way, the militant—formal subject of a practice of the will—seeks the exhaustive exploitation of being, the thorough appropriation of being to militant practice. The subject, as a singular absolute, works on the remainder of its autistic immanence, thinks of the world as the infinitely reducible, and affirms its own apotheosis in the closure of world into subject and subject into world. This is the figure of the liberal subject, which is also the communist subject: a progressive subject, a subject beyond the shadow of its own impossibility.

In the second way of ontotheological militancy, the militant emphasizes distance, dwells on the loss through which the subject finds its bliss through open, painful deconstitution. The subject is here pierced by its own insufficiency and must affirm a blind transcendence from that which, upon giving itself, is lost: from that which gives itself as loss. This is the reactionary subject, which is also the subject of personal identity.

In both cases, through both ways, the ontotheological ground of militancy is a *ground* because the world appears as an entity regarding which one must either insist or resist. Through the first militancy, insistence is a will for saturation: the world will reach proper totality, will be the One-All as it coalesces with a subject only upon which a world is possible. In the second militancy, the world is always already One-All, and the subject experiences it as it experiences its own expulsion toward nothingness. The world is experienced as possible through its very withdrawal, appears as an always vanishing horizon, and it is through this very vanishing that the subject can exercise its own overwhelming presence: the subject is nothing but a resistance against nothing, hence the subject is all.

So what possibilities remain beyond ontotheological, subjective militancy? Beyond progressivism and reactionaryism? In a way, this was Heidegger's political question, and from a very different perspective, it was also Zambrano's question. In *Heidegger y su tiempo*, Felipe Martínez Marzoa speaks about a distance from distance, a double distance, which would be the minimal distance provided by the very fact of understanding the game of appropriating presence and appropriating absence. But, Martínez Marzoa says, there is no "minimization" in that notion of minimal distance. Double distance—a distance from reactionary militancy, and a distance from progressive militancy, a distance from the insistence of subject/world and the resistance to its loss—is rather "enormous, immeasurable."[8] This double distance cannot form a new subject of the political, but it is the site for the appearance of that which dwells in the unthought of modern subjectivity. It is the promise of another constitution of the political.

Zambrano's concept of life without texture seeks the dissolution of every subjective insistence and of every subjective resistance. It seeks a possibility of experience beyond the autistic experience of ontotheological militancy. Zambrano says:

> [The action of nothingness] is a living action. One could call it life without texture, without consistency. Life with texture is already being, even though in life there is always more than texture, and so in man life is in excess of what it is in those for whom life is only texture. In man, life shows that it is more than being, being, that is, in the way of things, of objects. That is why in man, as being grows, so grows nothingness. And then nothingness works as a possibility. Nothingness *hace nacer,* brings into the world [I must point out the untranslatability of *hace nacer* here, since nothing could be more wrong than the obvious translation, "brings into being"]. (169)

What about this nothingness? For Zambrano, nothingness is precisely "what can not be thought as a function of being" (165). It is the dissolution of the thinking/being identity. Nothingness propitiates nihilism only for philosophical consciousness, and more properly for philosophy understood as a philosophy of consciousness, as a philosophy of subjectivity. But in Zambrano, nothingness does not announce nihilism. On the contrary, *la nada hace nacer,* "nothingness brings into the world," and what it brings is the *fondo sagrado,* "sacred ground": "The sacred ground from which man went on slowly awakening as if from the initial dream reappears now in the nothingness" (173). Nothingness is for Zambrano the excess of subjectivity, the absolute resistance to—as double resistance, as double distance—subjectivity, "a resistance that is not being, since the thinking subject knows nothing about any being that is not itself" (174). And that which is not being is nothing, "*mas es todo; es el fondo innominado que no es idea*" ("but it is everything; it is the nameless ground that is not idea") (174). To think through to this nameless ground, nothingness, since not-being, not-idea, is for Zambrano to think "the last appearance of the sacred" (162), the last god. This is for Zambrano the philosophical task of the present, understood as a "conversion" (164), insofar as it requires a renunciation. In fact, it requires a renunciation to the renunciation of the excess of being; it requires to give up having given up nonbeing, hell, or nothingness. Only in that renunciation to renunciation, in that double renunciation and double distance, will the totality of thought open up. Zambrano speaks of a *desmoronamiento,* a "falling apart of what is texture, of what is being in human life" (169) as an essential condition of that possibility of experience. This falling apart, this emptying out of being, will open the space for the harsh but redeeming unthought. Here is a translation of Zambrano's words: "Nothingness is like the shadow of an All that can not come into understanding, the void of such a compact fullness that it becomes its equivalent, the mute, unarticulated negation of all revelation. It is the pure sacred without any indication that it will allow itself to be unconcealed" (175).

How is the possibility of thinking the pure sacred, then, political, or how does it announce a new constitution of the political? The thinking of untextured life connects with the thinking of subaltern unlegacy. Something other than life shows up in untextured life, as life is not the limit of the thinkable. Beyond life there is a pure sacredness that remains close to the nakedness of nothing. The task today is to think or to undergo the experience of the pure sacred, to pass the test of the last god, that god that always already occupies the entire area of our life through our forgetting, and through our forgetting of forgetting. In life without texture, life without being, life without *bios,* accessible only through the experience of degrounding, in itself a consequence of the revelation of the death of God, the possibility and hence the necessity of an encounter with the last god—as the void of compact fullness—opens up. It is a remembering, but it is a remembering of what remains unlegated, and thus not the object of communitarian property. To remember life beyond life, against biopolitical subjectivation—that is the historical reserve of the vanquished as vanquished, and hence the promise of an altogether different politics, of another beginning: the other side of sacrificial politics. Zambrano gives us, against the sovereignty of ontotheological subjectivity, an antisovereign political a-theology. Is that the last or present sense of the Pythagorean white chapel at the heart of a thoroughly declined empire? Its promise for the abandonment of sacrificial history must still be thought out. For sacrificial history is always a history of the legacy, and of the life that is legated.

NOTES

1. There has been some attention paid to Zambrano's largely silent engagement with Heidegger's work. Certainly Jesús Moreno Sanz, perhaps the best Zambrano scholar, has insisted on the fact that Zambrano's work is in a constant dialogue with Nietzsche and Heidegger. See Jesús Moreno Sanz, ed., *María Zambrano. La razón en la sombra. Antología crítica* (Madrid: Siruela, 2004), 25, 27–28. In any case, important recent contributions to an elucidation of this crucial *Auseinandersetzung* by Sergio Sevilla, Oscar Adán, and Massimo Cacciari have cleared paths we must now follow.

2. María Zambrano, *Persona y democracia. La historia sacrificial* (1958; Barcelona: Anthropos, 1988), 42.

3. María Zambrano, *El hombre y lo divino* (Madrid: Siruela, 1991), 116–17. Subsequent references to this essay will appear in the text.

4. Martin Heidegger, "Letter on Humanism," in *Basic Writings,* ed. David Farrell Krell (New York: Harper & Row, 1977), 207. Subsequent references to this essay will appear in the text.

5. Friedrich Nietzsche, quoted in Martin Heidegger, *The Question Concerning Technology and Other Essays,* trans. William Lovitt (New York: Harper & Row, 1977), 101.

6. Ibid., 101.

7. Martin Heidegger, *Being and Time,* trans. Joan Stambaugh (Albany: State University of New York Press, 1996), 351.

8. Felipe Martínez Marzoa, *Heidegger y su tiempo* (Madrid: Akal, 1999), 45, 46.

IV

PSYCHOANALYSIS AND THE POLITICAL

10

Signification and Substance: Toward a Leftist Ontology of the Present

CHRISTOPHER BREU

What is a praxis? I doubt whether this term may be regarded as inappropriate to psycho-analysis. It is the broadest term to designate a concerted human action, whatever it may be, which places man in a position to treat the real by the symbolic.

—JACQUES LACAN, *Seminar XI*

A deadlock haunts contemporary theory. On the one hand, there is all the powerful work that has been enabled by social construction theories, by Foucauldian theories of discourse, and more generally by poststructuralist interventions into culture. On the other hand, there is the vital work undertaken by Marxist and globalization theories on the increasing inequalities produced by neoliberalism and post-Fordist capitalism. Although poststructuralism has advanced a salutary and important critique of ideas of nature and the natural as well as of philosophical idealism (and versions of materialism that represent merely an inverted form of such idealism), it is less effective at theorizing the limits, especially those of class and embodiment, placed on human life at any one time by the material dimensions of everyday life and the current organization of the political economy. Globalization and neo-Marxist theories, on the other hand, provide a much more compelling account of the material dimensions of existence, but are often in danger of advancing a hypostatized conception of the material and the political–economic.

So what do we do with this deadlock? It seems imperative to insist on the insights of both positions. It is crucial to maintain the poststructuralist critique of the discourses of nature and the biological; this critique has been central to the crucial advances made in theorizing gender, race, and sexuality in the last thirty years.[1] Yet it is equally essential to recognize the ways in which various forms of materiality—from the geopolitical and

socioeconomic to the biological—place limits on the discursive construction of everyday life, and indeed often produce the discursive meanings we
assume as autonomous.[2] Perhaps one way of beginning to work toward a
solution of this deadlock is to recast its terms in relationship to questions
of epistemology and ontology.

What we need at the present moment is a leftist ontology, but one that
attends to all the epistemological work that has been enabled by poststructuralist forms of critique. I want to suggest two perhaps unlikely places we
can turn to developing such an ontology: recent Lacanian work that emphasizes the category of the real, and the current writings of Michael Hardt
and Antonio Negri, with their concept of the biopolitical and their related
reworking of Foucault's notion of biopower to attend to the ways in which
late capitalist production shapes the very being of laboring and otherwise
managed bodies.[3]

Lacan's understanding of the real can be read in part as an elaboration
and radicalization of two early twentieth-century accounts of ontology,
those of Martin Heidegger and Georges Bataille. Central to Heidegger's
conception of ontology is his understanding of Being and its relationship
to existence. Being for Heidegger, to quickly and inadequately summarize,
is never reducible to representation or to any instrumental attempt to fix its
meaning. Thus it is extrinsic to language and exceeds any scientific account
of existence. It instead can only be grasped as it unveils itself as a nonre-
ducible, heterogenous totality (or "being-ness") that exists within a specific
history, location, and temporality.[4] Lacan's conception of the real draws
on this Heideggerian understanding of Being to theorize those aspects of
being and of existence that exceed the symbolic but that are central to the
historical constitution of subjectivity and human existence as such.

In developing this conception of the real, Lacan fuses Heidegger's understanding of Being with Bataille's conception of base materiality. Bataille
posits the notion of base materiality in a series of short essays written in
the late 1920s and early 1930s that critique both idealism and the mechanical materialism of positivist science and certain forms of Marxist thought.[5]
In contrast to the systematized materialism of positivism and orthodox
Marxism, Bataille argues for a conception of materialism that refuses dialectical sublation or the formal definitional procedures of science. It instead
puts forward a conception of materiality as brute, contingent, and intransigent; such materiality exceeds and exists in negative tension with any system of symbolic recuperation. In positing this notion of brute materialism,
Bataille doesn't reject the dialectic out of hand but instead radicalizes it,

positing this notion of brute materiality as a site of dialectical negation that refuses recuperation. In marking the radical rift between the material and the representational, Bataille puts forward an understanding of ontology that corresponds closely to Heidegger's celebrated distinction between earth and world in "The Origin of the Work of Art." However, in this case, the earth is not the nurturing natural foundation upon which worlds are constructed, but the site of the obdurately material that exists in opposition to such worlds.

Lacan, then, posits the real as that which is excluded, excised, or disavowed from the symbolic, and he emphasizes three different forms the real can take when theorized from the vantage of the symbolic, the imaginary, or the real: (1) a hole in the symbolic, (2) the unconscious and the drives, and (3) uncoded materiality.[6] In what follows, I will argue that this tripartite conception of the real forms the basis for a leftist ontology of the present, one that enables me to theorize the material underpinnings and exclusions of what Hardt and Negri describe as the emergent regime of biopolitical production. Although they compellingly theorize a new regime of production in which the body and its affects are central, this theorization, despite its emphasis on the body, remains surprisingly idealist. I will draw on Lacan's real to theorize the forms of materiality that are excluded from the circuit of biopolitical production as theorized by Hardt and Negri.

What Lacanian psychoanalysis has to offer, perhaps uniquely among contemporary theoretical perspectives, is a theory of the relationship between language and materiality that does not simply or immediately subsume the latter term to the former category or vice versa. Given this distinctive theoretical vantage, I want to suggest that certain tenets of Lacanian psychoanalysis can be radicalized, and at points extended through metaphor, to propose a discontinuous yet dialectical theory of the relationship between language and materiality that can help us rethink the relationship both to bodies and to the workings of the political economy in our present moment.

As with most terms in Lacanian psychoanalysis, the definition of the real is notoriously polyvalent and slippery. Indeed, the term, like all Lacanian concepts, underwent a series of revisions and redefinitions as Lacan's thought evolved from the 1940s through the 1970s. Hence it is hardly surprising to see that among contemporary Lacanians, the real is defined in a range of different and often contradictory ways. In his account, Tim Dean argues that it is important not to confuse "reality with the Lacanian real."[7] What we perceive as reality is largely a by-product of the interaction of the symbolic and the imaginary. The symbolic grants coherence to and effectively mediates what we term reality, but does so only at a price. The imaginary situates the subject within a visual field organized by desire, yet the field of the visual only gains coherence via the logic of the symbolic. In acceding to the symbolic, the subject is able to make sense of the world, marking the boundary between inside and outside and conceptually and perceptually differentiating the otherwise undifferentiated stuff of thought, affect, and the world outside the subject. Yet the very binary logic of language does violence to that which it attempts to describe, reducing the irreducible particularity, porousness, and (what is often less theorized) continuity of that which it attempts to represent to a set of discrete binary oppositions.

Slavoj Žižek at various moments characterizes the real as "the anomorphic stain" that represents the imaginary subjectification and distortion of "objective reality," as "the empty place" or "void" that marks the space where the symbolic breaks down, and finally as uncoded materiality, which from within the logic of the symbolic, appears as the abject, obscene, or contingent.[8] In *Enjoy Your Symptom!* he suggests that these are the different imaginary, symbolic, and real registers of the real, which indicates that these are different ways of describing or apprehending the same object or relationship. Other definitions of the term seem to be variations on this tripartite definition. Dean's definition of the term, for example, fully dematerializes it, arguing that it forms a "transcendental," nonsubstantial gap or empty space of contradiction to the symbolic. Elizabeth Grosz, on the other hand, presents a developmental and materialist definition of the concept in which "the Real is the order proceeding the ego and the organization of the drives" in the imaginary. In this definition, the real is "a space without boundaries, borders, divisions, or oppositions; it is a continuum of raw materials."[9]

Finally, Dylan Evans, in his dictionary of Lacanian psychoanalysis, likewise confirms the elusive dimensions of the term. According to Evans, from the 1950s onward, "the real is . . . no longer simply opposed to the imaginary, but is beyond the symbolic."[10] Citing key Lacanian texts of the mid-1950s, Evans goes on to argue that Lacan's definitions of the real coalesces as "'that which resists symbolization absolutely' (S[eminar] 1, 66); or, again, the real is 'the domain of whatever subsists outside symbolization' (E[crits], 388). The theme remains constant throughout the rest of Lacan's work, and leads Lacan to link the real with the concept of impossibility."[11] Although Evans's emphasis here is on the notion of the impossibility of the real, what also remains constant in the definition of the real is the notion that it represents the domain of that which exists outside of symbolization.

This of course begs the question: what it is that remains outside of the symbolic? There are any of a number of possible answers to this question. However, if we are to accept Žižek's tripartite account of the real, the answer itself is multiple. Dean emphasizes the transcendental dimension of the real, which would correspond to Žižek's definition of the hole in the symbolic. However, this definition represents only the symbolic dimension of the real and as such represents a largely dematerialized understanding of the concept; the imaginary and real dimensions of the real represent more materialist resonances of the concept. Indeed, it is these conceptions of the real that allow Lacan to contend that his version of psychoanalysis represents a form of materialism, because it "engages with ontological questions."[12] The imaginary dimension of the real signifies the domain of the drives and the unconscious both as it constitutes the structuration of the subject and the various objects of transference (including those objects that become phantasmatically associated with the *objet petit a*). It is in this context that Evans's definition of the real as that that lies beyond symbolization takes on its specificity. In Freudian psychoanalysis, symbolization is defined as a way of mediating the drives, functioning as that which can intervene in the acting out of the drives. So the drives and the way in which they shape embodiment and the organization of desire are another, more materialist, register of the real.

The third register, or what Žižek suggests is the real register of the real, is the domain that most thoroughly constitutes Lacanian psychoanalysis as a form of materialism. Both Žižek and Evans suggest that this represents the "material substrate underlying the imaginary and the symbolic."[13] This material substrate is only ever imperfectly indicated by the symbolic through the referential dimension of language. We often act as if the symbolic is fused with the material but this is one of the elementary ideological effects of the symbolic itself. To say this, however, is not to suggest that there is no relationship between the symbolic and this sense of the real. The symbolic, although overdetermined by language's differential organization, attempts to describe or represent the real. We call this activity by various names: science, philosophy, theory, or simply discourse.

The real register of the real is not merely the material substrate underlying the imaginary and the symbolic, although this is importantly its broadest definition, but more specifically the forms of uncoded materiality that elude symbolic definition or resist integration into the symbolic (and it is here that Lacan's borrowing from Bataille's conception of base materialism is most evident). As such, it functions as that which remains stubbornly contingent to the lawful and ordered universe of discourse and the symbolic. It is in this sense of the real that Žižek describes both death and ecological disaster as "answers of the real." Key to this conception of the "answer of the real" is how the *real* event gets subjectified and symbolized. Because the possibility of such events must remain disavowed for the smooth and seemingly noncontradictory functioning of the symbolic order to continue, our experience or fantasy of the *real* event is ordered by a whole range of different forms of enjoyment and attempts at symbolic control, from guilt, to blame, to denial, to repulsion, to perverse fascination, to ecstatic embrace.

However, it is at this point, when we begin to discuss the subjective response to the real, that the structural differentiation implicit in the tripartite definition begins to demonstrate its inadequacy. Although it is initially important to distinguish between these different registers of the real, Lacan's understanding of the concept can only be fully grasped when we conceive of the way in which all three registers work together. The subject has an imaginary orientation to the hole in the symbolic that is ordered by his or her unconscious and relationship to the drives; this orientation often works by disavowal, so that the hole in the symbolic remains invisible (filled by a fantasized big Other who/which represents the guarantor of symbolic meaning); this hole, and the resistant and contingent forms of materiality that exist outside of the symbolic, become perceivable when an event occurs that challenges or undoes the coherence of the symbolic system. Such an understanding of the real, with its continuous movement between the different registers, also works to keep the concept from being simply reduced to another reified symbolic structure.

I want to suggest that this definition of the real can help us to think through the deadlock of contemporary theory with which I began. For what is at stake in this deadlock are the contradictions produced between methodologies that are focused on epistemological questions versus those that are grounded in ontological concerns. What strikes me as most promising about recent Lacanian formulations of the real is the way in which they mediate, in a nonreductive way, between these registers. By attending to the productive and constitutive work done by language via the symbolic, while theorizing the limits of the linguistic and the equally constitutive dimensions of desire and materiality, Lacan's conception of the real maintains the epistemological critique advanced by poststructuralism while radicalizing Heidegger's and Bataille's understandings of ontology to produce an account that attends to the centrality of both materiality and desire to the constitution of the social. By drawing on Žižek's tripartite conception of the real as it intersects with the symbolic and the imaginary, we are able to theorize both the symbolic construction of everyday life and posit that which resists, eludes, and sets limits on that symbolic construction.

That which resists symbolic coding can be multiply theorized. One locus of resistance is the body itself, especially the forms of bodily materiality that remain outside what Freud describes as the body ego.[14] In *The Ego and the Id,* Freud asserts that the ego is not merely a metaphoric conception of the "I" that exists in a dynamic tension with the superego and the id, but it is also a symbolic and phantasmatic mapping of the materiality of the body, one that is shaped by visual and somatic perception.[15] Lacan's notion of the mirror stage is in many ways an extension and dialecticization of this conception of the body ego. The visual, and intersubjective, constitution of the "me" in the mirror becomes misrecognized as the "I" of the ego.[16] In Lacan, the real dimension of the body emerges as precisely those forms of materiality that differ or are excluded from this imaginary construction and its symbolic elaboration. This real dimension of the body forms one site of ontological significance that eludes the epistemological focus of social construction and poststructuralist theory.

The unconscious and the drives represent another ontological register of the real that challenges the epistemological preoccupations of poststructuralist theory. Central to the relationship of the real of the unconscious to the symbolic and imaginary is the workings of fantasy. One function of fantasy is a defensive one. What Žižek terms the "fundamental fantasy" works to maintain the fiction of subjective and symbolic coherence by keeping the intrusions of the real, which threaten to disrupt this coherence, at a safe distance. Žižek suggests that we can only break the power of the fundamental fantasy by way of what he terms the authentic act, a version of what Lacan terms "praxis" in the epigraph with which I started. The authentic act enables a traversing of the fantasy, the destitution of the subject, and a concomitant encounter with the real. It breaks with the terms of the symbolic by functioning in a way that is not comprehensible within its logic.[17] Central to the performance of the act is the process of subjective destitution, in which the subject recognizes the way in which her phantasmatic construction of the symbolic and masochistic positioning within it denies the freedom of her ability to act. Such acts can only take place when the very phantasmatic scaffolding of the symbolic and the subject's fantasized position within it appear to collapse. It is thus only by accepting symbolic death that the collective or individual subject can encounter the real (here both the real of her unconscious and of the un-coded or only partially coded materiality of the world around her) and come out the other side to produce the construction of a different sym-bolic universe.

The final ontological dimension of the real that challenges the exclu-sively epistemological focus of poststructuralism is the definition of it as uncoded materiality. It is here, I want to suggest, that a bridge can be built to the other important theoretical challenge to the epistemological preoc-cupations of poststructuralism: the forms of materialism posted by neo-Marxist and globalization theories. At first glance, Marx's understanding of materialism seems to be the opposite of the conception of materiality in Lacanian theory. Although the Lacanian understanding of the real as un-coded materiality is focused precisely on that which resists, lies outside of, or refuses to be reduced to various forms of symbolic coding, Marx's defi-nition of materialism is a dynamic one that focuses on the ways in which various material (and sometimes immaterial) properties of the physical world (which in Marx often go under the signs of "nature," "natural re-sources," or "material conditions") are transformed by labor, itself a mate-rial process—indeed, the most important material process—to produce various goods for social use and consumption.[18] Thus, Marx's conception of materialism is a transformative one, in which the materials of nature are socially coded and shaped, via the material process of labor, for social use. As such, they become fully integrated into the symbolic universe of the social. One way of conceptualizing the transformation that Marx names production is the successful transformation of raw materials into products that can be controlled by and contained within the logic of the symbolic. This process is what Marx theorizes as humanity wresting control of mate-rial circumstances from nature.

Yet it is precisely here, when the two concepts of materialism seem most at odds, that I want to suggest a relationship can be adduced. Slavoj Žižek has famously theorized the analogous relationship between the Freudian and Lacanian notion of the symptom and the logic of commodity fetish-ism.[19] Working through this analogy and charting its present implications for our increasingly globalized world will enable me to demonstrate the productive relationship that can be posited between Marxist materialism and the Lacanian conception of the real.

As I have theorized at greater length elsewhere, the crucial addition that Žižek makes to Marx's conception of commodity fetishism is that he sees the relationship between the subject (both collective, and individual) and the commodity as one structured by fantasy.[20] Marx's classic definition of commodity fetishism is that a relationship among people (that is, the social production and reproduction of the material underpinnings and relationships of everyday life) becomes misperceived as a relationship among things (the free exchange of money for commodities or one's commodified labor power for money).[21] What is then excluded from this commodified and individualistic understanding of the social is the very socioeconomic origin of labor and of the transformation of the material world itself.

What Žižek adds to this definition is that this misperception is phantasmatically structured in terms of the psychoanalytic logic of disavowal, with its classic Freudian articulation: "I know . . . but nevertheless. . . ." It is not that the subject is unaware of the social basis of commodity production but that this social basis must remain disavowed for the symbolic universe of capitalism to remain consistent. The same logic of disavowal holds true for the function of money within the capitalist economy: "I know very well that money is merely paper, or in our postmodern world, digits on a computer screen that have no relationship to any fixed international monetary standard, nevertheless it is the sublime guarantor of value that exists in a privileged relationship to all other commodities."

There are two crucial points to understand about this application of the Freudian notion of disavowal to commodity fetishism. First, the subject's relationship to the commodity is bonded through the workings of fantasy; indeed, fantasy here plays the role of the fundamental fantasy as elucidated above. Second, this phantasmatic relationship is inevitably a collective one. This second point is crucial because the transformation of this phantasmatic structure must inevitably be collective and not individual. To take just one example, the individual subject can stop believing in the collective fantasy that is money, yet he still lives in a world that is shaped and determined by this collective fantasy. The first point is crucial because it asserts that the subject's relationship to the symbolic of capitalism is not only discursive but, perhaps more importantly, imaginary and phantasmatic. Thus, what is excluded from the symbolic universe of capitalism may still be symbolically coded—for example, the productive labor of sweatshop workers in our globalized present is not unknowable and does not exist outside of the symbolic, broadly conceived—but it remains that which is disavowed or excluded on a phantasmatic level for the (ethical, philosophical, political) coherence of the symbolic system to be maintained. This is the significance of Žižek's turn to the notion of disavowal in explaining commodity fetishism. For that which is disavowed is initially symbolized, but in the very same moment, its significance is dismissed, and it is excluded from any real recognition within the symbolic universe.

In order to fully understand the value of this Marxian reworking of the notion of the real, we must demonstrate its relationship to the three registers outlined above. In terms of the symbolic register of the real, recognition of the excluded or disavowed term reveals the hole in the symbolic, demonstrating the way in which capitalism is neither inevitable nor philosophically consistent, but arbitrary and premised on a fundamental set of violent exclusions and consequent misrecognitions. The return of the excluded represents that which can only be experienced from within the symbolic as the contingent and the chaotic because its significance is disavowed. As my language of return already suggests here, the excluded term can also be allied with that which is repressed (for a disavowal requires the repression of that which is disavowed) and hence rendered unconscious. Thus, the excluded also embodies the imaginary register of the real; as I outlined above, this register indicates that which is unconscious and those aspects of the body and the drives that are not consistently part of the body ego. In this sense, we can talk about a social body ego. The real in this context represents those aspects of the socioeconomic body politic that are repressed within or excluded from society's collective ego ideal, or ideal image of itself. These aspects can be the social relations that are productive of the society's economic functioning, but also various identities (identities often—though not exclusively—associated with the denigrated aspects of production) that are, in Judith Butler's terms, abjected, that is, denied symbolic, and in the sense of a social body ego, *imaginary*, recognition.[22]

My emphasis on the body here suggests the third register of the real—the real register of the real, or that of uncoded materiality. Here the relationship between the excluded and the real is more complex. In Žižek's reworking of commodity fetishism in terms of the logic of disavowal, that which is excluded is not unsymbolized or uncoded; it is instead recognized and then disavowed, its significance excluded from the symbolic representation of the system to guarantee the latter's coherence. Thus, as I argued above, labor and the appropriation of surplus value are not excluded from the symbolic of capitalism; they rest at the very heart of the capitalist system, but their significance as a contradiction to the coherence of capitalism as the symbolic system is excluded on the level of fantasy. It is the work of the capitalist fundamental fantasy to ensure the continued working of this disavowal.

The concept of uncoded materiality, on the other hand, does not work via this logic of disavowal. Instead, it represents that which eludes or lies outside of symbolic coding altogether. As such, it posits a concept of materiality that seems to lie fully outside of the Marxist definition of materialism, with its emphasis on the transformation of the material world through labor. In an important sense, to the degree that it suggests a nontransparent or simply referential relationship between language and materiality, this third notion of the real does indeed present an important challenge to both the epistemology and the ontology of conventional Marxism, which emphasizes both the transparency of language and the knowability and manipulability of the material. In another sense, though, this notion of uncoded materiality can be allied with the category of "nature" in Marx. Nature is precisely that which resists and sets limits on, even as it contains the resources for, socioeconomic development in any given epoch. It is that which has not yet been socialized and symbolically reshaped through labor (physical and otherwise), and to the degree that human labor and knowledge have not reached the point of being able to socialize it, it represents the inert outside or ground of human society that can only be represented in metaphysical, speculative, or religious terms.

But although such a concept of nature may be compelling for work done in earlier eras, what is the fate of such a concept, and the conception of the real to which it is linked in our own postmodern era, in which as Fredric Jameson has argued, the last vestiges of nature and the unconscious have been colonized by the market, and thus seemingly fully socialized?[23] It is here that the aspects of the real that exceed the Marxian concept of nature become of critical importance. The Lacanian conception of uncoded materiality is not merely about that which lies outside of symbolization or socialization because it has yet to be socialized. It is even more crucially about that which, given the necessarily catachrestic aspects of language, eludes or resists symbolization precisely in the very act of symbolization itself.

This final understanding of the real posits a conception of materiality that is distinct from Marxist materialism, yet one that provides a necessary supplement to the Marxist paradigm in order to fully theorize the forms of biopolitical production that Hardt and Negri argue are central to our globalized, late-capitalist present. It also provides a paradigm for the relationship between language and materiality that partially reconciles, and makes productive, the contradiction between poststructuralism and materialism with which I began. Marxism and psychoanalysis, then, as different forms of materialism, work on the real to symbolize that which isn't yet symbolized and socialize that which isn't yet socialized or which is socialized only in exploitative ways. In this sense, both methodologies are forms of praxis as Lacan defines this notion in the epigraph with which I started: treating the real by the symbolic.

By contrast, the eschewing of the material for the symbolic and the concomitant effacement of the real is one of the main limitations of what is otherwise the most compelling theoretical synthesis of our present moment, one that works to theorize the new forms of capitalism and democratic, and potentially socialist, activism that have emerged in relationship to the late capitalist global economy: Hardt and Negri's theorization of empire, multitude, biopower, and the biopolitical in *Empire* and *Multitude*.[24]

In these two texts, Hart and Negri posit the emergence of a new political logic, empire, and a new economic dominant, what they term immaterial production, that works in relationship to what they term, after Foucault, biopower and to various forms of biopolitical production. Central to Hardt and Negri's account of contemporary capitalism is the nascent emergence of an entity called "empire," which they posit as a supranational regime of global sovereignty that works to reproduce the global division of labor through the logic of policing various extranational forms of resistance (embodied by everything from the progressive forces of World Trade Organization protesters and the Zapatistas to the deeply reactionary forces of various religious fundamentalisms). Linked to this conception of a new form of global sovereignty is their argument for the emergence of a new political–economic dominant: what they term immaterial production, which is developed through the biopolitical organization of everyday life. Although their political thesis has received the most attention, to my mind, it is this economic formulation that is the most compelling aspect of their new synthesis, for it suggests the centrality of bodies and the symbolic as such to contemporary global production. Whereas Foucault defines biopower as the locus of modern forms of administered power, Hardt and Negri's conception of the biopolitical transforms the notion of biopower into an economic conception of power, one that asserts the direct production of everyday life by various forms of immaterial production.[25] By immaterial production, Hardt and Negri do not mean that the labor involved in the production is immaterial—far from it. They are instead asserting that the end product is immaterial, such as the end products of intellectual, service, affective, and electronic labor, while an important part of the labor that produces this product remains material in the sense of being physically intensive.

On the face of it, this argument for immaterial production appears to merely rehash anti-Marxist notions of postindustrial society (such as those of Jean-Fançois Lyotard or Daniel Bell, to choose two politically divergent examples) and seems easily refutable by pointing to the shift of industrial production to free enterprise zones in the third world and ghettoized parts of the first world.[26] As Saskia Sassen has demonstrated, the growth of immaterial production is always underpinned by devalorized forms of labor that often have a more direct relationship to the material production and reproduction of everyday life.[27] However, Hardt and Negri recognize this shift in the location of industrial labor and are far from theorizing the simple superseding of industrial production by the immaterial. Instead, they are arguing that immaterial production represents a new globally dominant productive logic, one that reorganizes all other forms of production in its image. Thus it is not that immaterial production has become quantitatively the dominant form of production (this is still agriculture, as it was under industrial capitalism). Instead, the dominant is such because it represents the leading edge of the economy and catalyzes a reorganization of all other forms of production (agricultural and industrial) in relationship to its logic. Agribusiness represented an industrial reorganization of agricultural labor under industrial capitalism. Similarly, under immaterial production, both agricultural labor and industrial production are reorganized around the cybernetic, biopolitical, and communicative logics of immaterial production.

This concept of immaterial production is central to Hardt and Negri's vision of the multitude, which they define as a potentially emergent democratic collective that represents, in their paradoxical formulation, a "common social being" consisting of "singularities."[28] Drawing on early modern political philosophy, with its conception of the intersection between the body politic and the human body both invoked under the singular term *corpore,* Hardt and Negri theorize the multitude as a new collective yet stateless body made up of singularities. They argue that this collectivity—or, to use their preferred term, common—is made possible by the emergence of immaterial production that is built around forms of communicative interaction that produce an immanent and democratic shared existence.[29]

Because this existence is equally shared and entirely immanent on the economic level, it has the potential to produce a form of shared democratic governance that is entirely immanent and equally balanced between the connectivity of the common and the distinct differences of the singularities. This theorization, although dangerously idealist in ways I will shortly detail, has the virtue of thinking beyond the antinomies of the present moment, with the bankruptcy, or at least the growing ineffectiveness, of

conventional state-based forms of socialism and protectionism on the one
hand, and the hyperexploitative and unchecked economic violence of the
global "free market" on the other. The violence and instability of the latter
is all too painfully underscored by the recent global economic crash. Hardt
and Negri's theorization is also valuable for its convincing account of the
emergence of a new economic logic, one organized around a different and
potentially more immanent relationship between the human body and the
body politic.

Yet within this compelling account of the intersection of the human
body and the body politic, the human body itself remains surprisingly
untheorized. Although Hardt and Negri, citing Paul of Tarsus, argue for
the "power of the flesh" within the political economy of the present, this
flesh appears to have a peculiarly ghostly existence. It is here where the
Lacanian conception of the real represents an important addition to and
complication of Hardt and Negri's theorization of the contemporary global
economy. The real, as we have already seen, invokes notions of uncoded
and, just as significantly, unconscious materiality in relationship to the
body and the material substrate of production itself. Given its multivalent
resonances, the real can be invoked to theorize, first, that which eludes the
forms of socialization that Hardt and Negri associate with the immanent
forms of communicative production (in this case, aspects of the body that
cannot be controlled by or simply reduced to discourse), and second, the
aspects of production that remain stubbornly and resistantly material (and
thus also cannot be reduced to discourse).

Thus, on one level, my invocation of the real suggests the continuing
material basis and forms of material resistance that underwrite the global
economy with its increasingly immaterial end-products. We can think about
this material basis in terms of the forms of materiality and production that
are abjected from the idealized conception of the body politic produced by its
body ego, which under capitalism is shaped by collective, commodity-fueled
fantasy. On another level, however, we can also theorize the forms of materiality and the forms of unconscious or abjected resistance that remain
within the seemingly socialized economy of material production. Such a theoretical model enables us to attend to the ways in which the linguistic and
material not only saturate each other and interpenetrate, but also the ways
in which they remain in dialectical tension, at times eluding or resisting
each other, and at other times forcefully intruding on the other's domain.

Such a theoretical approach also suggests a model for praxis in our contemporary world: treating the real via the symbolic, while at the same time

not confusing the symbolic with the real or treating the two as ever simply coincident. Such a praxis would involve the domain of fantasy as well as that of action. Part of this work will be to work through our necessarily socially situated fantasies about the world—fantasies produced in large part by the symbolic of commodity culture and of the immaterial leading sectors of the economy. This work will function in part by critically interrogating our fantasies of the world (including left-wing fantasies of utopian transformation, such as those represented by Hardt and Negri) for traces of that which they work to exclude, cover over, and/or disavow. But it will also involve traversing the fundamental fantasy of capitalism itself, embracing the subjective destitution such a traversal entails, and thereby open up a space to act in order to produce a radically different collectively subjective and symbolic relationship to the real.

Part of such a Marxo-Lacanian ethics, then, would be the injunction to break out of our masochistic phantasmatic positioning within capitalism that tells us that we are powerless in the face of such a vast and systemic form of power, and that the current capitalist symbolic is the only relationship to the real that is possible. Breaking with this fundamental fantasy would also mean letting go of the forms of fantasy and disavowal that allow us to situate ourselves hierarchically in relationship to others within the world system, or, in other words, letting go of our fantasies of social class, cultural capital, and hierarchical racial, gendered, and sexual difference along with the bourgeois ethics that justifies them (while continuing to recognize the material inequalities that these categories underwrite) in order to fully recognize the randomness and arbitrary qualities of the market and our position in it. As Fredric Jameson argues, social class (as distinct from economic stratification) should be conceptualized primarily as a form of collective fantasy, one that we need to finally deprive ourselves of (even as we recognize its ongoing phantasmatic power) to begin to imagine a new relationship to the real.[30] Working through the fantasy in order to alter our relationship to the real and traversing the fantasy in order to produce a radically different relationship between the symbolic and the real— these are, then, the two aspects of praxis that emerge from the theoretical model I have been proposing here.

To conclude, I want to concretize some of what I have been arguing by providing two brief examples of how the model I'm proposing here can assist in theorizing materiality in late capitalism. My first example concerns the body and natural resources as they function within the global sweatshop economy; the second regards the overmedicalized intersex body as it exists in the overdeveloped first world. I choose both these examples because they demonstrate the way in which the bodily and the economic must be theorized together in the model I'm proposing.

As Saskia Sassen has demonstrated, the "informal" (that is, sweated or quasi-legal) sector of the last capitalist economy has grown hand in hand with the rise of the service, electronic, and financial sectors (what Hardt and Negri term immaterial production).[31] She argues that this growth of devalorized labor is not incidental to the overvalorization of immaterial production; indeed, she suggests that the same economic restructuring that produced the emergence of immaterial production as the leading sector of the economy also produced, as its dialectical flip side, the sweatshop economy of so-called free enterprise zones (that is, zones free of legal protections for workers and the environment) in the third world and the quasi-legal sweatshop economies in the global cities of the first world.

She goes on to argue that the informal economy is "a necessary outgrowth of advanced capitalism."[32] As such, this material economy of factory-based production does not just represent the work of an earlier stage that has been adapted, as Hardt and Negri argue, to the regime of immaterial production, but is also a necessary correlate to the growth of the symbolic- and communication-based system of biopolitical production that they celebrate as producing their immanent multitude.

The question then becomes: does this labor represent the excluded or devalorized real to Hardt and Negri's utopian celebration of a symbolic based on immaterial production? Although the two theorists would no doubt argue that the communicative basis of the multitude in immaterial production can extend and will extend to workers in the sweatshops, the question still remains as to the way in which their metaphor privileges certain sectors of the economy and thus certain workers (ironically, the ones who are already privileged) to the exclusion of the workers doing the material work that supports immaterial production. This question becomes more pressing when we realize that if Sassen is right, her analysis suggests that material production will always be a necessary correlate to immaterial production, even within Hardt and Negri's dream of the self-governing multitude.

This argument for tarrying with the real can be made on the level of bodies as well. The experience of sweatshop labor is a painfully embodied one.[33] Yet the embodied subjectivities, and the specifically material limits and forms of suffering that accompany these embodied subjectivities, of sweatshop workers are effaced from the symbolic not only of commodity culture, where production itself is effaced, but also from the symbolic calculus of theories of production—where the worker's body and its limits become just another mathematical input. In intimate opposition to the mathematization of the worker's body in terms of the employer's economic calculus, her body is also rendered brutely and often mutely material precisely because of the extralegal or quasi-legal status of the sweatshop and often of the worker. (I markedly use the female pronoun here, because as Sassen points out, women make up much of the labor force in contemporary sweatshops.)

It is important to recognize the way in which the materiality of the sweated body is socially produced by a socioeconomic system that could (and should) be organized differently, but also the way in which this materiality exceeds its symbolic coding, existing in a negative relationship to the symbolic against which it is situated. In this sense, the body of the sweatshop worker becomes the excluded real upon which the capitalist symbolic erects itself.

As this begins to suggests, the bodies of sweatshop laborers, even as they are central to the production of global life on a global scale, are also abjected from the imaginary body ego of the global body politic. Praxis in this context would be to challenge or alter this symbolic relationship to the real (this is in fact one important part of the work done by the creation of sweatshop unions and labor centers as well as international campaigns against sweatshops), a praxis that emerges precisely from the contradiction between the symbolic and the real.[34] A similar praxis is necessary in relationship to the intersex body.

Recent theoretical work on intersex by Anne Fausto-Sterling and Alice Dreger has emphasized the ways in which linguistic and ideological constructions of sexuality justify unnecessary surgical intervention on the intersex body.[35] Yet these surgical interventions can only be fully understood by addressing the larger political–economic context in which they take place; moreover, they can only be effectively theorized by attending to the tripartite relationship among language, materiality, and desire. The political–economic context can be adduced by recognizing the ways in which most of these surgeries are cosmetic—that is, unnecessary from the vantage of preserving life or enhancing sexuality. Instead, most of them are performed to make the body conform to the symbolic construction of sex as binary. As such, these surgical interventions must be theorized as the product not only of cultural fantasies of sexual biomorphism (or sex as it is produced by the differential logic of the symbolic), but also as produced by the overmedicalization of the first world bourgeois body. This over-medicalization can be theorized as being in dialectical contradiction, with the lack of medical resources and basic medical care in working-class, underclass, and third world contexts.

The materiality of the surgically altered intersex body has to be theorized as a form of materiality that is in part socially produced by the ideological workings of language and desire. Yet as is demonstrated by the various urinary tract strictures and other medical complications that are an un-intentional yet regular product of these unnecessary surgeries and that lead often to multiple necessary surgeries, the materiality of this surgically altered body does not merely conform to the symbolic notions of sex and the body that insists on its production. Instead, the real of the body asserts its own material imperatives—imperatives that differ from the linguistic and affective coding that medicine, culture, and our own bodily egoic con-structions place on it. These imperatives of the real not only elude cultural coding, but also force that coding to change to begin to attempt to account for them. The dialectical contradiction between these imperatives of the real and the symbolic codings through which we experience and compre-hend them becomes one site of the production of the larger social discourse around intersex, with its phobias and struggles for change, its disavowals, celebrations, and perverse fascinations. Thus, I want to suggest that it is again only by tarrying with the real, and not merely by theorizing it as entirely socially or discursively constructed, that the intersex body can be adequately theorized.

To shift back to larger political and economic questions, the model I have outlined also gives us perhaps a more complex and more resistant notion of biopower than we find in Foucault and even in Hardt and Negri. Both these theorizations of biopower tend to focus on the way in which the body, as a passive site of inscription, becomes saturated and reformu-lated by economic and discursive codings. Yet neither theorization attends to the ways in which the real of the body and of other forms of materiality may resist, challenge, deform, or contradict this coding, generating resis-tant as well as conformist desires, revolutionary possibility as well as the desire to better adhere to the dictates of power. Moreover, such a model theorizes the continued way in which various forms of materiality, not just bodily, but geopolitical and political–economic, underpin and exist in con-tradiction with the symbolic codings through which we apprehend them in late capitalism, despite all the emphasis on the postindustrial or symbolic nature of contemporary capitalism.

This, then, is the model that I want to propose as a leftist ontology of the present. It is an ontology that attempts to attend to all of the powerful epistemological questions raised by poststructuralist theory, while at the same time insisting on the twin forms of materialism asserted by psychoanalysis and Marxism. It recognizes that we only apprehend the material dimensions of life through the medium of language, yet it also marks the way in which the material underpins, shapes, and transforms the domains of language as well as fantasy and desire.

NOTES

I want to thank the following people who read and commented on multiple drafts of this essay: Waïl Hassan, Elizabeth Hatmaker, James Reid, Rebecca Saunders, Ronald Strickland, and especially Carsten Strathausen, who served as an ideal editor throughout this essay's gestation and development.

1. To name just two examples, think how impoverished contemporary theorizing about gender and sexuality would be without the work of Judith Butler, or theorizing about race would be without the work of Omi and Winant. See Butler, *Gender Trouble: Feminism and the Subversion of Identity* (New York: Routledge, 1990); and Michael Omi and Howard Winant, *Racial Formation in the United States: From the 1960s to the 1990s,* 2nd ed. (New York: Routledge, 1994).

2. This point is of course central to both Fredric Jameson's and David Harvey's different critiques of the ideology and cultural formation that is postmodernism. The biological limits of social construction, along with the latter's power, is theorized by Anne Fausto-Sterling. See Fredric Jameson, *Postmodernism; or, The Cultural Logic of Late Capitalism* (Durham, N.C.: Duke University Press, 1991); David Harvey, *The Condition of Postmodernity: An Enquiry into the Origins of Cultural Change* (London: Blackwell, 1989); and Anne Fausto-Sterling, *Sexing the Body: Gender Politics and the Construction of Sexuality* (New York: Basic Books, 2000).

3. Michael Hardt and Antonio Negri, *Empire* (Cambridge: Harvard University Press, 2000); Hardt and Negri, *Multitude: War and Democracy in the Age of Empire* (New York: Penguin Books, 2004).

4. Martin Heidegger, *Basic Writings,* ed. David Farrell Krell (New York: Harper & Row, 1977), 161.

5. The essays I have in mind here are "Materialism," "The 'Old Mole' and the Prefix *Sur* in the Words *Surhomme* and *Surrealist*," and "Base Materialism and Gnosticism." See Georges Bataille, *Visions of Excess: Selected Writings, 1927–1939,* ed. Alan Stoekl, trans. Stoekl, Carl R. Lovitt, and Donald M. Leslie Jr. (Minneapolis: University of Minnesota Press, 1985), 15–16, 32–44, 45–52.

6. Lacan's discussion of the gap in the symbolic can be found in Jacques Lacan, *The Four Fundamental Concepts of Psychoanalysis: The Seminar of Lacan Book XI,* trans. Alan Sheridan (New York: Norton, 1977), 20–23. Lacan also discusses the real as the unconscious and in relationship to the concept of drive in *Four Fundamental Concepts,* vii, 60, 184–86. Lacan discusses the real as uncoded materiality in Seminar III and in his discussion of "Das Ding" in Seminar VII. See *The Psychoses,*

1955–1956: The Seminar of Jacques Lacan Book III, trans. Russell Grigg (New York: Norton, 1993), 9; and Jacques Lacan, *The Ethics of Psychoanalysis, 1959–60: The Seminar of Jacques Lacan Book VII*, trans. Dennis Porter (New York: Norton, 1992), 43–70.

7. Tim Dean, *Beyond Sexuality* (Chicago: University of Chicago Press, 2000), 42.

8. See Slavoj Žižek, *Enjoy Your Symptom! Jacques Lacan in Hollywood and Out*, 2nd ed. (New York: Routledge, 2001), 224; Žižek, *Did Somebody Say Totalitarianism? Five Interventions in the (Mis)use of a Notion* (London: Verso, 2001), 183; Žižek, *Looking Awry: An Introduction to Jacques Lacan through Popular Culture* (Cambridge, Mass.: MIT Press, 1991), 21–32.

9. Elizabeth Grosz, *Jacques Lacan: A Feminist Introduction* (New York: Routledge, 1990), 34.

10. Dylan Evans, *An Introductory Dictionary of Lacanian Psychoanalysis* (New York: Routledge, 1996), 159.

11. Ibid., 159–60.

12. Ibid., 145.

13. Ibid., 160.

14. Although my methodology in this article finally differs from theirs, my thinking about the body has been deeply influenced by Elizabeth Grosz, *Volatile Bodies: Toward a Corporeal Feminism* (Bloomington: Indiana University Press, 1994); and Rosi Braidotti, *Metamorphoses: Towards a Materialist Theory of Becoming* (Cambridge: Polity Press, 2002).

15. Sigmund Freud, *The Standard Edition of the Complete Psychological Works of Sigmund Freud*, trans. James Strachey (London: Hogarth Press, 1955), 19:25–26.

16. Jacques Lacan, "The Mirror Stage as Formative of the *I* Function as Revealed in Psychoanalytic Experience," in *Écrits: The First Complete Edition in English*, trans. Bruce Fink (New York: Norton, 2006), 75–81.

17. Slavoj Žižek, *The Ticklish Subject: The Absent Center of Political Ontology* (London: Verso, 1999), 247–312.

18. On nature, see Karl Marx, *The Economic and Philosophic Manuscripts of 1844*, ed. Dirk J. Struik, trans. Martin Milligan (New York: International Publishers, 1964), 170–93. On this use of material conditions, see Marx, *Capital*, vol. 3, ed. Friedrich Engels, trans. Ernest Untermann (Chicago: C. H. Kerr, 1912), 944–45.

19. Slavoj Žižek, *The Sublime Object of Ideology* (London: Verso, 1989), 16–26.

20. Christopher Breu, *Hard-Boiled Masculinities* (Minneapolis: University of Minnesota Press, 2005), 177–80.

21. Karl Marx, *Capital*, vol. 1, trans. Ben Fowkes (New York: Random House, 1977), 164–65.

22. Judith Butler, *Bodies that Matter: On the Discursive Limits of "Sex"* (New York: Routledge, 1993), 3.

23. See Jameson, *Postmodernism*, 48–49.

24. My combination of Žižek and Hardt and Negri may initially seem strange, given Žižek's critique of the two in "The Ideology of Empire and Its Traps," but my own critique (via Žižek) of Hardt and Negri below will, I hope, restore the negative antagonism that Žižek argues is absent from their text. See Slavoj Žižek, "The

Ideology of Empire and its Traps," in *Empire's New Clothes: Reading Hardt and Negri*, ed. Paul Passivant and Jodi Dean (New York: Routledge, 2004), 253–64.

25. Hardt and Negri, *Multitude*, 186–87.

26. See Jean-François Lyotard, *The Postmodern Condition: A Report on Knowledge*, trans. Geoff Bennington and Brian Massumi (Minneapolis: University of Minnesota Press, 1984); and Daniel Bell, *The Coming of Post-Industrial Society: A Venture in Social Forecasting* (New York: Basic Books, 1976).

27. Saskia Sassen, *Globalization and Its Discontents: Essays on the New Mobility of People and Money* (New York: The New Press, 1998), xxiv. See also *The Marx-Engels Reader*, 2nd ed., ed. Robert C. Tucker (New York: Norton, 1978), 116.

28. Hardt and Negri, *Multitude*, 159. On some of the political dangers and epistemological limitations of this concept of the multitude, see Kam Shapiro, "The Myth of the Multitude," in *Empire's New Clothes: Reading Hardt and Negri*, eds. Paul Passivant and Jodi Dean (New York: Routledge, 2004) 289–314.

29. For a critique of Hardt and Negri's emphasis on immanence, see Ernesto Laclau, "Can Immanence Explain Social Struggle?" in Passavant and Dean, *Empire's New Clothes*, 21–30. As my own critique of Hardt and Negri to follow indicates, I very much share Laclau's suspicion of their recourse to immanence as a political logic.

30. Fredric Jameson, *Signatures of the Visible* (New York: Routledge, 1990), 22.

31. Sassen has commented directly on Hardt and Negri's conception of globalization and global citizenship. Although she agrees with much of what they argue, she argues that they have too dematerialized a conception of space. See Saskia Sassen, "The Repositioning of Citizenship: Emergent Subjects and the Spaces for Politics," in Passavant and Dean, *Empire's New Clothes*, 175–98.

32. Sassen, *Globalization and Its Discontents*, 155.

33. For an account of contemporary sweatshops and the conditions of labor and laboring bodies within them, see Robert J. S. Ross, *Slaves to Fashion: Poverty and Abuse in the New Sweatshops* (Ann Arbor: University of Michigan Press, 2004); and Ellen Rosen, *Making Sweatshops: The Globalization of the U.S. Apparel Industry* (Berkeley: University of California Press, 2002).

34. On the radical potential of these international campaigns against sweatshops, see Rosemary Hennessy, "¡Ya Basta! We Are Rising Up! World Bank Culture and Collective Opposition in the North," in *World Bank Literature*, ed. Amitava Kumar (Minneapolis: University of Minnesota Press, 2003).

35. See Fausto-Sterling, *Sexing the Body*, and Alice Domurat Dreger, *Hermaphrodites and the Medical Invention of Sex* (Cambridge, Mass.: Harvard University Press, 2000). My focus on intersex issues and the real of the body emerges in part out of personal experience. I was born with a severe form of a condition called hypospadias, in which the urethra does not extend to the tip of the penis, and which is usually categorized as a form of intersex. I underwent one unnecessary corrective surgery as a child, and the complications (primarily urinary tract strictures) from this initial surgery have produced fifteen more necessary surgeries. In part, I attribute my thinking about the need to move beyond social construction and poststructuralism to this formative experience.

11

A Politics of Melancholia

KLAUS MLADEK and
GEORGE EDMONDSON

MELANCHOLIA AND THE LEFT

To understand why leftist thought has traditionally held the melancholic in such deep suspicion, one need look no further than Walter Benjamin's brief essay "Leftist Melancholia." The trouble with leftist melancholic poets like Erich Kästner and Kurt Tucholsky, argues Benjamin, is that they have sold out to amusement, to the cult of eccentricity, and to the capitalist business routine. Prone to "fatalism" and "nihilism," devoted to the fetish of the "hollow form," they have lost their capacity for the kind of disgust with the world that would fuel a revolutionary engagement with it.[1] In a moment of crisis, when the "juices" of the social body have trickled to a standstill, the leftist melancholic is the first to betray the revolutionary object, almost as if he had been waiting for the chance to become a reactionary.

It may seem odd, considering the strong melancholic proclivities on display elsewhere in his work, that Benjamin should have written what amounts to a distillation of everything the left mistrusts not simply about the figure of the melancholic, but also about the melancholic disposition generally. Yet it seems to us that this is the most telling thing about his essay. When viewed in light of the rest of Benjamin's vast oeuvre, "Leftist Melancholia" cannot help but itself seem a deeply melancholic text, a worried, isolated work in which Benjamin turns all of his ambivalence about the left back on himself, in the process creating an inner-textual superego by which he chastises his ego's melancholic disposition. The essay simultaneously disdains and performs the guilty conscience of the left with regard to its own melancholia. The melancholic leanings that Benjamin attacks are the very leanings that his work, considered as a whole, clearly reveals to have been his own.

Why is this? Why has the left (to say nothing of the right) continued to mistrust, even to despise, not just the melancholic alone but its own melancholic tendencies? Perhaps the answer lies in Freud's initial distinction between "healthy" mourning and "unhealthy" melancholia. In melancholia, as Freud famously put it, "the shadow of the object [falls] upon the ego."[2] That shadowing of the ego, we want to argue, is what most seems to haunt political thinkers on the progressive left. In their common view, the melancholic errs by turning against his own ego all of the critical energies that ought to be directed outward against the powers of the status quo. According to this reasoning, the state goes so far as to induce melancholia in its subjects so that its own idealized forms can be dissimulated as a psychic state with a psychic topography.[3] Encouraged to draw all of his aggressions inward, away from the true source of discontent, the compliant melancholic sets up a superegoic agency harboring the ego's own former rage against the object. The norms and rules of the idealized state thus assume their psychic equivalent in an ego ideal that a demanding superego gauges against the ego. Introjection becomes a form of deflected critique. Meanwhile, the berated and debased ego, busy with its own internal insufficiencies and thoroughly discouraged from political activism, is not only fully censured but also is fashioned into a willing, productive—if ultimately impotent—participant in society. The whole Marxist discourse on alienation, fetishism, and reification *(Verdinglichung)*, culminating in Lukács's *History and Class Consciousness,* makes this point repeatedly. In a word, the ideal subject under capitalism is melancholic.

Because this peculiar contemplative stance, this reactive turn back onto itself, promotes passive self-observation and self-reification *(Selbstverdinglichung)*,[4] political philosophy has traditionally pathologized melancholia as anticommunitarian and, more suspect still, antipolitical. The melancholic is guilty of letting an active engagement with the social world be supplanted by a festering fixation on an object that he simply will not let go.[5] Invariably, the political dismissal of the melancholic congeals in tales of misdirected energies, of plugging up future openings, and of a generalized constipation of mind and act that holds him back from moving on. From the perspective of political philosophy, the melancholic is seen as epitomizing stasis, closure,[6] idleness—even, to return to Benjamin, flatulence. In short, the melancholic is obsessed with death, which is why Freud, in *The Ego and the Id,* calls the superego in melancholia "the gathering place for the death instincts."[7]

Given these many objections, it is perhaps not altogether surprising that until recently, nobody on the left (besides a certain Benjamin and a certain

Adorno) ever bothered to exploit the latent political thrust of melancholia: the melancholic's unerring fidelity to the object, his unconditional commitment beyond all considerations of the pleasure principle, his noninstrumental resistance. Within the past fifteen years, however, there has been a steady movement on the part of what might be called the poststructuralist left, represented by Derrida, Butler, and Bhabha, to name but the most prominent examples, toward a politics of melancholia. One proof text of that movement is Freud's statement in *The Ego and the Id* that the ego is "the precipitate of its abandoned object-cathexes."[8] For the Freud of the second topography, the ego is constitutively melancholic, a vital defense system of self-containment against a history of continuous loss. The ego, in fact, is said to "revolt" against the extinction of objects that are unmourned and unmournable. At its most extreme, this revolt "displays the ego's melancholic yet militant refusal to allow certain objects to disappear into oblivion."[9] But what type of revolt does the ego's "militant refusal" really constitute? Why has a whole tradition, stemming from Freud to Butler, understood melancholia as a rebellion carried out only under the shadow of its impending failure? And what object is it, specifically, that the melancholic cannot kill? Is melancholia, as Freud suggests, nothing more than the index of a suffocated, crushed rebellion, followed by feelings of impotence and resignation? Or could there be an affirmative, even proud dimension to the melancholic state—a dimension that recognizes doom itself as the engine of rebellion—that diverges from a certain model of political activism grounded, as we hope to show, in a leftist ontology of fullness and presence?

That ontology is perhaps best summed up in the introduction to the collection *Loss,* where the question "What is lost?" is turned "invariably" into the question "What remains?"[10] Although we consider ourselves generally sympathetic to the trend to seize on mourning and melancholia for political ends, we nevertheless think that the approach taken by the editors of *Loss* ends up draining melancholia of its most radical implications.[11] If the question of loss truly revolved around the contention that "what is lost is known only by what remains of it," then the most we could hope for would be a nostalgic effort to recuperate such remains for (mostly "hopeful") political projects capable only of describing "*how* loss is apprehended."[12] The crux of melancholia, however, is precisely that loss is unavowable, unconscious, and therefore radically unknown. For the melancholic, nothing is ever lost in the sense of having once been possessed, and so whatever remains of an object is utterly unknowable, its status too unclear to be adapted for any definitive political ends. Freud, for example, notes that "the melancholic knows whom he has lost but not *what* he has lost in him," meaning that the crucial aspect of the "object-loss is withdrawn from consciousness."[13] Something drives the melancholic's entire psyche, but it is something unknown to the melancholic herself. "The loss of the melancholic seems puzzling to us," writes Freud, "because we cannot see what it is that is absorbing him so entirely."[14] When Freud opposes the declared loss of mourning to the unspeakable loss of melancholia, he emphasizes not so much the threat of losing the object as being lost *to* the object, not so much taking tally of loss for political means, but being taken in by the pure loss of an unclear and undeclarable melancholic object. Something lacks, is insufficient, is not right, is out of joint. Melancholia suspends the verdict of reality that the object no longer exists. And in that, it confronts the polity with the insistence and obstinacy of an object that embodies lack, and that emerges only through its lack.

It is because of this crucial distinction between loss and lack that our privileging of melancholia over mourning goes well beyond what Žižek, for example, describes as a fashionable trend in academia. We harbor no romantic longings for transgression and worry that the fantasy of a lost object, whether "the same-sex libidinal object" of queer theory or postcolonial theory's "lost roots," dilutes the political sting of projects that could be more radical if transposed into affirmative terms.[15] That only means, however, that we remain faithful to the unfinished political business of melancholic fidelity that Žižek derides. Of course, the fidelity we mean is never willing to accept any substitutes or compensations for a lost object to which some might pledge an identificatory allegiance. Rather, this fidelity takes the form of an act of affirmative decompletion that, by extracting the public Thing from the symbolic plane, effectively redefines what counts as political in the first place. The melancholic fidelity we have in mind creates the political world by investing seemingly nonpolitical events or found objects with an imminently political charge. This means not that everything is political, but that anything, particularly what is not-all, can suddenly attain political significance, forcing the traditional concept of the political to implode. Contrary to the nostalgic, the melancholic is not interested in preserving the remainder of a lost object, as Žižek argues. His commitment, as we hope to show, is to the lack in and of the Other (as opposed to the economy of loss and the management of a lacking object) and, more radically, to the anxiety unleashed by the lack of lack. In embracing anxiety, the melancholic declares fidelity to the sudden overproximity of an object missing even from the place where it ought to be lacking. To further Eric

Santner's third way beyond the usual interpretations of melancholia,[16] we propose a three-pronged gesture: first, a turning away from the substitutional logic that subtends the position of the master; second, an extraction of the spectral and residual Thing in the midst of the political field; and third, an affirmation, at once destructive and transfigurative, of a master bereft of sovereignty, the master as neighbor.

If, on the other hand, the focus were to stay on the multiple dimensions of the "domain of remains,"[17] leftist politics would truly continue to be engulfed in a nostalgic image of the Other as whole—sutured by a lost object once possessed, then reclaimed—and not as radically *decompleted*.[18] For a politics of affirmative melancholia, by contrast, if anything remains—and this can in no way be taken for granted—it is the need to fully confront a psychic topology suffused with aggression and ambivalence, with the hauntings of anxiety and emptiness that impoverish or even threaten to annul both the ego and the object. In this, it opposes itself to most other strands of contemporary political thought, which seem to be inscribed in a manic teleology of the not-yet, incapable even of confronting the *horror vacui* of emptiness and immobility, the unconscious bearing of the Thing, that melancholia compels us to think.

The notable exception to this trend is Judith Butler. The ego, claims Butler, is itself a polity, a social text whose thwarted grief and illegible rage become legible as symptoms of a dissimulated sociality.[19] Patiently, methodically, Butler teases out the ways in which melancholia invents a whole psychological typography, a spatial constellation and a fable that Freud invented in *The Ego and the Id*: that of the split between ego and superego in the moment when the object is incorporated, and of the emergence of ambivalence at that moment. She demonstrates how the melancholic introduces not only an irreducible antagonism inside the psyche but how the grief of the melancholic bespeaks the violence of social regulation in general, the speech acts of power: the declaration of guilt, the demands of norms, punishments, and so on. It is precisely through these "circuitous" or "misdirected" expressions of social discontent that the social and political character of melancholia articulates itself.[20]

We would amend Butler's reading in the following ways. First, there is no "misdirected" melancholic expression of social discontent that could be supplanted by a more direct, outward mode of aggression (say, by reexternalizing the disavowed rage against the object, as Butler suggests). Melancholia's political thrust is neither nascent nor misdirected. The act of incorporation itself—an act that both preserves and destroys the object—

constitutes the melancholic's genuinely political, albeit unconscious, decision. Nor does the melancholic eclipse the social world, as Butler proposes.[21] The social world is made, altered—made *as* decompleted—in the act of decompletion, that is, in the very process of identification, incorporation, and transformation of the object. What Butler calls a detour, a withdrawn state,[22] is actually a way, the melancholic way, of relating to the public Thing. It is a particular response to the Other—and not just to the specular other, but to the Same in that other, now understood as a new universal: being mutually exposed to the self-estrangement of jouissance.[23]

Second, we resist Butler's characterization of the melancholic's political impulse as necessarily circuitous. This characterization derives less from the common pathologization of melancholia as a reactive, internalized, frustrated disposition (although echoes of this are noticeable) than from the fact that Butler adopts the whole of Freud's topography after 1919: the emergence of the superego as critical agency, the superego as gathering place of the death instincts, and so on. That is, Butler buys completely into Freud's fable of a reactive, circular psychic model, a model of exchange or reciprocity, with the ego working at the behest of the superego's enjoyment, and the superego providing moral guidance to the ego. The problem here is not simply that adopting this particular fictional—and speculative—topography means succumbing to a reactive moralism. It is that Freud's typological model in *The Ego and the Id* already recoils from the far more traumatic insight he had expressed earlier, in "Mourning and Melancholia." This is the idea, elaborated by Derrida in his foreword to Abraham and Torok's *The Wolf Man's Magic Word*, that the melancholic incorporates something entirely alien and foreign into the ego—an ex-timate object that is inside–outside of itself: a crypt.[24] For the melancholic, there is something so unknown, and so unknowable, that it cannot be captured even with the conception of repressed, negated, or disavowed unconscious speech. Melancholia insists that there is something more deeply buried, more thoroughly concealed, and infinitely more traumatic, than could ever be accounted for by fantasies of superegoic punishment, a sense of guilt or simple ambivalence. In short, melancholia affirms the fact that there is no relation, no common measure or symmetry, no possibility of specularity between subject and Other, that could be replaced or smoothed out by an intrapsychic drama of betrayal and revenge. In *The Ego and the Id*, the primordial antagonism or nonrelation—the impossibility of relating—is translated into a defensive battle: a relation of unequal powers that is a relation nonetheless, one designed to make sense of inexplicable pain and suffering. This typography, in other words, finds a seductive narrative (seductive because consoling) for a profound disturbance, an unnamable scar in the psychic apparatus: the way the object takes possession, the way the Other is possessed.

What the subject and the Other share between them is, instead, the paradoxical bond of mutual estrangement. Indeed, Freud's typography highlights that there is an unconditional investment in nonrelation. It is a trauma that cannot be abandoned, from which nobody can move on, and from which everybody must therefore proceed. This is what the melancholic holds onto; the cryptonymous grammar is his holdout against an economy of substitutional objects, beyond all considerations of the good and the useful. The melancholic, without necessarily meaning to in any active way, shows that nonrelation is the one thing that the social cannot do without, that it is the one Thing that concerns the social above all. The melancholic is thoroughly social in that, like the social, he cannot get past antagonism.

The third way we would amend Butler's position is by adopting, in turn, Lacan's amendment of Freud. In "Mourning and Melancholia," Freud claims that "an object-loss [is] transformed into an ego loss," that the shadow of the object falls upon the ego.[25] Lacan famously reverses this phrase by stating that "the wandering shadow of [the] ego structures the object"[26]—that is, in narcissistic identification, the image of man's body is the principle of every object perception. While in Freud and Butler[27] the ego contracts the object's loss, for us, elaborating Lacan's statement on narcissism for a melancholic reading, the shadow of the ego's self-loss falls on the Other. The Other contracts my encrypted lack, my emptied being. The unspeakable loss in the ego is imposed on the Other as well, inextricably binding them together through the embodiment of one another's lack. Homi Bhabha was surely correct when he called the incorporation of the other, above all, a "discorporation of the Master."[28] Incorporation not only desanctifies the ideality of authority by displacing, in repetition and metonymy, its seemingly unique place; it literally extracts the bare bones—the thingliness—from the master, stripping him of his flesh, aura, and sovereign splendor, conserving him as an entombed skeleton-master within the subject. The master's reemergence in melancholic incorporation—inside the psyche—resembles that of a specter whose ontological and ethical status remains always in question.

In the midst of our own moment of political crisis, it becomes all the more important to acknowledge that melancholia is not a slip back into a reactionary politics fixated on the past. Nor should melancholia be dismissed as forfeiting the emancipatory claims of leftist politics. On the contrary, the melancholic assumes the burden of what we carry on our back; he counts with what is not counted, what remains unnamed and drops out of symbolic representation. The scandal that the melancholic presents to a political activism rooted in modes of the not-yet is that one cannot count on him. Melancholia disrupts the tally-taking done in the accounting books of history and politics. It cannot help but address the wrong done to no-counts—the essential miscount that, according to Rancière, lies at the bottom of the political.[29] What induces that miscount is, emphatically speaking, the death drive. Only by identifying the other's death drive as our own can we assume the burden of political subjectivity.

NEGRI, DE TOCQUEVILLE, AND THE WAITRESS'S SMILE

It strikes us that the reflexive lashing out at melancholia is itself a symptom begging to be read, indicative of an identificatory hastening toward the place of the big Other, toward a master discourse that protects act, revolution, life, fulfillment against the impoverishing effects of the melancholic gaze. Although there are no doubt many other examples of this precipitancy, it is perhaps best exemplified by the concluding passage in Antonio Negri's essay "The Specter's Smile," which isolates a scene from de Tocqueville's recollections of the events of June 1848. "We're in a lovely apartment on the left bank, seventh arrondissement, at dinnertime," writes Negri.

> The Tocqueville family is reunited. Nevertheless, in the calm of the evening, the cannonade fired by the bourgeoisie against the rebellion of rioting workers resounds suddenly—distant noises from the right bank. The diners shiver, their faces darken. But a smile escapes a young waitress who serves their table and has just arrived from the Faubourg saint Antoine. She's immediately fired. Isn't the true specter of communism perhaps there in that smile? The one that frightened the Tsar, the pope . . . and the lord of Tocqueville? Isn't a glimmer of joy there, making for the specter of liberation?[30]

Negri's enabling gesture is to interpret the waitress's smile as a collective, rather than singular, Desire of revolution. Locating "there in that smile" the "true specter of communism," Negri attributes to himself the right not only to pinpoint which specters communism will summon as allies to haunt its foes, but also to define the terms and conditions under which that haunting will occur.

But are we really so free to pick and choose which ghosts we will allow near enough to trouble us? To go ghost hunting, as it were, upon the haunting grounds, populating our table with only the most compliant and well-mannered specters? And why is it that the communist specter always seems to haunt the foes of the left—"the Tsar, the pope . . . the lord of Tocqueville"—as if ghosts were merely instrumental as weapons or tools? Why is the "true specter of communism" never one that perturbs communism itself? What distresses us here is not Negri's longing to haunt the foes of leftist thought; it is his own refusal to be haunted. To be haunted, in fact, is from Negri's point of view necessarily to be a false Marxist— an assumption that effectively denies a figure like Walter Benjamin his rightful place in Marxist tradition. True Marxism, as Negri notes in "The Specter's Smile," by contrast, resides in "the rupture with memory" (14), in an eternal present where all specters are fellow travelers and no specters haunt the Marxism that has conjured them. The most authentic embodiment of such a specter, at once intimate and destructive, is the smile of the anonymous waitress fired by de Tocqueville and hired, so to speak, by Negri. "There in that smile," Negri assures us, is where we will find the public Thing, where the lost object of Desire will be recovered and where our true political subjectivity will finally emerge. Negri channels the traumatic energies of the public Thing toward teleological ends ("liberation"), treating the wound in the body politic with a rhetoric of optimism. It is thus the staging of that smile as the foundational revolutionary gesture that entitles Negri to speak with "passion" for "the new social force of mass intellectuality" and "a new practice" (15).

To a smile that others might find merely enigmatic, Negri attributes the very kernel of communist aspiration. And yet by turning the waitress's smile into both "a specter of liberation" and "the true specter of communism" (15), Negri in effect domesticates the communist specter at the very moment he acts to unleash it against its enemies. For with every qualification (joyful, liberating, youthful, destructive, passionate, "new," real) attributed either to the specter or, by implication, to the (old, rotten, decadent, outmoded, melancholic) opponents of Marxism, we get further and further away from the event of spectrality, the power of which is precisely that it seizes and shatters us unpredictably and without qualification. The reduction of the ghost is thus also a reduction of the political and of what Negri calls Desire, because he falls into the logic of what Rancière and Žižek call the metapolitical gesture of Marxism, one that represses the political (Rancière) and desire (Žižek) in the name of strictly socioeconomic relations.[31]

Seeking to liberate the real, Negri seeks liberation from the real—the Lacanian Real—of the waitress's desire.

Far from being self-evident, in fact, the smile of the waitress demands
to be read. Her smile is not a community-founding gesture but a symptom of the impossibility of community where the two scenes, the barricades and the dining room, are mutually conjoined as the contentious
battlegrounds of society's antagonisms. Those antagonisms, psychoanalysis tells us, designate the symptom of a societal impasse, the point where
aggression, contention, and powerful political sentiment collide and converge. This public Thing, this deadlock that makes community impossible,
is precisely what neither Negri nor de Tocqueville can bear. It is not that the
two thinkers are oblivious to this Thing. On the contrary, they rightfully
perceive the death wish playing on the waitress's lips, and to this extent,
the two men are uncannily like one another, insofar as each one eventually
recoils from the spectral apparition of the political Thing. The resounding
cannonade from the barricades, the events in the de Tocquevilles' dining
room: Each bears witness to the aggression, the destruction—in short, the
unbearable enjoyment of social antagonism—that continues to haunt the
political order.

Leftist melancholia, by contrast, cannot read the darkened faces, the
shivering diners, the cannons, or the events on the barricades simply as
joyful or threatening. If de Tocqueville fires the waitress and Negri hires
her as the midwife to revolution, the melancholic, like Benjamin's *Grübler,*
cannot stop contemplating the tear that runs through the midst of the
social fabric, a tear signified by the waitress's smile. Resisting the impulse
to guarantee the master's consistency, a leftist melancholic would detect,
in the social antagonisms that haunt the social order, material evidence
of the master's own spectrality. Her alliance is not to a master of either
the present or the future; it is to the aggression and enjoyment inherent
in the smile itself. What she demands is that the full measure of the master's spectrality be taken. Yes, the smile is anticipatory, promising a disrup-
tion of the status quo; yet it is charged with an unrealized potential whose
direction remains utterly uncertain, and its enjoyment is unbearable and
unpredictable to anyone working for the completion of the master. Ultimately, the waitress's provocation is not ours to claim. Her smile remains
enigmatic and singular, irreducible to either a project or a plot. It is not
a specular smile, offering validation or triggering immediate action, but a
disquieting, uncanny smile whose inscrutability intrigues us without ceas-
ing to haunt us.

There Is a Specter Haunting the Left

For all of Negri's efforts at exorcism, what is it, exactly, that distinguishes his fantasy of transformation and flux from capitalist mobility? Is it not his continuous devotion to the specter of a past revolution whose failure he attempts, retroactively, to salvage? A case in point is Negri's depiction of the waitress, whom, in an almost textbook fashion, he sets up as an agent in his psyche at once tantalizing and reproachful. "My smile has been frozen in anticipation for the past century and a half," she seems to scold. "How much longer will I have to wait for our dream to be realized?" Her smile, rather than being a placeholder for revolutionary desire, has hardened into a rictus, a petrified grimace—the smile of the corpse—that drops out of the symbolic order only to reappear in the real. Incorporating her as an object that cannot be mourned, whose claim has not been redeemed, Negri's fantasy of forward movement is arrested by an untimely turn to an unresolved past. Indeed, the waitress's smile seems to embody the guilty conscience that shadows all revolutionary movements, the stinging reminder that the longing to secure the future by redeeming the past may only end up betraying the present.

In Negri's case, that betrayal of the present takes a peculiarly melancholic form: a refusal to mourn the dead master. The source of Negri's melancholia, the thing he cannot get past, is that the master, rather than being "the constitutive spirit," "a real coming-to-be," "a new practice," or simply the waitress's smile, might commit perpetual suicide. What Negri refuses to think, then, is the possibility that there is no master to be killed, no master to elevate, no position of an omnipotent master to be filled. Indeed, Negri speaks of a specter of liberation as the new master: the apparition of a future freedom. We, on the other hand, speak of liberation itself as the specter. In short, we speak of liberation as being, in all its permutations, spectral, a ghost encrypted within our political aspirations. For us, the "new communist experiment" is not "born through the rupture with memory . . . [a] rupture distinct from melancholia or resentment," as Negri asserts in "The Specter's Smile" (14). Leftist melancholia, we contend, is the rupture *of* memory: the rupture within introspective, inculcated remembrance brought about by the impoverished dead letters, the ephemeral writing system, of materialist mnemotechnics.

The most colossal misreading Negri performs is thus, we claim, to separate the specters of the past from the communist specters of the future: regressive from progressive specters. It is the easy way out to interpret the apparition of a ghost as either clear injunction or direct command, to

translate a pressing political enigma into a political order. The more difficult course is precisely the one Negri charts out in "The Specter's Smile,"
only to avoid taking: embracing what Spinoza in his *Ethics* calls "*pathema*
of the soul*" (11). Negri's haunting presence of *pathema,* which he tries to
limit to "brief parentheses," lingers in one's memory longer than the optimistic reading of the smile meant to supplant it. *Pathema* is the figure of
melancholia. Negri is thus right to affirm *pathema* as the substratum of a
future politics because it, like melancholia, sets one on the path to haunted
Being.

   If we happen to isolate the melancholic dimension of Negri's text, it is
not because we are oblivious to the urgency of his call; it is because we
believe that the project of leftist analysis and that of melancholic politics
function as one another's repressed truth. Leftist politics is not sufficiently
haunted by its past failures, its lost opportunities, its unrealized potentials.
Now more than ever, it seems, there is a refusal on the left to mourn, aided
and abetted by a renewed call to thoughtless activism. Melancholia, meanwhile, has too often fled from itself, pursuing solipsistic pleasures while
failing to seize on its intrinsic politicizing impulse. Leftist analysis is in-
habited by a melancholic disposition of which it seems ashamed, while
melancholia, though usually dismissed as apolitical, often generates political effects of the most transformative kind. Melancholia's potency, of a
different order than that typically understood by the political, lies partly in
its capacity to turn memory against the official narrative of remembrance,
partly in the injunction of the unmourned and undead, whose ghosts are
unleashed at the very moments when monuments speak on their behalf,
and partly in its strict adherence to the death drive, which calls for an analysis beyond the fantasies of a governmentality obsessed with the reduction of
the political to the social. Traditionally, the political is defined so narrowly as
active that genuinely disturbing *Befindlichkeiten*[32] like *pathema* and melancholia are systematically barred from the polis. Hence the power of the
melancholic disposition: It forces us to rethink the very concept of the political as necessarily active, practical, productive, or decisionist.

   At the same time, to reorient the conception of the political toward a politics of melancholia is also to redeem melancholia itself from the charges
of intransigence and negativity with which it is traditionally burdened. The
properly melancholic stance is not the cynical or nostalgic "Nothing can
be done," but rather, "Nothing must be counted as one"—something very
different from the quest for political representation. By refusing to sacrifice interminable analysis for the sake of decision, a melancholic politics

instead promotes the active subtraction of oneself and of meaning from the political situation. What as yet remains unthought (surprisingly, given that Freud's profound horror of melancholia should have alerted us to melancholia's capacity for disturbance) is the conception of an affirmative—as opposed to circuitous, nostalgic, or introspective—melancholic politics genuinely worthy of the transformative nature of the event. A melancholic politics is nothing but the affirmation of the eternal recurrence of the Same, a movement directed toward the purging of the negative, moralistic, and reactive currents from political thinking in the name of a universal lack. A politics of melancholia thus consists of the strict politicization of psychoanalytical thinking, not as a retrieval of the lost bonds of community but as a meticulous, noninstrumentalist unbinding of all community bonds. To throw off the bans of the law also necessitates, for the melancholic, throwing off the logic of friend and enemy that sustains the law. Such is the work of affirmative decompletion.

AFFIRMING HAUNT(O)LOGY;
OR, THERE IS A SPECTER, HAUNTING

Leftist melancholia refuses to foreclose the future political dimension of haunting, of specters and ghosts. In this, it opposes itself to a long-standing tradition, of which Negri is a part, that has sought to reduce the disquieting political force of spectrality to a question of the past needing to be overcome, with no bearing on the future. As the examples of haunted houses and ghost stories suggest, one tends to think of ghosts as wanting nothing more from us than a proper burial—to be put to rest. The polis can only function effectively, it is assumed, in a world not just free of ghosts but also no longer in need of specters.

The melancholic must have three objections to this mind-set. The first is that the work of mourning, even if interminable, can never fully kill the dead.[33] Mourning is never reducible to the mercantilist terms of multistep debt service or repayment plans. The second is that ghosts, despite their common association with repetition and the spellbinding power of the past, are actually beings of futurity. The third, and arguably the most important, is that the urge to quiet ghosts ignores the dynamic charge of resistance uncovered by psychoanalysis. In clinical practice, resistance, rather than being perceived as an obstacle to analysis, is embraced as one of its primary aids: the crucial point at which the most significant insights will emerge. This genuinely psychoanalytic move, when translated into the realm of the political, allows us to see how the blockages that supposedly hamper progress are actually the truth of the political as much as the subject, open-ing for each a passage to the yet-to-come. Ghosts are nothing but the em-bodiment of such fruitful impasses in the psyche and in the body politic. By linking the analytical situation and the political sphere, ghosts compel both the subject and the political to move beyond their prescribed limita-tions, pointing them toward a heteronomous realm where the fundamental dependency on the other is acknowledged, where the subject is politicized and the political subjectivized.

In both instances, ghosts force us to risk the difficult passage from an initial rejection of their claims to an eventual acceptance that they and the living inhabit the same space. But whereas analysis has assumed that risk from its very inception, everyday politics—what Rancière would call the police dimension of the biopolitical order—has been reluctant even to acknowledge that this is the one risk it must always take. One of the chief purposes of everyday politics is to mourn the ghosts it daily produces. But at the same time, politics, sensing the threat posed by ghosts, knows that their appearance calls into question everything for which it traditionally stands—the sublime identity of the sovereign position, the sanctity of the communal bond, the figures of the enemy and the stranger. As beings of futurity, ghosts radically empty out illusions of plentitude, promises of fulfillment, and phantasms of a consistent master—in short, all of the guarantees of authenticity and markers of identification around which the polity traditionally rallies. Displacing, without ever claiming, the position of the master signifier, ghosts have been trying for generations to deliver the message that a future political space must be cohabitated, and that coexistence between the living, the anticipated, and the dead is not only possible but necessary. Thus, not only do we need to learn how to live with ghosts, but it is also incumbent on us to render visible their peculiar polit-ical status.

Ghosts are asynchronic, untimely beings that have fallen out of strict temporal succession. Nothing can demonstrate this better than the doubts they bring to bear on any discourse of the natural: any cycle of death and regeneration, any pattern in which the new emerges from the old, in which death gives rise to new life—lending, in turn, a new significance to death. Neither reasonable nor natural, their return challenges a long-standing faith in the reason of nature and the naturalness of reason. Their appearance, belying all procedures of naturalization, derails the biologistic myths em-powering ideological systems, historical continuums, psychological develop-ment, continuity, genealogical succession—any narrative of becoming that claims to show how the current situation derives from a natural sequence. Such automatic responses to the fact of change and becoming are a way of betraying the contingent nature of nonrelation.

The ghost's unpredictability explains why someone is always attempting to schedule when and how a ghost will return. "A crime has been committed! We have not paid our dues!" These are the exclamatory devices of society's professional mourners, working on our behalf to deny that ghosts cannot be made to participate in an economy of restitution. And if a ghost should haunt us nonetheless, it is only because we have failed to perform the symbolic rituals meant to put that ghost to rest in its proper time and place. Such is the deal struck by our professional mourners: "We will give you all the funeral rites you deserve, and you will leave us alone."

This way of giving structure to lack—propitiating our ghosts, acceding to their demands, making sacrifices on their behalf—is among the most exquisite disavowals of castration. In run-of-the-mill symbolic castration, the absence of the phallus merely reinforces the bedrock belief that the phallus ought to be present somewhere, the fundamental assumption being that that lack of the phallus is only temporary. The real acknowledgment of castration, by contrast, admits that the presence of the phallus, more than simply signifying the lack in the Other, may actually signify its own radical lack, its own permanent absence. Our anxiety surrounding the phallus is determined by the constant possibility that its lack is fundamental, that there is no fullness either forgotten or forthcoming. Negri's essay offers an especially graphic example of the disavowal of this more fundamental castration. The reason why the communist specters only haunt their enemies, designating their lack, is to retain the possibility of owning the phallus, even if it is currently missing. To attribute lack to an external agent, as does Negri (not to mention Marx), is to starkly signal communism's unconscious knowledge of its own spectrality, its own attachment to a primal lack. One might go so far as to claim, in fact, that the expectation articulated in Negri's not-yet falls back into a manic version of symbolic castration, where lack becomes a transient void keeping the infinite play of the signifying chain in motion.[34] By contrast, instead of buying into the fantasy of a *phallus absconditus* still present in its disappearing, any melancholic politics worth the name must insist upon the lack of the signifier of lacking (that is, the phallus).

None of this is to suggest that there are no crimes, whether individual or national, for which one must atone—far from it. But all too often, the real crimes we commit get drawn into the mythological circularity of lawmaking and law-preserving violence, reinscribed as the means that justify imaginary ends (the birth of nations, movements, institutions).[35] Rather than confronting the perverse enjoyment at the heart of crime, an enjoyment readily translated into imaginary acts of remembrance or over-coded with symbolic weight, we instead work even harder at refining the machinery of suffering and salvation. Is it not then particularly surprising that the more we service this machinery, the more ghosts we produce? Perhaps, then, we have invented an apparatus around the wrong set of questions and answers. Perhaps we need to raise the possibility that the anxiety ghosts provoke points to our complicity in a more fundamental betrayal. Perhaps, to paraphrase Lacan, one should not come to terms with that anxiety too quickly.[36]

In his late text *Inhibitions, Symptoms, and Anxiety,* Freud too grapples with the notion that anxiety, rather than alerting the Ego to some repressed content, might not have any determinate cause or object.[37] Anxiety, Freud implies, has no essence: It is itself nothing, follows from nothing, and so precedes the economy of repression that is constitutive of the Ego. Anxiety, the sudden absence of foundation—the recognition that there exists no Other that one must serve or support, run to or flee—inscribes a break in the causal chain, inserting the radical loss of meaning and significa-tion into the consistency of the symbolic order. Like Kant's respect for the moral law or the awe of the sublime, anxiety is a pure *Geistgefühl* (a spiritual sentiment, a sentiment without content),[38] and as such belongs among the most authentic witnesses of the death drive. The horror of anxiety stems from its capacity to remove the subject from its complete immersion in the symbolic order, thereby dislodging the psychic appara-tus ever so slightly from its entanglement in an environment or context—what Heidegger would call the anonymous structure of the *They*.[39] It is thus no surprise that for both Freud and Heidegger, anxiety (as opposed to the fear of a specific object) is never reckoned as a mere sentiment that must be shunned. On the contrary, it is the best humans have: a point of no return that can be neither fully remembered nor ever completely forgotten. The secret of anxiety, we might say, is that apart from its clini-cal significance, it also holds tremendous ethical, not to mention politi-cal, ramifications. For what anxiety announces is not mere terror. At once unraveling and binding the subject, anxiety announces an unconditional-ity without self-authorization, and so makes possible the commitment to a specific political cause without assuming the transferential trappings of mastery or sovereignty.

This unconditionality without sovereignty takes us to the verge of what Lacan calls "belief without belief."[40] As Lacan writes: "[The subject] is alerted (by the anxiety-signal) to something that is a desire [. . .] which does not address itself to me as to someone present but rather as to someone who has been awaited *(attendu)*, or even more, as to someone who has been lost, and whose loss is also urged *(qui sollicite ma perte)*, so that the Other may rediscover itself there—that is anxiety."[42] Anxiety, as that which summons both our desire and our resistance to desire, contemplates the radical loss not only of the subject but of the Other, the desire of which "does not recognize me, as Hegel believed."[42] The Other cannot find itself in and through my own desire, and thus remains hopelessly estranged from its own quest for self-identity via imaginary identification with a subject. As opposed to, say, the master–slave dialectic, where both parties engage in a death struggle for mutual recognition, each one craving validation from the other, anxiety instead points to the way in which the two parties are bound to one another by the estrangement of desire. Conjoined by the nonspecular inscrutability of the gaze, they are incapable of seeing one another. What ties them together is not the whole temporal dialectic of labor and enjoyment, but the atemporal lack of relation to which anxiety attests: the fact that rather than providing one another with the recognition they crave, they decomplete each other at the point of desire, the point where I do not know what object I am for the Other's desire. As Lacan puts it: "[A]nxiety manifests itself clearly from the very beginning as relating—in a complex manner—to the desire of the *Other*. From the very first I have indicated that the anxiety-producing function of the desire of the Other was tied to the fact that I do not know what object *o* I am for this desire."[43]

One limitation of political philosophy, we contend, is that it has for too long fantasized that the position of the master or the Other can be thought of apart from desire—that there could be a master capable of reducing desire to the level of manageable need. But anxiety tells us just the opposite: One cannot delegate the affect of anxiety away from some "Other" or to others (a community that once was or is not-yet), redirecting it to some place where its burden is shared or in any way evenly distributed. Anxiety's call is singular, addressed to you, to something in you that concerns you before "you" are ready to respond. That call may be uncertain, but it is never deceptive, and its direction is always unmistakable. Anxiety therefore signals not just the lack of a communal answer; because it always demands a singular answer, it pronounces the lack of community itself. This must be the irreducible point for any politics of psychoanalysis: Anxiety hints at the unconditional primacy of inherent antagonism as constitutive of the political.

It is for this reason that specters—and also, we would argue, ghosts—are inherently political beings. Above and beyond serving as the prime objects of anxiety, they insist on the impossibility of community, thereby forcing the decompletion of specular, imaginary relation. Literally, specters embody the space of nonknowledge, the point where one does not know what the Other wants or what one is for the Other. A specter, by virtue of its paradoxical nature—an obstinate presence that is also a haunting "Nothingness," an all-too-proximate hollow object with an uncertain ontological status—occupies the beloved place of lack. One must not take this to mean, however, that specters then somehow fill up or complete the Other. The scandal is that specters, as beings of nonbeing, as *phantoms*, empty out the place of lack that they possess. To be possessed by a specter, to find a specter already occupying the place where the subject ought to emerge, is really to be dispossessed, not only of one's subjective claim to wholeness or of one's recourse to the Other, but also of the bedrock (mis)assumption that the lack of the phallus is merely transient. This reformulates Lacan's definition of anxiety as the loss of the lost object, or "when the lack comes to be lacking"[44]—that we might lose our minimal distance to the master, the Other, the neighbor, and discover his Thing to be our own. Ghosts call upon us to know what we know, to listen to what anxiety has to tell us: The Other is always already dead.

All too often, leftist ontology serves as a defense mechanism against this fundamental insight. For example, Marx's and Negri's attitude toward specters is largely utilitarian, ensnarled in a logic of means and ends. Once the communist specters have gained full presence, once the smile of the young waitress has been redeemed and the communist specter has become a living presence in practice, labor, and production, then those specters will cease to haunt both communism itself and its enemies. At that point, the political has reached its end and is rendered superfluous. But if the essence of the political is to be inessential being, then it is all the more clearly the realm of the undead—that is, of the specter. The transient sphere of spectrality, in fact, is nothing but the fleeting, inessential essence of politics itself.[45] We cannot will away specters any more than we can will away the political. Yet it is precisely this spectral insistence of the political that the various modes of politicized exorcism undervalue, if not miss altogether. And in this defensive move, the secondary nature of traditional ontology becomes fully visible: Ontology positions itself against the political (as haunted field) only in a movement of exorcism.[46] Ontology is the supreme conjuration of soothing spirits to purge the ghosts and specters from the political. Its aim is to avert our eyes from a politics of hauntology.

The first insight of analysis concerns the fact that the political order, with all its hold over individuals, is haunted by its own spectrality, so that to fight for ownership of the symbolic plane is to battle over a spectral landscape. (Since 1848, this can be seen nowhere so clearly as in the spectral struggle for "authenticity" between the left and the right.) We recognize that the master as specter is still an enormously efficacious figure, producing material political effects at every turn. Yet even when accounting for those effects, the being of the master always remains in doubt. Is his status merely imaginary, a symptom of the symbolic, or a return of the real? That unclear ontological and epistemological standing is what invites our hesitant investigation. The specter in Marx assumes a political dimension that the ghost is thought to lack. But is it possible that the ghost, too, in its pathos, can be retrieved for political ends? The political has so far been entirely on the side of the specter, believing the specter to be dependable, predictable, trustworthy. Ghosts, meanwhile, seem out of place, lingering in a no-man's-land betwixt and between places and times. This might be another reason why Marx always chose the specter over the ghost. Specters are spirits that can be seen as conspiratorial, exchanging messages across ages and spaces, taking matters into their own hands. Ghosts, by contrast, in their unclear purpose and confused ontology, poised somewhere between Being and being, are often vulnerable and helpless. If we want to salvage the ghost for political ends, it is particularly for the slight twinge of pathos in the ghostliness of the master. In Marx, the place of the master is perceived as spectral, having the power to trouble its enemies or goad its followers, to seem immaterial yet all pervasive, virile, and robust. *But the master is only spectral because we have not yet revealed him to be a ghost.* Politics is not only the sphere of the undead, the specter. It is also the state of the pathetic, the anxious, the hesitant, the in between. It is the state where decisions are made not decisively or because of supreme resolve, as in Schmitt, but out of anxiety—that is, out of defense against the ghost.

Leftist Melancholia

There may be no better set of terms for describing the affirmative dimension of leftist melancholia than those developed by Alain Badiou in his short work *Ethics: An Essay on the Understanding of Evil.* That one should seize in her being that which has "seized and broken" her; that one should never forget what she has encountered; that a subject is always *"in excess of himself,* because the uncertain course of fidelity *passes through him,* transfixes his singular body and inscribes him, from within time, in an instant of eternity"; that a truth, "indifferent to differences," is "the same for all"; that one should resist opinions, which only work for the benefit of some, and instead stay faithful to an event that cannot be communicated; that the difficulty in any endeavor of thought lies in recognizing the Same: The melancholic has always known these things.[47]

There exists, in fact, something like a secret affinity between melancholia and what Badiou calls fidelity. Melancholia, in the manner of fidelity, refuses to give up on the political Thing. It will not move forward just because. This is not the same as wallowing in the past. It is, rather, to anticipate the yet-to-come as radically different from the not-yet. Melancholia, like fidelity, declares that our past is not done, that it can never be done, that the dead cannot be killed. This is not a call for Trotsky's *revolutio continua,* for a continual making of the new and for a progress that has a telos, albeit an unattainable one. Melancholia, opposed to a working toward, is akin to messianic time in the way that Kafka and Benjamin conceive of it: a constant preparedness that is a perpetual undoing of the present as a mere pathway to the future. "The Messiah," Kafka writes in his notebooks, "will only come when he is no longer necessary. He will only come after his arrival, he will come not on the last day, but on the very last day."[48] The master here comes after his arrival. That is, he comes too late: not at his appointed hour, the hour scheduled for him by the symbolic order. He is spectral, his power split between an arriving without coming and a belatedness without impact.

This primordial belatedness induces the melancholic political subject. There comes a moment when every subject-coming-to-be must assume the symbolic mandate in his own unique, irreducible manner. All are hailed; each must decide. All are haunted, each by his own ghostly master. What emerges is thus a decompleted subject without mastery or agency, fully exposed and appropriated to the event. Although the subject affirms the decompletion of the master, in return, the spectral master decompletes the subject. The community of melancholic subjects is then held together by the abyss of nonsubjective subjectivity. As opposed to Negri's vision of a robust, virile political agent enveloping the new in his embrace, the haunted subject is held in place, petrified, by the decision to hesitate, by a declaration of fidelity to the undead, the discarded, the unremembered—to all of those as yet unlisted in the account books of monumental history.

The melancholic is enveloped in the angel of history's awestruck gaze. It is for this reason that we cannot quite bring ourselves to join Badiou's jubilant hymn of the activist political subject, with its powerful romantic overtones. Specifically, we resist his reduction of the event merely to its future dimension, his unidirectional propulsion toward a future politics. The subject-coming-to-be in Badiou, having been seized and shattered by the event, is then forbidden to tarry at that moment of decompletion. Hesitation is but a momentary break on the path to political subjectivization. One is enjoined to maintain fidelity to that which has seized and shattered her, but never to the instance of seizing and shattering itself.

Thus the most traumatic figure for the political is always the melancholic: the figure snarled in the inability to move on, refusing to be healed. Contrary to the waiting endured by Kafka's man from the country, which only serves to strengthen the law, enhancing its sublime aura, the melancholic's refusal to move on more closely resembles Agamben's proposal that to break the ban of the law, one must close the door and interrupt the law. It only seems as though Agamben and Derrida are far apart on this point. In fact, Derrida also claims that a particular act or conclusion is necessary to loosen the law's hold over us—an act not of lingering hesitation but of affirmative interruption. The greatest mistake a melancholic can make, the one that robs him of his true political potential, is to think that he is actually progressing. Why pretend that you are running when in fact you cannot move on? In not wanting to move forward, in refusing to move, the melancholic frees himself to apprehend the stagnation of mere movement. The asynchronicity, the untimeliness, of melancholic fidelity— that is what turns the melancholic into the bête noire of both the left and right. The melancholic never rises to the demands of his time. He instead affirms that there is no metaguarantee in the Other. More a holding on than a holding out, the untimely meditation of the melancholic in the face of catastrophe is the last resort of politicized history.

Today, for example, world politics is haunted by the figure of the displaced: the undocumented worker, the migrant, the refugee, the camp dweller, the no-count, the have-not, the *sans papier*, the *Heimatlose*. Those who drop off the pages of ledgers and account books, who fall outside the lines of administrative graphs, who elude governmental surveys, who fall between the cracks and yet remain: They are the most poignant and intractable symptoms of contemporary politics. Such nonsubjects occupy the most powerful political ground precisely because they debunk the distributive, managerial logic behind everything from NGOs to development aid to debt relief—all of the programs and institutions that would turn the third world into a vast camp where traumatic desire is translated into legible, manageable need. Contrary to that, the melancholic reads such abject subjects, such ab-jects, as proponents of the Same. Although some might label them as victims in need of our salvation, they are in fact the Same, demanding by their very proximity that one dare to love the neighbor as oneself. Neither friend nor foe, such nonsubjects, often reduced to the form of bare life, make a travesty out of the fine distinctions by which we would ascertain communities and neighborliness. In this, they are the neighbor par excellence: not in the family, not in the polis, not familiar, not strange. They demonstrate again that—just as it is our ex-timate neighbor, the Thing, that makes the subject impossible—it is the neighbor who makes community impossible.

But more than this, no-counts are the undead of the current political situation: extimate, introjected, at once incorporated and repelled. Negri and Hardt would enlist these nonsubjects into the army of counterempire. We, on the other hand, would hesitate to enlist them at all, to appropriate their varying desires as reflective of an overarching agenda or revolutionary movement. The no-counts are radically the Same: our neighbors, our Thing—the embodiment of our own political question. Let us call them what they are: the purest manifestation of the death drive at the heart of today's political situation. Dead without ever having physically died, erased from the symbolic order without ever having occupied a place within it, they move between the two deaths in exactly the way Lacan describes.[49] Everyone is aware of their presence, their proximity. Everyone knows of their existence. Everyone acknowledges the indispensable part they play in the shadow economies of the world. And yet they are the site of unbridled hatred and aggression, thus revealing for all to see—and all to ignore—the autoimmunitarian tendencies that fracture every political order.[50] This is not to presume to speak on their behalf; that would be to draw them into symbolic order in such a way as to silence them even further. Indeed, if there is anything that the melancholic cannot abide, it is this very act of speaking for others. We are striving instead to remain faithful to the no-count's particular status as the traumatic object of the political, that which has fallen out, and which continues to fall out, of any social and political calculation.

Unlike the nostalgic, who refuses to kill the lost object, misinterpreting lack as the loss of something he once possessed, the melancholic refuses to kill the object as lacking, as damaged, as decompleted. The melancholic interprets lack as the lack by which he himself is possessed. Refusing to give up on the *objet a* as real, the melancholic thus acknowledges his dependence on the symbolic order even as he declares fidelity to the radical impossibility of the Thing as utterly lacking, outside any order of counting, threatening to efface even the *objet a* as our last refuge against annihilation. This is not the same thing as saying that the melancholic is exclusively on the side of the Thing. He is on the side of the symbolic order, but a symbolic order bereft of the consoling function of lack, with no recourse to compensation, substitution, or manic mobility.

Fantasy scenarios of a new future, free and unmarred by specters of the more disturbing kind, may appeal to the nostalgic and the mournful, but they are never for the melancholic. The melancholics are those who invite ghosts to the table, who welcome their arrival, who affirm their intrusion. By drawing forth the melancholic core of the political, ghosts burden us with a cause that has no guarantee of compensation. Rather, they make political subjects face up to a cause, the possibility of pure loss without reciprocity. Cause in this instance assumes its full Lacanian weight as that which goes missing. What we get instead are effects—laws, goods, compensation, a place in the symbolic order—that function as screens preventing us from confronting the traumatic fact that our cause is truly lost. Cause marks, in both senses of the word, the scar of the unconscious, triggering all of the evasive strategies meant to lead us away from this simple insight: "There is cause only in something that doesn't work."[51] And what emphatically doesn't work is the social relation, the lack of our relation to the neighbor. All social effects are arrayed against the traumatic lost cause of neighborhood and community. Nothing is more uncertain than the transition from subject to neighbor. But it is this gap in community alone that opens up the space for melancholic politics.

NOTES

1. Walter Benjamin, "Linke Melancholie," in *Gesammelte Schriften,* ed. Rolf Tiedemann and Hermann Schweppenhäuser (Frankfurt am Main: Suhrkamp, 1991), 3:283, 3:284. Translated as "Left-Wing Melancholy," in *Walter Benjamin: Selected Writings, Volume 2, 1927–1934,* ed. Michael W. Jennings (Cambridge: Belknap Press, 1999), 423–27.

2. Sigmund Freud, *The Complete Standard Edition of the Psychological Works of Sigmund Freud,* trans. and ed. James Strachey (London: Hogarth Press, 1966), 14:249.

3. See, for example, Louis Althusser, "Ideology and Ideological State Apparatuses (Notes Towards an Investigation)," in *Lenin and Philosophy and Other Essays* (New York: Monthly Review Press, 1971), 167.

4. See Georg Lukács, "Reification and the Consciousness of the Proletariat," in *History and Class Consciousness,* trans. Rodney Livingstone (Cambridge, Mass.: MIT Press, 1971), 83.

5. Melancholia is therefore often associated with degeneracy, sick enjoyment, impotence, suicidal tendencies, and, as Hegel would have it, homosexuality and effeminacy.

6. Even in leftist projects that make a serious attempt to recover mourning and melancholia for the question of the political, this objection is regularly leveled against a certain (regressive and reactionary) strand of melancholia. Reading Benjamin's critique of historicism's tendency toward an "indolence of the heart" *(acedia),* David L. Eng and David Kazanjian blindly follow Benjamin: "This indolence not only insists upon a hegemonic identification with the victor's perspective but also preempts history's other possible accounts." David L. Eng and David Kazanjian, "Introduction: Mourning Remains," in *Loss: The Politics of Mourning,* ed. David L. Eng and David Kazanjian (Berkeley: University of California Press, 2003), 2.

7. Freud, *Standard Edition,* 19:54.

8. Ibid., 19:29.

9. David L. Eng and Shinhee Han, "A Dialogue on Racial Melancholia," in Eng and Kazanjian, *Loss,* 365.

10. Eng and Kazanjian, "Introduction," 2.

11. Ibid., 6.

12. Ibid., 2, 6.

13. Freud, *Standard Edition,* 14:245.

14. Ibid., 14:245–46.

15. Slavoj Žižek, "Melancholy and the Act," *Critical Inquiry* 26, no. 4 (2000): 658.

16. Eric L. Santner, *On Creaturely Life: Rilke, Benjamin, Sebald* (Chicago: University of Chicago Press, 2006), 89–91.

17. Eng and Kazanjian, "Introduction," 4.

18. When we say that the Other is *decompleted,* and not simply *incomplete,* we mean that the subject's primal, ethical act of designating or isolating the Thing—of extracting the Thing from out of the substitutional economy of the symbolic order—plays an active role in decompleting the field of the Other. The subject's later apprehension that the Other is not whole affirms, from what Lacan calls the "point of view of the Last Judgment," that the Other has been decompleted from the very beginning. The subject's last judgment, in other words, affirms its first. See Jacques Lacan, *The Seminar of Jacques Lacan, Book VII: The Ethics of Psychoanalysis, 1959–60,* trans. Dennis Porter (New York: Norton, 1997), 313–14.

19. Judith Butler, *The Psychic Life of Power: Theories in Subjection* (Stanford: Stanford University Press, 1997), 179, 184.

20. Ibid., 180.

21. Ibid., 183.

22. Ibid., 181.

23. On the Same, see Alain Badiou, *Ethics: An Essay on the Understanding of Evil,* trans. Peter Hallward (London: Verso, 2001), 25–28.

24. Jacques Derrida, "Forward: Fors: The Anglish Words of Nicolas Abraham and Maria Torok," trans. Barbara Johnson, in *The Wolf Man's Magic Word: A Cryptonymy,*

trans. Nicholas Rand, ed. Nicolas Abraham and Maria Torok (Minneapolis: University of Minnesota Press, 1986), xiv–xxi.

25. Freud, *Standard Edition*, 14:249.

26. Jacques Lacan, *The Seminar of Jacques Lacan, Book II: The Ego in Freud's Theory and in the Technique of Psychoanalysis, 1954–1955*, ed. Jacques-Alain Miller, trans. Sylvana Tomaselli (New York: Norton, 1991), 166.

27. See Butler, *Psychic Life of Power*, 187.

28. Homi K. Bhabha, "Postcolonial Authority and Postmodern Guilt," in *Cultural Studies: A Reader*, ed. Lawrence Grossberg et al. (New York: Routledge, 1992), 66.

29. Jacques Rancière, *Disagreement* (Minneapolis: University of Minnesota Press, 1999), 21.

30. Antonio Negri, "The Specter's Smile," in *Ghostly Demarcations: A Symposium on Jacques Derrida's "Specters of Marx,"* ed. Michael Sprinker (London: Verso, 1999), 15. Subsequent references to this essay will appear in the text.

31. On the term *metapolitics* in Marxism, see Rancière, *Disagreement*, 81–93, and Slavoj Žižek, *The Ticklish Subject: The Absent Centre of Political Ontology* (London: Verso, 2000), 190.

32. Parallel to Heidegger, who shies away from calling angst simply an affect or an emotion, we call the spiritual–emotional state of melancholia a *Grundbefindlichkeit* ("fundamental state of Being"). See Martin Heidegger, *Sein und Zeit* (Tübingen: Max Niemeyer Verlag, 1953), 184.

33. Derrida, "Forward: *Fors*," xxi–xxii.

34. See Samuel Weber, *Return to Freud* (Cambridge: Cambridge University Press, 1991), 160.

35. On the circularity of law-making and law-preserving violence, see Walter Benjamin, "Critique of Violence," in *Reflections: Essays, Aphorisms, Autobiographical Writings*, trans. Edmund Jephcott (New York: Schocken Books, 1986), 278–89.

36. On this point, see Weber, *Return to Freud*, 162.

37. Joan Copjec also addresses Freud's pivotal text on anxiety. See her *Read My Desire: Lacan against the Historicists* (Cambridge: MIT Press, 1994), 118–19.

38. See Immanuel Kant, *Kritik der praktischen Vernunft* (Stuttgart: Reclam, 1961), 122–23.

39. Heidegger, *Sein und Zeit*, 126–29.

40. Lacan, *Ethics of Psychoanalysis*, 70. Cited by Copjec, *Read My Desire*, 119.

41. Cited by Weber, *Return to Freud*, 160.

42. Lacan, cited by Weber, *Return to Freud*, 160.

43. Ibid., 161.

44. Ibid., 159.

45. Jacques Derrida, *Specters of Marx: The State of the Debt, the Work of Mourning, and the New International*, trans. Peggy Kamuf (New York: Routledge, 2006), 127.

46. Ibid., 202.

47. Badiou, *Ethics*, 47, 52, 45, 27, 50–51, 25–28.

48. See Agamben's excellent reading of this enigmatic passage from Kafka. Giorgio Agamben, "The Messiah and the Sovereign," in *Potentialities*, ed. Daniel Heller-Roazen (Stanford: Stanford University Press, 1999), 174.

49. On the "space between two deaths" as a disjointed lag or interval between on the one hand biological death and on the other the symbolic death effected when one is no longer counted within or by the community, see Lacan, *Ethics of Psychoanalysis*, 320; but see chapter 21, "Antigone between Two Deaths" as well.

50. See Giovanna Borradori, *Philosophy in a Time of Terror: Dialogues with Jürgen Habermas and Jacques Derrida* (Chicago: University of Chicago Press, 2003), 94–101.

51. Jacques Lacan, *The Four Fundamental Concepts of Psychoanalysis,* trans. Alan Sheridan (New York: Norton, 1981), 22.

Thinking, Being, Acting; or, On the Uses and Disadvantages of Ontology for Politics

BRUNO BOSTEELS

Which imbecile spoke of an ontology of the revolt?. . . . The revolt is less in need of a metaphysics than metaphysicians are in need of a revolt.

—RAOUL VANEIGEM, *Traité de savoir vivre à l'usage des jeunes generations*

Faced with the ubiquitous return of the question of being in the field of political thought today, put into relief most eloquently by the present collection of essays, I am tempted to repeat Theodor W. Adorno's gesture when in part I of his *Negative Dialectics,* as he explains, "ontology is understood and immanently criticized out of the need for it, which is a problem of its own."[1] In keeping with this model, I too would want to ask in what way the answers of the ontological turn in self-anointed leftist circles today may be "the recoil of the unfolded, transparent question" and to what extent these answers also "meet an emphatic need, a sign of something missed," even if it does not, or no longer, correspond to what Adorno sees as "a longing that Kant's verdict on a knowledge of the Absolute should not be the end of the matter."[2] We need not stoop to the level of Adorno's blunt and for this reason often ill-understood attacks on the new fundamental ontologies in Germany (Martin Heidegger's in particular) to raise again the question about the need for a leftist ontology today. This would mean asking not only, What are the uses and disadvantages of ontology for politics, and a leftist one to boot? but also, Where does this politico-ontological need stem from in the first place?

The initial task would consist in outlining the general form or platform in which the question of being is presented to us today in the context of political thought. As opposed to Adorno's claim, the way this happens is

no longer—if ever it was the case—through an appeal to a supposed sub-
stantiality, or to some version or other of the absolute, surreptitiously
brought back to life behind Kant's back. In fact, if there is a common presupposition shared by all present-day political ontologies touched on in
this volume, it is that ontology is not, cannot be, or must not be a question
of substance or the absolute. It presupposes neither the presence of being
nor the identity of being and thinking as a guide for acting. On the contrary, ontology here is described as spectral, nonidentical, and postfoundational. It tries to come to terms not with present beings, but with ghosts
and phantasms; not with entities or things, but with events—whether with
events in the plural, or, alternatively, with the singular event of presencing as such, which should never be confounded with a given present, albeit
a past or future one. Consequently, there can be no determinate politics,
not even a democratic or radical-democratic one, that would simply derive
from ontology as a thoroughly desubstantialized field of investigation into
being and/as event—even though most commentators are quick to add
that democracy, often in the guise of a radical democracy or a democracy
to come rather than its historical shape, would be the only political formation or regime attuned to the horizon of ontology at the close of the metaphysical era. "This, then, is the argument: in the answers that they have
traditionally brought to bear on the 'special' question 'What is to be done?'
philosophers have relied, in one way or another, on some standard-setting
first whose grounding function was assured by a 'general' doctrine, be it
called ontology or something else. From this doctrine, theories of action
received their patterns of thought as well as a great many of their answers,"
Reiner Schürmann writes in one of the very first attempts at outlining
the practical and political implications of a postfoundational, or an-archic,
ontology. He continues: "Now, the deconstruction of metaphysics situates
historically what has been deemed to be a foundation. It thus closes the era
of derivations between general and special metaphysics, between first philosophy and practical philosophy."[3] The specifically leftist nature of such
a proposal, however, is not always clear, except insofar as some prior criteria are assumed to be at our disposal by which to judge what is leftist and
what is not.

I

Heidegger and Lacan, often in bold rereadings or creative misreadings, no
doubt name the two dominant strands in this revival of the ontological
question in a practical or political key, with added inflections taken from

the work of Carl Schmitt and Walter Benjamin. Heidegger's centrality in this context goes without saying, even as the political consequences of his ontology remain a topic of dispute, to say the least: "Our epoch can be said to have been stamped and signed, in philosophy, by the return of the question of Being. This is why it is dominated by Heidegger. He drew up the diagnosis and explicitly took as his subject the realignment, after a century of Criticism and the phenomenological interlude, of thought with its primordial interrogation: what is to be understood by the being of beings?"[4] But even Lacan's psychoanalytical work is concerned with ontology, as his son-in-law and soon-to-become executor of his intellectual legacy, Jacques-Alain Miller, perceived as early as in 1964, when he asked Lacan about his ontology, to which the latter responded rather coyly: "I ought to have obtained from him to begin with a more specific definition of what he means by the term ontology," only to go on stressing "that all too often forgotten characteristic—forgotten in a way that is not without significance—of the first emergence of the unconscious, namely, that it does not lend itself to ontology," and yet just a few weeks later he would seemingly contradict himself: "Precisely this gives me an opportunity to reply to someone that, of course, I have my ontology—why not?—like everyone else, however naïve or elaborate it may be."[5] However this may well be, we might conclude with one of Lacan's most astute contemporary readers: "Ontology or not, Lacan's psychoanalysis imposes a general rectification on philosophy, which touches upon nothing less than the way in which truth leans up against the real."[6]

Between Heidegger's destruction of the metaphysics of being qua presence and Lacan's subversion of the ideology of the subject qua ego, in any case there lies the general framework in which we could situate the authors whose writings dominate most discussions in this collection, namely Jacques Derrida, Giorgio Agamben, Ernesto Laclau, Chantal Mouffe, Alain Badiou, and Slavoj Žižek. Aside from the overarching legacy of Marxism, here represented above all in the figure of Fredric Jameson, the principal exception to this Heideggerian–Lacanian framework that immediately comes to mind would be the neo-Spinozist or Deleuzian ontology of substance as pure immanence, or life, which Antonio Negri and Michael Hardt, among others, offer as their gift to the communist Left in their two-volume manifesto, *Empire* and *Multitude*. But significantly though perhaps not surprisingly, this vitalist ontology, which otherwise claims to be an ontology of the event as well, is not only underrepresented in the present collection of essays; it also comes under serious attack in the last two of these essays, both for being dangerously idealist, insofar as it would eschew the dimension of uncoded materiality, and for being too confidently materialist, insofar as it would seek to exorcize the indeterminacy of ghosts whose uncanny smile turns out to be irreducible, all good intentions notwithstanding, to any preestablished political program, be it communist or otherwise. Christopher Breu thus writes: "While Hardt and Negri, citing Paul of Tarsus, argue for the 'power of the flesh' within the political economy of the present, this flesh appears to have a peculiarly ghostly existence," whereas Klaus Mladek and George Edmondson in a way argue that this existence is not ghostly enough: "The political has so far been entirely on the side of the specter, believing the specter to be dependable, predictable, trustworthy. Ghosts, meanwhile, seem out of place, lingering in a no-man's-land betwixt and between places and times," which is why a melancholic stance of fidelity haunted by anxiety-producing ghosts may be needed to subtract our leftist ontology from the illusions of mastery, movement, and militantism: "As opposed to Negri's vision of a robust, virile political agent enveloping the new in his embrace, the haunted subject is held in place, petrified, by the decision to hesitate, by a declaration of fidelity to the undead, the discarded, the unremembered—to all of those as yet unlisted in the account books of monumental history."

2

Here, in other words, ontology by and large is supposed to be postmetaphysical, if by metaphysics we understand the age-old discourse for which the principle holds that "the same, indeed, is thinking and being."[7] The problem with this characterization of metaphysics, which otherwise seems to me no worse than any other and which in any case has the virtue of concision, is that it ignores the extent to which not only Heidegger but also someone like Badiou—both of whom are widely perceived to be models of so-called postfoundational thought—might ultimately subscribe to this Parmenidean principle, even though Heidegger does so by displacing metaphysics in the name of thinking, whereas Badiou (like Deleuze and Negri, for that matter) openly embraces the notion that his ontology and theory of the subject signal a new metaphysics, bypassing as a nonissue the whole debate regarding the end of metaphysics or its closure. Even so, it is hard to ignore that today, with very few exceptions, most radical ontological investigations would seem to start from the nonidentity of being and thinking—we might even say from their alterity, in the Levinasian sense according to which an ethics of the other must disrupt the metaphysics of the same, or even from their subalternity, in the sense in which Gayatri Spivak argues that "the subaltern is necessarily the absolute limit of the place where history is narrativized into logic."[8] Being and thinking, but also history and logic, thus become delinked or unhinged in ways that perhaps are not even dialectical anymore in the older sense of the term. This has profound consequences for politics precisely insofar as there no longer exists a necessary linkage that would set the paradigm for practical forms of acting. Instead, it is to the very delinking or unbinding of the social that a leftist ontology would have to attune itself. Whence also the stubborn not to say hackneyed insistence on motifs—here we can forego the mention of proper names—such as the indivisible remainder or reserve, the constitutive outside, the real that resists symbolization absolutely, the dialectic of lack and excess, or the necessary gap separating representation from presentation pure and simple.

It is not, then, ontology as such that is either leftist or rightist, unless of course we were to ascribe a moral value—whether good or bad—to 'being qua being in a fashion that would more properly have to be called religious or theological, but rather the specific orientation given to the impasse or aporia that keeps the discourse of being qua being from ever achieving full closure. Badiou's distinction, explored in much of *Being and Event,* between three fundamental ontological orientations—constructivist, transcendent, and generic—should be helpful in this regard, especially insofar as the distinction does not correspond neatly to a leftist, rightist, or centrist tripartite division, nor should it be equated without further ado with the division that Laclau and Roland Végső, for instance, propose between immanence, transcendence, and failed or decompleted transcendence-within-immanence, although in this case the similarities and overlaps are rather striking indeed. Briefly put, the constructivist orientation seeks to reduce the impasse by bringing it back into the fold of a well-formulated language; the transcendent orientation raises the impasse to the level of a quasi-mystical beyond; and the generic orientation postulates the existence of an indiscernible with which to interpret the impasse of being as the effect of an event within the situation at hand—thus neither collapsing the event into the sum total of its constructable preconditions nor elevating the impasse to the level of a miraculous or monstrous-sublime Thing, as it were, taking the place once occupied by God.

Following Marx and Freud, whose doctrines take us beyond ontology in the strict sense and possibly open up a fourth option, we could furthermore argue that the generic or indiscernible orientation shows the extent to which the science of being, through its inherent deadlock or impasse, presupposes the retroactive clarification of an intervening subject without which the ontological impasse would not even be apparent to begin with. "Its hypothesis consists in saying that one can only *render justice* to injustice from the angle of the event and intervention. There is thus no need to be horrified by an un-binding of being, because it is in the undecidable occurrence of a supernumerary non-being that every truth procedure originates, including that of a truth whose stakes would be that very unbinding."[9] Indeed, it may very well be the case that the defining polemic behind the present collection of essays—its principal contradiction or its fundamental line of demarcation—depends not so much on the elaboration of a leftist ontology in one form or another as much as on the possibility of a leftist (or communist—not necessarily the same) theory of the subject. The latter, actually, turns out to be barred or blocked, put under erasure, or kept at the level of virtuality or potentiality without actuality, by some of the most radical arguments for a leftist ontology in this volume.

In any case, returning to a simpler alternative, the unspoken presupposition behind those essays in this volume that accept the option—if not the need—of a leftist ontology seems to be that a leftist orientation in ontology is one that acknowledges, exposes itself to, or accepts to come to terms with the inherent gap or ghostly remainder in the discourse of being qua being, whereas a rightist orientation would be one that disavows, represses, or displaces this gap or remainder. "A leftist ontology therefore recognizes that everyday political practice—and not just 'the political'—is defined by this daily struggle about the very nature of our world and its lines of communication, about who possesses the right and the power to delineate its borders and enforce its rules," as Carsten Strathausen writes in his introduction: "However, at stake is not just any ontology, but one that acknowledges and thinks through its paradoxical, antifoundational horizon." This means that, perhaps against the author's wishes, even Adorno's own negative dialectics, which hinges upon the gap between the concept and nonconceptualities, might fit the profile of a leftist ontology. "Regarding the concrete utopian possibility," he writes as if to enable this posthumous rereading, "dialectics is the ontology of the wrong state of things. The right state of things would be free of it: neither a system nor a contradiction."[10] However, this does not free negative dialectics itself, as a reflection of and on nonidentity, from the charge of hypostasizing its fundamental ontological principle—a charge that Adorno himself levels against Heidegger and that an Adornian approach could level against philosophies of difference coming from thinkers who try critically and responsibly to take up the Heideggerian legacy.

3

As I hinted at a moment ago, though, not all contributors to this volume agree that there is a need for an ontological grounding of politics—not even if, as is most often the case today, this grounding actually takes the form of an ungrounding, a degrounding, or a precipitation into the abyss of an absent ground. Many contributors raise doubts about the very standard or index that would allow us to gauge the leftist or rightist nature of any ontology whatsoever, insofar as the discourse of being qua being cannot but be subtracted from all empirical specifications, including political ones. As Benjamin Robinson writes: "The problem, or antinomy, is this: one cannot empirically commit to one 'thing world' over another (say, socialism, whatever that might be, over liberalism) if there is no shared index of reality to decide between them. At the same time, a purely theoretical or normative commitment is empty as long as the choice is not proven on the practical level where the things in a chosen system have a self-evidence— what I will call apodictic force—that lets them serve as their own index of validity." This antinomy is constitutive of the very project of a leftist ontology. Indeed, speaking of the latter, we might ask what possible relation there could well be between being qua being, which presumably is generic if not indeterminate, and the particular seating plan of the 1791 French legislative assembly, which historically lies at the origin of our modern divide between Left and Right? Several authors in this volume, expressing similar doubts, wonder whether we should not reinstate the question mark following the title of the original conference behind the collection. Almost all, finally, reject the simple derivation of a leftist politics from a postfoundational ontology as a non sequitur at best and a performative contradiction at worst. "Since one of the basic insights of deconstruction is that the primary ontological terrain of the constitution of subjectivity is that of radical undecidability, it is impossible to found politics on an ontology," as Végső usefully summarizes. "That is, there is no logical move from radical undecidability to a leftist politics. This is why deconstructionist ontology (or hauntology) cannot be inherently leftist."

Some authors, however, explicitly or implicitly take ontology to refer not so much to the science of being qua being in the strict sense so much as to the basic presuppositions behind a given politico-philosophical stance— what we might call the bedrock of their fundamental assumptions and unshakable commitments, never mind that the term *ontology* is perhaps less suited to name this value-laden and affect-imbued dimension than *political anthropology* would be. One author even goes so far as to reject the ontological need in politics altogether. William Rasch thus opens the volume with a bang: "There is no Leftist ontology. Let me phrase this less ontologically. There *ought not* be a *Leftist* ontology." Still, the same author does not for this reason abandon the call to clarify his basic underlying commitments, such as to the ontological primacy of conflict and violence over consensus and public deliberation.

Rasch and Eva Geulen, in part I, go a long way in highlighting both the enchanting appeal and the real danger involved in radical ontological orientations of politics of the kind that can be found in Benjamin or Agamben. In fact, both seem to argue that the ontological need in political thinking today stems precisely from a eschatological, even catastrophic desire for radicalization—whether by arguing for a purified politics that would step wholly and completely out of the modern administered world or by seeking a turning point where danger and salvation coincide as the power of ambivalence. "This, of course, is its danger, for the temptation becomes one of thinking the political precisely in theological, which is to say, in messianic and redemptive terms," says Rasch, who would rather argue with Max Weber for a modest and decidedly more secular view of the political: "A political ethics that recognizes the ever-present possibility of violence, rather than its glorious self-immolation, is the ethics of the human being in an unredeemed, and unredeemable, fallen state. Civil peace, not civil perfection, is the goal of such politics." Geulen likewise warns against the entanglement of redemption and catastrophe that, in the case of Agamben's discussion of Auschwitz, "instrumentalizes the pseudoeschatological figure of thought in a way that neither Adorno nor Heidegger were familiar with," and yet Agamben also offers his own remedy against this danger: "If the price for grounding politics in ontology is the perpetuation of the very kind of ambivalences that Agamben's own critical account of ambivalence helps to analyze and dispel, then one ought to resist the temptation to ontologize. It is quite possible to separate Agamben's ethical speculations in the Auschwitz book from his sober analyses of the sacred and his critique of the ambivalence theorem."

The quest for a leftist ontology, in other words, risks producing an ontologization of leftism that is as radical as it is empty. Was not the young Marx himself fond of recalling that to be radical means literally to go to the root of things, which for him meant the essence of the human being?

What, then, could be more radical than in the name of contemporary onto-logical interrogations to forego all humanist anthropologies so as uncon-ceal the uprootedness of the human essence that is its absent ground? The price to be paid for this radicalization, however, is either the expulsion of the politics to come beyond the social realm altogether, or else its sin-ister and undialectical conflation through a figure of ambivalence with world-historical horrors such as the Holocaust. This enormous risk can be avoided only by reinscribing politics—let us say once again dialectically—in the present situation. Instead of seeking a pure or purified form of the polit-ical, no matter how violent and catastrophic, what is needed then amounts to some kind of ontology of actuality, as in the essays in part II.

4

When Michel Foucault, in his programmatic elaboration on Kant's "What Is Enlightenment?" essay, coined the expression "ontology of actuality" to designate the task of his lifelong endeavor, as different from an "analytic of truth," he himself perhaps could not have predicted the enthusiasm this coinage would generate among contemporary thinkers.[11] Figures as widely different as Gianni Vattimo and Fredric Jameson thus have come to classify the overall aim of their work under this umbrella term.[12] And yet, beyond this unexpected success, have we fully understood the paradox encapsulated in the very project for an ontology of actuality?

For Foucault, the task of a "historical ontology of ourselves" or a "criti-cal ontology of the present" amounts above all to an archaeological and genealogical criticism of our modes of doing, thinking, and saying: "Archae-ological—and not transcendental—in the sense that it will not seek to identify the universal structures of all knowledge or of all possible moral action, but will seek to treat the instances of discourse that articulate what we think, say, and do as so many historical events. And this critique will be genealogical in the sense that it will not deduce from the form of what we are what it is impossible for us to do and to know; but it will separate out, from the contingency that has made us what we are, the possibility of no longer being, doing, or thinking what we are, do, or think."[13] The task of criticism then ultimately no longer consists only in drawing up limits but also and above all in enabling one to pass beyond them. In this sense, the ontology of actuality is nothing less than the work of freedom in action. As Philip Goldstein concludes in his contribution to this volume: "Although Foucault also develops Heideggerian theory, he interprets it in positive terms whereby its historical ontologies or epistemes enable the subject to assert itself. Moreover, as Macherey maintains, he allows the subject an indeterminacy or self-fashioning that permits progressive action." In Foucault's wake, however, the conjunction of both terms—ontology and actuality—to describe the task at hand has become increasingly paradoxical, especially with the advent of the so-called postmodern condition and the rise of late or finance capitalism.

On the one hand, as discussed above, the most radical ontological investigations today tend toward spectrality, virtuality, potentiality—and not toward actuality. "Higher than actuality stands possibility," Heidegger notes in *Being and Time*, not unlike Agamben, who insists that the most radical potentiality is a potential not to become actual: "It is a potentiality that is not simply the potential to do this or that thing but potential to not-do, potential not to pass into actuality."[14] Going against the grain of these tendencies, there is thus something intrinsically uncanny, not to say oxymoronic, at least today, about an ontology of actuality, if we take into account the dominant orientations of postfoundational thinking. Foucault's provocation, in this sense, also consisted in enabling a historical ontology of ourselves that would not have to shy away from speaking about the present situation in the name of some knee-jerk aversion to the metaphysics of presence.

On the other hand, however, there can be no doubt that the ontological themes of difference, multiplicity, event, becoming, and so on are the product of late capitalism as much as, if not more than, they are counteracting forces. Marx himself, after all, was always quite enthusiastic about the power of capitalism to destitute and break down old feudal, patriarchal, or idyllic bonds and hierarchies. "It is obviously the only thing we can and must welcome within Capital," Badiou comments, referring to those well-known passages from *The Communist Manifesto:* "That this destitution operates in the most complete barbarity must not conceal its properly *onto-logical* virtue."[15] But if it is indeed capitalism itself that reveals all presence to be a mere semblance covering over random multiplicity, then this also means that the categories of a postfoundational ontology not only are not necessarily leftist; they also might turn out to be little more than descriptive of, if not complicitous with, the status quo. "In this case, 'critical' thought is in fact precisely adequate to its moment, just not in the way it imagines itself to be. It reiterates, no doubt in sublimated or misrecognized form, accepted social structures and political presumptions—effectively canceling out real critical reflection," Nicholas Brown and Imre Szemán warn us, and, later, referring to what might well be the quintessential category of a leftist ontology, they conclude: "The primacy of 'difference' in fact outlines an identity—the unacknowledged frame of the monoculture, global capitalism." Difference, multiplicity, or the primacy of events or becomings over subjects and objects, far from giving critical leverage, thus would define our given state of affairs under late capitalism and its attendant cultural logic.

Jeffrey T. Nealon, in his periodization of the 80s, similarly wonders whether the theoretical dramas opposing essentialism versus constructivism, or stasis versus flux, are not a hangover from the 60s: "At this point, we'd have to admit that privatized finance capital has all but obliterated the usefulness of this distinction: to insist on the hyridity and fluidness of x or y is the mantra of transnational capital—whose normative state is the constant reconstitution of value—so it can hardly function unproblematically as a bulwark against that logic." Transnational finance capital desubstantializes ontology even more thoroughly than the nineteenth-century bourgeoisie could have dreamed. Flexibility, difference, and innovation are of the nature of dumb facticity today. In these circumstances, which define our actuality, how radical can a postfoundational ontology claim to be? Is it not rather the spontaneous ideology of late capitalism?

We could argue, though, that the return of the ontological question in political thought today is also, at least in part, an attempt to respond—by way of a retreat or a step back—to this complicity, which is easier to intuit than to undo, between the desacralizing tendencies within capitalism itself and the drive toward difference, multiplicity, or becoming in the critique or deconstruction of metaphysics. Frequently, such a response leads to the introduction of a conceptual split *within* the notion of politics, that is, a split between politics (*la politique* in French, or *die Politik* in German) and the political (*le politique* in French, or *das Politische* in German). This distinction, present in quite a number of essays in this volume, is most explicitly discussed in part III.

5

Common to thinkers as diverse as Schmitt and Arendt, the distinction between politics and the political has recently been championed as a common feature that would unite contemporary figures such as Laclau, Nancy, Lacoue-Labarthe, Lefort, or Badiou into a form of "Left Heideggerianism."[16] In the present volume, this reading can be found in the essays by Roland Végső and Sorin Radu-Cucu, both of whom follow a lead in this regard from another disciple of Laclau's, Oliver Marchart. "With regard to current political theory," Marchart argues in *Post-foundational Political Thought*, "the conceptual difference between politics and the political, *as difference,* assumes the role of an indicator or symptom of society's absent ground. *As difference,* this difference presents nothing other than a paradigmatic split in the traditional idea of politics, where a new term (the political) had to be introduced in order to point at society's 'ontological' dimension, the dimension of the institution of society, while politics was kept as the term for the 'ontic' practices of conventional politics (the plural, particular and, eventually, unsuccessful attempts at grounding society)."[17] The search for a more radical or a more fundamental level or dimension, thus, continues to be what grounds, regrounds, and degrounds the politico-ontological need.

The so-called political difference between the political and politics, modeled on the ontological difference between being and beings, should nonetheless be handled with certain reservations. "These reservations have to do mainly with the possible misconstrual of the distinction—its transformation into a rigid bifurcation between structure and superstructure, between foundation and derivations, or between noumenal and phenomenal spheres of analysis," Fred Dallmayr writes in *The Other Heidegger:* "As can readily be seen, the distinction relates obliquely to Heidegger's notion of the ontic-ontological difference—but with the proviso that the ontic can never be a derivation or simple application of the ontological dimension."[18] Above all, the two terms are not external to one another, nor should one all too hastily be used to denigrate the superficiality or inauthenticity of the other. If this last risk cannot always be avoided, Végső reminds us that Derrida already tackled the possible misconstrual of Heidegger's own distinction, which allegedly undergirds the difference between the political and politics: "Derrida criticizes the very category of ontological difference, the absolute separation of the ontological and the ontic, and the concomitant philosophical and political project of the recovery of an authentic and originary temporality," just as Radu-Cucu insists on the radical impurity of each of the two terms: "Thus, the difference between politics and political functions in analogy with the ontological difference, while the displacement caused by the logic of the trait (by *différance*) suggests that nothing is pure—neither politics nor the political—and that these categories exist only to have their identity threatened." Even when subject to constant cross-contamination, however, the retreat from politics into the political cannot fail to endow really existing political processes with a negative aura of being merely positivist, sociologist, empiricist, or ontic—that is to say, as so many examples of the ongoing oblivion of being now translated as the essence of the political.

The retreat of the political, in other words, is a welcome gesture in the face of the banal reassertions according to which everything is politics and politics is everything. It is from this complete suture of politics into the social that the ontological turn seeks to release itself by taking a step back to delve into the founding moment of society, which is the moment of the political as such as radical dislocation or antagonistic institution. In so doing, however, the gesture of radicalization may very well have disabled in advance the pursuit of truly emancipatory actions, insofar as the latter will necessarily appear far less radical, not to say blind to their own quasi-transcendental conditions of possibility, which are also always already conditions of impossibility.

Ultimately, then, the question with which I would want to address the ontological need today concerns the fate of the various "others" of ontology, that is, those domains from which the ontological dimension splits off, including the ontic, the empirical, and the epistemological, but also the dialectical and the historical-materialist. How can a critical or leftist ontology of the present be articulated with these others without denigrating them or condemning them to the dustbin of metaphysical (pre)history?

6

Perhaps the most fundamental tension that runs through the entire volume, though, is the one that brings together or separates the project of a leftist ontology and the theory of the subject. On the one hand, there can be no doubt that a psychoanalytical approach to this question allows a theorization of the process of subjectivation, for example, through the notion of hegemonic articulation and/or identification, including at the level of ideological recognition and misrecognition. But on the other hand, it would seem as if the most radical deconstructive and even psychoanalytical inquiries had to come to the conclusion that no leftist or emancipatory agenda can be complete without also questioning the centrality of the category of the subject with all its metaphysical baggage.

Végső may still conclude his essay by suggesting the possibility of a deconstructive theory of the subject that would be compatible with a de-grounding of ontology: "Even if this theory does not yet exist, its outlines are readable within the Derridean corpus. And what these dim shapes suggest is not only that such a theory is possible, but that it is also necessary." But, pushing this suggestion one step further, Alberto Moreiras as well as Klaus Mladek and George Edmondson, writing, respectively, from a post-Heideggerian or Derridean and a Lacanian point of view, seem to conclude that a radical leftist ontology would necessarily have to include a theory of the nonsubject. For far too long, in fact, the Left has clung to an idea of subjective militantism that is based on notions of fullness, affirmation, productivity, and life, without considering the extent to which these notions, tied as they are to centuries of mythic and religious violence, have been responsible for the sacrifice of innumerable victims among both friends and enemies. The interruption of this sacrificial history thus requires at the same time an interruption of the entire subjectivist paradigm of politics. "If subjective militancy is at the same time a condition and a result of ontology, to go beyond ontology—and that means beyond the subjectivity of the subject as the current horizon of political thinking—is also a condition and a result of an ethical position where every possibility of a nonsacrificial politics is sheltered," Alberto Moreiras writes in his essay on María Zambrano. But this is not possible without the nearly impossible task of approaching the legacy of history in an entirely new way by disremembering the forgotten and the vanquished: "The abandonment of subjectivity, the accomplishment of a thinking that abandons subjectivity, is not possible in the wake of the resolute acceptance of a historical legacy. Rather, it fundamentally presupposes a thought of unlegacy, a thought of disinheritance, of disheritage, a thinking of the forgetting of that which will not be remembered." For sure, nothing could be further removed from the populist call for hegemonic or counterhegemonic articulation than this appeal to the disinherited and the subaltern. In fact, the paradigm of subjectivism is so all-encompassing, ranging from liberal and communist militantism in the name of appropriation all the way to reactionary attachments to identity and its loss, that little more can be offered by way of alternative than the announcement of a promise of another constitution of the political outside of subjectivity.

Mladek and Edmondson, in their much longer but equally breathtaking essay, finally propose that for the sake of a theory of the nonsubject, what is needed is a bold reevaluation of melancholia and anxiety. They start by asking: "Is melancholia, as Freud suggests, nothing more than the index of a suffocated, crushed rebellion, followed by feelings of impotence and resignation? Or could there be an affirmative, even proud dimension to the melancholic state—a dimension that recognizes doom itself as the engine of rebellion—that diverges from a certain model of political activism grounded . . . in a leftist ontology of fullness and presence?" If the answer to this question entails affirming the second option, it is because Mladek and Edmondson find in melancholia the model for an unerring fidelity to the part of those who have no part, to use Jacques Rancière's expression: "The scandal that the melancholic presents to a political activism rooted in modes of the not-yet is that one cannot count on him. Melancholia disrupts the tally-taking done in the accounting books of history and politics. It cannot help but address the wrong done to no-counts—the essential miscount that, according to Rancière, lies at the bottom of the political." Rancière (or Moreiras, for that matter) may not follow these authors in their argument, drawn from Freud and Lacan, that what ultimately induces this miscount is the death drive. But all of them would certainly agree that what is at stake now that the classical models of political activism and partisanship have entered into a profound crisis, closely tied to the crisis of the party form of politics and the state, is finding new ways of relating to the primordial antagonism or nonrelation—that is, new ways of relating to the impossibility of relating, to use the words of Mladek and Edmondson, or to the degrounded relation, in the terms that Moreiras borrows from Zambrano. "What emerges is thus a decompleted subject without mastery or agency, fully exposed and appropriated to the event," Mladek and Edmondson write, before concluding with the evocation of a community of leftist melancholics: "The community of melancholic subjects is then held together by the abyss of nonsubjective subjectivity." Like Moreiras, finally, they claim that fidelity to this rather strange and uncanny community requires that we refuse to give up, that we refrain from the urge to move on and instead stubbornly stick to the remembrance of the unmourned and the undead: "This is not to presume to speak on their behalf; that would be to draw them into symbolic order in such a way as to silence them even further. Indeed, if there is anything that the melancholic cannot abide, it is this very act of speaking for others. We are striving instead to remain faithful to the no-count's particular status as the traumatic object of the political, that which has fallen out, and which continues to fall out, of any social and political calculation."

Here then, it seems to me, is the great either-or that comes at the end of a detailed and painstaking investigation into the possibility of a leftist ontology: Can emancipatory politics today still take the form of militant subjectivation, or should the deconstruction of metaphysics also include all theories of the subject among its targets? Is every subject necessarily enmeshed in the history of politics as a history of sacrificial violence, or can there be a form of subjective fidelity to the very traumas and anxieties that bear witness to those vanquished and sacrificed? And furthermore, can we even ask this concluding question without in turn sacrificing the radical nature of the question of being to one of the many "others" of ontology? If we cannot, then should we not also question the emphatic need for a leftist ontology as a sign of something missed, namely, a truly emancipatory politics?

NOTES

1. Theodor W. Adorno, *Negative Dialectics,* trans. E. B. Ashton (London: Continuum, 1990), xx. See also Adorno, *The Jargon of Authenticity,* trans. Knut Tarnowski and Frederic Will (Evanston: Northwestern University Press, 1973).

2. Adorno, *Negative Dialectics,* 61–63.

3. Reiner Schürmann, *Heidegger on Being and Acting: From Principles to Anarchy,* trans. Christine-Marie Gros (Bloomington: Indiana University Press, 1990), 9. Schürmann himself, despite his insistence on a "necessary ignorance" as to Heidegger's question "how a political system, and what kind of one, can at all be coordinated with the technological age," does not fail to suggest that the experiences of direct democracy, no matter how short-lived, would after all be most attuned to an economy of being qua event of presencing and expropriating. To use the words of Roland Végső in this volume: "Democracy, as a particular political formation, is the only universalizable paradigm because it is capable of turning its own foundational principle against itself."

4. Alain Badiou, *Deleuze: The Clamor of Being,* trans. Louise Burchill (Minneapolis: University of Minnesota Press, 2000), 19.

5. Lacan, *The Four Fundamental Concepts of Psychoanalysis,* ed. Jacques-Alain Miller, trans. Alan Sheridan (New York: Norton, 1981), 29, 72.

6. Alain Badiou, *Théorie du sujet* (Paris: Seuil, 1982), 153. For a detailed account of Lacan's early ontological reflections, see François Balmès, *Ce que Lacan dit de l'être* (Paris: PUF, 1999). For Žižek's elaborations on the ontology of Lacanian psychoanalysis, see Adrian Johnston, *Žižek's Ontology: A Transcendental Materialist Theory of Subjectivity* (Evanston, Ill.: Northwestern University Press, 2008).

7. Parmenides, fragment 3. Friedrich Nietzsche in this context can be said to inaugurate the closure of metaphysics when in a note from 1888, included in *The Will to Power,* he writes: "Parmenides said, 'one cannot think of what is not';—we are at the opposite extreme, and say 'what can be thought of must certainly be a fiction.'" See *The Will to Power,* trans. Walter Kaufmann and R. J. Hollingdale (New York: Vintage, 1967), aphorism 539. For a commentary on the significance of this note, see Philippe Lacoue-Labarthe, "La fable" (1970), in *Le sujet de la philosophie (Typographies 1)* (Paris: Aubier-Flammarion, 1979), 7–30.

8. Gayatri Chakravorty Spivak, "Subaltern Studies: Deconstructing Historiography," in *Selected Subaltern Studies,* ed. Ranajit Guha and Gayatri Chakravorty Spivak (New York: Oxford University Press, 1988), 16.

9. Alain Badiou, *Being and Event,* trans. Oliver Feltham (London: Continuum, 2005), 284–85.

10. Adorno, *Negative Dialectics,* 11.

11. Michel Foucault, "What is Enlightenment?" ("Qu'est-ce que les Lumières?"), in *The Foucault Reader,* ed. Paul Rabinow (New York: Pantheon Books, 1984), 32–50.

12. See, for instance, Gianni Vattimo, "Postmodernity, Technology, Ontology," *Nihilism and Emancipation: Ethics, Politics, and Law*, ed. Santiago Zabala, trans. William McCuaig (New York: Columbia University Press, 2004): "The expression is meant to be taken in its most literal sense: it does not simply indicate, as Foucault thought, a philosophy oriented primarily toward the consideration of existence and its historicity rather than toward epistemology and logic—that is, toward what would be called, in Foucault's terminology, an 'analytic of truth.' Rather, 'ontology of actuality' is used here to mean a discourse that attempts to clarify what Being signifies in the present situation" (3–4). Roberto Esposito, on the other hand, goes so far as to speak of an "ontology of actuality" to describe the best of what *all* Italian philosophy has to offer: "If one considers those Italian authors who are known internationally—from Machiavelli to Vico, to Croce, and to Gramsci—we can assert that all of their reflections are placed at the point of encounter and tension between history and politics. Unlike the Anglo-Saxon analytic tradition or for that matter German hermeneutics and French deconstruction, the continual problem for Italian philosophy has been thinking the relationship with the present day *[contemporaneità]*, that which Foucault would have called 'the ontology of actuality,' which is to say an interrogation of the present interpreted in a substantially political key. Thinking above all of Vico or differently of Gramsci, history and politics have constituted the obligatory point of transition from which and through which the dimension of thought generally has been constituted in Italy." See Timothy Campbell's interview with Esposito in *diacritics* 36, no. 2 (2006): 49. As for Fredric Jameson, we should think of the subtitle to his *A Singular Modernity: Essay on the Ontology of the Present* (London: Verso, 2002). Another forgotten figure in this context, aside from Italian "weak ontology," is Georg Lukács, who saw his magnum opus as moving in the direction of an "ontology of social being." See his *Zur Ontologie des gesellschaftlichen Seins,* 2 vols., ed. Frank Benseler (Darmstadt: Luchterhand, 1984–86).

13. Foucault, "What Is Enlightenment?" 45–46.

14. Martin Heidegger, *Being and Time*, trans. John Macquarrie and Edward Robinson (New York: Harper & Row, 1962), 63; Giorgio Agamben, *Potentialities: Collected Essays in Philosophy*, trans. Daniel Heller-Roazen (Stanford: Stanford University Press, 1999), 179–80

15. Alain Badiou, *Manifesto for Philosophy*, trans. Norman Madarasz (Albany: SUNY Press, 1999), 56–57.

16. For a devastating attack, with which I am overall in agreement, on "Left Heideggerianism" as a contradiction in terms, see Geoffrey Waite, "Lefebvre without Heidegger: 'Left-Heideggerianism' *qua contradictio in adiecto*," in *Space, Difference, Everyday Life: Henri Lefebvre and Radical Urban Theory*, ed. Kanishka Goonewarda et al. (New York: Routledge, 2008), 146–81.

17. Oliver Marchart, *Post-foundational Political Thought: Political Difference in Nancy, Lefort, Badiou and Laclau* (Edinburgh: Edinburgh University Press, 2007), 5.

18. Fred Dallmayr, *The Other Heidegger* (Ithaca, N.Y.: Cornell University Press, 1993), 50–51.

ACKNOWLEDGMENTS

This project has been many years in the making, and I thank all of our contributors for their dedication to this topic. It truly was a pleasure working with you, and I have profited enormously from the close intellectual relationships that developed over the past few years. Special thanks go to Bill Connolly and Alberto Moreiras for their spirited support of this and related projects. The main idea for this volume goes back to a conference panel I organized for the American Comparative Literature Association in 2005. Although Bradley Butterfield, Max Pensky, and Lynn M. Ta were unable to join us for this book, I thank them for their lively contribution during our initial discussion at the ACLA. *A Leftist Ontology* would not have succeeded without the tireless support of Richard Morrison, Executive Editor at the University of Minnesota Press, who gave me much-needed advice throughout the publication process. I am deeply grateful for his guidance. I also thank Adam Brunner and Karen Hellekson for taking excellent care of many details and editorial nuances that surfaced before and during the production of this book. Finally, I want to express my sincere gratitude to Jennifer Arnold, our departmental administrative associate at the University of Missouri, who helps me navigate through the administrative labyrinth of this university every day so I can find the time to write.

This book is dedicated to all of us who believe that thinking is a political act, the significance of which can only be recognized retrospectively through the changes it rendered possible.

CONTRIBUTORS

BRUNO BOSTEELS is associate professor of Romance studies at Cornell University. His numerous essays focus on modern Latin American literature and culture and on contemporary European philosophy and political theory. He is the author of *Alain Badiou o el recomienzo del materialismo dialéctico* (2007) and *Badiou and Politics* (2009). He is translating three books by Alain Badiou.

CHRISTOPHER BREU is associate professor of English at Illinois State University. He is the author of *Hard-Boiled Masculinities* (University of Minnesota Press, 2005). He has published essays on Maryse Condé, Frank Sinatra, Dashiell Hammett, Chester Himes, intersex issues, and contemporary popular music and is working on a book project on the body and biopolitics in postmodern literature.

NICHOLAS BROWN is associate professor of English and African American studies at the University of Illinois at Chicago. He is the author of *Utopian Generations: The Political Horizon of Twentieth-Century Literature*, which argues that modern literature is most usefully understood within a Hegelian framework.

WILLIAM E. CONNOLLY is Krieger–Eisenhower Professor of Political Science at Johns Hopkins University. His numerous books include *Identity/Difference: Democratic Negotiations of Political Paradox; The Ethos of Pluralization; Why I Am Not a Secularist;* and *Neuropolitics: Thinking, Culture, Speed,* all published by the University of Minnesota Press. His most recent book is *Capitalism and Christianity, American Style.*

SORIN RADU-CUCU was awarded a PhD in comparative literature at the State University of New York—Buffalo, where he worked with Ernesto Laclau on the philosophical foundations of political radicalism on the Left. His dissertation studies possible encounters between contemporary political thought and contemporary American fiction.

GEORGE EDMONDSON is assistant professor of English at Dartmouth College. He has published on Middle English poetry and is now working on a book on Troilus and Criseyde.

EVA GEULEN is professor of German at the University of Bonn. She has published essays on Adorno, Benjamin, Nietzsche, Grillparzer, and Walser, and she is author of *The End of Art: Readings in a Rumor after Hegel* and *Giorgio Agamben zur Einführung*. She is coeditor of *Zeitschrift für deutsche Philologie*.

PHILIP GOLDSTEIN is professor of English at the University of Delaware. He is author of *The Politics of Literary Criticism: An Introduction to Marxist Cultural Theory; Communities of Cultural Value: Reception Study, Political Differences, and Literary History; Post-Marxism: An Introduction;* and, recently, *Modern American Reading Practices: Between Politics and Aesthetics*. He is editor of *Styles of Cultural Activism: From Theory and Pedagogy to Women, Indians, and Communism* and coeditor (with James Machor) of *Reception Study: From Literary Theory to Cultural Studies* and *New Directions in American Reception Study*.

KLAUS MLADEK is assistant professor of German at Dartmouth College. He has written essays on Kafka, Kant, Hegel, Freud, Nietzsche, Heidegger, Adorno, and Baudrillard, as well as on topics in law, literature, and psychoanalysis. He is editor of *Police Forces: A Cultural History of an Institution* and is working on a book on politics and the police in German literature and thought during the nineteenth century.

ALBERTO MOREIRAS is Sixth Century Professor of Modern Thought and Hispanic Studies at the University of Aberdeen, Scotland. He is author of *Interpretación y Diferencia, Tercer Espacio: Duelo y Literatura en America Latina* and *The Exhaustion of Difference: The Politics of Latin American Cultural Studies*, and coeditor (with Nelly Richard) of *Pensar en/la Posdictadura*. He is coeditor of *Journal of Spanish Cultural Studies*. His work now focuses on political philosophy and Spanish imperial reason.

JEFFREY T. NEALON is professor of English at Penn State University. He is author of *Foucault Beyond Foucault, Double Reading: Postmodernism after*

Deconstruction, and *Alterity Politics: Ethics and Performative Subjectivity;* co-author (with Susan Searls Giroux) of *The Theory Toolbox;* and coeditor (with Caren Irr) of *Rethinking the Frankfurt School: Alternative Legacies of Cultural Critique.*

WILLIAM RASCH is Henry H. H. Remak Professor of Germanic studies at Indiana University. He is author of *Niklas Luhmann's Modernity: The Para-doxes of Differentiation* and *Sovereignty and Its Discontents: On the Primacy of Conflict and the Structure of the Political.* He is editor of *Niklas Luhmann: Theories of Distinction: Redescribing the Descriptions of Modernity* and coedi-tor (with Cary Wolfe) of *Observing Complexity: Systems Theory and Post-modernity* (University of Minnesota Press, 2000). His interests now center on the work of Carl Schmitt.

BENJAMIN ROBINSON is assistant professor of German Studies at Indiana University. He is the author *of Other Systems: Alternate Germany, Social-ist Modernity.* His essays have been published in *Critical Inquiry, German Studies Review, Modernism/Modernity,* and *New German Critique.*

CARSTEN STRATHAUSEN is associate professor of German and English at the University of Missouri. He is author of *The Look of Things: Poetry and Vision around 1900* and has published essays on media history, literary theory, and Continental philosophy. He is working on a book about aes-thetics, art, and politics in the digital age.

IMRE SZEMÁN is Senator William McMaster Chair of Globalization and Cultural Studies at McMaster University, Canada. He is author of *Zones of Instability: Literature, Postcolonialism, and the Nation;* coauthor of *Popular Culture: A User's Guide;* and coeditor of *Pierre Bourdieu: Fieldwork in Cul-ture, The Johns Hopkins Guide to Literary Theory and Criticism,* and *Between Empires: The Canadian Cultural Studies Reader.* He is working on a project that assesses the politics of global anti-Americanism.

ROLAND VÉGSŐ received his PhD in 2007 from the English Department of the State University of New York—Buffalo. He is assistant professor of literary and critical theory in the English department of the University of Nebraska–Lincoln. His articles on American literature, literary theory, and psychoanalysis have appeared in *Amerikastudien, Hungarian Journal of English and American Studies, JNT: Journal of Narrative Theory, Arizona Quarterly, Psychoanalyis,* and *Culture and Society.* He is also the translator of numerous theoretical articles.

INDEX

abandonment of sacrificial structuration of history, 170–73, 174
abandonment of subjectivity, 248
Abraham, Nicolas, 213
actuality, ontology of, 243–44, 251n.12
Adán, Oscar, 184n.1
Adelphia, 70
Adorno, Theodor W., 19, 24, 29n.10, 33, 35, 36, 44, 52n.5, 52n.13, 53n.16, 90, 96n.4, 96n.9, 96n.11, 97n.18, 119n.11, 250n.1; aesthetics of, xxxvii–xxxviii, 80–84, 94; condemnation of Heidegger's notion of Being, 86; cultural pessimism, xxxvii–xxxviii; ethics of, 25; on institutional settings out of which thought grows, 42; negative dialectics, 23, 35, 235, 240; notion of instrumental reason, 80–84, 85, 95; on ontology, 235; parallels between Heidegger and, 84–88, 96n.12, 97n.15
aesthetic, recent change in political significance of, 37
aesthetic regime, 93
aesthetic theory: of Adorno, xxxvii–xxxviii, 80–84, 94; of Heidegger, 84–88
affirmative decompletion, 220; melancholic fidelity in form of act of, 211

Agamben, Giorgio, xxvi, xxxiv–xxxvi, 8–11, 13, 17, 17n.5, 18n.11, 28n.4–5, 29n.12, 144n.15, 228, 232n.48, 251n.14; attempt to disengage Heidegger's philosophy and National Socialism, 19, 22–28; attempt to found new ethics on Auschwitz and *Muselmann*, 24–26, 242; form-of-life concept, 21–22; invocation of catastrophe, 10–11; polemics against Derrida, 26; proposal to break ban of law, 228; rejection of Leftist critique of state, 20; reontologization of politics, function of ambivalence in, 19–29, 242; review of attempts to reconcile dual attributes of *homo sacer* (impossibility of sacrifice and possibility of unpunishable murder), 26–27; temptation of thinking redemption, 8, 16; tendencies to fuse politics and ontology, skepticism regarding, 19
agribusiness, 199
Althusser, Louis, 230n.3
ambivalence: in Agamben's reontologization of politics, function of, 19–29, 242; power of, xxxv–xxxvi; power of, coincidence of danger and salvation as, 23–24
American cultural imperialism, 43–44

259